D0185560

Understanding Social Theory

Understanding Social Theory

Second Edition

Derek Layder

SAGE Publications
London • Thousand Oaks • New Delhi

Understanding Social Theory

Second Edition

Derek Layder

⑤SAGE Publications

London ● Thousand Oaks ● New Delhi

© Derek Layder 2006

First published 1994. Reprinted in 1994, 1995, 1996, 1998, 2000,
2001, 2003, 2004

 SAGE Publications Ltd
1 Oliver's Yard
55 City Road
London EC1Y 1SP

SAGE Publications Inc
2455 Teller Road
Thousand Oaks, California 91320

SAGE Publications India Pvt Ltd
B-42, Panchsheel Enclave
Post Box 4109
New Delhi 110 017

British Library Cataloguing in Publication data

A catalogue record for this book is available from the
British Library

ISBN 0 7619 4449 4
      0 7619 4450 8

Library of Congress control number available

Typeset by C&M Digitals (P) Ltd., Chennai, India
Printed on paper from sustainable resources
Printed in Great Britain by The Alden Press, Great Britain

Contents

Preface   vii

Preface to the First Edition   ix

1   A Map of the Terrain: The Organisation of the Book   1

PART 1   THE VIEW FROM ON HIGH   13

2   The Legacy of Talcott Parsons   15

3   Varieties of Marxism   39

PART 2   WHERE THE ACTION IS   67

4   Meanings, Situations and Experience   69

5   Perceiving and Accomplishing   91

PART 3   BREAKING FREE AND BURNING BRIDGES   111

Introduction   112

6   Foucault and the Postmodern Turn   115

7   Beyond Macro and Micro: Abandoning False Problems   139

8   Giddens's Structuration Theory   155

PART 4   ONLY CONNECT: FORGING LINKS   189

Introduction   190

9   Linking Agency and Structure and Macro and Micro   193

10 Habermas's Lifeworld and System   213

11 Varieties of Dualism   239

12 New Directions: The Theory of Social Domains   271

Glossary   302

References   311

Index   319

Preface

The reader of this second edition may wish to know in what respects it differs from the first edition. Since it was originally published (1994) there have been some developments in social theory that relate to the central themes of the book and I have incorporated some reference to them in this new edition. Also, in the intervening years I have changed some of my views as they appear in the earlier book so I have taken the opportunity to amend or reformulate some of the ideas expressed in it. The practical impact of these changes is as follows. What was originally the final chapter (12) has disappeared from this new edition, although substantial parts of it have been redistributed to other chapters in the second edition (specifically Chapters 7, 8, 10 and 11). I have repositioned Chapters 10 and 11. The 'old' Chapter 11 on Habermas now appears as Chapter 10, while Chapter 10 has become Chapter 11 in this new edition. This was necessitated because I have added new material to what is now Chapter 11 (and also re-titled it 'Varieties of Dualism'). Now joining the original discussions of Goffman and Turner are additional commentaries on Mouzelis and Archer. These changes make for a much smoother transition to the issues discussed in the new final chapter (12).

The new Chapter 12, entitled 'New Directions: The Theory of Social Domains', provides a more definite conclusion than did the original, which was somewhat tentative and speculative. My own work on social theory and social research strategies was only at the mid-point of its development when the first edition was published so I largely refrained from referring to it in that book. However, my work on the 'theory of social domains' and 'adaptive theory' has subsequently acquired a more fully developed form and so I have taken the opportunity to organise the concluding chapter largely around themes and issues deriving from this work. Of course, many of the authors and perspectives dealt with in the foregoing chapters arise as topics of discussion in this new chapter, and so it serves both as a conclusion to the book as a whole and an introduction to alternative ideas and new directions for social theory. Since my own ideas focus centrally on issues relating to the dualisms of individual–society, agency–structure and macro–micro, the final section of Chapter 12 ties the discussion back to the central organising themes of the book as a whole.

Apart from these 'major' alterations, throughout the whole text I have made minor amendments, revisions and refreshments to the discussion where I have thought appropriate and they reflect the way in which my views have changed since the first edition. There are two other significant changes to the original. Every chapter now has a 'preview' at the beginning and a 'summary' at the end which provide overviews of the topics and issues as they appear in the chapter concerned. I have also added a 'glossary' of the main social theory terms and concepts that recur throughout the text. Hopefully these two additions make the book (even) more reader-friendly than the first edition. Finally, I'd like to thank Chris Rojek at Sage (and the Sage staff generally) for suggesting a second edition. The more I have thought about and worked on this project, the more convinced I have become that the changes it has enabled me to make are both necessary and important.

Derek Layder 2004

Preface to the First Edition

This book is an introduction to key issues in modern social theory. Although it does give a general overview of social theory it does not sacrifice depth of analysis in an attempt to cover absolutely every topic. Rather, it concentrates on the work of major authors, perspectives and key issues in social theory. I believe that although there can be no eventual great synthesis in social theory, there are, nonetheless, many different strands which can be usefully drawn together. Thus, while not underestimating the obstacles and incompatibilities, I stress the unities and points of connection in social theory. This moves away from the idea that social theory is necessarily diverse and irredeemably fragmented. I think that the only way forward is to stress the cumulative nature of sociological knowledge and the co-operative dialogue of those involved in its production.

I have tried to emphasise the empirical and social research implications of the theoretical issues that I raise. My guiding assumption is that theory is never completely isolated from problems of empirical research, any more than empirical research is free from theoretical assumptions. The really interesting questions concern the nature of the relations between theory and empirical research and not whether either domain has some divinely given priority. Similarly, I do not think that sociology is beleaguered by 'false' problems and divisions (such as those expressed in the pairings of 'individual and society', 'agency–structure' and 'macro–micro'). In my opinion these dualisms represent not so much false problems as contested issues about which are the most adequate ways of thinking about the interconnections between different features of social life. The most enlivening and important questions facing social theory today are concerned with *how* different aspects of social reality are related to each other. Both classical and contemporary theorists have produced an interesting diversity of answers to these questions. It is the sorting through of competing and complementary claims in the search for sound and adequate solutions that provides much of the creative impetus, excitement and controversy in modern social theory.

I would like to thank Karen Phillips of Sage for her patience, help and constructive advice throughout the writing of this book. Also, two anonymous reviewers from Sage were instrumental in defining the form and content of the book prior to writing. I thank them for this and their subsequent perceptive and useful comments on a completed draft of the book. I owe a lot to Alison Drewett, who went through the manuscript in great detail. Although I have not incorporated absolutely everything she suggested, I found her observations to be invaluable.

While not directly involved in the writing of this book, a number of people have generally influenced my thinking about social theory and I would like to acknowledge them here. Paul Secord of the University of Houston and John Wilson of Duke University have over the years provided collegial support and enthusiasm. Stewart Clegg's influence has been both practical and intellectual and, although he may be unaware of it, he bears some responsibility for broadening my theoretical horizons! I also learned much from Tony Giddens while writing a previous book.

David Ashton has always provided important support and helpful advice. In particular our collaboration on an article that combined theory and empirical research stimulated my thinking about crucial aspects of the macro–micro problem. Conversations with William Watson and Simon Locke always proved to be productive and stimulating. Also, I would like to thank the students who attended my sociological theory lectures at the University of Leicester between 1986–91. They provided an extremely inquisitive and attentive audience and 'sounding board' for many of my views. Finally, I wish to thank Julia O'Connell Davidson, John Williams, Dominic Strinati, James Fulcher, Stephen Small, Steve Wagg, Terry Johnson and John Scott – all colleagues at Leicester – for their friendship, but above all for their sense of humour.

Those who wish to obtain a full picture of the overall argument are encouraged to read the book straight through. However, those who wish to dip into it to gain an impression of a particular author's main ideas or to obtain a preliminary understanding of a particular perspective are encouraged to do so. I have tried to help in this respect by making each chapter fairly self-contained. However, before plundering various parts of the book it is probably best to read Chapter 1 first, since this defines key terms and themes and gives an outline of the chapter contents.

1

A Map of the Terrain:
The Organisation of the Book

The Main Story:
Key Dualisms in Sociology

This book provides an overview of the major issues in social theory but the organisation of the discussion is unlike that found in most textbooks. Instead of presenting the discussion in the form of a list of issues or authors in social theory, this book is organised around a central theme and problem-focus. This concerns how the encounters of everyday life and individual behaviour influence, and are influenced by, the wider social environment in which we live. The book explores this basic theme in terms of three dualisms which play a key part in sociology; individual–society, agency–structure and macro–micro. These three dualisms are all closely related and may be regarded as different ways of expressing and dealing with the basic theme and problem-focus of the book. The dualisms are not simply analytic distinctions – they refer to different aspects of social life which can also be empirically defined. It is important not to lose sight of this fundamental truth since the sociological problems they pose cannot be solved solely in theoretical terms any more than they can by exclusively empirical means. In this sense, both empirical research and 'theorising' must go hand in hand (see Layder, 1993, for an extended argument).

Some authors have suggested that the dualisms that abound in sociology – and there are quite a few others that I have not yet mentioned – express divisions between separate and opposing entities that are locked in a struggle with each other for dominance. These authors object to this because they believe that social

```
┌──────────────────────────────────────────┐
│  Macro         ───────────  Micro          │
│                                            │
│  Agency        ───────────  Structure      │
│  (action)                                  │
│                                            │
│  Individual    ───────────  Society        │
└──────────────────────────────────────────┘
```

Figure 1.1   *Three key dualisms*

life is an interwoven whole in which all elements play a part in an ongoing flux of social activity. Dualism, on this view, is simply a false doctrine that leads to misleading and unhelpful distinctions which do not actually exist in reality.

However, I would side with those theorists who suggest that sociological dualism must not be understood as inherently tied to such a view. The entities referred to in the dualisms must not be thought to be always separate and opposed to each other in some antagonistic manner. Whether or not they are thought of in this way will depend upon which authors or schools of thought we are dealing with. But we must recognise that some authors see dualisms as referring to different aspects of social life which are inextricably interrelated. That is, while possessing their own characteristics, they are interlocked and interdependent features of society. In short, they mutually imply and influence each other. They are not opposed to each other in some kind of struggle for dominance.

In Figure 1.1, the individual–society dualism comes at the base of the diagram with agency–structure above it and macro–micro at the top. This is deliberately arranged to indicate that as we ascend the list we are dealing with more inclusive distinctions. To put this another way, I am saying that the macro–micro distinction comes at the top because it 'includes' within its terms some reference to the two underneath. So, by starting with the individual–society distinction I am dealing with the simplest and most basic dualism.

The individual–society distinction is perhaps the oldest and represents a persistent dilemma about the fitting together of individual and collective needs. This is expressed in sociological terms by the problem of how social order is created out of the rather disparate and often anti-social motivations of the many individuals who make up society. As one of the oldest dualisms in sociology, this has been rightly criticised for its tendency to see individuals as if they were completely separated from social influences. This view fails to take into account the fact that many needs and motivations that people experience are shaped by the social environment in which they live (see Chapters 4 and 7). In this sense there is no such thing as society without the individuals who make it up just as there are no individuals existing outside of the influence of society. It has been argued, therefore, that it is better to abandon the individual–society distinction since this simply reaffirms this notion of the isolated individual (or perhaps more absurdly, society without individuals).

Now, there is some merit in the argument against the notion of the pristine individual free from social influences. Some non-sociologists still speak fondly but misguidedly of people as if they stood outside of collective forces. More importantly, some sociologists tend to view the individual's point of contact with social forces as one which is 'privatised' – a straight line of connection between the individual and the social expectations that exert an influence on his or her behaviour (see Chapters 2 and 3). In these cases it is important to view the individual as intrinsically involved with others in both immediate face-to-face situations and in terms of more remote networks of social relationships. In this sense, the individual is never free of social involvements and commitments.

However, as I shall argue throughout, it would be unwise to simply abandon the notion of the individual as 'someone' who has a subjective experience of society, and it is useful to distinguish this aspect of social life from the notion of society in its objective guise. To neglect this distinction would be to merge the individual with social forces to such an extent that the idea of unique self-identities would disappear along with the notion of 'subjective experience' as a valid category of analysis. This is a striking example of the difference between the cautionary use of dualisms, as against their misuse by the creation of false images. Thus, if the individual is not viewed as separate or isolated from other people or the rest of society, then the individual–society distinction has certain qualified uses. As I have said, one of the drawbacks of speaking of 'individuals' as such is that this very notion seems to draw attention away from the fact that people are *always* involved in social interaction and social relations. This is where the agency–structure dualism has a distinct advantage.

The agency–structure dualism is of more recent origin and derives rather more from sociology itself, although there have been definite philosophical influences, especially concerning the notion of 'agency'. In Figure 1.1 you will notice that I have put the word 'action' in brackets below the word agency. This is meant to indicate that these two words are often used interchangeably by sociologists. In many respects 'action' is superior to the word 'agency' because it more solidly draws our attention to the socially active nature of human beings. In turn, the fact that people are actively involved in social relationships means that we are more aware of their social interdependencies. The word 'agency' points to the idea that people are 'agents' in the social world – they are able to do things which affect the social relationships in which they are embedded. People are not simply passive victims of social pressure and circumstances. Thus the notion of activity and its effects on social ties and bonds is closely associated in the terms 'action' and 'agency'.

Another advantage over the individual–society dualism is that action–structure focuses on the mutual influence of social activity and the social contexts in which it takes place. Thus it is concerned with two principal questions: first, the extent to which human beings actively create the social worlds they inhabit through their everyday social encounters. Stated in the form of a question it asks: How does human activity shape the very social circumstances in which it takes place? Secondly, the action–structure issue focuses on the way in which the social context (structures, institutions, cultural resources) moulds and forms social activity. In short, how do the social circumstances in which activity takes place make certain things possible while ruling out other things? In general terms, the action–structure distinction concentrates on the question of how creativity and constraint are related through social activity – how can we explain their coexistence?

Having said this, I have to point out that I am presenting the agency–structure issue in a form which makes most sense in terms of the overall interests and arguments of this book. That is to say, different authors use varying definitions of the two terms and understand the nature of the ties between them in rather different ways. For instance, some authors suggest that agency can be understood to be a feature of various forms of social organisation or collectivity. In this sense we could say that social classes or organisations 'act' in various ways – they are collective actors – thus the term 'agency' cannot be exclusively reserved for individuals or episodes of face-to-face interaction. In some cases and for some purposes I think it is sensible to talk of the agency of collective actors in this way, but I shall not be primarily concerned with this usage. For present purposes, the most important sense of the term 'agency' will refer to the ability of human beings to make a difference in the world (see Giddens, 1984).

Similarly, I am using the notion of structure in the conventional sense of the social relationships which provide the social context or conditions under which people act. On this definition social organisations, institutions and cultural products (like language, knowledge and so on) are the primary referent of the term 'structure'. These refer to objective features of social life in that they are part of a pre-existing set of social arrangements that people enter into at birth and which typically endure beyond their lifetimes. Of course they also have a sub-jective component insofar as people enact the social routines that such arrange-ments imply. In this sense they are bound up with people's motivations and reasons for action. Although activity (agency) and structure are linked in this way, the primary meaning of structure for this discussion centres on its objective dimension as the social setting and context of behaviour.

There are other meanings of structure, some of which refer to rather differ-ent aspects of social life (for example Giddens defines it as 'rules and resources'), and some refer to primarily subjective or simply small-scale phe-nomena. I shall not be dealing with these usages in this book but this issue does highlight a difference between the agency–structure and the macro–micro dualisms. That is, whereas agency–structure can in principle refer to both large-scale and small-scale features of social life, the macro–micro distinction deals primarily with a difference in level and scale of analysis. I shall come back to this in a moment but let me just summarise what I mean by the agency–structure dualism. My definitions of these terms follow a fairly conventional distinction between people in face-to-face social interaction as compared with the wider social relations or context in which these activities are embedded. Thus the agency–structure issue focuses on the way in which human beings both create social life at the same time as they are influenced and shaped by existing social arrangements.

There are other differences in usage such as the degree of importance or emphasis that is given to either agency or structure in the theories of various authors and these will emerge as the book progresses. However, the important core of the distinction for present purposes hinges on the link between human activity and its social contexts. By contrast, the macro–micro distinction is rather more concerned with the level and scale of analysis and the research focus. Thus it distinguishes between a primary concentration on the analysis of face-to-face conduct (everyday activities, the routines of social life), as against a primary con-centration on the larger scale, more impersonal macro phenomena like institu-tions and the distribution of power and resources. As with agency–structure, the macro–micro distinction is a matter of analytic emphasis, since both macro and micro features are intertwined and depend on each other. However, macro and micro refer to definite levels of social reality which have rather different properties – for example, micro phenomena deal with more intimate and detailed aspects of face-to-face conduct, while macro phenomena deal with more impersonal and large-scale phenomena.

There are considerable overlaps between structures and macro phenomena, although there are important differences in emphasis. Macro phenomena tend to deal with the distribution of groups of people or resources in society as a whole, for example, the concentration of women or certain ethnic groups in particular kinds of jobs and industries, or the unequal distribution of wealth and property in terms of class and other social divisions. However, macro analyses may include structural phenomena like organisational power, or cultural resources such as language and artistic and musical forms, which may have rather more local significance. The common element in both structures and macro phenomena is that they refer to reproduced patterns of power and social organisation. There is also some overlapping between micro analysis and the concern with agency and creativity and constraint in social activity. The main difference is that micro refers primarily to a level of analysis and research focus, whereas a concern with agency focuses on the tie between activity and its social contexts.

I think we can see from these brief preliminary definitions, that not only is the individual–society problem closely related to the agency (action)–structure issue, but that both are directly implicated in the macro–micro dualism. That is, if micro analysis is concerned with face-to-face conduct, then it overlaps with self-identity and subjective experience as well as the idea that people are social agents who can fashion and remake their social circumstances. Similarly, if macro analysis concentrates on more remote, general and patterned features of society, then it also overlaps with the notion of 'social structure' as the regular and patterned practices (institutional and otherwise) which form the social context of behaviour. So, my point is that these different dualisms overlap with each other and that the macro–micro dualism includes elements of the other two. This is the reason that it is the principal focus of this book, although I shall have something to say about them all throughout.

As I have tried to make clear, these are not distinctions without substance. They all mean something quite definite even though they overlap to some extent. They all refer to divisions between different sorts of things in the social world, and it is important to remember that these may be complementary rather than antagonistic to each other. As mentioned earlier, some sociologists object to the influence which these sorts of dualism have had on sociological thinking, and this is something we shall go on to consider. However, the whole point of presenting them and being clear about what they mean right from the start is that it is the only way of evaluating the arguments both for and against this point of view. We can only really understand why some sociologists have objected to them, and judge whether their arguments are sound, if we know what it is they are objecting to.

Apart from these three key dualisms there are a number of others that have played an important role in social analysis such as 'objectivism–subjectivism', 'dynamics–statics', 'materialism–idealism', 'rationalism–empiricism'. I shall not be discussing these here, I simply wish to indicate that they are fairly widespread and ingrained in routine social analysis. It is important to be aware of this because it is part of the context against which the 'rejectors' of dualism are protesting. Also, since this book is organised around the theme of the macro–micro dualism, it is important to have some sense of the wider context of dualistic thinking in the social sciences.

The Organisation of the Book

Let me now turn to the way in which the book is organised from Chapter 2 to 12. One of the main themes which group certain writers and schools of thought together is based on the extent to which they reject or affirm dualism in social theory, especially those of agency–structure and macro–micro. With regard to this basic organising principle we can see that the book is divided into four parts. Each part deals with approaches to theory which either affirm or reject these dualisms in different ways.

In Part 1, I examine the work of Talcott Parsons (Chapter 2) and the variety of theoretical work that has stemmed from the writings of Karl Marx (Chapter 3). It is often thought that the work of these authors is diametrically opposed and, to a large extent, this is true. However, there are common features in their work which become more apparent as we compare them with other approaches. One of these common features concerns their views about the role of social structural (or macro) features in the shaping of social activity. In this sense they are both 'affirmers' of dualism insofar as they make a distinction between the realm of social activity and the realm of institutions, which represent the social conditions under which such activity takes place.

However, both Parsons and Marx (and the schools of theory they gave rise to: 'functionalism' and 'Marxism'), tend to affirm dualism in a rather one-sided manner in the sense that they give priority to the macro realm in determining the form of social activity. So, despite their many political and theoretical differences, Parsons and Marx (and their later followers) are in agreement about the importance of objective social structures (Parsons prefers the term 'system') in setting the terms in which social activity is played out. It is largely for this reason that I have entitled Part 1, 'The View from on High'. This points to the fact that these authors stress the idea that the external (macro) social conditions, to varying degrees, influence the form of social action ('agency' or the 'micro world').

Although this book is primarily about modern social theory, the influence of the work of classical authors (Marx, Durkheim and Weber) on contemporary theorists is evident throughout. In Part 1 the work of Durkheim and Marx is stressed while in Part 2 the influence of Weber comes to the fore. This is because of Weber's interest in incorporating the 'subjective understanding' of the people that we, as sociologists, study into a more general analysis of social structure. Other authors have taken this interest in the micro social world to an extreme with which Weber might have felt rather uncomfortable. Thus, in Part 2 my discussion centres around those theorists who have taken subjective experience and social interaction as their focus of analysis. I have entitled Part 2 'Where the Action Is' in order to highlight this focus of interest and to contrast it with Part 1, where the micro world is subsidiary to an interest in macro features of society.

In Part 2, I deal more with schools of thought (or 'approaches' and 'perspectives') rather than with single authors (although particular authors are often taken as representatives of different approaches). In Chapter 4, I discuss the 'symbolic interactionist' approach, which emphasises the role of meanings, situations and experience in social life. In Chapter 5, I deal with what are known as 'phenomenological' approaches (including 'ethnomethodology'), which emphasise social life as something which is in a continual state of construction and reconstruction by the people involved. These approaches, therefore, tend to react against the priority given to macro-structural matters which is evident in the work of those theorists discussed in Part 1. In fact, they stress the opposite by suggesting that the world of social interaction and subjective experience is the only one with real importance in understanding social life. Some of these authors suggest that the macro world is simply a neutral 'background' against which the key elements of action and meaning emerge and are enacted. Some go so far as to say that the whole notion of a macro world of social structure is simply an invention of theorists!

Thus, the authors and approaches dealt with in Part 2 could be said to be 'rejectors' of dualism in the sense that they believe that action and meaning are of paramount importance and, as a result, largely dispense with the idea of an external macro world. There is some overlap with the sociologists that I discuss in Part 3, insofar as they too reject dualism. However, those in Part 3 tend to 'reject' it for different reasons and in different ways. Even among themselves there is quite a variety of preferred approaches which hinge around different 'solutions' to the dilemmas created by dualistic thinking. Alternatively, they can be thought of as responses to dualistic forms of theory. I have called Part 3 'Breaking Free and Burning Bridges' because this suggests that the sociologists involved want to abandon completely the traditional terms of reference of social theory. Central to this aim is the rejection of philosophical dualism which views such distinctions as 'macro and micro' and 'action and structure' as if they were separate and opposed.

As indicated earlier, the idea of criticising this type of dualism is a creditable one, but it rather misses the point by implying that all sociological thought necessarily fits in with the philosophical type of dualism. However, this is something which I shall be arguing in detail throughout and here I want simply to give an overview of the general argument. Now, having said that there is an overlap with Part 2 in the sense that those in Part 3 reject dualism, I must highlight the fact that this is a somewhat different form of rejection. Those in Part 2 reject the macro–micro dualism by putting all their eggs in the one basket of the micro world of interaction – and therefore still uphold at least one term of the dualism. This contrasts with those in Part 3 who wish to reject dualism more fundamentally by abandoning any reference to either of its sides. These authors typically invent their own terms and language of social analysis, which are meant to replace the traditional dualistic forms.

Thus in Part 3, Chapter 6, I discuss Foucault, whose work can generally be understood as a response to, and ultimate rejection of, Marxism in its various guises. In particular, Foucault is against those theories which envisage society as a monolithic structure in terms of which people play preordained roles. Thus Foucault is an example of the post-structuralist movement which emphasises the localised and fragmented nature of society. Foucault is also associated with post-modernism, which overlaps with post-structuralism in its rejection of 'structural' theories as well as those which centre their analyses around the individual 'subject'. Foucault's work thus represents an attempt to transcend what he takes to be the limitations of dualisms such as macro–micro and action–structure by analysing a 'middle ground' of social practices and how they express relations of power.

As with the other authors discussed in Part 3, Foucault makes a good deal of headway in breaking free and avoiding some of the pitfalls of more traditional ways of thinking but, by so conclusively burning the bridges that link older and newer forms of theory, he leaves much unresolved. The same is true of Elias (Chapter 7) and Giddens (Chapter 8), although I feel that Giddens allows for more continuity in this regard. While I suggest that Elias's work has much to offer in many other respects, it fails on the specific task of pulling together different strands of theory into a more adequate synthesis of macro and micro levels of analysis.

I find Giddens's 'structuration theory' to be the most persuasive and compelling attempt to move 'beyond' traditional dualistic thinking, not least because Giddens argues a detailed case in relation to existing theories even where he disagrees with them. Despite the fact that it is generally undogmatic in form, structuration theory is based on certain assumptions which prevent it from entering a dialogue with particular approaches to social theory and research. In this respect, Giddens's theory tends to insulate itself from those approaches (discussed in Chapters 11 and 12) which suggest that there are social structures and systems which exist to some extent independently of the motivations and reasons that people give for their conduct. I argue throughout that there needs to be dialogue between this kind of 'objectivist' theory and those which concentrate on the form and dynamics of social behaviour. Such a dialogue cannot take place if we prematurely reject certain aspects of dualistic thought in sociology. This brings us to Part 4 in which I discuss the work of other contemporary theorists who tend to 'affirm' dualism by attempting to forge links between the different domains. Obviously, this is a very different strategy from that adopted by those in Part 3 who wish to abandon dualism root and branch.

To some extent, this theme of linking agency and structure and macro and micro domains connects with the discussion in Part 1. However, the crucial difference in Part 4 is that it is not assumed that agency or micro elements are of only subsidiary importance. Most contemporary theorists who affirm dualism do so by stressing that agency and structure and macro and micro domains are of equal importance. Thus I begin Chapter 9 with a brief discussion of Bourdieu's attempt to link objective and subjective aspects of social life in a theory of social practice. I follow this with a rather more detailed analysis of the work of Dorothy Smith. This is an example of feminist theorising which attempts to understand the links between macro and micro features of social life from the viewpoint of women. In a sense, both Bourdieu and Smith are ambiguous on the dualism issue. While they wish to overcome the opposition entailed in philosophical dualism, they both seem to stress the links between definite domains of social life.

However, there are some who, while acknowledging the existence and importance of both domains, either insist on, or at least tend to assume, the primary importance of one or the other. The work of Alexander and Munch (also Chapter 9) is interesting for its bold assertion of the importance of objective and collective aspects of social life. However, while they both recognise the necessity of integrating macro and micro elements, their work tends to veer towards the macro side. This is perhaps an inevitable result of their commitment to the theoretical programme initiated by Talcott Parsons. Randall Collins (also Chapter 9) is an example of a theorist who formally acknowledges the importance of both macro and micro domains but who goes on to suggest that the macro domain can be explained in micro terms. Collins has important things to say about the dynamics of interaction, but I agree with the other writers discussed in Part 4 who insist that macro and micro phenomena cannot be reduced to one side of the dualism or the other.

In Chapter 10, I discuss Habermas's ideas about the relationship between the 'lifeworld' and 'system'. Habermas's views on the 'colonisation' of the lifeworld by system elements brings sharply into relief the question of the interpenetration of agency and structure and macro and micro domains. It also brings back a concern with a critical theory of society as an essential ingredient of social analysis in general. In Chapter 11, I examine the work of four authors (Erving Goffman, Jonathan Turner, Nicos Mouzelis and Margaret Archer), all of whom support dualism in some guise or other. However, it is important to stress that each of these authors has very different views on the nature of dualism and the sorts of social analysis they support. Thus they represent a diversity of views on the best overall framework for understanding the interconnections between agency and structure and macro and micro dimensions of social reality. In the final chapter I discuss my own contribution to the debate in the form of the 'theory of social domains'. Clearly, much of what I say about domain theory is consistent with the views of those authors discussed in Chapters 9, 10 and 11.

However, there are certain crucial respects in which domain theory takes its own distinct direction and form. In particular it suggests that social theory and analysis should take the next crucial step beyond 'analytic dualism' and understand social reality as a complex unity of the influences of four principal domains of social reality. While these social domains are distinct from and partly independent of each other, they are at the same time closely interlinked and mutually influential.

part one

the view from on high

2
The Legacy of Talcott Parsons

PREVIEW

- The influence and legacy of the work of Talcott Parsons on sociological thought.

- The social system, its sub-systems and their functional 'needs'.

- Individuals, social roles and the pattern variables.

- The problems of determinism, over-conformity and social harmony in Parsons's analyses.

- Critical issues around social inequality, material interests, power and ideology.

- The problem with Parsons's view of social interaction.

- Social action and the emergent nature of social systems.

- The continuing relevance of Parsons.

To begin our journey through the terrain of social theory I shall examine the work of Talcott Parsons. Parsons's work has been extremely influential in sociology in several ways. After the Second World War his ideas were held in high esteem and tended to dominate the intellectual scene until around the mid-1960s, after which they declined in significance. The imprint left by this influence can be seen in three distinct senses. First, Parsons's work set the terms for a model of society which stressed the primary importance of the macro elements as against micro elements. This was expressed as the power of the social system to influence the social behaviour of individuals. Secondly, when the popularity of Parsons's ideas declined, the theories that replaced them were often expressed in the form of a critical dialogue with them, or could be seen as a deliberate attempt to construct alternatives to them. Thirdly, although the influence of Parsons's work was subdued for a large stretch of time, there has now been a resurgence of interest in his work and some authors have attempted to develop the theoretical ideas that he originally proposed.

There are two things to bear in mind as I discuss Parsons's work. First, my focus of interest will be on the manner in which he construes the relation between individual social behaviour and the larger social environment in which it occurs. In this respect I shall ignore much of what he has to say on such issues as social evolution and the nature of the relation between institutions. Secondly, in confronting Parsons's work one immediately comes up against the problem of the difficulty of the language that he uses. There is no doubt that reading Parsons can be extremely frustrating and productive of headaches. Nonetheless, there is a great deal of value in his work and it deserves closer scrutiny. As a consequence, I shall, where possible, substitute simpler terms and phrases for some of Parsons's more impenetrable prose.

The Development of Parsons's Framework

If we consider Parsons's work from his first major publication in 1937 (*The Structure of Social Action*) to his second in 1951 (*The Social System*), it is clear that his ideas underwent a significant change in emphasis during this time. This is partly due to the fact that the earlier book was largely a critical review of previous authors' work and provided, as it were, a platform on which Parsons was to build his later, very original, theoretical framework. In *The Structure of Social Action*, Parsons reviews the work of a number of writers (including Durkheim and Weber but, notably, omitting Marx) and concludes that it is possible to construct a general theory of social action. Such a theory must reject the assumptions of those economic theories which insist that human activity is simply economically motivated – that people act solely on the basis of rational self-interest. These assumptions tended to take the general 'orderliness' of society for granted.

Parsons insisted that orderliness was largely the result of the influence of certain values (such as the belief in family, or the sanctity of human life). It is the fact that people embrace such values that curbs tendencies towards self-interest and reduces (although not entirely) the necessity for external sanctions (such as legal punishments or social ostracism and so on). These values are expressed in rather more concrete and immediate ways by the 'norms' or rules of behaviour that operate in certain situations. For example, in families 'fathers' and 'mothers' are expected to care for their children and not to abuse or neglect them. Social 'norms' suggest guidelines for behaviour and are based on the values that refer to more general features of social life. In this respect Parsons was drawing on the work of Durkheim, who stressed the role of collectively held beliefs and values as a kind of social 'glue' which created cohesiveness and order in society.

Gouldner (1971) has argued that it is important to understand Parsons's work as an attempt to defend capitalist society against the criticisms contained in Marxist analyses. Although both Marx and Parsons see capitalism as a 'social system', their assessments of it are very different. Marx envisioned capitalist society as basically exploitative (of the working classes), conflict-ridden, and governed primarily by the profit motive inherent in the economic system. On the other hand, while Parsons recognised that capitalism was still striving towards its ideal form, he saw it as a basically fair and meritocratic system in which individuals are rewarded according to the efforts that they are willing to expend. In this sense, Parsons was keen to dislodge Marxist criticism as well as to dispel some of the pessimistic ideas about the future of capitalism that were being put forward by writers who were critics of Marxism (notably Weber and Sombart).

Instead of giving a pessimistic image of a repressive society in which the mass of people are exploited and controlled by the dominant capitalist class, Parsons was keen to emphasise the potential for individuals to benefit from the system and to control their own future. Thus he stressed 'voluntarism' in social life, that is, the capacity for people to act on the basis of their own decisions, desires and choices and not on requirements enforced by the brute workings of an economic system that thrived on inequalities of wealth and power. At the same time, Parsons emphasised the importance of core values as a means of social integration. Such values and norms had an independent role to play in society since they were not simply a reflection of, or determined by, the requirements of the economy.

The Idea of the Social System

Parsons's earlier work also suggested that society exists on different and quite distinct levels of organisation. This is referred to as the principle of emergence and feeds directly into his later work in which he develops an elaborate model of the 'social system'. Parsons employs the principle of emergence in order to describe the four different layers of social organisation that underpin the social system. Each is a level of organisation in its own right, and corresponds to a

System or level	Aspect of experience
1 The physiological system	The body
2 The personality system	Individual psychology
3 The social system	Roles and positions
4 The cultural system	Knowledge, literature, art and other human products

Figure 2.1   *System levels in Parsons's work*

recognisable aspect of our experience of social life. They are represented in Figure 2.1. The model highlights the contribution of four system levels which are related to each other in various ways. This analytic model is simply a tool to help us investigate the empirical features of social life. The difference between it and reality is that in actual social life the levels are not neatly separated out as they are in the model, they are interconnected and overlap with each other in a number of ways. This is very much in line with our actual experiences.

Clearly, we experience or 'feel' the effects of our bodies, our psychological impulses, social conventions and cultural traditions and so on, but we do not experience them as if they were clearly distinguishable from each other. Thus actual reality is always a complicated and 'messy' affair that poses difficulties for our understanding. Nevertheless, the great virtue of a theoretical model such as Parsons's is that it allows us to investigate this complexity by separating out the component units and viewing their workings in a systematic manner. However, we must always be aware that, in this sense, the model is, necessarily, a simplified version of reality. Bearing these points in mind let us now move on to a discussion of the way in which these system levels throw light on the relation between society and the activities of individuals.

The Physiological or Organic System

Although Parsons distinguishes the physiological or 'organic' level of the human body, he does not discuss it in great detail. For Parsons the body is a 'basic foundation' upon which other systems operate. In particular, there is much overlap between the body and the 'personality system' in Parsons's framework, in that the human body is a precondition for the development of the human psyche. In this sense the body is a 'container' for a fund of impulses, drives and motivations that make up the personalities of individuals. However, the personality of an individual cannot be understood simply in terms of his or her body (although without doubt a person's image of their body may play a pivotal role in their personality). The personality system has to be understood as a 'level of reality' in its own right. It has properties and characteristics which cannot be explained in terms of other levels, and this is an example of the principle of 'emergence' that I referred to before.

The Personality System

This is composed of motivational elements such as a person's beliefs, feelings, emotional attachments, wishes, desires, goals and objectives. These have been incorporated into the individual's attitudes and subjective responses to other people and the social world as a result of their own unique personal biographies. Such biographies trace an individual's experience of growing up in their families and subsequent social contexts like peer groups and work groups that have had a formative effect on their personalities. They also include various 'internalised' beliefs and moral standards that are current or dominant in society.

The individual's motivational 'needs' push him or her to seek gratification generally in terms of the 'solutions' laid down in socially acceptable forms and standards of behaviour. Thus, the individual seeks emotional attachments in the context of the family or romantic love, or seeks great wealth through hard work. In this way the personality system overlaps with the other systems. Nonetheless, it is a unique amalgam that results from this complex of influences. Thus, it too has to be understood as a system in its own right with its own 'emergent properties'.

The Social System

Confusingly, Parsons sometimes uses the term 'social system' (as in the title of his 1951 book) to refer generally to 'society' (society as a social system). At other times, he speaks of the social system as simply one dimension of society which has its own distinct 'emergent properties'. Parsons illustrates this by imagining how the first social systems arose. This 'thought experiment' involves the idea of two (or more) individuals interacting with each other. In order to communicate and co-operate effectively with each other they establish certain understandings and agreements about the nature of their relationship and the sorts of things it will include. In short, they develop a set of common 'expectations' about their mutual behaviour which, over time, tend to shape their orientations to each other.

An example of this can be seen in the development of a friendship relationship. When they first meet, people tend to be rather tentative towards each other but, over time, understandings emerge around mutual interests and passions. Sometimes 'private' languages or meanings are 'created' in order to exclude others and to enhance the depth of shared commitment to each other. In an analogous manner, we can see that social systems emerge from interactions which are repeated over time and which produce durable expectations about the behaviour of those involved. In a fully developed social system such as modern society, these expectations become 'institutionalised'. That is, they become part of the accepted fabric of society which people have to take into account when formulating their behaviour.

Crucially, such expectations revolve around roles and positions in society that have proved to be important to its continuous and efficient functioning. Such networks of positions and roles can be seen in all sectors of society, from the more formal occupational sphere with its authority positions and work roles, through the governmental and economic institutions into the more private and informal worlds of family, love and friendship. In the family and school, and in later socialising agencies, individuals are introduced to the expectations that surround different roles and thus learn how to play them. Many roles, such as that of 'mother', 'father', 'friend' and so on, do not involve any formal training so to speak, rather they are learned without conscious effort. Other more formal roles, like those in the work world or in the realm of politics, have to be more consciously learned and adopted.

The Cultural System

To understand the nature of the cultural system we have to view processes of 'emergence' in a longer-term perspective. Human interaction over long periods of time creates cultural products not only in terms of artifacts, like furniture or buildings of different styles, but also in terms of different forms of knowledge, literature, art and traditions. A specific characteristic of modern societies is that there is a vast wealth of written knowledge (as opposed to the oral cultures of simpler societies).

In this sense, the cultural system is the 'store-house' of the cultural forms and human products that represent the history and traditions of particular societies. The cultural system 'contains' the core values and other normative elements which give each society its cultural distinctiveness. Thus, the 'emergent' features of the cultural system are reflected in the sedimentation of values and tradition;

in short, the cultural heritage of society. As such, the cultural system is unlike the social system in that it is not as closely tied to the interactions between people. Nonetheless, the values and traditions of society indirectly underpin and inform much of this day-to-day behaviour.

The 'Needs' of the Social System

Although the four systems interpenetrate and overlap, the social system is the centrepoint of Parsons's framework. It is here that the stuff of everyday life is routinely enacted; it is here that the substantial weight of society lies. As we shall see, this is reflected in Parsons's more specific vision of the relationship between the individual and society. However, Parsons also suggests that particular systems have 'needs' that must be met in order for them to remain in good and continuous working order. The analogy that Parsons employs here is that of a living organism. Unless certain requirements are forthcoming, such as food and water, and some kind of mechanism exists to convert these things into energy (like a digestive tract), then the organism will die. So, too, will a human society and its various parts. Thus, the social system has its 'needs' or requirements that must be serviced in order to remain properly operational. Parsons suggests there are four principal social system needs which are met by various sectors of society. These are as follows:

Social system need	Fulfilled by
1 Adaptation	The economy – money
2 Goal attainment	The political system – power
3 Integration	Social controls, legal and informal – influence
4 Pattern maintenance	Socialisation – commitment

Figure 2.2 *System needs and their fulfilment*

By using this classification, Parsons is, in effect, 'making sense' of the immediately recognisable major institutions in society in terms of his wider framework. Each institutional sector services important needs which are essential for the survival of the society as a whole. The first, adaptation, is concerned with the economic production of commodities and wealth by manipulation of the environment. The resource that drives this sector is money. The political sector takes care of goal attainment by co-ordinating activities through the legitimate use of power.

If these two sectors concentrate on 'external' problems, then the other two focus on the internal needs of society. The requirement that a society does not fall into disarray through internal conflict and dissent is handled by the influence of the social community. Thus, formal legal controls as well as informal sanctions (such as ostracism, gossip and so on) help to cement individual members of society to the groups to which they belong. These integrative mechanisms are supplemented by more psychologically based forms of commitment. Processes of socialisation serve to instil the central values and norms of society in its members. These 'pattern-maintaining' elements reinforce the core values in society, by promoting consensus and by ensuring that there is a basic level of conformity.

The Individual and Society: The Macro–Micro Link

Let me now tie all the pieces together to give a general impression of Parsons's solution to the problem which is the principal focus of this book: the connections between macro and micro elements of social life. Parsons himself generally does not speak in terms of 'macro' and 'micro' levels of analysis. His favoured terminology is that of the relation between the individual and society. In effect, Parsons's solution to the individual–society question also provides answers to the macro–micro dilemma (as well as the relation between agency and structure). This is because these oppositions basically refer to the same things in Parsons's work, and therefore the same solution applies to them all.

As we have seen, Parsons views society as a series of interconnected layers or 'system levels'. Thus it is not surprising that his view of the relation between the individual and society involves pinpointing the mechanism which is principally responsible for binding together these different levels. Parsons is very clear that it is the notion of social role which is of primary importance in establishing the connection between individual personalities and social systems. For Parsons, 'role' is the bridge between the individual (both as a biological organism and as definite personality), and the rest of society as represented in the social and cultural systems. By enacting the social roles that constitute the day-to-day substance of society, the unique needs and motivations of people are met by social arrangements. Conversely, the cultural values and norms that give society its distinctive character find their way into the lives of people via the system of social roles.

According to Parsons this meshing of individuals to their social context occurs partly because people feel the need to fulfil the expectations associated with various roles. These needs arise for two main reasons. First, during the process of socialisation, parents and other significant people inculcate their children with moral values, appropriate patterns of behaviour and so on. As adults, the same individuals tend to adhere to these learned 'role expectations' as blueprints for their ongoing behaviour, thereby reducing uncertainty and giving direction to behaviour. They provide, as it were, a shared set of 'rules of the game' and a stock of background knowledge which people may draw upon to enable them to achieve their goals and intentions in their dealings with others. Secondly, by adhering to the standards and rules of behaviour associated with roles, the person gains the support and trust of others and this in itself reinforces the conforming response. Thus, people become locked into a set of mutual obligations by being committed to the rewards associated with them.

The Pattern Variables

Parsons's wish to retain the idea that people are free to choose their own courses of action, and the idea that the social system (in the form of role expectations) influences and guides their initial choices, creates a certain tension in his framework. This is further emphasised by the addition of what he terms the 'pattern variables', which refer to the range of options open to people in various kinds of situation. The pattern variables are more general than role expectations, and represent the dilemmas that confront people in various situations. Nonetheless, they also represent the wider context in which particular role expectations are shaped. Before I endeavour to explain this in more detail let us examine the pattern variables as they are described by Parsons.

Affectivity versus Affective Neutrality   In simple terms, this refers to the extent to which people become emotionally involved in particular kinds of social relationship. In some relationships, such as family and friendships, we feel emotionally close and open to others. In more 'business-like' relationships we adopt a more emotionally neutral attitude. This is the case in professional–client relationships (such as that between doctor and patient).

Specificity versus Diffuseness   Some of our relationships are very specific in that they are based on a single thread of interest, such as our momentary connection with the ticket collector at a rail or bus station. In contrast, our relationship with a marriage partner is based on a large number of common interests, and thus could be described as being more diffuse in nature.

Universalism versus Particularism   In some contexts we relate to people in terms of general rules which apply to everybody, in other cases we deal with individuals in terms of whether they belong to a special group or category. Racial and sexual discrimination are good examples of the application of particular, rather than objective, general criteria.

Quality versus Performance   This is similar to the one above and refers to whether we treat people in terms of what or who they are rather than in terms of what they can be expected to achieve. Again racial and sexual discrimination are examples of this.

Self-orientation versus Collectivity-orientation   This underlines the dilemma between acting primarily in terms of one's self-interest, or sacrificing this for the greater good of the community. In short, do we seek individual gain from our actions and relationships, or do we strive to support the interests of the wider community?

These pattern variables are meant to express real dilemmas for people in their everyday activities in the sense that they have to 'decide' how to relate to others in terms of the alternatives. Here we can clearly see the significance of Gouldner's argument that Parsons directly opposes the Marxist assumption that human behaviour is more or less determined by the economic and political structure of capitalist society. In this sense, the choice between alternative courses of action is meant to underline the 'voluntarism' or freedom of action of people in their daily lives. However, further reflection suggests that in many cases the solutions to these supposed dilemmas are not simply the product of free choice by the individual. Rather, it is often the nature of the relationship or the situation that implies, or sometimes even demands, a certain kind of solution.

Parsons provides a good example of the manner in which roles and the pattern variables intersect, through an analysis of the doctor–patient relationship in modern society in Chapter 10 of *The Social System*. According to Parsons the doctor must treat his or her patient in a fair and open-minded manner (universalism). The doctor must not be tempted to give preferential treatment to certain people because of their personality, or because they have the same social background as the doctor (particularism). Furthermore, the role has very clearly defined limits (specificity). This ensures that the doctor focuses solely on the patient's illness rather than the broad spectrum of their lives (diffuseness). This removes from the spotlight the many other aspects of their patients' lives which may be irrelevant to (and get in the way of) the job of restoring them back to health.

Similarly, a doctor is not expected to become emotionally over-involved with patients (affectivity), since this would make it impossible to treat them in the most appropriate and rational manner (affective neutrality). Finally, doctors are expected to act in terms of the best interests of their patients (collectivity-orientation), rather than their own private interests (self-orientation). For Parsons then, these (pattern variable) characteristics give shape and direction to the role and this, in turn, allows the doctor to delve sufficiently deeply into the patient's affairs in order to help them combat their illness.

Parsons's portrayal of doctor's behaviour in modern societies has been criticised for presenting a rather idealised view of medical practice and for neglecting the empirical variability associated with the role. However, the example shows the way in which the pattern variables are intimately tied to role expectations. Whereas the expectations themselves refer to the details or 'substance' of behaviour which is appropriate in particular situations, the pattern variables refer to the general parameters of the role. The example also clearly indicates that, in the main, the social system provides the 'solutions' to the dilemmas of action supposedly faced by people in their day-to-day behaviour. Thus in his later work Parsons regards the influence and demands of the social system as taking precedence over the voluntary aspects of social behaviour (Scott, 1963; Bohman, 1991).

This is as far as I want to take my description of Parsons's work at this point. In the following sections I shall deal with some of the main criticisms of Parsons's work as they bear upon the problem of the relationship between macro and micro elements of society.

Human Puppets:
The Problem of Determinism

The vision of the human being as a role-player who 'internalises' the norms and values of society allows Parsons to say that people are 'social' and 'individual' at the same time. However, the way that Parsons actually achieves this linkage has led to the charge of 'determinism'. As Garfinkel (1967), Blumer (1969) and others have pointed out, in Parsons's system people passively assimilate the rules and roles that they have been socialised into and unthinkingly behave in accordance with the established cultural guidelines. People's own reasons, accounts, justifications, motives and so on, play no part. A creative dimension to human behaviour seems entirely missing.

Giddens (1976) has expressed a similar view in a rather different manner. He suggests that Parsons (along with other sociologists who have focused on institutions), concentrates on the problem of social 'reproduction' at the expense of social 'production'. In other words, Parsons is more successful in accounting for the manner in which social institutions persist over time through the activities of the people who operate them. This can be seen, for example, in the way that the day-to-day activities of hospital personnel and patients constantly reproduce the organisational patterns which make it recognisably a hospital in the first place. However, Giddens's point is that this sort of approach neglects the very important 'productive' aspects of people's activities. For instance, personnel and patients are constantly bending or reinventing the hospital rules and procedures. In creatively applying their knowledge in the local circumstances of wards, both staff and patients produce new social arrangements in the hospital. Clearly, therefore, Parsons's framework (and others like it) cannot account for this creative aspect of day-to-day interaction.

Over-emphasis on Conformity

Dennis Wrong (1967) complains that Parsons has created an 'oversocialised' image of the human being as a passive conformist. He suggests that although people may indeed 'internalise' various norms and values, this does not mean that they will automatically conform to them. Even if someone feels guilty about breaking the law or some social convention (and we should not assume that this is always the case), this is no guarantee that it will stop them. In Wrong's view Parsons provides no understanding of the way in which elemental impulses and motivations constantly jostle with the requirements of social conformity and discipline, and often win out in the struggle. Parsons gives too much credence to the idea that people are basically 'acceptance seekers' in the sense that they seek the approval of others by conforming to shared norms.

Wrong asks about motives born out of material interests such as sexual drives and the quest for power, including the power to impose one's own definitions of what is appropriate and 'right' upon other people. It is true that people are 'social' in the sense that they know a lot about the culture in which they are born and that they are able to operate efficiently or 'get by' in social life. The point is that it does not follow that they are completely moulded by the norms and values of their culture. Wrong points out that it was Freud who drew attention to the fact that biologically based drives, to some degree or other, always break through social and psychological mechanisms of control. This is somewhat ironic since Parsons felt he was incorporating Freud's emphasis on motivation in his notion of personality needs. Unfortunately, these personality needs are shorn of the self-centred preoccupations that inevitably come into conflict with social convention and discipline.

Over-emphasis on Harmony, Integration and Consensus

Gouldner (1971: 220–1) points out that there is far too much emphasis on the harmonious nature of the process of self-development in Parsons's work. While the approving responses of other people are a central means of developing self-esteem, conflict with others is also a necessary part of the development of self-identity and self-regard. By stressing difference from others through tension and conflict, an individual's identity becomes more distinct and clearly defined. Parsons's fundamental image of the human as an acceptance-seeker who eagerly co-operates with others is, therefore, questionable. A more appropriate view would stress that people are also confrontational and need to define their own individuality by marking their differences from others.

At the collective and society-wide levels too, Parsons continually underplays the importance of conflict and dissensus amongst groups and between parts of society (Dahrendorf, 1959; Rex, 1961; Gouldner, 1971). In this respect Parsons is essentially a conservative thinker who ignores the exploitative and unequal character of capitalist society, along with the resulting division and disharmony. Certainly it does appear that Parsons over-stresses the amount of consensus and integration between social groupings such as managers and workers in industry. Similarly, when he speaks of the core institutional spheres such as family, economy, polity and religion and so on, Parsons seems to assume a high level of integration between them based on mutual co-operation and overlapping interests.

Neglect of Inequality and Material Interests

Parsons's lack of focus on issues of conflict and disharmony in society is not simply a matter of unequal emphasis. At the heart of the matter is a very different view of the nature of society and the forces that bind it together as a coherent whole. In an important paper, Lockwood (1956) noted that Parsons's view of society neglects the role of the material interests of certain groups of people, as opposed to interests structured around core values and norms. This directs our attention to the fact that inequalities exist in society (for example, class, gender and ethnic inequalities) and that they significantly influence people's lives. Thus, the inability of the lowest ranking groups to command various resources like money, property and goods and services impinges on the quality of their lives and directly influences their general life chances. Coupled with the discrimination suffered in terms of employment opportunities, harassment and housing opportunities, we can see that such situations can produce non-normative or material interests.

In this sense there is a material basis for resistance to, and conflict with, central values and norms, producing tension and disharmony in society. Also, volatile situations may be created in which, at one and the same time, forms of consumerism are stressed, such as having an expensive car or owning household gadgetry, but where people are also denied the means of access (money, jobs) to these goods. This often results in the adoption of 'illegitimate' means (crime, delinquency) in order to obtain the goods or achieve the valued lifestyle (Merton, 1967). Certainly, Parsons is guilty of missing out the material interests that motivate people by focusing on central values in modern society, such as 'equality of opportunity', 'reward for effort' and 'individual initiative'. By ignoring barriers to the achievement of the things stressed in these values, Parsons fails to understand that various groups of people may be motivated by interests other than normative ones.

Having mentioned it in passing, let me dwell on Merton's work a little longer because it gives us some impression of the variations in the 'functionalist' school of thought in sociology at this period of time. Although Merton shared a commitment to many of Parsons's fundamental concerns, he attempted much more to grapple with social processes that produce strain and conflict, and offered an image of the social actor as much less of a conformist. In Merton's work on deviance there is a real sense of the role of material interests and social inequalities in producing responses other than conforming ones. For instance, he identifies the kinds of situations mentioned above where people are influenced by pervasive success goals like the acquisition of wealth, but where they are also denied access to the means of achieving these goals (because, perhaps, of a disadvantaged class position). Merton argues that this kind of situation may produce a range of responses including conformity, innovation (breaking norms and criminal behaviour), ritualism, retreatism ('dropping-out' of society – tramps and down-and-out alcoholics) and sheer rebellion.

Merton suggests that the actual response that is chosen depends upon a number of factors, including the amount of pressure that a person is subjected to, the values they hold and the degree to which the local circumstances (including class) 'prohibit' the use of illegitimate means like crime. For example, those who opt for the retreatist response (alcoholism, drug addiction and psychotic withdrawal) choose this means of 'escape' because of failure to achieve success goals and a disinclination to break social rules and conventions. Such is the case often with downwardly mobile persons or retired middle-class types. However, retreatism may also result from unsuccessful attempts at innovation (crime) by those in the lower social classes or from slum areas. Moving away from the details, it is clear that Merton offers a vision of social activity as the product of the creative and adaptive responses of people to the social circumstances in which they find themselves. In this sense, Merton's version of functionalist sociology escapes from the extreme determinism of Parsons's framework as well as taking into account some fundamental dimensions of social inequality.

Also, Merton's work on role conflict and strain provides us with a version of role theory which is less tied to the conformism, consensus and harmony that is a feature of Parsons's work. Merton (1967) points out that many roles (such as that of school teacher) are surrounded by a complement of other roles (such as school board members, parents, children), all of whom have their own expectations about the teacher's role behaviour. In many cases these expectations come into conflict and cause strain and dissension amongst the members of the 'role set'. Other functionalist writers (notably Gross et al., 1958) took up Merton's lead here and investigated the degree of consensus (and thus also of disagreement) and conflict among those involved in defining particular roles. In Merton's work in particular, there is a strong sense of the influence of material interests and the role of power differentials in society which is absent in Parsons's work. This brief discussion of Merton has served to reinforce the view that, while Parsons is perhaps the most influential of functionalist theorists, it is unwise to view functionalism as a uniform school of thought. Thus many of the weaknesses identified in Parsons's framework cannot be assumed to be equally applicable to other writers within the functionalist tradition.

The Issues of Power and Ideology

For Parsons, the power structure of society is seen as a legitimate means through which the existing social order, based on reward for effort (and the inequalities this produces), is secured and maintained. Governments elected on the basis of democratic political systems exemplify this legitimate use of power. In this sense, governments are consensually agreed upon instruments which are empowered by the general populace to utilise, co-ordinate and distribute society's resources. It has been pointed out that Parsons neglects the coercive (or, at least, 'ambiguous') uses of power that often lie 'behind the scenes' of official business (Giddens, 1977). While Parsons emphasises the enabling features of power, the ability of the authorities to get things done, he neglects its constraining features. He overlooks the fact that power can be a means of securing the control of certain groups over others who also have legitimate claims. In this sense, power is a means of maintaining inequalities, regardless of their legitimacy. Parsons's understanding of power does not take into account that, even in democratic governments, political manipulation may be used as a means of securing the trust and compliance of those over whom power is wielded.

Furthermore, Parsons avoids the question of how the legitimacy of power may have been achieved in the first place. Many forms of power (and not just 'democratic', governmental power) have been achieved through coercion, struggle and conflict between groups with divergent interests. It is because Parsons defines power itself as part of the legitimate and overt authority structure of society that he tends to overlook these aspects.

More generally, Parsons is unable to view power as founded in entrenched and divergent group interests. He is almost wholly concerned with power as it is expressed in the relation between the individual and society. He views it as the 'power of society' confronting the individual (Giddens, 1977: 347). Parsons also neglects to examine the role of ideology in the establishment and maintenance of power relations. Insofar as ideology refers to sets of beliefs and values that serve to explain and justify existing power relations, then Parsons has no real need for the concept in the first place. For him, power is already legitimate, since it is an expression of trust and confidence in power-holders by subordinates. In this sense 'legitimacy' is simply an extension of the general agreement about central values.

In a more radical sense, ideology refers to beliefs and values (and the practices they embody), which may serve to legitimise power relations in an indirect and manipulative manner. On this definition, ideology serves to justify the inequalities created by power relations (and the means through which they are secured), by 'covering over' or disguising them. In this sense, ideology masks the exploitative nature of power relations and represents them as 'natural' and 'inevitable'. (An example of this is the way in which men's power over women (patriarchy) is justified on the basis that women are genetically programmed as the 'weaker' sex, rather than as a result of the systematic exclusion of women by men from positions of power.)

Of course, for Parsons to admit to the necessity of a conception of ideology in this sense would be to undermine his notion of the inherent legitimacy of power. All in all, then, we can appreciate that Parsons views the integration of society – the way it is 'knitted together' so to speak – as founded upon the twin ideas of consensus on central values, and the legitimacy of power arrangements. This diverts attention from central issues relating to the way in which power and ideology may be used as means of securing and maintaining inequalities that serve sectional rather than 'collective' interests.

The Problem of Informal and Unofficial Practices

In face-to-face interaction people depart from tried and tested ideas and conventions far more than Parsons envisages. In this sense we have to be aware that unofficial and informal 'expectations' grow up in and around even the most routine and seemingly rule-bound activities, such as those involved in work and occupational tasks. For example, in their studies of police work, Bittner (1967) and Preiss and Ehrlich (1966) have noted that police officers routinely act in accordance with informal and unofficial 'rules of thumb' which depart from, and often contradict, the official guidelines outlined in training, or emphasised in official manuals. These rules constitute informal, on-the-job knowledge which has grown up out of the practical experience of police officers. As Bittner observes, in their day-to-day contacts with the down-and-out residents of skid row, the police are less concerned with upholding the letter of the law than they are with 'keeping the peace'. Importantly, this may involve ignoring minor infractions of the law or even arresting someone on a trumped up (but minor) charge so as to keep them out of trouble.

In this respect, Turner (1988) suggests that despite Parsons's talk about developing a 'theory of action' he is primarily concerned with classifying the basic elements of action in a fairly abstract manner (as in the pattern variables), rather than with describing the ways in which people actually interact with each other. Thus Parsons often ends up concentrating on what role players 'ought' to be doing rather than on what they actually do.

The Emergent Nature of Interaction

Face-to-face interaction is far more dynamic than Parsons supposes. In specific situations, people are actively involved in creating understandings between themselves and others on the spur of the moment and in the light of the unfolding circumstances. Whatever purpose they have in mind (for example, to control the situation, to influence a particular person or simply to create a congenial atmosphere), any one person has to take into account the intentions and wishes of the others involved, otherwise their own may be thwarted. In the 'give and take' that occurs in interactions between several people, there emerge working definitions and rules of thumb about how the participants will conduct themselves. These emergent definitions (as reflected in, for example, a 'tense' situation or a light-hearted encounter), generally 'fade away' as the people involved go their separate ways. However, such emergent definitions and the local practices based on them have to be regarded as emerging from 'within' the situations in which they occur, as creations of the participants, rather than as given, external and binding rules (Garfinkel, 1967; Cicourel, 1973).

Giddens (1979: 117) offers a related but somewhat different form of criticism by suggesting that we must understand social systems as *reproduced practices* rather than roles. The notion of practice has a much wider connotation than 'role' and enables us to think in terms of what people are actually doing, and what is 'really' going on in various situations. The notion of role tends to restrict our focus by concentrating on what 'should' be happening from the point of view of various parties with vested interests. In this sense, it is practices rather than roles that are the primary point of connection between people and social structures. The idea that societies are composed of sets of 'reproduced' practices simply means the practices are recurrently used by people in their day-to-day lives, rather than unique occurrences. This connects with Turner's (1988) point that Parsons's account of interaction is rather thin. To properly render the relation between macro and micro phenomena, social activity has to be depicted in a 'thicker', more textured manner.

The Relation between Theory and Empirical Research

In certain basic respects, Parsons's work was not directly derived from empirical research, it is rather more the product of thinking through certain ideas and issues in a fairly abstract way. On the basis of this Glaser and Strauss (1971), among others, suggest that Parsons's work is therefore inherently 'speculative'. In other words, they imply that it is of dubious merit because it has little obvious connection with 'the facts' as they apply directly to people's lives. Of course, there is something in the charge that Parsons paid too little attention to the world of facts and empirical data. However, it is far too sweeping to suggest that his work is 'speculative' in the sense that it lacks any grounding at all in the real world.

It is precisely because Parsons's work does make some recognisable claims about the social world we experience that it cannot be written off as a purely speculative endeavour. Rather, it has to be appreciated that such work is couched at a high level of generality and abstraction. Its empirical anchoring is, therefore, of a different kind from theory which has emerged directly from empirical data (see Layder, 1993, for an extended discussion of this issue). This kind of criticism is related to another type which claims that Parsons's framework is more concerned with description and classification than with explanation. Here critics (for example Craib, 1984) point to the fact that Parsons appears preoccupied with constructing a set of analytic categories (types of action, types of system and sub-systems, pattern variables and so on), to the exclusion of other (particularly empirical) concerns.

To a certain extent it is true that Parsons gives undue attention to these seemingly endless conceptual refinements. This may create the impression that his framework is an elaborate system of classification (rather like scientific exhibits in a display case), instead of a theory which explains how things work. Certainly there is a tendency in Parsons's work towards 'filing', or otherwise 'arranging' aspects of the social world under various conceptual labels. However, beyond this it is equally true to say that Parsons's framework is a genuine attempt to explain social mechanisms and processes. For example, as we saw with the analysis of the doctor role, Parsons's 'pattern variable' analysis does attempt to explain some features of doctor–patient interaction. In this sense, doctors are expected to focus on the patient's illness, to be emotionally uninvolved and so on. Now the point is not necessarily that Parsons is offering us the 'right', or even the most adequate, explanation here. This would depend upon the type or depth of explanation required and this may in turn depend upon the presentation and weighing up of various kinds of evidence. Rather, the point is that he is offering us an *explanation* which tells us why doctors behave the way they do, rather than a description which simply outlines various aspects of their behaviour.

The same is true for almost all aspects of Parsons's framework, such as the relationship between the different system levels and the way in which he accounts for social integration. They all represent attempts to explain various features of society. We do not have to believe that Parsons's ideas are right beyond all doubt or that they are the only possible ones to be considered, in order to accept that they are genuine attempts to explain. In any case, more often than not it is difficult to separate out aspects of explanation and description in any clear way. Thus, it is far too easy to undervalue the importance of Parsons's work as a form of explanation. More generally, being aware of the different types of explanation that are employed by various sociologists is likely to be a more fruitful way of distinguishing between theories and evaluating their importance. It must be noted that Merton's (1968) work on the relation between theory and research is much more committed to the role of empirical research as a direct means of developing and establishing the validity of social theory. Thus, again, it is important to note the variability in the functionalist school of thought that Parsons's work has come to exemplify.

The Difference Between Action and System

I think there is also a possibility of misunderstanding the nature of Parsons's project with regard to his overall vision of society. This has a direct bearing on the macro–micro problem. It is true that Parsons does not distinguish between what Lockwood (1964) refers to as social integration and system integration. This highlights a distinction between the way in which people are socially related, as compared with the way parts of society – institutions – are related to each other. Clearly, this makes it difficult for Parsons to talk about, for example, the possibility of an economic recession (disturbance of system integration) occurring in society without it having any effects on people's adherence to values and norms in society (maintenance of social integration). However, I do not think it is accurate to generalise from this and say that Parsons has no conception of social structure 'underlying people's actions and meanings, but separate from them' (Craib, 1984).

In this respect, the claim that Parsons views the social system as 'congealed action' is something of an overstatement. Although Parsons does move from a general concern with actors' choices and meanings to a focus on the way in which these are determined by the social system, it does not follow that he takes action and systems (or structures) to be the same thing. It is unwise to argue that Parsons starts with action and then works up to structures and systems and thus to conclude that he believes that the latter are simply forms of congealed action.

This is to neglect the importance of what Parsons referred to as the 'emergent properties' of different action systems (the social system being one of them), and which I mentioned in my initial discussion.

The Emergent Nature of Systems

One of the conclusions that Parsons drew from his review of classical theory in his book *The Structure of Social Action* (1937), is that a viable sociological theory of action must be based upon the assumption of the emergent properties of social systems. Like Durkheim (1982), Parsons believed that social phenomena exist in their own right at their own (social) level of reality and must be explained in terms of this particular level. Durkheim had in mind principally the notion that psychological aspects of people's behaviour must not be mixed up with the social aspects. For example, collective phenomena like values, norms and culture have socially produced characteristics which are misunderstood if it is imagined that they are the products of individual psychology. In sum, the 'general' nature of social phenomena (their spread and range of applicability), their ability to influence behaviour and their continued existence beyond the lifetimes of individuals are uniquely social in character. For Durkheim (and for Parsons), this means that they cannot be explained in terms of the motives, intentions or needs of individuals.

This notion of emergent properties can be seen in Parsons's analysis of system levels. The needs and personal meanings that shape a person's behaviour do not constitute the social system or vice versa, even though each services the needs of the other to some degree. However, it must be remembered that there is a heavy emphasis on the need for social acceptance (through conformity) in Parsons's theory. In this sense, it is logically possible for an imbalance of 'dependency' to exist between the two systems. It is feasible to imagine, for example, that a person may be extremely conformist, even though this may be unusual. Thus, the individual may be dependent upon social encounters and relationships to meet his or her personality needs. However, the social system does not rely on specific individuals for its continued existence. Rather, it depends upon sizeable networks of individuals who routinely reproduce its features in their daily activities.

Also Parsons was well aware that, over time, social systems evolve complex structural features (Parsons, 1966). Over many generations, and through large networks of people, 'emergent' aspects become established and relatively stable features of the social system. In this sense, people are confronted by an already existing system and are 'forced' to deal with it in many different ways. On the one hand there are those who reluctantly fit in with society, or actively resist such incorporation through deviance and rebellion. On the other, the different styles of conformity range from those who 'go along' with the system because it is the only reasonable alternative, to those who whole-heartedly endorse and identify with the central values and institutions of society.

The Layered Nature of Society

Parsons does not view structures and systems as composed of basically the same stuff as action, rather he sees social processes as 'layered'. It is Parsons's commitment to a layered view of society that partly rescues him from criticisms which suggest that he 'reifies' society. 'Reification' refers to the mistaken assumption that the products of human endeavour (material objects as well as social arrangements such as institutions) are, in fact, the work of non-human entities, such as Gods or mystical forces. In relation to society, this involves the idea that social structures and systems 'seem' to have a life of their own, somehow disembodied from human beings absorbed in their daily business. It is a mistake to talk about society in this way since 'in reality', it is composed of human individuals. Those who make this criticism of Parsons often confuse the fact that he attempts to construct a layered model of society with the idea that this involves reification. Thus they miss the fact that the point of such a model is to distinguish between different features of society and their appropriate levels of analysis.

A similar confusion is entailed in the claim that Parsons's theory enforces a false 'split' between the individual and society (Elias, 1978a; Burkitt, 1991). I shall deal with this claim in more detail in Chapter 7, but two brief points need to be made here. First, according to Wrong's criticism, Parsons is, in fact, rather more guilty of proposing an 'oversocialised' individual. In this sense, Parsons tends to assume too close a relation between the individual and society (rather than a split), and this creates an image of the over-conforming acceptance-seeker. Secondly, the idea that there are different system levels (individual and social) with distinct characteristics may be misconstrued as a split or separation. Certainly, Parsons is a 'dualist' in the sense that he views activities and institutions as partly independent features of society. But this does not involve a separation or split between the individual and society.

In Parsons's theory people are interlinked and dependent on each other via networks of social roles. In this sense, the theory has much in common with other sociological theories. It is the specific manner in which the linkages and connections between activity and institutions are formulated (or modelled) that distinguishes Parsons's theory from others. As before, Parsons's inattention to the subtleties and complexities of interaction is the crucial weakness here, and not that he falsely separates society from individuals.

What Can Be Learned from Parsons?

Although Parsons's framework is often seen as outmoded and in dire need of radical revision, some modern theorists have taken Parsons as the central point of reference for a revived interest in his brand of 'functionalist' theory (Alexander, 1985a; Munch, 1987). Also, Parsons's work has left its imprint on the work of a central figure in modern social theory, Jürgen Habermas. The importance of Habermas's work lies in its attempt to reconcile some of Parsons's ideas on social systems with other strands of theory which emphasise the 'action' elements of society (see Chapter 10). Parsons's 'layered' model is directly pertinent to Habermas's ideas about a fundamental distinction in society between the 'lifeworld' and 'system'. I shall go on to argue that Habermas's theory deals more successfully with the linkages between macro and micro aspects of society. However, it must not be forgotten that elements of the Parsonian framework reappear in Habermas's work.

It is undeniable, as various critics have pointed out, that there is a tendency for Parsons to construe 'action' in rather static terms. Of course, attention needs to be directed to the dynamic qualities of social activity (also, as we have said, to the more textured interpersonal aspects) in order to fully link macro and micro phenomena. However, perhaps the great virtue of Parsons's theory is its appreciation of society as something which has 'ontological depth'. This is really a technical way of referring to what I have otherwise termed the 'layered nature' of society.

Just as in our everyday lives we experience physical reality as a series of distinct but connected substances or entities, then so is society composed of distinct aspects. We know that mountains are quite different and distinct from the air we breathe or the animals and cars with which we coexist. Nonetheless, we are equally sure that all these things are interrelated and mutually dependent on each other. We find this way of thinking about such things quite natural and to some extent 'obvious'. In a similar manner, society is made up of elements of fundamentally different kinds, but which are completely and inescapably linked to each other. It is this aspect of social reality that is highlighted in Parsons's work.

SUMMARY

- Parsons's influence on sociological thought was once very strong and although it has subsequently waned, there is continued interest in his work as a whole as well as particular aspects of it.

- Parsons views society in terms of its constituent sub-systems: the physiological system, the personality system, the social (role) system and the cultural system. The survival and smooth running of the social system as a whole depends on its 'needs' being fulfilled.

- The link between individuals and society (or the social system) is fashioned through social roles. These are structured around social expectations about appropriate behaviour associated with different roles as well as 'pattern variables' which express wider 'dilemmas' of action.

- With his emphasis on the overwhelming influence of the social system, Parsons has been criticised for his image of human beings as 'oversocialised' conformists whose behaviour is largely determined by system constraints.

- Parsons's critics point out that he over-emphasises harmony, integration and conformity in society and that he neglects reproduced inequalities and the material interests, power and ideological elements that underpin them.

- As symbolic interactionists and phenomenologists have highlighted, Parsons's account of social interaction neglects situational and emergent factors. While Parsons does sometimes employ over-elaborate classifications of social phenomena, it is easy to overlook the explanatory importance of his conceptual framework.

- Although deficient in certain respects, Parsons's work has had enduring influence on social analysis. Prominent are his notion of the emergent nature of systems, his 'dualist' vision of activities and institutions as partly independent features of society, and his view of society as possessing 'ontological depth'.

3

Varieties of Marxism

PREVIEW

- The different strands or interpretations of Marx's ideas.

- Basic themes in Marx's work: historical materialism and social development; the importance of the economic base of society; material interests; class divisions and sectional interests; power and domination; the alienating effects of capitalism; the functions of ideology.

- Structural Marxism: its account of everyday life, the rejection of the individual creative subject, people as 'bearers' or system supports. Marxism as an objective science, the relation between theory and evidence.

- Humanistic Marxism: individual personality as moulded by the economy, the family and the state. The individual's 'dialectical' relationship with the social order, the importance of resistance and dissent.

- The weaknesses of structural Marxism and the rise of post-structuralism and postmodernism.

- The lasting contribution of Marx's thought; the importance of history and group interests; the analysis of power and domination, processes of social transformation; the nature of social order and social integration; the agency–structure and macro–micro problems.

In this chapter I draw attention to the various strands of Marxism in social theory which have played an important role in the debate about the relations between the individual, society, and social activity. I shall begin by outlining some of Marx's basic ideas which have served as the foundation for later interpretations of his thought. In the following three sections of the chapter I concentrate on a strand of thought known as 'structural Marxism'. I want to show that despite the many marked differences between this and Parsons's theory, there are some striking similarities in its view of the relation between macro and micro elements. The term 'structural Marxism' is a bit of a mouthful, but it does highlight important features. First, it refers to a central connection with the work of Karl Marx and, secondly, it indicates that it is one strand of the wide variety of ideas that can be grouped together under the label 'Marxism'.

The 'structural' part of the term refers to the fact that this particular brand of Marxist theory emphasises the importance of the structural or macro elements of society as opposed to the interactional or micro features. (There are variants of Marxism that give more weight to micro aspects, and I deal with these in later sections.) Structural Marxism came to prominence in the 1970s (although its influence has since dwindled) and is particularly associated with the work of Louis Althusser. I shall only concentrate on those aspects of this work that relate to central issues covered in this book. Thus, I shall leave aside many of the complexities, especially the more exclusively structural issues.

After evaluating structural Marxism I turn to a consideration of other forms of Marxism that are less extreme and allow more room for creative social activity. I then move on to a preliminary consideration of poststructuralism and postmodernism, two perspectives which in many ways have developed as a reaction against structuralism (the more general school of thought that goes under this name, rather than simply the Marxist version), and Marxism itself. Much of the critical attack from poststructural and postmodern ideas centres on a dissatisfaction with the general nature of Marxist theory – its attempt to give a comprehensive overview of history and society. I conclude the chapter with a general assessment of the contribution of Marx's ideas and those of later commentators. I suggest that, although there are serious shortcomings in Marxism, it nonetheless does raise some issues which are absolutely central to an adequate understanding of the macro–micro link.

The Background: Some of Marx's Basic ideas

Let me outline some of the principles underlying Marx's thought as a series of points. These not only serve as a background to the immediate discussion of structural Marxism, but will also provide the basis for a discussion of some other strands of modern theory. These have either drawn on Marx's work and have been incorporated into new theories (such as Habermas's), or have been formulated in direct opposition to some of the central ideas of Marxism (Foucault).

Historical Materialism

This has several aspects, but its most basic assumption is that social activity is profoundly influenced by the material problems of producing food, clothing, shelter – the basic requirements of human existence. From the earliest of human (tribal) societies, these problems have 'set the tone' for social activity in general. How these problems of material production are solved varies from one historical era (and its corresponding type of society) to another. In modern (capitalist) society the sphere of work and its organisation into specialised occupations handles the requirements of human existence. Not only basic needs like food, clothing and housing, but other more 'sophisticated' goods and services are produced in an industrial and technologically advanced economy.

In stressing the importance of these material problems, Marx was reversing the emphasis found in the work of economists and social philosophers who were his contemporaries. Marx felt that these writers unduly stressed the importance of current ideas about politics, morality and economic theory as if they were 'pure' and detached from the pressing concerns of material existence. Moreover, this emphasis on the primacy of ideas as against material factors led them (perhaps unwittingly) to justify the social injustices and inequalities that resulted from the capitalist organisation of production. Marx clearly wanted to uproot this 'false' line of thought which implied that ideas themselves were more basic than, and independent of, material problems of existence. He proposed, in fact, that ideas actually derived from fundamental problems of production and the sphere of work. If we want to understand the current ideas and popular forms of thought of any historical era (including the modern one), we have to first understand the economic organisation upon which social relationships are based. In this sense, the economic foundation of society is the most important factor in understanding its overall functioning, and for social analysis generally.

Social Development

Another aspect of 'historical materialism' is the idea that modern society has emerged historically from previous forms of society. Marx envisaged a progressive movement from the earliest tribal societies, through ancient societies like Greece and Rome, to the feudal societies of medieval times, and then to the modern form, capitalist society. (Marx also often referred to this as 'bourgeois' society, because of the dominant role of the bourgeoisie or middle-class owners of industry.) For Marx, the final phase of the historical development of human society would be the overthrow of capitalism (through the revolutionary uprising of the working classes), and its replacement with communist society. The questions of the accuracy and usefulness of Marx's general ideas about social development raise some additional complex issues which have been the subject of much debate (Hindess and Hirst, 1975; Giddens, 1981b). However, for our purposes we need not pursue these issues. We simply need to register that Marx proposed this historical progression and that he suggested a certain inevitability about the movement of societies through it.

Societies as Historical Products

The first two points highlight the importance of a historical dimension to social analysis. That is, for Marx, it has been all too often forgotten that the form of society (its dominant social relationships) are a product of historical processes involving actual human activity, especially in the economic sphere. In this respect, we have to understand modern capitalist society in the context of the societies (and the social relations) that preceded it. The forms of class inequalities and power relations that support them have to be seen as historically specific (and potentially changeable) products, not as eternal and naturally given social circumstances. Marx emphasised that social arrangements are human products. History is not some impersonal process moved simply by great ideals or political objectives removed from the grasp of human activity. However, Marx also stressed that we must be constantly aware that history is the history of struggle between groups (primarily social classes) for dominance in the sphere of production and politics.

Importance of the Economic Base

Much of Marx's theoretical framework rests on the idea that economic institutions are of primary importance in society. Those who own the industries and factories that produce goods and services (the middle classes) are particularly powerful in this respect. They obtain profits by exploiting the labouring classes who work in their factories. According to Marx, this economic relationship of exploitation is the bedrock of capitalist society. Specific political, legal and religious social institutions arise out of this basic foundation, and serve to justify and mask the underlying and economically rooted power relationships. Without going into the ramifications of this, it suffices for our purposes to note that Marx proposes a distinction between an economic underlay (sometimes referred to as an 'infrastructure') and an institutional overlay (often referred to as a superstructure').

This relates back to the distinction that was raised in the previous chapter on Parsons. I pointed out that Lockwood criticised Parsons for placing too much emphasis on the way in which behaviour is influenced by the central values and norms of a society. Lockwood suggests that, in this sense, Parsons leaves out of account the influence of the 'substratum' of material factors and interests. This refers to much the same thing as is implied in Marx's notion of an economic infrastructure, although Lockwood does not seem to envisage it as exerting quite the same strength of influence. Unlike Parsons, Marx seems to place undue emphasis on the influence of the economic base. As Gouldner suggests, it is perhaps in relation to this that we must understand Parsons's preoccupation with the legitimacy of norms and values.

Class Divisions

As part of Marx's distinction between base and superstructure, he also highlights the class divisions in society. His basic model of class in modern societies is a two-class one, with the owners of the means of production (the bourgeoisie) exerting power over the property-less workers. All intermediate groupings become absorbed into either of these two principal classes. Their division is based on an exploitative relationship with the owners extracting more value from the workers in the form of profit than is returned to them in the form of wages. This relation of domination is sustained by the inequality of power resources at the disposal of the two groups. The owners have money, property and the law on their side, while the workers have only their own (physical) labour power at their disposal. Thus, the relationship is based on a conflict of interest and frequently lapses into actual conflict. The two are locked into an antagonistic relationship. Under certain conditions (the specifics do not concern us here), Marx predicted that the workers would realise the true nature of their exploited position and rise up against the oppressive regime which imprisoned them. Thus, in a revolutionary uprising, the working classes would displace the bourgeoisie and take over the reins of power in an egalitarian 'communist' society.

Such was the theory. I do not want to dwell on the many inadequacies and weaknesses involved in Marx's overall scenario. Much of what he foresaw did not happen. Much did happen which he did not foresee (such as the growth of 'intermediate' groupings like the new middle classes of managers, clerks and so on, or the emergence of skilled working-class groups). This ground has been extensively covered elsewhere (see Dahrendorf, 1959; Goldthorpe et al., 1968, 1969; Giddens, 1973) and, in any case, takes us away from our main concerns. What is of interest for present purposes is that Marx draws our attention to several important issues which are absent from Parsons's work (and others of similar persuasion like Robert Merton and Kingsley Davis).

These are first, a focus on issues of sectional (in this case class) interests. This raises the possibility of social conflict and dissension as a routine feature of modern societies and the necessity of accounting for, and studying such things. Secondly, Marx draws our attention to an examination of power and domination as a means through which social integration generally, and the consent of subordinate groups in particular, may be secured. It is also precisely these issues that have continued to play an important role in various interpretations and branches of Marxism, especially Althusser's 'structural' version.

Alienation under Capitalism

Marx also drew attention to some of the psychological consequences of living in a world where there are sharp divisions of interest and power. For subordinate groups in particular, the problem of being relatively powerless is a pressing one. 'Alienation' is the term that Marx uses to describe several related psychological conditions that afflict individuals and groups who have little control over their living conditions, working lives and future prospects. However, for Marx, alienation reaches its full destructive potential under capitalism and thus is historically emergent.

The most dehumanising conditions of work, and thus of life itself, are realised under the free market, profit-driven system that capitalism introduces. In such a system people are measured primarily by their labour value – how much profit they can produce for employers by expenditure of physical and mental labour – other personal aspects are ignored or become irrelevant. Thus, a loss of humanity is incurred. People may become 'estranged' and feel that there is a lack of 'connectedness' with their real selves or with other people (see Seeman, 1959; Blauner, 1964, for extensive discussions of these issues).

The Analysis of Ideology

The final aspect of Marx's framework that I want to touch on is his analysis of the role and functions of ideology in modern societies. Ideology is, in fact, the other side of the coin of Parsons's notion of a general consensus on values and norms. Marx's view is that values and norms are never simply neutral and 'innocent' expressions of the will of the majority. In this sense, values and norms are ideological in that they represent the interests and values of dominant groups. In the case of capitalism they represent the values and interests of the ruling bourgeoisie. However, ideological elements such as religious, political and moral ideas manage to secure the broad 'consent' of subordinate groups by masquerading as 'general' or 'universal' values and interests. Thus, for Marx, dominant values and norms are ideological in that they serve to justify the power position of ruling groups.

This they do by suggesting that the inequalities in society are natural, eternal and universal. Thus, present power arrangements are not viewed as the historical outcome of power struggles between groups in society and hence potentially changeable through further struggles. In this way attention is deflected from the reality of power and its consequences for subordinate groups in society. As a consequence, ideologies serve to mask power relations and prevent subordinate groups realising their true interests. In this respect then, Marx's notion of ideology sets up the possibility of a distinction between 'truth' and 'falsity' in the realm of ideas.

From this perspective, the truth can only be grasped by recognising and 'seeing through' the ideological facades that operate to conceal the reality that lies behind them. For the following discussion it is important to appreciate that Althusser develops and extends Marx's notion of ideology to account for the linkage between individual and society. Also, in a rather different way, Althusser uses the notion of ideology to demonstrate the validity of certain forms of theory as opposed to others. Further on still, we shall see that Foucault views this notion of ideology as one of the central weaknesses of structuralist Marxism.

People and Everyday Activity in Structural Marxism

People as Supports or Bearers of the Capitalist System

Since I have other more pressing objectives, I do not want to dwell on all aspects of this strand of Marxism. Therefore I shall go straight to a consideration of the problem of the relationship between action and structure. There is a sense in which

Marxism in general is concerned rather less with individual activity, and more with the possibilities of collective action. Thus one of Marx's principal concerns was with the working class (proletariat) as a collective force of political, and ultimately revolutionary social change. Specifying the conditions under which such collective action could be facilitated thus became (and to a certain extent still is) a central feature of all forms of Marxism. Nonetheless, some account of the role of the 'individual' in all this has always been required to fill out the picture completely.

Also, since not all phases of a society's history are characterised by social change or charged with revolutionary potential, it has always been necessary for Marxism to attend to the more routine and stable features of capitalism. It is in this respect particularly that Althusser's work (1969, see also Althusser and Balibar, 1970) has contributed. The question for Althusser is, how does the social system of capitalism reproduce itself? In other words, if we consider societies over time, what mechanisms ensure its continuity and give the impression that it remains pretty much the same sort of society? This is both a strength and weakness of Althusser's framework. While the question of reproduction is a crucial aspect of any social analysis, Althusser takes this to an extreme and thereby tends to neglect issues of change.

In order to handle the question of social reproduction, Althusser has to deal with it in the context of his vision of the general nature of society. Like Parsons, Althusser uses a layered model, but the layers are, in crucial respects, quite different. In particular, the bottom layer is occupied by the economic organisation of production. As is consistent with more general Marxist theory, this layer determines (in the final instance) the general character of the upper layers, as well as the perceptions and thoughts (consciousness) of people in general. The upper layers (political and ideological), however, are not simply derivatives of the economic base. There is a complex mutual reinforcement of economic, political and ideological organisation. Thus Althusser gives the impression that society is a rather durable structure which is highly resistant to change. Even though he is committed to the idea of eventual revolutionary change, it is difficult to see how this is possible in a framework of ideas which stress the rigidity of the general social system and the vice-like grip of its central power structure.

This stress on social reproduction in Althusser underlines a parallel with Parsons's work, despite the many other differences. Like Parsons, Althusser emphasises the binding nature of society and its dominant institutions for individual activity. It could be argued, however, that in Althusser's framework the space for the freedom, creativity and discretion of the individual virtually disappears. In this sense the theory is more extreme than Parsons's. However, instead of 'roles',

Althusser posits the idea that people occupy 'positions' in society. For Althusser and Balibar (1970), 'real' people are of secondary importance to the functions they serve in society. These functions are provided for through the positions that people occupy in society.

In this respect the economic institutions (work and its hierarchical relations of authority) are a dominant feature. Individuals are assigned to particular (work and occupational) positions within the productive processes of the economy. Other core positions centre around the state (government, administration, army and police and so on). In Althusser's framework (see also Poulantzas, 1975, 1976) these play a fairly repressive role in keeping the general population, and in particular the labour force, pliable and submissive. Other, more dispersed institutions, such as the family and religious and educational organisations, are directly responsible for purveying and disseminating ideology.

The Role of Ideology

To ensure a skilled and willing labour force, labourers need to be trained to acquire specific skills, but they also need to be willing to accept their subordinate position in society. They must be presented with appropriate 'models' of behaviour which stress the natural and inevitable nature of the power system which entraps them, otherwise they will begin to realise its true nature and begin to question it, and even actively resist it. It is ideology working through the institutions of family, education, the state and so on, which serves these needs and ensures that the capitalist system continues to operate undisturbed. Ideology provides people with 'commonsense' sets of beliefs and ways of viewing the world and their position in society which justify their subordination by making it appear natural and inevitable. It expresses an imaginary relation between people and their real conditions of existence (Althusser, 1971).

Ideology thus binds people to the social structure in a similar manner to core values in Parsons's theory. A crucial difference is that, for Parsons, people are not 'deluded' about the nature of society and the power structure. In Parsons's terms, people by and large come to accept society as providing a legitimate system of incentives and rewards for effort. Thus their adherence to values and norms is not 'coerced' or constrained by the distortions of ideology. Rather, it is the result of a willing conformity to a system which they believe to be fair and legitimate. However, considered as individuals, people suffer a similar fate in terms of the operation of the system. Thus, as Althusser stresses the binding and directive nature of ideology on social behaviour, so Parsons views core values as having a similar 'mechanical' effect on behaviour. In short, social activity is an almost 'automatic' reflection of the determining effects of the social structure.

Again, a crucial difference is the causal role that Althusser assigns to the economic base in the construction of the ideological and institutional 'overlay'. In Parsons's framework the 'cultural system' which defines and sets the terms of norms and values is only attached to the economic and political system in an 'adjacent' manner as a separate but complementary aspect of the social system. In this sense norms and values reflect the forms of economic conduct that mesh the social system with the material environment by transforming the material environment into commodities and wealth. In Parsons's theory the economy is not allied to a social and political system of inequality. Thus, in opposition to the general Marxist position, the economy does not generate institutional forms that ideologically justify the imbalances of power upon which they 'supposedly' rest.

The Disappearance of the Human Subject

As Althusser's emphasis on ideology implies, the human being as a creative person is almost entirely absent from this kind of theory. The individual is thought to be simply a 'support' (although perhaps an unwitting one), of the economic and political system in which she or he is enmeshed through ideological delusion. This veering away from the individual as the centrepoint of analysis is a deliberate ploy and something which structural Marxism shares with other kinds of structuralism. Here, it must be said that 'structuralism' is a wider school of thought than is represented by the work of Althusser and other Marxists. In fact, much structuralist thought has been influenced by the work of Lévi-Strauss, an anthropologist. This work centres on the structure of the human mind and the way in which it classifies things in the social world.

Other structuralist work, such as that of Roland Barthes, concentrates on the analysis of cultural items such as films, books, newspapers, fashion and so on, and emphasises the ways in which these forms exhibit underlying logical patterns. While this is an interesting line of analysis, it takes us away from our main theme, which is how the organisation of society (social structure) relates to individual behaviour or social activity more generally. We can see that Althusser's work, with its emphasis on the nature of the capitalist social system, intersects rather more with our present concerns than do other forms of structuralism. To a certain extent Althusser dissociates himself from these other branches of structuralism.

However, it is clear that there is an overlap in terms of a common distrust of 'individualism', or the idea that the human being (sometimes referred to as the human 'subject') should be the starting point of social analysis.

According to Althusser the basic flaw in what he termed 'bourgeois' social analysis was its preoccupation with individual action and consciousness. Jean-Paul Sartre, the French existentialist thinker, exemplified this view by emphasising that people are 'free' to act and thus are responsible for the consequences of their own activity. As we shall see in the next chapter, the premise that the social world is constructed out of the interactions of individuals is a basic feature of social theories which focuses on the more subjective elements of activity. However, Althusser sees this as a general problem of 'bourgeois' social science, that is, all positions other than the 'scientific' standpoint of Marxism!

I shall deal with this somewhat arrogant claim in the next section. For the moment let us attend to Althusser's insistence that Sartre, among others, has fallen prey to the bourgeois myth of 'individualism'. This myth supports the idea that people are equally free to do what they want and to achieve all that is possible in society. However, because of its inherent inequalities, society actively denies this to its members. Rather than being free, according to Althusser, people are hedged in by power, inequality and constraint. People are extremely 'unfree' because they are yoked to a system which allows them to be nothing other than 'supports' or 'bearers' of the needs and demands of capitalism.

The Importance of an Objective Science of Social Behaviour

Another facet of this concerns the idea that 'real' people are not, and cannot be, the objects of analysis in social science. A focus on individuals merely moves attention away from the fact that social analysis has to be about the *social relations* that define the social functions that people occupy under capitalism. In this sense, social analysis must be about the objective distribution of positions and functions in society, not about the subjective thoughts, feelings and intentions of 'free' individuals. While rejecting Althusser's wilder claims, I do feel that there is a kernel of truth in the idea that social analysis must accord a central place to social relations and that they must not be confused with, or thought to be the same thing as real individuals and their social activities.

However, Althusser takes the argument to an extreme and ends up with an exaggerated claim about the importance of 'objective' social relations. In fact,

Althusser completely rejects the view that social analysis should take into account the subjective experience of individuals. The only psychological inner life that interests Althusser is the way in which individuals unconsciously internalise the effects of ideology. Clearly, we have here an even more serious case of the human actor as an unthinking automaton than we encountered with Parsons! With regard to the question of the overriding constraining influence of the social system on activity there is definitely a parallel in the work of Parsons and Althusser. Nonetheless, closer scrutiny will reveal some persistent differences.

For example, 'roles' tend to straitjacket individual initiative and creativity in Parsons in much the same way as 'positions' do in Althusser's work. However, if we look at the way these two important concepts are defined by the respective authors, we find that Parsons does not abandon the notion of the individual (or 'subject'). Whereas Althusser concentrates on the objective social relations through which positions are defined, to the eventual exclusion of 'real' people, in Parsons we find a more humanist solution. For Parsons, roles are the bridge between personality and social systems and therefore they contain both subjective and objective features. It is true that these subjective features tend to be rather rudimentary in Parsons's work and, moreover, they are tied to a notion of social action which lacks texture (the dynamic and interpretive aspects of activity). Nevertheless, a space exists for the individual as a necessary part of the overall theory. In this sense Parsons manages to grapple with the issue of the macro–micro relation, whereas Althusser simply abandons the micro level along with the notion of the subject.

'Scientific' Analysis and the Question of Evidence

As mentioned above, structural Marxism makes the claim that it is the only 'true' scientific analysis of society; all the rest are infected by 'bourgeois ideology', and thus false. I do not want to dwell too much on the sensationalist, headline-grabbing side of this. It suffices to say that one way of commanding attention is to be deliberately controversial even if, in the final analysis, the issues concerned are superficial. This said, there are nonetheless some important questions which may be disentangled from the welter of spurious claims in which they are embedded. (See Benton, 1984, for an extended review of this and other detailed matters connected with structural Marxism.)

Perhaps the main claim in this respect is that structural Marxism goes beyond the limited horizons of conventional social analysis. This it does by rejecting the idea that we should study only those things which are immediately observable and for which we have definite empirical evidence. In this sense, social theory must describe things in (empirical) terms which may then be confirmed or disconfirmed by the application of research procedures. That is to say, social theory must be judged on its ability to make statements that can be tested against the observable evidence. As opposed to this 'empiricist' view, the structural Marxists adopted a wholly 'rationalist' position which allows the study of unobservable social structures through the positing of conceptual and theoretical models (see Hindess, 1973, 1977; Hindess and Hirst, 1977). In this sense, such theories have to be judged more in terms of their logical coherence and their explanatory power (how much they explain), rather than their conformity with empirical evidence.

The structural Marxists argued that such a position is necessary in order to overcome the problem of the 'individualist' focus of conventional analyses. In an effort to understand the objective nature of the social relations which compose the social system of capitalism, we must go beyond the sensory limitations which are inherent in human experience. We can only understand social structures which are, in every respect, so much larger than human beings, through the use of abstract theoretical concepts which depict the objective nature of social systems. Thus, abstract theory and theoretical models come to replace the kind of analysis, which relies on the researcher's ability to observe empirical facts, about concrete human activities.

In a very real sense then, the structural Marxists tended to concentrate on the internal character of theoretical discourses (consistency, coherence and so on), to the exclusion of external empirical data or evidence (see for example, Hindess and Hirst, 1977). This had the apparent 'advantage' of neatly precluding the micro world of individual experience and the observable facts of social interaction, and so conformed with the necessity of 'abandoning the subject'. Although this is an extreme version of 'rationalism', which eventually turns its back on the world of experience, activity and observation, this need not be so. There is no need to reject the external world of experience and observation in order to 'go beyond' the limitations that they impose on our abilities to understand the social world.

So, despite all its drawbacks, structural Marxism does raise an important issue but fails to solve it satisfactorily. The 'realist' approach (Keat and Urry, 1975; Bhaskar, 1979) has attempted a more satisfactory resolution of this problem. Realists suggest that social analysis should include both underlying (and to some extent unobservable) social phenomena, without rejecting the importance of subjective experience. This is an important step forward; nevertheless, problems still remain. First, what exactly is the relation between theory and evidence? Are there, in fact, different types of relationship depending on the type of theory and the kind of evidence concerned? For example, should we treat theory which is about social structures and systems differently from theory which is about certain kinds of activity?

I have tried to tackle these questions in my own work. First (Layder, 1990), I have suggested that it is important to include a rationalist element in social theory in order to be able to describe things which are not easily experienced or observed. However, we must avoid the extreme version of rationalism, which insulates concepts and theories from the external world of empirical evidence. There must always be a link between theory and evidence, although we must be aware of the possibility that the nature of this link may vary from problem to problem. Also, I have tried to develop specific social research strategies which attempt to link macro and micro elements by drawing upon different types of theory and evidence (Layder, 1993, 1998).

Other Kinds of Marxism and the Problem of the Individual

Of course, not all Marxism has gone down the road that structural Marxism has travelled. Some would even argue that this type of Marxism is a perversion of true Marxist thought. In this respect, the structural version is instructive in that it represents an extreme. The individual (or subject) is dissolved completely into the structure (the institutional requirements) of society. The micro world of interaction in everyday life is forever sidelined by the 'more important' issues of structural domination. In more conventional forms of Marxism there is a stress on the importance of action, and collective action in particular, as a means of effecting the social changes required by the inequities of capitalism. Nonetheless, there is still a stress on the primacy of the economic, political and social structure, in setting the terms and tone of daily social life (Swingewood, 1975; Miliband, 1987).

Yet other forms of Marxism have taken more care to develop a specific theory of the individual. For example, Lucien Sève (1978) has attempted to do this, and so has Peter Leonard (1984), who draws on Sève's work and extends his ideas. In this version the importance of historical materialism and the role of ideology remain persistent themes. The original aspects of this approach lie in the thesis that the individual's personality is affected by a conjunction of three social determinants: the economy, the family and the state. Leonard argues that in contemporary 'bourgeois democracies' the family and the economy are more important than direct state intervention.

The economy affects individual personality in several ways. These include the oppressive demands of wage labour (work) and domestic labour (housework and child rearing), and the low level of pay and working conditions for the subordinate classes. These conditions restrict the time available for private use (particularly for the development of skills like writing and public speaking). Also, the pervasive effects of consumerism link identity and social status to the market for commodities. This may take two forms: either, the compulsive buying of new fashions and new products, or the inability to purchase such items attended by consequent negative feelings. The family household affects personality by providing the location in which parental control over children is established. It also prepares children for the gender and status hierarchy that exists in society in general. In this respect, female children are familiarised with roles such as housework and the nurturing of children, while males are psychologically and ideologically prepared for wage labour and fatherhood.

In Leonard's view, the extent to which the state intervenes in the individual's experience is determined by wider considerations such as class, gender and ethnic group membership. The politically weakest groups (such as certain ethnic minorities) will have their interests least represented in state activities. State practices such as educational initiatives, social security services, immigration legislation and so on, serve to reinforce the gender, class, ethnic and age hierarchies which already exist. The economy, family and state, then, penetrate the personal biographies of everyone and produce personal identities formed around the person's structural location in class, gender, ethnic and other hierarchies. These factors and elements combine to 'produce' individuals who are sensitive to their own subordination (inferiority, lack of confidence) or their advantaged position (feelings of superiority, self-confidence).

Resistance and Dissent

In this framework, as in other brands of Marxism, the emphasis is on the way in which the individual's personality is moulded and penetrated by the institutions and ideologies of the social order. However, an important difference revolves around the idea that the individual has a 'dialectical' relationship with the social order and may actively resist its effects. The space for individual resistance, avoidance and dissent is created because social relations contain contradictions and there is never a perfect 'fit' between the individual and the social order.

For example, ideologies stressing the legitimacy of the existing core institutions are generally successful in inculcating a particular 'world view' in individuals. However, people's daily existence may indicate that the system' is perhaps not as fair as it is made out to be by the authorities. In this sense, the grip of ideology on the personalities of people in subordinate positions is imperfect. There is a contradiction between the ideology (official explanations and justifications of the social order) and the reality of people's everyday lives, experiences and material interests. This can lead (although not inevitably) to acts of deviance such as theft, industrial sabotage or even unusual sexual preferences.

Similarly, Leonard argues that the social order may be resisted in a psychological sense through the rejection of the conventional standards of behaviour and an acceptance of stigmatised and marginal identities. This 'breaking through' the accepted fabric of social life may lead to anxiety and even mental illness. Finally, resistance may occur on the level of individual behaviour, in the form of the development of a person's own capacities such as skills and knowledge. In this sense, the individual is resisting or deflecting the dehumanising and restrictive effects of wage labour.

Resistance on an individual level may be complemented by other forms, based on collective action. In this manner, says Leonard, there is a move away from the competition and rivalry of individualism to more altruistic forms of activity (for the collective good). This is born out of a recognition that personal needs can only be met through a transformation of social relations which, in turn, can only be achieved through co-operative activity with others. The experience of collective action provides the individual with the opportunity for the development of his or her capacities such as writing, organising and public speaking. This enhancement of personal powers may, in fact, lead to an altered conception of self. In effect, a sense of subordinacy may be resisted and eventually dislodged by the acquisition of self-confidence and the ability to 'make things happen'.

Clearly, this kind of Marxism has significant advantages over the structural kind insofar as it does leave space for individual creativity in the form of resistance and avoidance of the demands of the social order. There is, indeed, a 'dialectic' between the individual and the social order, and this may be mediated by forms of collective activity. The capacities of human beings to 'act back', to resist and transform the social circumstances in which they find themselves, are important features of any theory which links macro and micro phenomena.

Also important is the idea that a person's 'consciousness' of their society and their place in it may contain contradictory elements. The notion that people are not necessarily consistent, unified and rational beings is also necessary to an adequate theory of the individual (or 'the subject'). (As we shall see later, this is also a central proposition of 'post-structuralist' and 'postmodernist' theories which have grown out of a reaction to structuralist theories like Althusser's.) Having said this, however, there are drawbacks and weaknesses in this kind of theory which are also applicable to Marxism in general.

The Weaknesses of this Brand of Marxism

In this brand of Marxist theory the freedom and creativity of individuals is tightly defined in terms of an opposition to an otherwise monolithic system which penetrates every aspect of life. This misses out forms of creativity and freedom (as well as attempts to change society) which are not born out of 'resistance' as such. Forms of artistic endeavour like painting and sculpture, many forms of literature (from 'pulp' to 'elite'), popular and classical music, various forms of entertainment and so on, cannot be thought of simply as resistance, avoidance or deviance. Similarly, the creative and transformative effects of interpersonal encounters have to be viewed in more diffuse and fragmented ways. An underpinning of such activity by some form of consent, or endorsement of existing social circumstances, cannot be simply ruled out.

Secondly, as with many forms of Marxism, this version suffers from an over-reliance on a centralised and unified notion of power. As we shall see, particularly in the discussion of Foucault's work, power is much more fragmented, dispersed and localised. Power in this sense is not 'caused' by some central mechanism like the economy, the class system or the state.

As a corollary to this, the theory is primarily concerned with an analysis of the productive and labour processes and with the working class as a subordinate group. While these are important in any overall account, in general this is a rather narrow focus. First, it leaves out other marginalised, relatively powerless groups such as the mentally ill, women, children, homosexuals, and ethnic minorities. Yet other groups are also overlooked, such as patients and consumers, who are not normally thought of as subordinate groups, but are nevertheless engaged in power struggles. Also, intermediate and more powerful groups are important to an understanding of the overall balance of power in society. These groups cannot be seen simply in the same terms as the working class. Also, such groups (and the working class for that matter) cannot be analysed exclusively or primarily in terms of their relationship to production and the labour process. To restrict analysis to this narrow province (no matter how important it is) is to falsify the complex and variegated nature of society.

The restricted focus mentioned above runs into a more general point about the analysis of 'everyday life'. Although it is true that people's lives are significantly influenced by the economy, family and state, this does not exhaust the full range of possibilities. The fullness and complexity of social life in the modern era means that it cannot be grasped simply in terms of the oppressive drudgery of wage and domestic labour. The range of cultural and counter-cultural activities that are a routine feature of the everyday world indicates a diversity of forms of life that go well beyond the exclusive and narrow terms of a critique of political economy.

Street culture, youth culture, high culture, as well as the range of activities that go on in pubs, clubs, restaurants, cafes and sporting venues, leisure pursuits, hobbies, travel and tourism, are just a few of the social activities and involvements that constitute life beyond the confines of family and work. Moreover, family life and work themselves have to be regarded as areas in which emotional relationships are fashioned in ways which cannot be thought to be simple reflections of economic and political subordination. To suggest otherwise would be to vastly under-rate the capacities of human beings to create possibilities for themselves, even if they possess only limited resources. The ability to 'make things happen' and to create cultural, counter-cultural and oppositional forms, even in the most dire of circumstances, is a central and defining characteristic of human activity.

It is true to say that while this brand of Marxism does not discount the creative and productive capacities of people, it does not do them full justice. In a slightly more technical sense, this amounts to much the same criticism as that applicable to Parsons's framework. In short, there is a very thin account of the nature of interpersonal activity because it ignores the sense in which people create localised 'realities' by endowing their experienced world with meaning. Also, to some extent, people actually create and sustain their own sense of orderliness in their routine dealings with others.

I shall discuss the full nature and implications of agency and meaning in the next chapter, on theories concerning the nature of interaction and subjective experience. However, it remains as a limitation of the general Marxist position that, in its own terms, it is unable to accommodate these finer and more complex characteristics of interaction. In this sense also, in order to provide a full and adequate account of the macro–micro relation we have to consult other theoretical traditions and schools of thought.

The Rise of Post-structuralism and Postmodernism

At the beginning of this chapter I indicated that the influence of structural Marxism had waned somewhat. This coincided to some extent with the decline in influence of the wider school of thought loosely grouped together under the term 'structuralism' and including the work of Lévi-Strauss in anthropology and that of Saussure in linguistics. Its place has been occupied by a group of writers who could be said to be post-structuralist insofar as they reject, among other things, the concept of structure and the pursuit of scientific 'objective' truth (two of the central characteristics of Althusser's work). Writers such as Jacques Lacan, Jacques Derrida and Michel Foucault questioned the basis of Saussure's linguistics (on which much structuralist thought was based) and, as a result, have been responsible for developing what has become known as the post-structuralist strand in social analysis.

I shall mainly be concerned with the work of Foucault, since his work directly touches on some of the issues I discuss in this book. Foucault has also been labelled a postmodernist, and this reflects a good deal of overlapping in the two terms. Insofar as all postmodernists reject most of the main assumptions of structuralism (except the critique of the human subject) they can be said to be post-structuralist as well. Postmodernism has recently become very fashionable and is to some extent the latest 'buzz' word in the academic community. However, behind the superficial 'in' nature of the term there are a number of important issues. The term 'postmodernism' refers to three related areas of concern which are worth distinguishing.

Three Dimensions of Postmodernism

First, 'postmodernism' refers to a stage of societal development beyond the modern era. Thus the modern era is said to coincide with the advent and establishment of advanced industrial societies. The characteristics associated with this, such as urbanism, and the influence of legal-rational forms of bureaucracy, distinguished these societies from the pre-modern or traditional types from which they emerged. Consequently, in this sense, postmodernism refers to a distinctive type of society that has supplanted the modern type. This newer form relies on a different technology, that of the computer, and is based on information storage and retrieval. Postmodernists (like Lyotard and Baudrillard) argue that these and other changes have radically affected the nature of social relationships and social life.

However, the question of how far these changes can be said to constitute a radically new form of society is a controversial question. Some writers such as Giddens (1991) have argued that it is more appropriate to speak of 'late modernity' rather than postmodernity. The debate about whether a new type of society has come into being will not directly concern us. However, some of the social changes that lie behind and constitute the 'subject matter' of the debate will intersect with aspects of our more general concern with the macro–micro issue. I shall deal with these as they become relevant to particular sections of the discussion.

The second area to which the term 'postmodernism' has been applied concerns the nature and objectives of social analysis. In this regard postmodernism is associated with a specific group of ideas about the nature of social analysis which include the following: a rejection of conventional approaches to historical analysis; the death of the subject and the rejection of humanism; a critique of comprehensive, total theories (particularly those emphasising causality and structure); a questioning of the validity of science and its search for objective knowledge or truth (Sarup, 1988; Rosenau, 1992).

As may be already apparent, I feel that many of these forms of rejection are quite untenable. In many cases the claims upon which they are based are too sweeping and ill-founded. Nevertheless, they represent a challenge to existing approaches to the study of society and, as such, they must be evaluated in a fair-minded way in relation to the range and depth of understanding that they can offer. Thus, again, I shall draw attention to the implications of these things for the central themes of this book as the discussion unfolds.

Finally, the term 'postmodernism' has been used to describe a set of cultural styles which have replaced those associated with the modernist movement in art and architecture. In this respect, artistic forms of all kinds, film, painting, sculpture, photography, architecture, literature, novels, fashion and so on, have come to be described as 'postmodernist' in style. Perhaps the major characteristic of this 'style' is, in fact, the rejection of a single unified style. Instead, postmodernism borrows from, and toys with, a diversity of styles and genres to produce a collage or patchwork effect. In this sense, pastiche is the watchword of postmodernism. Clearly, there are connections between these three strands of postmodernism, but it is also quite apparent that they represent distinct emphases. The third meaning of postmodernism, as a cultural form, will be the one we will be least concerned with in the present context. Nevertheless, it is important to be aware of its relationship to the others since, as I have said, there is some mutual influence between the three areas.

The aims of this brief discussion of post-structuralism and postmodernism have been twofold. The first has been simply to introduce them as topics that will reappear at later stages of my overall discussion. Secondly, and perhaps more important for my immediate concerns, I have attempted to highlight the link between the structural Marxism which has been the main focus of this chapter, and the post-structuralist and postmodernist movements that grew out of a critical response to structuralism in general.

The Contribution of Marxism in General

Although the principal theme of this chapter has been the influence of structural Marxism, I have also discussed other forms of Marxism. I suggested that while these less dogmatic variants managed to avoid some of the grosser errors and excesses of the structural brand, nonetheless, they themselves were subject to certain shortcomings. In conclusion, let me now spotlight the stronger features of Marx's thought in general in relation to the macro–micro problem.

History and Group Interests

One of the central tenets of Marx's materialism is the idea that human history must provide a central place for the analysis of the pursuit of sectional interests. As long as this is not interpreted in a restricted manner as referring exclusively to the analysis of class interests and class struggle, then it draws attention to an important and general feature of social life. Any theory of social activity, especially one which hopes to describe and account for macro–micro linkages, must take the pursuit of sectional interests into account.

Historical developments have witnessed the emergence of divisions of interest based around differential access to scarce goods and resources (money, power, property, status, material possessions and so on). Such developments define the general characteristics of societies (that is, endow them with their historical 'stamp') and help us to identify the distinctive features of societal types (capitalist, feudal and so forth). However, they also allow us some purchase on the patterning of inequalities and divergences of interest that constitute the developed form of specific societies. Thus, the analysis of social activity has always to be seen against the backdrop of the shifting pattern of group interests.

An essential feature of this must be the understanding that interests should not be exclusively defined in economic and market terms. Interests may be formed around the quest for, and defence of, many different resources other than money and property. The quest for authority, honour and recognition in all walks of life may be the origin of divergences of interest. As Max Weber, one of the great classic sociologists, suggested (partly as a critical response to Marx), 'status' groupings of all kinds serve to complicate any analysis of interests based simply on class. Even knowledge itself may become the site of struggles to defend some interests, say, the belief in a particular theory, against the interests of those who adhere to opposing theories.

The Analysis of Power and Domination

By taking into account the various interests that groups and individuals pursue and defend in the context of historical change, Marx highlighted the importance of understanding how certain interests become entrenched and established in society. This led him to underline the dimensions of power and domination that had the effect of stabilising general conditions of inequality which favoured the interests of some groups rather than others. Again, an emphasis on power and domination is absolutely essential to an understanding of the wider social conditions under which people live out their daily lives.

However, the important limitation of Marx's approach lies in the fact that he proposed a one-dimensional view of power and domination as exclusively linked to his class theory. Power and domination have to be understood in much more dispersed and fragmented ways. Also, it must not simply be assumed that single sources of domination (like that of class) will have some overall and deterministic influence on society. These are matters to be decided by empirical investigation. They cannot be settled in advance by a priori theoretical assumptions.

History as Process

Marx's own writing stresses that the unit of social analysis must be the activity of 'real people in their real life-process' (Bottomore and Rubel, 1963: 90). Moreover, he views the historical process as an emergent and dynamic one. It is this ingredient of general Marxist thought that must be retained in the analysis of social processes rather than the rather static and closed notion of a structure frozen in time that is implied by Althusser's model (Thompson, 1978). Much the same can be said of Parsons's view of society and social evolution (Parsons, 1966).

Although both these authors understand it in rather different ways, they view social reproduction itself as the dominant effect of social activity. For them, social activity serves, in the end, to reproduce the very social forms and institutions that give rise to this activity in the first place. Such a view does not do justice to the capacities of individuals and groups to transform the social circumstances in which they find themselves. This latter view is certainly evident in Marx's writing. As I said in the previous section, the main problem here is that analysis of creativity and the productive effects of activity are restricted to the sphere of production and politics. This leads to an inadequate account of interaction in everyday life.

Social Order and Social Integration

Marx's own thought, as opposed to that of later interpreters (such as Althusser), offers us a vision of the nature and basis of social order in general which differs from that offered by Parsons's work. While both have something to contribute in this regard, they should be viewed as complementary rather than competing ideas. In one sense, Parsons's social theory provides answers to the twin questions of how social order is possible in the first place, and if it is, how it is maintained. Stated another way, why is it that society does not fall apart as a result of people's pursuit of their own self-interests? (Hobbes, the political philosopher, depicts this as a 'war of all against all'.)

Parsons's answer is that people are committed to the establishment and maintenance of community interests as a whole, through an adherence to core values. This allows the co-operation and co-ordination of the separate parts of the community and makes possible the pursuit and achievement of everyone's interests in a fair and open way. Of course, there will be winners and losers in any meritocratic system, but it is, importantly, a regulative body which guarantees that people will adhere to the 'rules of the game'. Core values, and core institutions based on them, ensure that naked conflict and disharmony will not result from the untrammelled pursuit of self-interest. An essential by-product of this is the prevention of 'illegitimate' and tyrannical forms of domination.

On the other hand, Marx envisioned a social order that had already been fashioned historically and had emerged from power struggles and conflict between groups revolving around the defence of sectional interests and the ownership of scarce resources. For Marx, the existing social system was held together by power, coercion and the ideological masking and distortion of its true nature. It was certainly not held together as a result of some orderly establishment of a just system of merit based on a 'gentleman's agreement'. Certainly, these emphases in Marx are an important counterbalance to Parsons's somewhat naive scenario in which the darker and less altruistic side of human nature is totally ignored. However, it is also essential that one extreme and incomplete view is not simply replaced by another. Just as Parsons neglects the material interests that underpin norms and values, so too Marx neglects the 'legitimacy' of certain forms of power relation and the degree to which some subordinate groups are incorporated into the social community.

In sum, to understand social order we must have a model which combines the binding nature of norms and values (in their non-ideological guise), as well as a notion that social order always depends upon a pattern of power relations. These power relations will always represent a 'balance' constantly in tension and liable to tip in one direction or the other. As I said in the previous section, power and its workings must be seen as much more diffuse and dispersed than in Marx's writing. Nevertheless, the workings of economic and other markets and the quest for scarce resources (symbolic as well as material) and the strategies used by individuals and groups to acquire and maintain them, are key features of modern societies. Also, the divisions of interest that give rise to, and flow from these must be part of any analysis of social order.

The Agency–Structure and Macro–Micro Problems

In the above discussion I have been talking of social order in terms of processes that are conventionally thought of as macro phenomena. That is, attention has been largely concentrated on larger-scale, more impersonal social processes rather than the interpersonal dealings of daily activity. In this respect both Parsons and Marx are similar; they both tend to endorse a *dualist* model of social reality. As such, they both display the advantages as well as some of the limitations of dualism. We have already seen how Parsons's theory and that of structural Marxism both lapse into deterministic views of social activity. In both, individual creativity and the internal dynamics of interaction are collapsed into the (objective) operational needs of the social system.

Marx's own work, on the other hand, allows for a more interesting and complex view of the dualist position. However, this statement is subject to two qualifications. First, it is a theoretical argument which Marx himself never worked out in any detail. Secondly, it has to be borne in mind that Marx's overall framework is subject to the inherent limitations that I have already spelt out. Notwithstanding these qualifications, it is possible to find in Marx's writing indications of a dualist position which allows for an adequate synthesis of macro and micro elements.

In this respect, Marx distinguished between individuals and the objective social relations in which they are enmeshed, and which come to assume a power over them. In the *Grundrisse* Marx argued strongly against the idea that 'individuals' are essentially separate from their society. For example, Marx states that

> society does not consist of individuals; it expresses the sum of connections and relationships in which individuals find themselves ... To be a slave or to be a citizen are social determinations, the relationships of Man A and Man B. Man A is not a slave as such. He is a slave within society and because of it. (McLellan, 1973: 89)

Moreover, says Marx, 'In the social production which men carry on they enter into definite relations that are indispensable and independent of their will' (see Bottomore and Rubel, 1963: 67). Here we can see that Marx clearly understood society to be composed of two intersecting orders that intertwine with each other. These two quotations highlight the 'objective' social relations which are independent of the control and manipulation of specific individuals. In this respect, individuals are shaped and influenced by the social relations that constitute society.

On the other hand, Marx was equally vehement that social relations themselves were the products of human activity, and could be changed by human activity. This, in fact, was behind his call for revolutionary action on the part of the working class. In much of his writing Marx castigates the political economists and philosophers of his day for diverting attention from the real activities of people, by writing of social relations as if they were examples of natural or supernatural intervention (God's) which were unchangeable and thus inevitable. In a very famous and oft quoted passage Marx is clear about the dualist position that he advocates. He says that people 'make their own history, but they do not make it just as they please; they do not make it under circumstances chosen by themselves, but under circumstances directly encountered, given and transmitted from the past' (Marx and Engels, 1968: 96).

It is precisely the encounter between creative (and transformative) human activity and the (objective) social relations that are inherited from the past that forms the continuous link between activity and social structure. However, as I have made clear, this formulation of agency–structure, macro–micro links was not something that Marx elaborated in any full and unambiguous manner. Thus, various authors have interpreted its implications in different ways. For example, Giddens reworks this insight into a theory which abandons 'dualism' (see Chapter 8), but

Marx's statement is consistent with Archer's (1995) defence of dualism (see Chapter 11) as well as my own work (Layder, 1997, 2004b) on the theory of social domains (see Chapter 12). Nevertheless, Marx's comments provide an interesting standpoint on, and insight into, the complexities of the macro–micro relation.

SUMMARY

- Marx's ideas have given rise to a number of variants, some of which lead to rather different conclusions about the nature of capitalist societies.

- Marx's own ideas are founded on the importance of material human needs (for food, clothing, shelter). His 'materialism' stands in stark contrast to 'idealism', which stresses the overriding influence of political, moral and economic ideas, values and theories.

- In Marx's view, society has developed historically through several types – tribal, ancient, feudal – to reach its present capitalist phase. Marx hoped that through the revolutionary efforts of the working class, society would move beyond capitalism to communism.

- Class inequalities and relations of power are historically specific. Economic institutions are of primary importance and generate material interests and class divisions. Modern capitalist societies are based on a two-class model in which the owners of the means of production (the bourgeoisie) hold power over, and economically exploit, the propertyless workers.

- Under capitalism, workers are measured by their labour value and little else, hence they become 'alienated' from their work, themselves and other people. Ideology serves to rationalise and justify the power position of ruling groups.

- Structural Marxists emphasise the processes through which the capitalist system reproduces itself. Individuals are viewed as (unwitting) 'supports' of the system while ideology plays an important role in binding people to it.

- Structural Marxists wish to avoid what they see as the myth of 'bourgeois individualism', and therefore remove ('decentre') the individual as a focus of interest in order to produce an 'objective' analysis. They have a 'rationalist', rather than 'empiricist' view of the relation between theory and evidence.

- There are other, more 'humanist' versions of Marxism that have a more moderate and embracing view of individual personality formation. For Sève and Leonard, for example, while historical materialism and the role of ideology remain important, the individual is 'dialectically' related to the social order in the form of the economy (work), the family and the state. This dialectical relationship is characterised by creative resistance and dissent.

- Many strands of post-structuralism and postmodernism have emerged out of a dissatisfaction with structural Marxism. The work of Foucault and others, who may be described as post-structuralists or postmodernists, can be seen as a response to the weaknesses of structural Marxism, particularly its centralised and unified conception of power. Foucault and others have suggested that power is much more fragmented, dispersed and localised.

- The enduring contribution of Marxism can be traced back to the basic ideas of Marx himself. These are expressed in his central themes such as: the historical emergence of sectional interests (not only class interests); his analysis of power and domination (although it has shortcomings); the development and transformation of societies through power struggles; and the underpinning of social order by power and ideology. Finally, Marx stressed the 'dialectical' (dualistic) interplay between social activity and social structure, or between transformative (collective) agency and 'objective' social relations inherited from the past.

part two

where the
action is

4

Meanings, Situations and Experience

PREVIEW

- Rejecting dualism and the concept of structure. The humanist view of society as 'people doing things together'.

- Symbolic interactionism and the active, creative individual – the importance of mind, self and society.

- The role of language in the construction of meaning.

- Motivation as commitment to a line of activity rather than an inner force or compulsion.

- The positivistic 'Iowa School' of symbolic interactionism compared with the humanist 'Chicago School'.

- The seamless join between the individual and society, and the 'emergent' features of interaction.

- Role distance, the presentation of self and joint activity.

- The nature of social organisation according to the different schools of symbolic interactionism and the associated problem of reification.

- Critical issues for symbolic interactionism: emotions, irrationality and the unconscious; alleged concern with minutiae; the problem of meaning; power, inequality and conflict.

Rejecting Dualism

In this chapter we move away from those schools of thought which have relied on a dualism of action and structure, in which the structural side dominates the activity side. In this respect I shall deal with what I described in Chapter 1 as the 'rejectors' of dualism. As I said in that chapter, we have to be aware that particular writers or schools of thought do not necessarily reject dualism in a deliberate and formal manner. On the other hand, many of the writers dealt with in this chapter imply this very strongly. The main issue that divides these authors from the ones already discussed is their rejection of the notion of an objective social 'structure'. Thus these writers are wary of using the term 'structure' at all, since it usually refers to the idea of a 'social system' (as in Parsons and Althusser) which 'determines' from above, so to speak, the activities going on 'on the ground'.

The 'symbolic interactionists', who are the main subject of this chapter, reject the idea of structure because its use in social theory tends to 'dehumanise' people. That is, it seems to rob people of their essential characteristics as human beings and regard them as mere 'effects' or 'reflections' of the encompassing structure. Most importantly, the term 'structure' seems to neglect the 'meanings' with which people imbue their lives and which colour their relations with others. Such writers argue that we should dispense with the idea of an 'objective structure' since it plays no useful role in the analysis of social life.

These 'humanists' (I shall use this as a shorthand term for an otherwise diverse group of thinkers) view social activity itself as the prime topic of concern for social analysis. Society is nothing other than people 'doing things together' as Howard Becker (1970) has described it, and therefore there is no point in suggesting that external structures play any part in the conduct of social life. For authors like Becker, such things as 'structures' and 'systems' are simply the 'inventions' of sociologists; they are mythical entities that correspond to nothing that can be observed or experienced in social life. Humanists believe that social life can only be understood by reference to the situations that people experience and which they believe to be meaningful. In this sense, social life is constructed by individuals themselves in their interactions with others. It is not produced by some impersonal entity such as an 'objective structure' which exists 'outside' their experiences.

Later in the discussion I shall suggest that many of the humanist arguments against the notion of structure miss the point somewhat. Moreover, they are based on an unduly restricted view of what is possible in social study. For the moment, however, let me simply underline the fact that they reject dualism insofar as they reject the idea of a social realm beyond that of activity itself. This means that they reject not only the idea of a division between action and structure, but also the macro–micro distinction. From their point of view such distinctions are false, the artificial products of an untenable approach to social analysis. Let me now explore in more detail the reasons for this, and some of the wider assumptions made by humanists. I shall concentrate on a framework of ideas that has become known as 'symbolic interactionism'.

Symbolic Interactionism: Mead's Social Behaviourism

The perspective of symbolic interactionism developed from the work of the American philosophers Mead, Cooley and Dewey, writing in the first three decades of this century. George Herbert Mead, in particular, is seen as the main originator of this perspective, although the term 'symbolic interactionism' was coined much later by a student and follower of Mead called Herbert Blumer. Mead's most important work was a collection of his lectures entitled *Mind, Self and Society*, published in 1934, three years after his death. In this work Mead described his general approach as 'social behaviourism'. By this he meant to indicate that he was breaking with the traditions of behaviourist psychology, which viewed human action as learned responses to stimuli in the environment.

This behaviourist approach made little distinction between the behaviour of animals and humans in this regard. Both animal and human actions were seen as 'conditioned responses to various external stimuli. For instance, dogs who salivate at the sound of a bell have learned to associate the sound with the arrival of food; likewise, an experimenter can teach pigeons to peck levers of a certain colour in order to receive a pellet of food. In both cases the animal learns to associate a particular response (salivation or pecking) with a particular stimulus (the sound of a bell, a lever of a certain colour), by being rewarded with food. Thus the coupling of the stimulus with the response is reinforced by the manipulation of rewards. No reward, or even a 'punishment' may produce another kind of response.

For the behaviourists, the same principles apply to human behaviour. Thus human behaviour is thought to be an observable response to an external stimulus. Using this method, the observer could be rigorously 'scientific' and objective about the analysis of human behaviour. Such a procedure avoids all the subjective (non-scientific) references to internal psychological states such as mind, meaning, emotion and so on. According to the behaviourists, such references interfere with the detachment and precision of definition required by the 'scientific method' (as it is used in the natural as opposed to the social sciences).

Mead was radically opposed to the view that people mechanically respond to external stimuli. He wanted to incorporate some notion of an inner mental life or subjective experience in his view of social interaction. For Mead, people respond to stimuli in the social environment by reflecting on what particular stimuli 'mean' and by selecting a line of behaviour that they think is appropriate to the situation at hand. People are able to do this because they have 'minds' and 'selves' which allow them to respond in a more deliberate and thoughtful manner than that envisaged in behaviourism.

The Active, Creative Individual

Mead's interest in such inner mental processes like minds and selves was not oriented towards recording a person's unique subjective experience. Rather, he viewed them as the key to understanding the link between individuals and the society to which they belong. It is through mind and self that people are merged with the social customs and habits of their society and social group. In Mead's view, there is no such thing as an individual who is separate from society; the two are firmly interlocked. The individual is born into an already formed society and thus she or he emerges from, and is defined in terms of, an ongoing flux of social activity. A person's self and mind are, therefore, intrinsically social processes.

Mind and self allow the person to 'think through' the possibilities and probable consequences of a line of action before committing themselves to it. People do not respond in an automatic way to a social stimulus such as being asked a question. Instead they anticipate how the situation will unfold and then choose an answer that best reflects this anticipated state of affairs, and which 'fits in' with the person's aims and intentions. Of course, the response or answer that the person makes will depend on the kind of situation they are in (an emergency, a routine meeting, a family argument and so on). It will also depend on the kind of relationship that the people involved have with each other (for example, friends, parent and child, strangers on public transport). Nonetheless, for Mead, people's ability to interact skilfully with each other is the direct result of the 'inner', but no less *social* workings of the mind which the behaviourists dismiss.

Also, compared with Parsons's work and the structural Marxists, there is a much greater emphasis on the creative and self-determining aspects of human behaviour. However, there is disagreement among symbolic interactionists as to the importance of social institutions and their influence on behaviour. In general, the more humanist strand of symbolic interactionism (the 'Chicago School') views society much more as a dynamic process of co-operative activity among individuals. For these writers, society is an emergent and ever-developing network of relationships, not an objective system or structure. In this respect, Mead's work views social behaviour neither as the result of the outer influences of an objective structure nor as the result of fixed personality types or instinctive drives. He believed that, while it is underpinned by biological entities such as the central nervous system, behaviour itself is something that always *develops* during the course of interaction.

Mead's work is an unabashed and unremitting affirmation of the importance of the individual subject. This is the classical humanist position, which centres the analysis of social life on the thinking, reflective subject. Moreover, this subject is more appropriately conceptualised as an 'individual' or a 'person' and is seen to possess the capacity for constructing the social world in a way that is meaningful to her or him. It is precisely this notion of the individual as the centre of the social universe that is the object of such vehement criticism by structuralism and its post-structuralist and postmodern offshoots. This, therefore, represents a radical distinction between humanist and postmodern forms of thinking. Despite this crucial divergence, however, there are other points at which there is some overlap between humanist schools of thought and postmodernism. In particular, there is an emphasis on the local and the fragmentary nature of meaning, an anti-theoretical strain and a distrust of the search for objective truth which is the hallmark of conventional scientific enquiry.

The Importance of Language and Meaning

Mead suggests that the distinguishing feature of the behaviour of humans, as compared with that of the animals, is their language-using capacity. Animals are 'trapped' in a form of communication that relies on the presentation of gestures like the snarling and baring of teeth in dogs. In this sense, animals respond to each other automatically without any interpretation of each other's actions. In some sporting activities, like fencing or boxing, this kind of automatic response is a characteristic feature. It is also present in some non-verbal forms of communication like smiling or gesturing with the hands. However, by far the most important means of communicating between humans is through language.

Linguistic communication has a number of advantages over gestural forms. First, the signs and symbols that constitute language allow people to tap into a large reservoir of common understandings and meanings and this allows much more complex forms of 'negotiation' between people. This, in turn, allows more complex interactions to take place because people can communicate their intentions to each other prior to acting. Subtle and complex levels of understanding may occur because language enables individuals to view things from the standpoint of others. Although this may not guarantee agreement between the parties concerned, it does allow them to anticipate each other's behaviour and, in the light of this, modify their own actions.

Additionally, by 'talking to ourselves' – the internal conversation that goes on when we are thinking something through – we are able to see ourselves through the eyes of others and anticipate how they will respond to us. Thus language (or 'symbolic' communication) creates the conditions for far more subtle and complex forms of interaction. It also provides a most important vehicle for the expression of meaning, and for the interpretation and understanding of the meanings of others. The notion of meaning and its influence on social behaviour is pivotal to the symbolic interactionist (SI from now on) position. Blumer (1969), in fact, suggests that this emphasis on the importance of meaning is the key distinguishing feature of SI.

Blumer argues that there are three aspects to this. First, people act towards things on the basis of the meanings that these things have for them. These may be physical things such as flags, badges, uniforms, tears or clothes and so forth. On the other hand, these 'things' may be social situations like a wedding ceremony, a party, a courtroom trial. More than likely the things that are meaningful to people involve combinations of physical and social aspects, such as a car assembly line in a factory. Blumer insists that social behaviour has to be understood in terms of the meanings that these things have for the people involved. This distinguishes SI from both traditional psychology and sociology (particularly the Parsonian variety) insofar as they ignore meaning. This they do by assuming a neutral link between behaviour and the factors that are said to produce it, such as roles, or attitudes, or personality. According to Blumer, the analysis of social behaviour is falsified unless meaning is taken into account.

The second premise of SI is that meaning arises out of social interaction itself. This view is set against the idea that meaning is contained in the object in question. For example, the meaning of a drug for the user is not given in the drug itself, but arises out of the user's experience of the drug in the context of interaction within a community of users (Becker, 1953). Similarly, meaning does not arise from a person's initial attitude or psychological predisposition towards something. For example, the experience of being high and the view of a drug as a source of pleasure, do not arise from a person's initial 'deviant' attitude. They arise from a learning process in which the 'strange' and ambiguous sensations induced by a drug are redefined as pleasurable and controllable.

Again, this is produced through contact and interaction with a community of established users. The novice drug user gradually changes his or her view of themselves from non-user to habitual user. The meaning of the drug, therefore, is bound up with the situation of its use and the emergent self-concept of the user. 'Meaning' does not come from the drug itself, nor from a person's initial motivation to experience the drug. Rather, it emerges out of a process of interaction in which the person has to learn to correctly use the drug and to perceive its effects (as pleasurable rather than frightening) and so on. Becker's analysis of the development of habitual marijuana use clearly highlights the points emphasised by Blumer. People act in terms of meaning which arises out of interaction.

It also illustrates Blumer's third premise: that meaning is handled in, and modified through, an interpretative process. This refers to the fact that meaning is not a permanently fixed and stable thing. It can change in the light of changing circumstances. For example, the meaning of a kiss shared by two people may change according to the 'state' of their relationship. What was at one time a prelude to a more passionate embrace may, at a later stage, indicate a more platonic relationship. As we can see, meaning as it arises in the give and take of interaction, and through the interpretative and flexible responses of the participants, is central to the perspective of SI. Meaning, especially as it is formed through the use of language, is what holds people together socially; it is the social glue that allows action to proceed in the form of conflict or co-operation.

This is an important counterpoint to rather simplistic criticisms of SI, which stress that it concentrates too much on co-operation and consensus. (In this light it is often seen, wrongly in my opinion, as the micro counterpart to Parsonian 'functionalism' at the macro level. However, more of this later.) There is nothing in the SI perspective which inevitably commits it to harmony and consensus. The establishment of meaning is merely the vehicle through which the 'substance' of the business between people is allowed to go forward. Depending on the exact meaning of the situation involved (a hold-up at a bank, a meeting between old friends or close relatives, a courtroom encounter between divorcing spouses), the encounter may go either smoothly or disruptively.

Meaning and Motivation

Meaning is also the focus of the motivational and emotional interplay of interact-ing individuals. As far as possible, writers in this tradition steer away from the idea of 'mysterious' inner forces that are said to motivate or impel individuals to do things (as is the case with Freud's theory of the unconscious'). For SIs, individuals are primarily conscious and rational beings who are largely in control of their social performances. In this sense, their 'reasons' for doing certain things or taking a particular 'direction' in their lives are to be found in the social process itself, and not in some prior motivational drives. Both Mills (1940) and Becker (1960) have tried to draw attention away from the question of what initially prompts activity, to a concern with the way in which individuals become committed to particular courses of action through social involvements and entanglements.

Becker suggests that commitment to a line of activity may be for positive reasons (such as remaining in an occupation because it brings rewards in the form of fulfilment and status). On the other hand, a person may become 'entrapped' in a particular form of work for negative reasons such as having family responsibili-ties, or being too old to start over. In this sense, people are locked into courses of action for socially grounded reasons, not because of personal needs or drives. Certainly, this form of analysis is an important contribution to understanding why people become committed to certain activities and directs attention to the way in which much 'motivation' is socially constructed. However, there is no need to con-clude from this, as some SIs do, that all motivation is socially constructed, or that there is no room for the analysis of personality factors in social interaction.

What I have suggested here about the nature of meaning (such as motivation and commitment) as a focal point for SI, implies a quite coherent theoretical per-spective. However, SI is not a tightly integrated set of theoretical ideas like other theories. Although Mead and Blumer have been very influential in setting the tone of SI, the framework itself has been developed in diverse directions by a number of other writers. This invests SI with rather more variability than theo-retical schemas which tend to pivot around the work of a particular author.

Major Schools of Symbolic Interactionism

Perhaps the major distinction within SI is that between the 'Iowa School' and the 'Chicago School'. While both centre around the concepts of SI, such as the nature of the self and interaction, the Iowa School does this in the context of a more traditional approach to scientific analysis. In this sense it is associated with positivism – the idea that it is possible to obtain objective knowledge of the social world through detached study and the application of quantitative techniques. By contrast, the Chicago School (of which Blumer and Becker are prime representatives) has embraced a far more humanist approach to social analysis. This stresses the involvement of the researcher and the idea that he or she should try to unravel the 'meaningful worlds' of those social groups that are the topic of interest (see Rock, 1979). In short, the researcher is charged with attempting to get as close as possible to the subjects of analysis and to give an 'insider' account of what it is like to be a member of a particular group (drug user, musician, nurse and so on).

This division along methodological lines coincides with another which concerns the role of structural elements in social life. This is particularly important for our present purposes since it directly bears upon the issue of dualism. I shall come back to this point in due course, but let me say here that the Iowa School is more inclined to view social life and society in general as more structured than the Chicago School. Thus some writers like Stryker (1981) have advocated the need for a more 'objective' account of SI which stresses the constraining nature of structural (macro) features of social life. As I said at the beginning of this chapter, the humanists radically oppose this idea and stress the 'free' emergence of interaction.

Another reason why SI should not be viewed as a tightly unified theoretical perspective has to do with its attitude towards empirical research. SI has always been regarded by its proponents as first and foremost a research tradition rather than an overarching theoretical framework. That is, the emphasis has always been on SI's contribution to empirical knowledge generated by field research. However, beyond this basic assumption there is a certain amount of disagreement about the place of theory in the research process. Some writers like Becker (see comments in Rock, 1979) have even suggested that SI is basically anti-theoretical in the sense that it is not interested in theory-building for its own sake. According to this view, such conscious efforts at theory-building actually get in the way of empirical investigation by distracting the researcher from the concrete empirical world and concentrating attention on abstract 'speculative' ideas.

However, other writers working within the general SI tradition have argued that it is not enough to be interested in the accumulation of empirical facts. In this vein, Glaser and Strauss (1967) have further argued that only by generating theory from empirical data can there be any real cumulative progress in our knowledge of the social world. They suggest that, while empirical research must be a central concern, sociologists should try to generate formal theories out of the empirical data of their research. This will ensure that our knowledge of the social world is firmly anchored in the 'real' empirical world. Thus 'grounded theory' avoids the problems of speculation that plague other approaches to theory. Given these differences of emphasis in SI, it is clear that, although we may speak generally of a loose framework called SI, this should not blind us to some of the very marked differences within it.

The Merger of Individual and Society

Bearing in mind the diversity within the SI tradition let us now move to a consideration of the way in which it deals with the macro–micro dualism. What I say will, however, be more pertinent to the humanist strand than to the approach of the Iowa School. This is because the humanists clearly reject any dualist position and attempt to construct a viable alternative. In this respect we can say that, to a far greater extent than the Parsonian and the structural Marxist theories, SI attends to the delicate interweaving between the institutional features of society and the creative capacities of people. As Cooley (1902), one of the originators of the perspective, has pointed out, individual and society are an indivisible whole. There is no such thing as an individual separate from society any more than there is such a thing as society apart from the individuals who constitute it.

This is a basic plank in the SI's attempt to overcome the dualisms between individual and society, and macro and micro levels of analysis. If there is a general merger of the individual and society then it follows that the distinction is a false one in the first place. Similarly, if there is no such thing as society apart from the individuals who produce it in their daily interactions, then the so-called distinction between macro and micro processes is also bogus. Such distinctions (and dualisms) simply direct our attention away from the fact that social activity *is* society. Moreover, when we use the noun 'society' we are simply referring to the interlinking of the social activities of many individuals. The idea of thinking of individuals (activity) and society (structures or macro processes) as separate entities is a mistaken enterprise. It is a cul-de-sac that we have been led into unwittingly by linguistic convention.

The SIs have been particularly successful in providing a social psychology which attempts to depict the seamless join between individual and society. This is mainly the result of concentrating analytic attention on the point of view of the person actually involved in the activities in question and is very apparent in the analysis of role behaviour. Writers such as Turner (1962, 1985) and Goffman (1961) have successfully managed to portray a notion of role behaviour which departs considerably from the image of puppets being manipulated by the demands of an overarching system. Ralph Turner, for example, insists that people actively create their roles in interaction. Unlike the unthinking conformism which is the dominant image in Parsons's theory, Turner's version views norms and expectations simply as starting points for action. Roles only exist prior to the action, so to speak, in the sense that they provide guidelines for behaviour.

For example, a 'parent' has in mind what is expected of him or her while they are acting in that role and while other people are judging them in relation to that role. However, interaction is unpredictable and, in the give and take of encounters with others, there arise circumstances which exert pressure for the role-player to go beyond tried and tested solutions to problems thrown up by the situation itself. The person is thus required to improvise, interpret and create aspects of the role on the spur of the moment. In a sense, the unique experience of the individual is brought to bear on the problems posed by trying to get along with others and in eliciting their help in so doing.

The Emergent Nature of Interaction

This emphasis on 'making' roles within the interactive process, rather than simply 'taking' them by conforming rigidly to expected behaviour, highlights one of the basic and distinctive assumptions of SI – that interaction itself has a life of its own which is repeatedly invigorated by the energies of the people involved. Each person brings with them to the encounter their own social experiences and their own needs and intentions. The intermeshing of several such lines of energy in the context of a social encounter creates new aspects of shared experience that could not be predicted in advance. These new aspects are emergents from the flux and dynamics of the interplay of individual inputs in the encounter. In a sense, these are a 'negotiated outcome' of the interaction. This means that each individual is a party to collective decisions and plays some part in the outcome even if it does not reflect their own wishes and intentions. This holds even if a person does not appear to be taking any active role in the 'business' of the encounter, since silence or inactivity may be very effective means of influencing others.

Take, for example, a group of friends or acquaintances who have met up with each other at a particular venue, say a club or a bar. After exchanging greetings and pleasantries they begin to discuss whether they should remain together for the rest of the day or the evening as the case may be. Having decided to stay together they then begin to 'negotiate' with each other about what they should do and where they should go. Obviously, in such discussions individuals have their own preferences and seek to persuade the others to go along with their own. However, in the interests of keeping the group together and enjoying the rewards that come from sociability, certain compromises are made in order to accommodate the needs of everybody concerned.

In the end, a sort of general agreement is worked out which is roughly accept-able to all, although each person is called upon to adapt to collective wishes and needs. It is the conjunction of the flexible responses of all those involved that produces a vibrant and ever-changing shape to the encounter. Nonetheless, the fact that each individual's contribution is neatly dovetailed into the group dynam-ics gives the encounter a distinctive social definition. As with Turner's view of role behaviour, people are 'dragged into' the emergent give and take of social activity 'in spite of themselves'. In the example just described a person must, to some extent, 'fit in' with the others unless he or she is prepared to forgo the obvi-ous benefits of sociability. Being 'unsociable' may even court the sanctions that others may impose on them (such as being shunned or 'dropped' from a circle of friends). In such a case there is no real option but to relinquish oneself (partially at least) to the collective will. The same is true of Turner's notion of role behav-iour in that people are 'forced' to adapt to the emergent, and often unforeseen requirements that attend our dealings with others.

Role Distance and the Presentation of Self

Goffman's work on 'role distance' (1961) also offers a view of human action as lying more within a person's conscious control than is the case with structural theories. Goffman argues that people do not slip on a kind of straitjacket of role expectations when they play roles like parent or surgeon or whatever. In this regard, a person's self-identity is a central component of the behaviour they dis-play. In Goffman's eyes, a person's self-identity is not limited to a singular 'core' image. Rather, people have many different sides to their personalities and they reveal different aspects of themselves to different people on different occasions. In this sense, people are conscious of the impressions they are giving to others who witness their behaviour in certain settings. As a consequence, they seek to control this by displaying certain attributes of themselves which they hope will be valued by others (Goffman calls this 'impression management').

According to Goffman (1971), people are to some extent involved in giving scripted 'performances' to their social audiences rather like dramatic actors in a play. By sticking largely to a 'script' appropriate to the kind of person they wish to convey to others, people can carefully edit out those aspects of themselves which seemingly 'contradict' the self-image they are currently trying to establish or sustain. This kind of ploy involves an awareness of the fact that different 'audiences' may have different preconceptions of the actor. Therefore, performances that may lead to contrary impressions need to be carefully segregated. One of Goffman's illustrations of this is the example of men serving in the armed forces who, whilst away from home, lead a rugged 'he-man' life, in which the use of swear words is routine. By contrast, at home their parents may have a view of them as rather more cultured and sensitive individuals. Thus, to be 'caught out', so to speak, asking one's mother to 'pass the fucking butter', tends to puncture what might otherwise have been a carefully cultivated impression of themselves.

It is this constant implication of self-image and its management in front of others that distinguishes Goffman's view of role-behaviour from those who see it as the somewhat inevitable outcome of prior expectations. Thus people are able to preserve a space for themselves, even when they are engaged in role-playing, by standing apart from the role at the same time. Thus adult riders on fairground rides sit stiffly and nonchalantly in order to convey that they are only there as 'good parents' to ensure the safety of their children. In this sense they distance themselves from the role of 'rider' (and the self-image it implies) by appearing to be less than immersed in, and preoccupied with enjoyment of the ride. Goffman also cites the example of surgeons in operating theatres who joke or engage in domestic gossip when a critical incident has occurred during an operation. This distancing from the role by invoking identities other than 'surgeon' has the effect of draining away the tension and seriousness of the situation.

Although these two examples of role distance have rather different social effects, in both cases they indicate the way in which the individual avoids the straitjacket of 'demands' and 'expectations' that are normally associated with role-playing. Thus, in Goffman's view, there is a pivotal interplay between the desires and intentions of the individual and the kinds of social pressures to which he or she is subjected. In both Goffman and Turner then, there is a move away from understanding role-behaviour in terms of describing the assumed content of roles in the form of prior expectations. Instead, they turn attention to the everyday features of role behaviour. Moreover, they view such behaviour from the actor's point of view and attempt to grapple with the problem of how and why people actually 'produce' such behaviour. This has led some commentators (notably Giddens, 1984), to suggest that such perspectives tend to concentrate all their attention on the problem of social production at the expense of the problem of how institutions and social practices are *reproduced*.

Although this aspect of Goffman's work overlaps with the SI tradition and has been 'claimed' for SI (Meltzer et al., 1975), I think it unwise to try to package all his work in this manner. I shall argue later that other aspects of his work clearly distinguish it from the general SI perspective. This particularly relates to a distinction he makes between the 'interaction order' and the 'institutional order', and I shall deal with this in Chapter 11.

Society as Joint Activity

As Blumer points out, the only things that are capable of acting are individuals and groups. Structures and systems do not act and do not interpret meaning as people do. To talk in such terms is to *reify* society, to treat it as if it were a static, thing-like entity which is largely independent of people. Instead, society must be viewed dynamically in terms of processes of social interaction. If this is so, then how is the patterned nature of social life maintained and continually recreated with the passage of time? The SIs answer this partly in terms of the idea of 'joint activity'. Society cannot be understood simply from the 'actor's point of view', it has to be understood as the convergence and the fitting together of individual lines of activity. Importantly, the term 'joint' is meant to convey not only those forms of activity involving two or more co-operating individuals who share common aims and values, but also forms of joint activity which involve the pursuit of diverging and conflicting objectives. For example, in a robbery or hold-up both perpetrator and victim have different interests and aims, but they are both engaged in joint activity.

The notion of joint activity is closely associated with that of 'career' in SI. Freed from its exclusive association with occupations, 'career' conveys the sense in which joint activities and relationships have a 'history' which can be traced through time and space. In this general sense, it refers to a series of linked stages or phases of social activity that a person or a group goes through in a progressive fashion on the way to some end point or goal (Roth, 1963). Thus, there may be careers associated with being married, or becoming a drug user, as well as the more conventional work careers. In short, any activity in the daily round can be analysed as a connected sequence over time and against the backcloth of various social settings (see Layder, 1993).

As Hughes (1937) pointed out, the concept of career is two-sided. It may refer to an individual's subjective experience (their perceptions, hopes, fears and so on) of a career such as marriage, illness, occupation and so forth. On the other hand, it can also refer to the objective series of statuses, positions or stages that the person (or group) is going through (such as a promotional hierarchy, variations in severity of an illness, a 'bad patch' in a relationship such as a marriage or friendship). As such, the term 'career' promises to bring together the two sides of social reality into a conceptual whole.

Used together then, the notions of joint activity and careers give the analyst some understanding of how specific patterns of interaction emerge and are sustained on a larger scale than simple face-to-face encounters. Some joint actions become orderly and relatively fixed and are continually repeated. This is what gives institutions and organisations such as government bureaucracies or hospitals their enduring qualities. The notion of meaning and the interpretative capacities of people are again central. It is because all those who work, say, in a hospital, behave in terms of a common (previously established) framework of definitions and meanings that the regularity, stability and repetitiveness of the joint activities which we define as a hospital is maintained.

Social Organisation: Differences in Emphasis

It is at this point that there is a difference between the Iowa and the Chicago schools of SI. I noted before that the Iowa School tended to view social life in more structured terms than the Chicago School. In relation to the present discussion this concerns the extent to which people can be said to influence and mould their social environment. Writers such as Becker, and Glaser and Strauss, are much more inclined to view social organisation as continually 'in process' in the sense that people actively create the social order as they negotiate meaning in the flux of daily life. In this sense, there is nothing 'prior' to the action so to speak, which externally governs its form. If there is any point at all to the notion of structure then, it is strictly something which is constantly 'in process' and entirely within the flow of events.

In their empirical studies of dying patients in hospital, Glaser and Strauss (1965, 1968; Strauss et al., 1973) speak of the hospital as a 'negotiated order' or as an example of 'structural process'. Both phrases convey the idea that the social organisation of hospitals (and indeed other organisations) are continually changing and adapting to different circumstances. Nurses, doctors, patients and administrators are ceaselessly negotiating and bargaining with each other about the 'rules', meanings and circumstances that impinge on their activities. For example, the interaction in and around the patient is coloured by the 'awareness contexts' that surround the dying patient – this refers to which people know of the patient's impending death (Glaser and Strauss, 1965).

Much manipulation of information and bargaining takes place around such issues. Also, changing circumstances affect the ward structure in relation to dying patients. Changing types of treatment, changing awareness of the patient, increases or decreases in the rate of progress of illness are, according to Glaser and Strauss, instances of 'structure in process'. This account leads to a view of social organisation as somewhat less organised than sociologists often make out. The 'order' of the hospital is continually being negotiated and the people involved are creating and recreating this order ever anew.

A somewhat different picture emerges from those symbolic interactionists who give more emphasis to the constraints imposed by already established social settings and contexts. For example, in formulating ideas about role behaviour, both Ralph Turner and Sheldon Stryker employ a distinction between 'making' and 'taking' (or simply playing) roles. Stryker also suggests that the 'degree to which roles are "made" rather than simply "played" ... will depend on the larger structures in which interactive situations are embedded'. Further, he states that 'all structures impose some limits on the kinds of definitions that may be called into play and thus limit the possibilities for action' (Stryker, 1981: 55).

Turner's and Stryker's ideas certainly go some way towards meeting objections that may be raised with regard to the rather more 'free-form' version of a negotiated order. They do attempt to come to terms with the constraints that existing or established forms of social organisation exert on people's social behaviour. This is a manifest weakness of the idea of an unfettered negotiated order. Clearly, as Marx pointed out, people do not make their own history under circumstances of their own choosing. However, Turner and Stryker do not go far enough and deal with issues of power and structural inequality as part of the political and economic context of activity. Furthermore, they are also limited by their commitment to the idea of social role. As I argued in the chapter on Parsons, the concept of role only allows a rather 'thin' account of interaction and thus does not do justice to its diversity and textured quality.

This is a bad trade-off. In the free negotiation scenario we have a more rounded, denser account of interpersonal behaviour, but a weak sense of institutional constraint. While with the more structural version, constraint is acknowledged but the complexity and fullness of social activity is rather understated. Thus neither achieves the kind of balance between objective and subjective aspects of society which would be the hallmark of an adequate and comprehensive theory. This is a pity because the concept of 'career', which I mentioned before (and which plays an important role in much empirical research in SI), has considerable potential in this regard.

The Problem of Reification

As I indicated at the beginning of the chapter, many SIs, especially those of a more humanist persuasion, would argue that there is no distinction between macro and micro phenomena in the first place. It is precisely this conviction that upholds their belief that terms like 'social organisation' are nothing more than convenient labels to express the unfathomable complexity produced by the knitting together of the social activities of many individuals.

This brings us to the issue of 'reification'. As I said earlier, SIs often object to terms like 'structure' and 'system' because they wrongly imbue social life with an objective nature and thus imply that it is not susceptible to human attempts to change or rearrange it. Certainly there are some instances in which notions like 'structure' and 'system' are used injudiciously by various authors, with the implication that they operate independently of human intervention. However, this is not *always* the case. Some authors use concepts like 'structure' and 'system' as ways of describing the more objective aspects of social life without denying that they are human constructs which may be transformed by human (probably collective) effort. This is a very important distinction in usage and must not be confused or forgotten. Unfortunately, most SIs do not acknowledge this difference and thus are sceptical about the use of such terms at all.

Criticisms of Symbolic Interactionism
Emotions, Irrationality and the Unconscious

Insofar as SI attempts to bring together both psychological and sociological issues, it is no surprise that criticisms of SI come from both directions. On the psychological side it is asserted that SI does not deal sufficiently with emotional and irrational features of human behaviour. To some extent this is true, in that the model of the human actor in SI stresses the rational and self-controlled aspects of behaviour. In the SI framework, people are creatures formed by their social environment, who respond sensitively to it in the light of consciously held plans and intentions. This view is carried to the extreme in Goffman's work, where people are thought to be engaged in carefully staged social performances.

This rather rational, manipulative model of human behaviour would seem to neglect its more 'subjective' unpredictable side. This has been somewhat offset by more recent studies of emotion (see, for example, Hochschild, 1983). However, these have tended to stick to analyses of the social construction of emotion rather than deal with its more individual manifestations (for example, as stressed in Freud's notion of the 'unconscious'). Furthermore, the SI interest in the self has often raised more questions than it has resolved. For example, the relationship between the 'impulsive' and the socially conformist aspects of the self (the 'I' and the 'me' in Mead's work), has never been adequately defined. Also, the question of the 'unity of the self' has never been fully resolved. That is, do people have dominant core selves (to which other satellite selves are loosely attached), or do they have a number of different and fully formed selves which are displayed on different occasions? SI is capable of supporting both views.

Also, feminist sociologists (Lengermann and Niebrugge-Brantley, 1992) have pointed out that in interactionist sociology the notion of subjectivity is subsumed under the micro analysis of face-to-face interaction. They insist that, particularly from the point of view of women, individuals' interpretations should be taken into account. Thus subjectivity should be a distinct level of analysis in its own right. This is because women (and others who are treated as subordinates) often experience the world in very different ways from those who dominate (men) and from the prevailing and culturally established definitions. Here the issue of power and the distribution of resources becomes relevant to the understanding of subjective experience in general, but also to understanding how women (and other subordinates) become virtually excluded from certain arenas of interaction.

Concern with the Minutiae of the Micro World

According to some sociological critics, SI pays too much attention to the transient, episodic and fleeting aspects of interaction rather than the more durable structural features (Gouldner, 1971; Brittan, 1973). However, it is not true that

SI is always concerned with fleeting (and thus, seemingly unimportant) aspects of social activity. Many empirical studies focus on patterns of interaction or types of social relations that are routine and 'typical' of the particular location under study. This is illustrated in the studies of dying patients by Glaser and Strauss, and Becker's study of habitual marijuana use, noted previously.

Also, although some aspects of interpersonal encounters are by their very nature fleeting or episodic, it does not follow therefore that they are somehow less worthy of study. As Giddens (1987) has pointed out, such apparently insignificant details of everyday behaviour are intimately connected to the larger-scale institutional aspects. The two are directly implicated in each other, and thus the seemingly more transient aspects must not be discounted. In this light, a more accurate criticism of SI would be that it very largely fails to do what Giddens implies. That is, it fails to connect the face-to-face aspects of behaviour to their structural contexts.

The Nature and Sources of Meaning

Blumer's idea that meaning arises out of social interaction in specific situations is something of an over-generalisation. In one sense, meaning arises from face-to-face situations in that we assess the meaning of other people's intentions during the course of the encounter. However, this is not true of the more general class of meanings through which we classify or identify the specific aspects of another's intentions (a threat, an agreement, a prelude to romance). Also, the meanings which we attach to the social circumstances and situations in which others find themselves (poverty, affluence and so on) have a more established and mandatory character. In many cases, such institutionalised meanings are subject to the manipulation and control of power-holders in society, particularly those who are able to command access to the mass media.

Related to the question of power, feminist theorists have noted that meaning is often obscured or rendered invisible for subordinate groups like women. Very often they are excluded from areas of meaning shared by dominant groups and are required to learn the expectations of these dominant others (Lengermann and Niebrugge-Brantley, 1992). On a slightly different tack Deborah Tannen (1992) has suggested that men and women use different conversational styles and are thus often prevented from understanding what each has to say. Tannen's larger point is that, coupled with the power differential between men and women, the use of different styles of communication tends to create worlds of mutually exclusive meaning.

Power, Inequality and Conflict

The way in which meaning is influenced by structural inequalities of wealth and power is not easily broached within the strict terms of SI. Very often this criticism is extended to suggest that SI allows no role at all for factors such as stratification and the analysis of economic and political power. This is not entirely correct, even though it may be true to say that SI is not generally concerned with such issues. A more precise criticism is that SIs deal with these things inadequately. For example, Luckenbill (1979) defines power as an emergent and flexible relationship between two or more people. Now, although individuals do try to control each other in situations by the exertion of forms of power, it is unwise to conceptualise power entirely in terms of face-to-face situations.

Such a view does not take into account structural features such as society-wide inequalities based on class, gender and ethnic divisions. These features represent *prior* and unequal distributions of power and power resources which, to some extent, limit and determine how power operates at an interpersonal level. Moreover, forms of power other than interpersonal ones may reside in the structural features of organisations (in the form of hierarchies of control and appraisal of members). These structural forms of power are not as visible and readily apparent as power manifest in face-to-face situations, but they are, nonetheless, present and highly influential. This tendency to miss the 'deeper', less easily observable aspects of economic and political power is a persistent weakness in SIs' analyses.

Much the same is true of their analyses of conflict. SIs do tend to stress the co-operative nature of human behaviour in a general sense. Nevertheless, they have also produced empirical studies which highlight the nature and importance of social conflict (for example, Gold, 1952, on janitors and tenants, Hearn and Stoll, 1975, on cocktail waitresses and their customers). However, as these studies bear out, SIs tend to concentrate on local interpersonal conflicts rather than society-wide conflicts between class or ethnic groupings or worker-management relations. Of course, since one of the central topics of any social-psychological perspective must be interpersonal dealings, then it is not surprising that SI tends to focus on localised interpersonal disruptions which have no serious effect on the status quo of the wider society.

The weakness of SI is that it does not postulate any connection between these localised, face-to-face issues and wider structural features. In a very real sense, structural features provide the wider backdrop against which interpersonal dealings take place. It is the inability of SI to properly come to terms with this structural domain that limits its contribution to the macro–micro issue. Nevertheless, I have dwelt on SI at some length because I believe that there is much in it that could be directed towards the resolution of the macro–micro problem, even if its proponents themselves are less than enthusiastic about such a project.

While the emphasis on empirical analyses is a strong feature of SI, it is often taken to an anti-theoretical extreme. The belief that knowledge and social analysis generally is based on direct observation and experience (empiricism) severely limits the SI contribution to the macro–micro issue since it has both empirical and theoretical dimensions. Nonetheless, I believe that much of what SIs have to say is complementary to, and thus may be fruitfully integrated with, other strands of thought. That is, on its own it does not provide an adequate account of macro–micro links. However, if its stronger features are properly integrated with more structural theories, then some aspects of SI could be brought to bear upon our understanding of the links between macro and micro phenomena. Some of these same considerations also apply to what are known as 'phenomenological' theories to which I shall turn in the next chapter.

SUMMARY

- Humanist schools of social theory such as symbolic interactionism, phenomenology and ethnomethodology reject concepts of structure (or system) as false constructs. Thus they reject the dualisms of individual–society, agency–structure and macro–micro. Society is simply people doing things together (symbolic interactionism) and social study involves the study of local practices (ethnomethodology).

- George Herbert Mead's symbolic interactionism rejects behaviourist psychology which regards human action as learned responses to environmental stimuli. Mead stressed the importance of the inner life – people's minds and selves.

- The individual in symbolic interactionism is reflectively aware and responds flexibly and creatively to situations. This is a strong affirmation of the importance of the individual subject (which is the focus of vehement criticism by structuralism, post-structuralism and postmodernism).

- Herbert Blumer suggests that a focus on 'meaning' is the most important feature that distinguishes symbolic interactionism from sociological functionalism (Parsons) and traditional psychology. For Blumer, (a) people act on the basis of meaning, (b) meaning arises out of social interaction, and (c) meaning is modified through interpretative processes.

- For symbolic interactionists it is of little interest to understand human motives as 'mysterious' inner forces or impulses. It is more useful to understand them as socially acceptable rationalisations for questioned conduct and/or in terms of the way people become committed to (or entrapped by) particular lines of activity.

- The 'Iowa School' of symbolic interactionism has a more positivist approach to research methods and views society as more structured. The 'Chicago School' has a humanistic approach to social research and rejects concepts like 'structure' and 'system' as applicable to society. There are also important differences within and between the schools as to the importance of theory construction in social research.

- Symbolic interactionists affirm the idea that individuals and society are seamlessly joined. They are of the view that there is no society apart from the individuals who compose it, just as there are no individuals apart from society.

- Individuals are able to distance themselves from the roles they play (Goffman) and are generally able to edit and shape their self-presentations for particular audiences.

- The patterning of social organisation is produced by the fitting together of lines of action in 'joint activity'. However, some symbolic interactionists view social order as the result of processes of 'negotiation' (Glaser and Strauss), whereas others (Stryker, for instance) believe that the wider structures in which interactive situations are embedded impose constraints on behaviour. This difference of emphasis raises the issue of reification.

- Symbolic interactionism has been criticised for not attending to emotion, irrationality and the unconscious. Although some of these criticisms are well founded, the real point is that symbolic interactionists often propose unsatisfactory or inadequate explanations for such phenomena.

- The criticism that symbolic interactionism is unduly concerned with the minutiae of the social world is somewhat misplaced. Rather, it fails to adequately connect the analysis of face-to-face behaviour with wider institutional contexts.

- Symbolic interactionists have an unnecessarily restricted view of meaning as a purely interactive construction. This ignores the notion of meaning as the expression of individual subjectivity, or as being defined, imposed or manipulated by powerful groups, including the mass media.

- Although it is inaccurate to claim that symbolic interactionists do not attend to power, inequality and conflict in society, it is true that their focus is primarily on localised, face-to-face issues. Thus, they underplay the important and close connection between these issues and wider structural features.

- Symbolic interactionists do not adequately resolve the individual–society, agency–structure and macro–micro problems, although they make a valuable contribution to understanding them.

5

Perceiving and Accomplishing

PREVIEW

- Phenomenological strands of sociological thought focus on people's consciousness, perceptions and experience – how they understand their world.

- Schutz and the notion of subjective understanding as constructed from a shared intersubjective world; common stocks of knowledge; the reciprocity of perspectives; the practical attitude and the fiduciary attitude; exchanging gifts or offerings; lived experience.

- Laing's phenomenology of mental illness. Mental illness as a 'reasoned' response to an intolerable situation.

- Critical evaluation of phenomenologists' and ethnomethodologists' claims to resolve or transcend the agency–structure or macro–micro issues. Evaluation of their claim to be indifferent to these and other concerns of 'conventional' sociology.

- Garfinkel's ethnomethodology. The rejection of positivism and the idea of an objective social world. The hidden rules and assumptions of social interaction. Meaning as fragile and ambiguous – its situated character (indexicality).

- Empirical studies of social organisation. Bittner on police work and peace-keeping on skid row. Zimmerman's study of public assistance case workers.

- Berger and Luckmann's early, phenomenologically inspired attempt to link subjective and objective features of social life.

- The positive contribution of phenomenological and ethnomethodological strands of social analysis – social interaction cannot be regarded as a simple reflection of more 'important' structural features. The major drawback of these schools of thought – their inability to deal with wider structural and macro features and hence their inability to transcend or resolve the agency–structure or macro–micro debates/problems.

Phenomenological Strands of Thought

In many ways, phenomenological sociology overlaps with SI, especially in its concern with 'everyday life'. In other respects there are a number of distinguishing features. Perhaps the main difference is that phenomenology takes a rather more subjective stance. While SI is careful to address the 'point of view of the actor', phenomenology takes this as the central concern. Consequently, phenomenology is even more radical in its rejection of social structures as external and constraining. How the social world appears to the individual is the only legitimate topic for the social analyst to study. This is the only reality; anything else is an artificial construction of sociologists.

Thus phenomenology (deriving from the philosophy of Husserl) concentrates its attention on people's consciousness and experience of the world they live in through the use of their senses. It is individuals' perceptions which colour their social experiences and which thus become the central focus of interest. In the first part of this chapter I shall deal briefly with the work of Schutz, who is the most important sociological writer within this tradition. This will serve to lay the ground for the two following sections. The first of these focuses on Ronald Laing's work on mental illness (particularly schizophrenia) as an empirical example of the application of phenomenological analysis. The final section discusses 'ethnomethodology', a branch of sociology that has been heavily influenced by Schutz's phenomenology.

Schutz's work, particularly *The Phenomenology of the Social World* (1972) received its original impetus as a critique of Max Weber's work. Weber's classical studies (of world religions and comparative social structures, among other things) were influenced by two convictions: first, that sociological analysis should attempt to unearth the meanings, or 'subjective understandings', which motivate and impel people to act in the way that they do; secondly, this must be done in conjunction with an analysis of the social-structural and historical circumstances that provide the context in which those meanings are realised. For instance, in *The Protestant Ethic and the Spirit of Capitalism* (1930), Weber attempted to reconstruct the typical motivations of early capitalist entrepreneurs by examining the writings of Calvin on protestantism. Here Weber was attempting to trace the effects of religious ideas on the emergence of certain kinds of economic behaviour.

The details of this study are not important for our present concerns. However, it is a good example of Weber's attempt to combine the analysis of subjective understanding with an awareness of the social, political, economic and religious circumstances in which it arises. It is exactly this insistence on a tie between subjective understanding and specific historical circumstances that Schutz objected to in Weber's work. In Schutz's terms, Weber overlooks the way in which meaning is constructed out of an individual's stream of experience. Schutz felt strongly that to treat subjective understanding as something that could be 'reconstructed' from historical documents and 'imposed' by the researcher misses out an essential fact – that meaning arises from the world of daily experience as it is lived by the different individuals who try to make sense of it and come to terms with it.

The Intersubjective World

Although I have said that the way the social world appears to the individual is emphasised in phenomenological sociology, this does not mean that the individual is somehow treated as isolated or separate from society. Society and social life are 'intersubjective' phenomena. This refers to the fact that much of daily life is a taken-for-granted affair which assumes that other people think, perceive and otherwise understand things in pretty much the same terms as we do ourselves. That is, the social world is one that we share with others on the basis of common knowledge (stocks) and procedures (recipes). It is the mutuality of such knowledge that allows us to interact with others. As with symbolic interactionism, language is for Schutz essential for this process. It allows us to 'typify' things and people in our environment by providing names and labels for them. This, more than anything, provides for a 'reciprocity of perspectives' and aids us in dealing with others' needs and demands in social life.

Since we all have unique biographical situations our 'stocks of knowledge', as Schutz calls them (all the bits of information and knowledge we have accumulated throughout our lives), will not be identical with other peoples'. Furthermore, knowledge is socially distributed in the sense that different people know different things because they deal with different things on a day-to-day basis (accountants know more about accounting than they do about nursing). Nevertheless, there is a core of commonsense knowledge which binds the everyday world together (language is an important part of this) and allows us to understand each other. Through typification we construct a shared world on a face-to-face basis, as well as with other groups which are more removed from our sphere of influence. Phenomenological sociology, therefore, is concerned with how this variegated social world appears to us as individuals and how we deal with it in terms of our knowledge at hand. (This includes the 'recipes' we employ to deal with both practical and social situations.)

Schutz concentrates on the problem of intersubjectivity in terms of what he calls 'the practical attitude'. That is, he tends to see people as 'problem-solvers' in a rather practical sense. We arrange to dine or have a meal if we are hungry, and we deal with this 'problem' in terms of the application of rules of thumb about cooking or inviting friends over for dinner. That is, we apply our stocks of knowledge at hand to solve the practical and organisational problem of eating (either alone or with others). However, Schutz's emphasis on the predominance of the practical attitude has been questioned recently by others working on the area. Vaitkus (1991), for example, suggests that we approach others from a point of view of trust and openness (which he calls a 'fiduciary' attitude).

This applies even if we are concerned with solving a practical problem. This trusting attitude implies a sharedness of an 'offering' or a 'gift' which is accepted by the other person. Examples of giving and receiving a social gift can be seen in such things as offering someone a place to sit, opening up a conversation, praising or complaining to another, telling secrets and so on (Vaitkus, 1991: 166). The point about these things lies not in their practical value but in the fact that they signify the general intention of giving and receiving during the encounter. Thus we never encounter others simply in terms of the practical attitude, we are always conscious of the way in which others go about dealing with the problems of daily life. How we evaluate the 'performances' of others in this regard will have consequences for our own attitudes toward the encounter and, consequently, how it turns out (whether, for example, everyone is satisfied or an argument ensues).

Vaitkus is here pointing to the fact that the attitude of basic trust is intimately tied to the question of meaning. In this sense, practical problems are overlaid with meanings which flow from acts of giving and receiving performed in attempting to solve such problems. For example, when we invite someone around for a meal, the practical problem of hunger is subsidiary to the trusting and gift-giving context of dining with others. That is, when we dine with others we are attempting to create a situation in which the conversation and sharing of food is the main point. Clearly, moods and emotions such as excitement, fear and depression are closely related to the extent and nature of our trust and 'belief' in others. Also, such responses as teasing, flattery, sarcasm and rivalry which are common features of general 'socialising' are connected to the nature of our attitudes to others. In this sense they are examples of giving, receiving, requesting, rejecting and withdrawing of social offerings (Vaitkus, 1991: 167).

This kind of analysis provides an important adjunct to the sorts of analyses provided by SIs. Perhaps even more than SI it stresses the humanistic nature of social analysis and the rejection of the idea that people can be regarded as 'things' or 'objects' that respond almost mechanically to their environment. Furthermore, it wholeheartedly rejects the notion that there can be any impersonal 'science' of social life that can specify general laws of behaviour. Social analysis must take into account the meaning that the social world has for the individual based on how the person understands and responds to their lived experience. The way people construe their social existence helps them formulate their plans and intentions. They make choices about the direction in which their lives should go on the basis of their experience. As such, persons are 'intentional', self-reflective and capable of making some difference in their world.

The Phenomenology of Mental Illness

Ronald Laing has developed some interesting ideas about mental illness (particularly schizophrenia) based on a phenomenological approach. Laing's ideas perhaps have more in common with Sartre's existentialism than Schutz's work, but nonetheless they highlight similar points. Existentialism focuses on human existence and a person's being-in-the-world. In essence, according to Sartre (1966), people are free to choose what they are and what they will become. They are not programmed by, and thus prisoners of, unconscious drives as Freud insisted. Nor are they inevitably forced to be exactly as others want them to be. In the final analysis even people who are obviously unfree in a literal sense, like slaves or prisoners, are 'free' to choose how to respond to their circumstances of subordination. That is, they can be willing victims, resigned fatalists or active resisters in such circumstances.

To understand the specific course of action that a person takes in such situations we also have to understand the plans, strategies and purposes which lie behind their actions. Even if they are unclear or somewhat confused, they will reveal something of the reasoning behind a person's choice to be a particular sort of person. This existential analysis assumes that people are not only free to choose, but also that they are rational inasmuch as they do the things they do with at least some awareness of why they are doing them. In this sense, even those who are seemingly 'irrational', as some mentally ill people often appear, they have their own reasons for what they think and for acting the way they do (see Roche, 1973).

Laing's work on schizophrenia in *The Divided Self* (1969) suggests that the mentally ill have reasons (good or bad) for acting the way they do. In order to help a mentally ill person come to terms with the illness the therapist has to talk to them in order to reconstruct the world as that person sees it. Furthermore, the therapist must understand the reasons for the ill person's 'strange' behaviour as directly reflecting their experience of, and existence in, that world. This makes a radical break with the traditional view, which sees the schizophrenic as a diseased object which has 'broken down', rather as a machine may break down, and which needs to be restored to good working order. Laing, however, argues that mental illnesses like schizophrenia cannot be understood in this way. The schizophrenic has to be regarded as a person first and foremost. Moreover, as human beings, people have to be understood as existing within a connected series (a nexus) of social relationships. This nexus of relationships with friends, family, colleagues and so on, is important in understanding the mental illness from the sufferer's point of view. In a sense the 'illness' reflects the quality of these relationships because it is in this context that the person experiences 'problems in living'.

In a later work (Laing and Esterson, 1964), Laing pinpoints the family as crucially important in this regard. The different kinds of communications (especially the indirect forms) and the shared assumptions that develop within a family context can be a source of difficulty. This is so in situations where a person's true feelings and wishes are being thwarted by other family members and where communications are confused or ambiguous. Laing and Esterson document a number of cases of this in the families of schizophrenic women. Denial and repression of the women's autonomy and sense of personal security within the setting and history of their families had taken its toll in the form of a mental breakdown.

In this sense, becoming mentally ill represents the person's response to an intolerable situation. The lapse into a private world of delusion and imagination is the only way of preserving a sense of integrity and personal identity that is otherwise being undermined. What is learned and formed within the family is then generalised into feelings towards the whole social community. Other people are regarded both as a threat to one's personal identity and as the only possible source of fulfilment. This represents an extreme in which mental illness is 'taken on', so to speak, by a person in order to cope with an impossible situation. In this specific sense the individual makes a 'reasoned' response to the situation and is not simply reacting mechanically to either social forces or deep psychological needs (although these do exist in some form or the other). The point is that the person becomes what they eventually become (in this case mentally ill) because they see this as the only way of coping with the world as it appears to them. Since other people are potentially a threat to their sense of identity and security then avoidance, aloofness and lack of emotional responsiveness may be the most rational means of preserving whatever still remains.

Quite clearly, this type of analysis is extremely perceptive and not only touches on the pathology of social experience (like that of mental illness), but also says something about social existence in a more general and routine sense. For example, the duality between the experience of 'relatedness' and 'separateness' is something we all experience; it is a generic feature of social life. Problems associated with feelings of being alone and isolated or of needing the company of others so much that one cannot stand to be on one's own are at the heart of our experience of life in modern society. Tannen (1987, 1992) has even suggested that men and women experience and value this duality differently and that this accounts for different styles of communication between them.

Indifference to the Macro–Micro Problem

In the light of these insights, we can conclude that the general phenomenological and existential framework has a great deal to say about social experience which is not catered for within the SI tradition. In particular, it tells us much about people's experience of social life, their feelings, hopes, plans and perceptions. Thus this perspective enables us to probe into the intersubjective world from a truly human point of view. However, even more than with SI, we have to be aware of the limitations of this line of thought. Certainly it has a lot to say about the relationship between the feeling states of people and the social web of 'other people' in which they are involved both intimately (friends and family) and more impersonally (strangers, outsiders, 'authorities'). This clearly is an essential aspect of the more general question of the relation between the individual and society.

However, this concentration on the individual's experience is at the expense of an awareness of the influences of wider and more impersonal structural factors. In a strict sense, these are external to activity and an individual's experience of it, in that they exist beyond the confines of individual control and awareness. Thus, in phenomenological sociology there is very little analysis, if any, of social forms like organisations, political and economic institutions and their structures of power and so on, which are partly (though not wholly) independent of the activities of particular individuals and groups. Of course, they are not completely separate from people since they are human constructs and depend on people in general for their continuance. However, in my view the partial independence of reproduced social forms must be taken into account in any theory which hopes to embrace both macro and micro phenomena. It is exactly these things that the more structural theories (like Parsons's, and those influenced by Durkheim and Marx) are good at coping with.

It is important to remember this since phenomenological writers often assert that their position is one which either resolves the macro–micro issue or transcends it in some way. Vaitkus (1991), for instance, feels that because the focus on intersubjectivity occupies the middle ground between the person and the 'external' world, it suggests a 'final overthrow of the very macro–micro distinction in the social sciences'. Such claims are based upon several rather dubious assumptions, for example, that intersubjectivity is an adequate way of conceptually handling macro or structural phenomena. This is patently not the case since intersubjectivity remains locked into an interpersonal focus, with particular emphasis on individual experience and consciousness. This simply reduces macro phenomena to the level of interactions between people.

In this sense, macro phenomena are defined out of existence and thus conveniently 'disappear' into thin air. This is a strategy that has been used by writers from other theoretical perspectives and we shall have occasion to mention it again. What is needed, as a number of authors have noted, is some theory of linkage between the two domains (Layder, 1981, 1997, 1998; Archer, 1995; Mouzelis, 1995), not a theory that simply abandons the distinction in the first place. Doing away with the macro–micro distinction by claiming that it is false does not prove it to be so. It merely avoids making the effort to work out the relations between the two domains. (In fact, in my own work I suggest there are multiple domains rather than just two – Layder, 1997, 2004b.) Phenomenology also implicitly claims to be a radical breakthrough, providing insights that effectively replace existing knowledge. For this to be the case it must be conclusively shown that existing knowledge (in this case the macro–micro distinction) no longer has anything to offer. This is usually what is lacking in most claims of this kind.

In the light of this lack of evidence a more modest and realistic proposal would be to suggest that new insights could be integrated with existing theories. Unfortunately, many proponents of 'radical new breakthroughs' get carried away with the romance of being on the cutting edge of discovery, rather than dealing in a systematic and careful way with what theoretical knowledge we already have and using its valuable aspects in a cumulative and co-operative manner. This brings us to the subject of ethnomethodology, many of whose adherents claim to have redefined the subject matter of sociology and respecified its methods.

Ethnomethodology:
A Revolution in Sociology?

Ethnomethodology is a sociological perspective based on the work of Harold Garfinkel in the late 1960s and draws upon the work of Schutz among others. Ethnomethodology refers to the 'methods' by which people make sense of the situations in which they find themselves and how they manage to sustain an orderliness in their dealings with others. The title of this section is taken from an article by John Goldthorpe (1973) in which he reviews the work of ethnomethodologists and concludes that their claims to have provided a revolutionary new approach to social analysis are rather inflated. Goldthorpe argues that many of their insights can be easily incorporated into, and operate alongside, traditional approaches.

While ethnomethodology has made substantial contributions to the understanding of social interaction, these add to the corpus of sociological theory rather than demand its abandonment. However, some of the more radical authors claim that ethnomethodology is indifferent to the concerns of 'conventional' sociology, and that it has transcended the terms of the macro–micro debate (Hilbert, 1990). Indifference to the established corpus of sociological work, both theoretical and empirical, simply ignores the issues rather than truly grapples with them. Thus the claim that ethnomethodology 'goes beyond' the boundaries of existing knowledge is quite unfounded.

Garfinkel's *Studies in Ethnomethodology* (1967) lays out the basic tenets of ethnomethodology which have since been expanded upon by a number of other writers. Garfinkel was influenced by Parsons's work on the problem of order but subsequently came to reject the basic premises upon which it is based. As we saw in Chapter 2, Parsons, following Durkheim, deals with the problem of order by relying heavily on the idea of externally defined norms and values which people learn and incorporate into their behaviour. In this sense, in Parsons's theory, people are conformist to a seemingly unhealthy degree. Garfinkel and others (such as Douglas, 1970) reject this conventional positivist idea that there is an objective social world which externally influences behaviour in favour of the idea that social order is accomplished from *within* settings through the practical activities of those involved. The proper focus for the study of everyday life and social order is commonsense knowledge and the unstated 'rules' and assumptions which people draw on to make their own actions understandable to themselves and to other people.

The basic and puzzling feature of everyday behaviour is that it appears so routine and stable and ordered even in situations where there is the potential for misunderstanding and ambiguity. Garfinkel insists that people are not simple automata responding to the dictates of an external social system. In fact, people are highly knowledgeable about social life and employ this knowledge in a creative manner to bring a certain sense of smoothness and order to day-to-day social behaviour. This surface orderliness, however, is undergirded by unstated, unwritten assumptions about the *dos* and *don'ts* of social life. Garfinkel devised a number of 'experiments' (more like natural 'demonstrations' than laboratory set-ups) to reveal this largely hidden, taken-for-granted knowledge. Thus he got his students to disrupt the normal and ordered routine of everyday social situations in order to reveal the taken-for-granted assumptions on which they are based. Students would enter shops and bargain about the prices of goods like magazines or cigarettes, or they would act as if they were lodgers in their own homes. Such disruptions naturally cause confusion and bewilderment; nonetheless, they expose the commonsense assumptions and principles underlying everyday behaviour.

Apart from a concern with the implicit taken-for-granted 'rules' on which routine behaviour is based, Garfinkel was interested in the meaning of behaviour for individuals. Garfinkel's ideas about 'rules' and 'meaning' are very different from both conventional structural theories (like those of Parsons, Durkheim and Marx) and the other humanist strands like symbolic interactionism. Rules are not to be thought of as definitive guides to action which have to be followed. Rather, they are more in the manner of starting points or background assumptions (Cicourel, 1973) about what might be appropriate and relevant in particular situations. The real business of behaviour begins with the way in which people use, bend and elaborate on such raw materials to create new rules, or at least substantial reworkings of the established ones.

Meaning and Activity as Context-Bound

Although meaning is central to symbolic interactionism, ethnomethodology goes some way further than this by suggesting that it is always a fragile and ambiguous thing. Meaning is always problematic and has to be continually 'worked at' and developed by those immediately involved. Meanings are a practical accomplishment on the part of members of society, they are not objectively given or unambiguous. Like 'rules' they 'emerge' from the situations in which they are employed. However, they do not become detached from the situations of their use, they remain intimately tied to the immediate circumstances of behaviour, including the specific people involved. Garfinkel refers to this as the *indexical* nature of meaning: the fact that it is tied to a particular context of use.

Examples of this can be found in ordinary conversational expressions like the use of 'he', 'she' or 'there' or 'here', the meaning of which depends upon the listener knowing exactly who 'she' is, or where 'there' is. The indexical nature of meaning requires that we have intimate contextual knowledge of who is doing what to whom, and under what circumstances before we can claim to know the meaning of an action or a conversation. Another source of indexicality derives from the *way* people say and do things. For instance, tone of voice, facial expression and the use of gestures all convey subtle aspects that contribute to the meaning of a statement, sometimes quite independently of the words used. For example, the sentence 'I will come at 5 o'clock' can be uttered in certain contexts in certain ways such that it could be 'heard' in several different ways, and thus, taken to mean different things. It could be taken as 'a promise', or 'a warning' or even 'an appeal' (Wootton, 1975).

In this sense, action and meaning are always tied to particular contexts and cannot be understood from an external or objective standpoint. The orderliness of interaction has to be understood as an ongoing 'accomplishment' created by people from within situations. Much importance is therefore attached to the accounts that people give of their behaviour, that is, how they describe and explain what they are, or were, doing in particular situations. These accounts are, in fact, the actual 'methods' that people use to produce and manage situations. As a result, the analysis of conversations both naturally occurring or as part of some in-depth interview, has become a central area of ethnomethodological inquiry.

Clearly, Garfinkel's work and the work that it has inspired is a valuable and insightful counter to over-zealous structural theories, which tend to discount the creativity and knowledgeability of people and the internal texture and dynamics of interaction. While in many respects similar to SI, overall it is rather more radical in its implications. It emphasises the importance of taken-for-granted and commonsense knowledge, the uniqueness of meanings and activities, the intentionality of people and their ability to create and manage the social forms they inhabit.

Empirical Studies of Social Organisation

Apart from conversational analysis, ethnomethodology has produced a number of empirical studies which highlight some of the basic premises of the approach.

Egon Bittner's (1967) study of police work on skid row is a classical example of this. Bittner points out that police work among a city's down-and-out population (including alcoholics, petty criminals, tramps, drug pushers and so on) has to be understood as 'peace-keeping' rather than 'law enforcement'. That is, instead of enforcing the law by attending to every legal infraction, the patrolmen merely use the law as a resource to solve practical problems of keeping the peace in this area of the city. Thus, a man may be arrested on a minor charge in order to save him and others associated with him from a lot of potential trouble. The police proceed against persons by assessing the *risk* of trouble rather than on the basis of strict culpability. Thus, the overall peace in the area is the major concern rather than individual cases.

The police's perception of their role results from two things. First, the nature of skid row and its inhabitants (people who do not lead 'normal' lives) meant that the usual means of policing were just not feasible. Secondly, the police operated with limited resources of time and personnel, and thus they had a view of their job as doing what was possible in the circumstances. In this context, peace-keeping was a realistic possibility whereas law enforcement was not. This approach was geared to dealing and coping with life on skid row, which is unpredictable and extremely changeable. Bittner highlights three elements of the patrolmen's strategies for dealing with trouble. First, the officers use detailed personal knowledge of the inhabitants as a means of maintaining control and making decisions in specific cases. Secondly, they make practical decisions which the law does not recognise as valid and, finally, they make decisions based on particular circumstances as they arise in the immediate situation.

Both this study (and others like Zimmerman's 1971 study of case workers in a Bureau of Public Assistance) emphasise the point that social order does not necessarily reside in the organisational structure or the formal rules that are meant to 'govern' occupational activity. Rather, it is the practitioners themselves, faced with the typical situations that their jobs entail, who develop ways of dealing with practical problems. The 'rules', such as the legal framework of policing or the formal 'first come first served' intake procedure of the public assistance caseworkers, are simply resources to be used. This may mean that they are reversed or 'flexibly applied' according to the developing situation as the practitioner sees it. These are clearly important correctives to the bland assumption that 'structural' features automatically influence the direction of behaviour.

Such studies underpin many of the theoretical insights of ethnomethodology and demonstrate its use in empirical research. However, this merely leads to the conclusion that it complements existing approaches to interaction. In themselves such studies do not endorse the claim of some ethnomethodologists that it represents a revolutionary change of approach. It is precisely those who claim this who are unwilling to recognise the profound limitations of ethnomethodology as a separate discipline in its own terms. In the previous chapter we saw how SI struggled with the problem of dealing with structural factors such as economic and political power, and forms of inequality based on class, gender and ethnicity and so on. Although restricted in its ability to do this and limited in its capacity to expand in this area, SI nonetheless has attempted to give room to such factors.

Ethnomethodology, as an even more radically subjective approach, actually rejects structural phenomena as a legitimate topic of interest in the first place. In this respect ethnomethodology has two rather contradictory views on structural phenomena. The first underlines (and probably overstates) the importance of human knowledgeability. This suggests that, unless people are aware or somehow conscious of structural factors like power or class, such factors have no place in social analysis. Researchers and theorists who use structural concepts are operating with creations of their own imagination. They are not real empirical phenomena. The second view somewhat contradicts this by saying that anyway, even if lay people (as opposed to sociologists) believe structural factors like class and power to be real, this does not mean that they are real. The first view takes the lay perspective to be the most authoritative while the second denies this.

The ethnomethodological conception of social organisation and social structure, then, is one which is even more extreme than the 'negotiated order' of the SIs of the Chicago School. There is no such thing as 'objective structure' and social order is a construction which is continually sustained and managed by those involved – it is created and recreated from moment to moment. Some ethnomethodologists have pushed this further to claim that their position therefore takes them 'beyond' the macro–micro debate (Hilbert, 1990). In this sense, they are 'indifferent' to structure at any level (either micro or macro) and thus they conduct their arguments from a transcendent vantage point. The transcendence is achieved only by abandoning the terms of the debate, not by resolving the substance of the issues.

An Early Attempt at Linkage: Berger and Luckmann

By way of conclusion I should like to look briefly at Berger and Luckmann's *The Social Construction of Reality* (1967). Although this work treads an independent path, it also draws on SI and phenomenology in trying to bring together macro and micro levels of analysis. As an early example of this, Berger and Luckmann's work anticipates some of the later attempts at synthesis and linkage that we will examined further on. It needs to be said, however, that although, in this work, there are continuities with the phenomenological and interactionist traditions, there is also a radical departure in that it endeavours to build a bridge between the objective and subjective features of social life.

That is, unlike the other traditions, Berger and Luckmann's work accepts the reality of both these aspects of social life and the macro–micro levels of analysis that go with them. The authors' intention, therefore, is to describe and explain some of the linkages between them, and not to advocate the primary importance of one aspect as against the other. Although there are problems with Berger and Luckmann's theory, in my opinion this bridge-building approach is a very constructive one. As a result it is more adequate and sophisticated than those which seek to ignore or denigrate alternative approaches.

A preliminary consideration is that Berger and Luckmann subtitle their work 'A treatise in the sociology of knowledge'. This area of concern takes it somewhat away from those we have already considered. Berger and Luckmann's work, therefore, is not concerned primarily with the nature of social interaction as such and its relation to its wider context (social structure). Rather, it is concerned with how groups and individuals know things and perceive things in the social world. In particular, Berger and Luckmann have a broad definition of 'knowledge' as anything which passes for knowledge in society. Thus they have a keen interest in commonsense knowledge and the general stocks of knowledge (practical or otherwise) that people rely on to give them a personal feeling of solidity and a sense of the reality of the social world around them.

This clearly relates to the phenomenological strands of thought which I discussed earlier. Berger and Luckmann's work concentrates on everyday knowledge (how to conduct oneself in social situations, or the problems of identity that arise during adolescence) as a resource which is available for people to draw on to inform their conduct. However, they do not go on from this to focus on the way in which such knowledge is actually employed in activity and how this connects with its settings and contexts. Instead, their framework is rather static and removed from the dynamics of face-to-face behaviour. In this sense, their analysis shifts away from the more encompassing issues of the macro–micro debate that we have so far considered. Nonetheless, the question of knowledge and the construction of social reality is connected in some way to activity. Also, since Berger and Luckmann's work is an attempt to bridge objective and subjective levels of analysis it has some interesting facets.

The Basics of the Theory

In essence Berger and Luckmann's analysis of the social construction of reality revolves around three interrelated ideas. First, through social activity, human beings create external features which emerge over time. This is rather like Parsons's notion of the emergence of shared understandings and role expectations from the interaction of two (or more) people. In this way institutions like family and kinship systems are developed. The importance of historical processes is underlined by Berger and Luckmann in that, through historical development, legal, political, economic and religious institutions become enshrined in traditions and rituals. Over generations such institutions become established as external realities which confront new generations of people.

The sedimentation of tradition which evolves through time endows such external realities with an objective quality in people's eyes. This is buttressed by the effects of language and other symbolic forms which allow people to think of them in detached, objective ways. Thus flags, emblems, rules of kinship, legal and governmental procedures and rituals all become means of expressing the independent reality of such things. Language is very powerful in this regard in that it enables people to speak and think of things which are removed from everyday situations of face-to-face behaviour. This ability to understand and refer to social institutions in a removed manner reinforces the 'objective' nature and power of these things.

This 'objectivation', then, is the second of the three interrelated ideas. This and the fact that social activity gives rise to social products which are external to individuals are linked to the third which involves the manner in which such products become incorporated in the individual's consciousness ('internalisation'). This concerns the question, how do social institutions, and the symbols, ideas and knowledge that go along with them, become a subjective reality for individuals? Berger and Luckmann suggest that this is accomplished first through 'primary socialisation', by which they mean the manner in which children are taught about the nature of society and the rules and regulations that are part of being a member of it.

Also, there are later forms of socialisation in which people acquire different forms of knowledge from friends, colleagues and acquaintances. For example, people learn how to do certain jobs, or how best to commit a crime and so on, depending on the sort of people they regularly encounter and the groups to which they belong. Finally, the nature of a person's identity and general social activity reinforce such subjective understandings of social reality. In line with their interest in everyday knowledge, Berger and Luckmann even suggest that casual conversations (again highlighting the influence of language) are important in maintaining 'subjective reality'. This is achieved by, 'the accumulation and consistency of casual conversation – conversation that can *afford to be casual* precisely because it refers to the routines of a taken-for-granted world' (1967: 172).

Berger and Luckmann suggest that the three elements are closely tied together in a manner which makes them mutually influence each other. Thus individuals create society while at the same moment society creates individuals in an unending chain of reciprocal influences. However, according to the authors, society is never anything other than a human product and thus society itself is simply human activity which has become externalised and objectified in the form of knowledge. Now this is an important qualification in their argument and considerably weakens their claim to have successfully bridged the macro–micro gap. Berger and Luckmann's intention here is to move their theory away from the 'reification' involved in saying that society is 'something other' than human activity. Here again we have the exaggerated reaction to the issue of reification.

Weaknesses of the Theory

Very few sociologists would claim that society is the product of supernatural forces, or forces completely outside the human sphere. Clearly human society is a human product. The crucial question is, 'Is society *the same thing as* people and activity?', as Berger and Luckmann think? Not so. It is perfectly in order to say that society is a product of human activity while at the same time suggesting that people and society are very different. To say that they have different properties and characteristics – for instance people fall in love while societies do not; societies exist beyond the lifetimes of people – is not to suggest that society is a non-human construct. Of course, people may experience society as oppressive and beyond their control. They may feel alienated from society, but this is a different matter. To say that people and society (social structures) are different things is merely to point to different aspects of social reality. This is similar to making distinctions in the natural world – such as those between air, earth, fire and water.

Unfortunately, by viewing individuals and societies as if they were the same as each other, Berger and Luckmann tend to repeat the two main errors from which they had intended to escape. On the one hand they try to avoid the trap of viewing individuals as mechanically determined by society (an error they see in Durkheim and Parsons). At the same time they try to avoid the implication that society is somehow a creation of individuals (an error they detect in Weber).

However, as Bhaskar (1979) points out, instead of avoiding them they reproduce both mistakes in their own theory. That is, by suggesting that society is simply an externalisation created essentially through language, they repeat the mistake of viewing society as a creation of individuals. By suggesting that individuals are subjective reflections of these 'objectivations', they endorse a rather mechanical view of the person.

So, despite a very promising and constructive starting point, Berger and Luckmann's theory founders on a number of formidable problems. In a sense, their belief in an objective world is not strong enough to enable them to deal adequately with structure and institutional phenomena. On the other hand, their view of the subjective side of social life is rather one-dimensional. On the subjective side they neglect a number of things. First, they tend to speak of 'individuals' as if they were separate from interaction with other people. As we have seen already, this does not do justice to the emergent dynamics of *social* activity. Secondly, there is little talk of activity as such. Individuals seem strangely static (as in Parsons). As a consequence there is little reference to the range of social practices in which people are engaged.

On the objective side of the equation, there is too much emphasis on the importance of knowledge and symbolic forms (idealism) and too little on the way in which material factors are related to, and have an effect on, these things. There is no appreciation of how material resources are distributed unequally in societies in specific historical circumstances (despite their emphasis on the importance of history). Thus there is no analysis of the manner in which goods, power, authority and money are distributed throughout society and the way in which certain kinds of knowledge reflect this. Finally, because they do not see organisations and institutions as different from people, Berger and Luckmann are unable to provide an account of how they operate in partly independent terms.

Conclusion: Phenomenology and the Macro–Micro Problem

The various strands of phenomenology that I have discussed in this chapter have undoubtedly provided much value to our understanding of the nature of human social activity. In particular, phenomenology has directed attention to the pivotal role of meaning, subjective experience and the purposiveness of human behaviour. The nature of social interaction is illuminated by these emphases and the idea of an intersubjective world underlines the special characteristics of situated activity. Such an approach rescues social analysis from the often inappropriately 'objective' and impersonal stance of positivism. It also underlines the fact that social interaction can never be thought of simply as a reflection of 'more important' structural influences.

However, phenomenology has tended to veer in the opposite direction, denying the role of structural factors beyond the observable and empirical 'local practices' that constitute the subject matter of social analysis. Ethnomethodology, in particular, has adopted this view, suggesting that it is indifferent to, and suspends belief in, institutions, classes, organisations – in short all the phenomena associated with structural studies. Moreover, Hilbert (1990) claims that ethnomethodology is indifferent to structure of any 'level' or 'size', and thus suspends belief in persons, individuals, subjective content, interaction processes and patterns as well. Hilbert believes that Garfinkel's notion of the artful production of local practices is the only legitimate focus of social analysis. So, like Vaitkus with his conception of the intersubjective world, ethnomethodologists believe that a focus on local practices transcends the macro–micro debate.

This of course is entirely illusory. The pose of 'indifference' to any 'level' of analysis simply masks a very decided bias towards the analysis of micro phenomena and an inability to cope analytically with macro phenomena like power, structures and institutions. In particular, the notion of constraint in social life is considerably underplayed while freedom of choice, the ability to create meaning and to pursue purposes are seemingly unhindered by larger structures of domination. Feminist theorists have highlighted the problems with this general stance by suggesting that women's lives cannot be understood in terms of the ability to pursue purposes in a self-controlling manner. For instance Dorothy Smith (1988: 66) argues that an effect of patriarchal domination under capitalism is that women's lives 'are organized and determined external to them' and that they 'have little opportunity for the exercise of mastery and control' in the ordinary situations of their lives. Phenomenology is unable to adequately take into account the effect of macrostructural features like forms of power and domination on the (micro) interactions of people in their everyday lives.

Clearly local practices are important, and my point is not to deny this in the least. However, to reduce power, institutions, organisations and the distribution of various resources to local practices is to confuse and conflate very different kinds of social phenomena. It leads to a one-dimensional vision of society and a form of social analysis that lacks penetration, explanatory power and empirical scope. Such a position does not transcend the macro–micro debate – to do this it would have to explain more about the social world more adequately than existing accounts. Instead, it constricts both the form of explanation and the subject matter of social analysis to one all-embracing principle – 'artful practices'. Such one-dimensionality overcomes the difficulty of understanding macro–micro linkages only by ignoring half the problem!

SUMMARY

- Phenomenological stands of social analysis focus on individuals' perceptions and responses to their lived experience of the world.

- In Schutz's view, the social world is fundamentally intersubjective – we relate to each other through common knowledge, reciprocal perspectives and the typifying capacities of language. Schutz deals with intersubjectivity in terms of 'the practical attitude'. However, commentators have suggested that to understand people as practical problem-solvers overlooks the way in which we deal with each other from a standpoint of trust and openness (a 'fiduciary attitude'). This is exemplified in the exchange of social 'gifts' or 'offerings' that are a common feature of everyday life, such as opening up a conversation, inviting someone round for dinner, complimenting someone or giving advice.

- Laing offers a phenomenological and existential account of mental illness (schizophrenia, in particular). The 'strange' behaviour of the person who is mentally 'ill' can be rendered understandable by seeing it as a response to the person's experience of the nexus of social relationships in which he or she finds him or her self.

- We must be wary of claims that a phenomenological focus on intersubjectivity somehow transcends or resolves the issues and problems implicit in the individual–society, agency–structure or macro–micro distinctions. Claiming that such distinctions are false does not prove or demonstrate that this is the case. A more fruitful approach would be to work out the relationships between the different domains of social reality. Ethnomethodologists claim to have gone beyond (transcended) the 'limitations' of conventional sociology. However, their insights are best understood in less revolutionary terms – they complement so-called 'conventional' approaches, rather than replace them.

- Garfinkel's original statement of the principles of ethnomethodology suggests that social order is accomplished from within settings through the practical activities of those involved. This is a rejection of the idea of a macro or structural order that externally influences behaviour. Garfinkel focuses on the taken-for-granted rules on which routine behaviour is based and the manner in which meaning emerges from, and is tied to, the situations in which it arises (indexicality).

- The work of Bittner on police attempts to keep the peace on skid-row and Zimmerman's on caseworkers in a Bureau of Public Assistance are good examples of the valuable empirical insights that have emerged from studies employing an ethnomethodological perspective.

- Berger and Luckmann's *The Social Construction of Reality* (1967) was a pioneering attempt to link objective and subjective features of social life and was influenced by phenomenology and interactionism. However, unlike these latter schools of thought, Berger and Luckmann take seriously the idea that objective aspects of society exist in the first place. They are not 'indifferent' to the distinction between objective and subjective domains and, moreover, they endeavour to trace out their interrelationships. They set out with a positive attempt to avoid the error of viewing society as the creation of individuals, as well as the mistake of understanding individuals as if they were mere reflections of the objective (structural, macro) features of society. However, despite their best intentions they tend to fall prey to these problems rather than come up with genuine solutions.

- Phenomenology, existentialism and ethnomethodology redirect sociological attention to the importance of intersubjective experience, the role of situated or local practices, and the ambiguity and indexicality of meaning in social life. However, claims that a focus on intersubjectivity 'overthrows' or 'transcends' debates around the individual–society, agency–structure, macro–micro distinctions should be treated with the utmost caution. The same is true for the ethnomethodologcal 'suspension of belief in' and 'indifference to' structures, institutions, classes, organisations and so on. Such analytic strategies merely side-step or ignore central problems in social analysis, they do not resolve or overcome them in a constructive manner.

part three

breaking free and burning bridges

Introduction

In Part 3, I examine the work of a number of authors who have attempted to break away from the three related dualisms that form the core themes of this book: the individual and society, action and structure, and macro and micro analysis. What these writers have in common is a desire to bring the elements involved 'together' by insisting that their separation into dualisms is a basic mistake. In this sense, social theory has taken a wrong turn so to speak, and has ended up with a false image of social life and social reality in general. A form of analysis and a descriptive language must be adopted for social research which does not make 'false' separations between individual and society, macro and micro, and action and structure.

For these writers, the elements involved in the dualisms are so neatly and completely interwoven with each other that we need to capture this quality in our theories and the analytic language we use to describe them. Thus we must abandon such terms, or at least move them out of the 'spotlight' which they seem to have occupied in our thinking. This is why I have entitled Part 3 'Breaking Free'. All the authors concerned want to break free from what they take to be the false assumptions that are contained in our 'dualistic' descriptions and analyses. This refers back to the theories considered in Parts 1 and 2 which have tended to emphasise the importance of action as opposed to structure, or macro rather than micro analysis.

The writers considered in this part of the book are all against the idea that these elements are somehow separate and stand in opposition to each other. Such ideas must be resisted at all costs. Nonetheless, the point is to overcome these false separations and produce a form of analysis which is more in line with the actual reality of society and social life. The 'Burning Bridges' part of the title indicates that these authors want to abandon dualistic thinking in order to construct a fresh and more adequate analysis.

This contrasts significantly with the ideas of the writers we shall consider later in Part 4. They feel that there is some point and use in dualistic thinking, as long as we do not make the more obvious mistakes that it may provoke. (Such as believing that everything can be explained in terms of 'action', as opposed to 'structure' or the reverse, and so on.) The main point is to describe and account for the *links* between the elements (such as agency and structure and macro and micro). They think that the way forward is to try to overcome the false separations by bringing them together in our analyses in order to understand how they are linked in reality. So, while they believe that the elements are tightly interwoven (as with the authors in Part 3), they also insist that the distinctions between action and structure and macro and micro in particular, are pertinent and interesting.

However, although there is broad agreement between the theorists in Part 3 at a very general level about 'Breaking Free and Burning Bridges' there are profound differences in the theoretical and analytical frameworks that they propose in order to achieve these aims. Thus, there is a wide variety of 'solutions' on offer within this category. I feel that no one of these solutions is complete and satisfactory in itself although I have a great deal of sympathy with much of what they suggest. However, I feel that, at best, they offer only partial answers which must be supplemented, extended or radically revised. Furthermore, in my opinion, their attempts to 'go beyond' the traditional terms and problems of social theory (including the reliance on dualisms), are not wholly successful either.

In this sense, the old problems remain on the sidelines to continually haunt (and taunt so to speak) the new solutions. This is the underlying reason why I feel that some aspects of the 'dualistic model' (although I am not completely happy with this term) must be retained and integrated with other theoretical strands. In accord with this, I feel that some of the ideas of the writers considered in Part 4 must play a part in any comprehensive attempt to deal with these issues. From these comments it could be concluded that I am advocating a form of eclecticism, that is, an attempt to reconcile disparate and sometimes conflicting ideas belonging to different schools of thought.

Eclecticism is only an inadequate strategy if one borrows from different shools in an arbitrary, haphazard or opportunistic way. Such an approach would ensure a ragbag assortment of ill-matched ideas. However, if one draws upon different strands of work as a result of rigorous and reasoned choices, then I believe that eclecticism is a viable way of proceeding. This is, in fact, the only possible way forward if one is primarily concerned to create a co-operative dialogue between apparently antithetical strands of thought. (In this sense forms of theoretical synthesis and integration may naturally result from such a dialogue, but are not 'forced' or artificially imposed by an initial expectation that this will automatically follow.) However, there are problems associated with this kind of approach. The main difficulty arises from the need to take care not to wrench ideas or concepts out of their original context (of an author's work in general, or the whole framework of which they form a part) while at the same time attempting to do just this by promoting dialogue and co-operation across such boundaries.

6

Foucault and the Postmodern Turn

PREVIEW

- The interdisciplinary character of Foucault's work, his break with Marxism and his association with post-structuralism and postmodernism.

- Foucault's attack on subjectivism and individualism and the attempt to decentre the subject.

- Foucault's emphasis on the close relation between language, discourse, power and social practices.

- The forms of power: sovereign power, disciplinary power and bio-power. The 'capillary' nature of modern forms of power.

- The break with Marxism and 'total' or 'grand' theories. Power as plural and fragmented. The rejection of the concept of ideology.

- A critical evaluation of Foucault. The problem of power as more or less stable forms of domination. The vagueness and elasticity of Foucault's conception of power. The lack of clarity about the relation between power, discourses and practices. Dualism and Foucault's inability to resolve the problems and issues associated with it. Power and the self. Foucault's neglect of situated activity and intersubjective meaning.

Michel Foucault's work represents a number of influences and trends and it is therefore difficult to fit it into any simple categories. His work cuts across the disciplinary boundaries of philosophy, psychology, psychiatry, sociology and history and it reflects the influence of all of them. Above all, Foucault's disinclination to develop a systematic theory (as a result of his opposition to 'grand' theory) provides a formidable obstacle to dealing with it as a framework of thought comparable to those with which we have already dealt. Also, Foucault's most substantial work has been of a historical nature (the history of madness, punishment, sexuality, for example), and this works against any simple comparisons with other schools of theory.

With regard to our central topic of interest (the dualisms of action and structure and macro and micro) the complex nature of his work poses difficulties. In one sense Foucault's work can be understood as an effort to overcome these dualisms. That is, his analyses attempt to bring action and structure and macro and micro together in relation to specific empirical issues. However, he does not explicitly address the problem in the rather formal way I have so far. He tends to deal with it indirectly and leave it as an implicit part of his substantive or empirical analyses. Of course, this is consistent with his anti-theoretical stance, but we shall have occasion to question this and ask whether such an extreme stance is necessary. Moreover, we shall be forced to ask whether Foucault's repudiation of theory (and the search for truth) simply masks some rather serious shortcomings in his attempt to go beyond dualism.

More often than not Foucault's work has been associated with poststructuralism and postmodernism; two 'movements' in social science which I initially noted in previous chapters. It would be an oversimplification to view Foucault's work entirely in these terms, but it is also undoubtedly true that it has many connections with them. For this reason I shall attempt to relate his work to these more general movements when relevant and necessary. It is in relation to poststructuralism that we find many significant resonances in Foucault's work. In particular, such a starting point serves to situate his work as an attack both on structuralism and interpretative (or action) theories. Foucault's break with Marxism and Althusser's structural version of it, highlights his dissatisfaction with structural theories. However, it also underlines one important and enduring continuity: the attack on theories which centralise the importance of 'the subject'.

Decentring the Subject

Although in his early work Foucault flirted with phenomenology, he came to reject it totally because it wrongly asserted that the individual was the origin of meaning and the natural centrepoint of any social analysis (a position known as subjectivism). In this sense, Foucault's work shares much in common with structuralism even though he goes on to reject most of the other important features of structuralism. He would therefore reject the interaction theories dealt with in the previous two chapters, although his main target was Sartre's existential theory. There is a close link between these two thinkers in terms of their common interest in Marxism in the 1960s and 1970s and a general 'critical' approach to social analysis. Both were left-wing intellectuals who were critical of the status quo and the forms of oppression and domination to be found in Western capitalist societies. Also, both thinkers wanted to develop analyses which adequately accounted for power, domination and resistance in modern societies.

However, Sartre's position was always tied up with his general existentialism, which emphasised the freedom of the individual (to resist forms of domination) and individual consciousness as the centre of meaning. Sartre's focus of interest remained on the analysis of the obstacles that confront individuals in their efforts to recognise and realise their freedom (Poster, 1984). Like the structuralists, Foucault felt that this was an error. The human subject was not inherently free but hedged in on all sides by social determinations. The very idea of the subject is a social construction, produced through social discourses (language, thought, symbolic representations) which position subjects in a field of power relations and within particular sets of practices.

Moreover, to view the individual as the originator of meaning was, according to structuralism and post-structuralism, a further error. The humanist view held that human consciousness radiated out from its individual centre and created meaning as the person confronted and grappled with his or her social world. However, this simply ignored the social distribution of meaning through social discourses. In this sense, meaning is a product of the internal relations between elements of the discourses which define and facilitate the social practices of individuals. People live their lives through the socially constructed meanings that are available to them. Certainly, the practices that people engage in in daily life act back upon, and thus come to shape, discourses, just as the discourses themselves shape practices. But these are social phenomena; individuals themselves do not create these meanings or the practices that they inform.

So Foucault is concerned to centre his analysis at a level of objectivity and to steer away from the error of subjectivism. (That is, wrongly adducing social causation to individuals.) This involves two aspects. First, as we have just mentioned, Foucault is interested in a level of objectivity that he calls discourse/practice and which moves away from a concern with the motivations of individuals. Thus he breaks decisively with the sociological traditions which involve some notion of subjective understanding (Weber, Schutz and phenomenology, Sartre, symbolic interactionism) as a starting point and a central ingredient of social analysis. (Later I shall suggest that, although there is no doubt that interactionism is concerned, at some level, with subjectivity, it is questionable whether it can be so easily dismissed as an oversimplified 'subjectivism'.)

The second aspect of this is Foucault's concern with giving an account of the nature of modes of domination or 'technologies of power' that 'escaped the attention of classical Marxism' (Poster, 1984: 26). I shall say more about this presently, but this emphasis on objective power relations is pivotal to Foucault's work. In both his interest in discourse/practice and technologies of power, Foucault sustains and continues the assault on 'the subject' which is also a defining feature of structuralism. In short, Foucault is against all forms of humanism which centralise the individual as the 'source' of meaning and as the building block for social analysis. In this sense, the individual has to be 'decentred' or removed from centre stage. Instead, attention should be given to the objective social forms which constitute society and 'construct' the subjectivities of individuals.

Another essential feature of this 'decentring' refers to what lies at the heart of the psyche (the subjectivity) of the person. The notion of the 'individual' in social analysis dates from the Renaissance when the term was first used. Not only was this individual thought to be autonomous (free from the obligations and demands of social life), but also rational and fully conscious. Thus, the individual is a coherent being, self-aware and in full control of him or her self. The individual is a centred unity who experiences and deals with the social world as a complete and rational agent. Foucault (along with other post-structuralists) objects to the idea of a coherent and unified subject.

First, such a view vastly exaggerates the degree of control that individuals exert over their own destinies and the social environment against which they are worked out. Conversely, it neglects the role of history and social-structural factors which shape individual subjectivities. Furthermore, the idea of a coherent and rational subject implies that human beings are unaffected by irrational and contradictory feelings and drives over which they have little control. From a post-structuralist standpoint it is important to understand that individuals have a psychic interior which is many-faceted and deeply layered. The unconscious forces of which Freud spoke (such as sexual, aggressive and generally anti-social drives) play a significant part in human experience and produce tension and contradiction in people's behaviour and in their attitudes and perceptions. In this sense, people are not completely rational and coherent unities; they are riven with tensions and forces which pull in different directions. People do not behave according to some uniform logic of 'reason'; they behave in certain ways for a multitude of 'reasons' which may be conscious or unconscious and irrational.

The fact that people exhibit contradictory aspects in their behaviour reveals that the self is a fragmentary and multiple phenomenon that varies according to both social circumstances and social position, as well as unconscious forces. The self is constituted within the play of language (and discourse more generally) and the field of practices and power relations that define the social locations in which people live out their daily lives. This takes Foucault's perspective away from that of Althusser in the sense that there is no mechanical relation between the individual selves ('agents' or 'subjects') and the class, occupational and authority positions they occupy in society. The role of ideology as an irresistible 'shaper' of individual psyches into uniform containers is abandoned. The self is the product of a number of cross-cutting discourses and practices.

Language and Discourse

We have seen that language is central to Foucault's approach dependent as it is on the notion of discourse. However, it is important to understand that language is never 'innocent'; it is not a neutral medium of expression. Discourses are expressions of power relations and reflect the practices and positions that are tied to them. A discourse here refers to all that can be thought, written or said about a particular thing such as a product (like a car, or a washing detergent), or a topic or specialist area of knowledge (such as sport or medicine). In this sense, the ability to employ a discourse reflects a command of knowledge of a particular area. It also implies that this facility is employed in relation to people who lack such command and have no legitimate claim to such knowledge. For instance, command of a particular discourse, such as that of medicine or law, also allows control over those who do not, such as patients and clients.

Employment of a discourse, therefore, enables a speaker to deploy knowledge about a particular area (such as health or legal procedure) in a way which claims to be correct (or true) according to the criteria laid down in the discourse. A doctor is able to define a patient's general state of health, or lack of it, in terms of a body of medical knowledge based on scientific evidence and information about the structure and functioning of the human body. The patient, on the other hand, usually has to take the doctor's word for it, and comply with his or her instructions as to the steps required to alleviate any illness. Thus the discourse of medicine (reflected in the doctor's training) becomes a means through which a power relation between doctor and patient is established and maintained. It is the medium through which a form of control is exerted and made possible in the first place.

Examples of professional discourses like this (and others such as teaching, social work and psychiatry) vividly highlight the power to control others which they confer upon users. But discourses are many and varied. In particular, many discourses are not systematically codified as formal bodies of knowledge or principles of practice (as they are in law and medicine). Nor are they necessarily accorded any special or legitimate place in society. Nonetheless, such discourses (examples of these might be 'commonsense', or sexism or racism) function to empower some people while subordinating others. Clearly, different kinds of discourse function in diverse ways and perform multiple roles. For example, racism and sexism are also ideologies which attempt to justify forms of inequality, while 'commonsense' may have broader connotations and perform rather more diffuse functions. This is not the place to detail all the differences. Here I simply want to point to the essential connection between discourse and power and control.

In these sections I have pointed to two aspects associated with the idea of decentring the subject to which Foucault subscribes. The first focuses on the idea of moving the individual from the centre of social analysis. According to this view, any position which begins with subjective understanding or a concern with individual meaning and motivation is bound to prove inadequate in its account of social phenomena. Secondly, the idea of the individual as a consistent, coherent and rational being must be resisted since it rules out the subtlety and complexity of the human psyche. In the next section I shall consider Foucault's position on power in more detail, since it is perhaps the key to his work in general.

The Forms of Power: Sovereign Power

Foucault approaches the subject of power from the standpoint of a historian attempting to trace the emergence of specific forms of power over time and the manner of their social evolution. In *Discipline and Punish* (1977) Foucault charts the development of modern forms of power, particularly disciplinary power, which supplanted the 'sovereign' or monarchical power that preceded it. Foucault suggests that under feudal and monarchical systems, power is embodied in the person of the sovereign who has unlimited power over his or her subjects. Crime in this type of system was considered to be a threat to the absolute power of the monarch and had to be punished in a public and spectacular way. This would reaffirm the power of the monarch and the ruling class by striking terror into the hearts of those who witnessed it. As an example of this, Foucault opens *Discipline and Punish* with an account of the horrific public torture and execution of a regicide in pre-revolutionary France. Poster (1984: 97) comments that such torture was not an act of gratuitous cruelty but a regulated practice consciously designed as 'a ritual enactment of the king's power before the world'.

Generally, the feudal monarch or lord exercised power only intermittently in specific episodes to ensure the periodical transfer of the product of labour from the labourers themselves. Power was not continuously exercised to subjugate people in their day-to-day lives (Bauman, 1982; Clegg, 1989). This notion of power as something which is exercised intermittently and, moreover, as something negative which prevents and prohibits, can be seen in the work of political philosophers like Hobbes and Locke, as well as modern social theorists like Dahl and Lukes (see Clegg, 1989). Foucault (1980: 121) suggests that this conception of power is tied to the emergence of monarchical rule, which developed during the Middle Ages against the background of chronic competition, conflict and struggle between feudal lords. As Foucault says, the monarchy

> presented itself as a referee, a power capable of putting an end to war, violence and pillage and saying no to these struggles and private feuds. It made itself acceptable by allocating itself a juridical and negative function, albeit one whose limits it naturally began at once to overstep.

Disciplinary Power

However, Foucault demonstrates that in the seventeenth and eighteenth centuries there emerges a new, more efficient and profitable form of power. This 'disciplinary' form attempted to place people under continuous surveillance rather than to subject them to specific physical punishments. Within the space of eighty or so years the method of punishment by torture disappeared to be replaced by a pervasive and impersonal system of surveillance which concentrated attention on the psychology of the individual. From its application in prisons, army barracks, asylums and monasteries this system of disciplinary power was extended through many organisational forms including hospitals and schools and eventually to the factory system. The disciplinary power moved the focus of control to individuals themselves. That is, by understanding that they are constantly under surveillance, individuals begin to oversee themselves, to regulate their own behaviour in the light of its assumed visibility to others.

This type of power is exemplified, for Foucault, in Jeremy Bentham's ideas about the Panopticon. The Panopticon was a circular building with a centrally elevated watch-tower around which radiated a number of cells illuminated from within. Thus all those in the cells could be subject to surveillance by a single observer centrally situated in the watch-tower, while the observer could remain unseen by those being observed. Those within the cells realised that it was impossible to avoid the gaze of the observer and that they were always (potentially) subject to it. Therefore, in effect, the principle of surveillance became internalised. In this sense, the functioning of power becomes automatic rather than the result of a conscious exercise by some external agency (such as a sovereign). It is indeed the general principle on which the Panoptican worked and which gave the the new disciplinary form of power its distinctive stamp which was the important analytic point for Foucault.

The pacification and control of large bodies of people in particular institutions (like prisons, schools, factories and so on) is brought about by increasing the predictability of their behaviour within such settings. Thus individuals within them become subjected to forms of training and correction set in the context of a routine in which each individual is treated in a like manner. In short, there is pressure upon the individual to conform to some standard of 'normality' whilst within the domain of surveillance, and indeed the purpose of disciplinary technique is to achieve 'normalisation'. Again, the individual's own self-monitoring is absorbed as part of the general system of surveillance. This is exemplified in the use of dossiers, marking and classification systems (and other forms of appraisal and monitoring) in schools, hospitals, prisons as well as factories. As Poster remarks 'capitalist society thus has available a means of control – a "technology of power" – that can be deployed at many locations' (1984: 103).

This fact is very important in understanding Foucault's break with general Marxist principles while retaining an interest in developing a 'critical' approach to social analysis. However, Poster further points out that Foucault fails to mention that bureaucracy and the computer 'both foster the principles of disciplinary control' (Poster, 1984: 103). As such, these extend and expand the nature of disciplinary control into the late twentieth century. The mechanisms of information processing involved in bureaucracy (using people) and the computer (using machines) mean that the ability to monitor behaviour is extended beyond the idea of regulating bodies in a limited area space as Foucault envisaged. Poster observes that the electronic age overcomes the limitations of space imposed by the necessity for controlling hierarchies.

All that is needed are traces of behaviour; credit card activity, traffic tickets, telephone bills, loan applications, welfare files, fingerprints, income transactions, library records, and so forth. On the basis of these traces, a computer can gather information that yields a surprisingly full picture of an individual's life. As a consequence, Panopticon monitoring extends not simply to massed groups but to the isolated individual. The normalized individual is not only the one at work, in an asylum, in jail, in school, in the military, as Foucault observes, but also the individual in his or her home, at play, in all the mundane activities of everyday life. (Poster, 1984: 103)

Bio-power

The other main type of power which has come to the fore in the modern era is what Foucault calls 'bio-power'. Again, like disciplinary power, bio-power is quite different from sovereign power. However, unlike the disciplinary form, bio-power focuses on the body and targets whole populations instead of particular individuals or collections of individuals. In *The History of Sexuality* (1984) Foucault argues that governments perceived that they were dealing with the problem of controlling whole populations in terms of such variables as birth and death rates, life expectancy, fertility, state of health, frequency of illnesses, patterns of diet and habitation. In the eighteenth century therefore, the area of sexuality became the focus of intense discursive interest designed to regulate and administer sexuality by defining its 'normal' forms. From the early nineteenth century onwards there was a great outpouring of talk and writing (discourse) on sex, which attempted to define the range of sexual responses and types of sexual identities that are permissible and possible within specific social contexts.

Foucault is concerned to make the point that this happens contrary to the conventional assumption that the Victorian era was one of extreme repression in terms of sexuality – far from it; and this illustrates vividly a more general point about modern forms of power (and discourse) for Foucault. Modern forms like bio-power open up possibilities for the implementation of control and subjugation, rather than close down, prohibit and generally negate. The development of a range of professional discourses of psychiatry, medicine, social work as well as disciplines like sociology and criminology 'contributed to the development, refinement, and proliferation of new techniques of power' (Best and Kellner, 1991: 50). Again, these discourses carry and disperse forms of power and control into the everyday lives of the populace. That is, they normalise certain practices, habits and routines whilst creating deviations and perversions out of those that they exclude.

The Nature of Modern Forms of Power

Both disciplinary power and bio-power are new forms that are ever-present in the social body at large and represent an alternative to sovereign or monarchical power. Such power (also reflected in state power or class power) intermittently exercised from the top down from some central agency, provides an extreme contrast to the new forms, which are continuous, dispersed and localised. This 'capillary form' of power is exercised *within* society rather than *from above it*. Foucault is less interested in where power comes from, who has power and what intentions they have, and rather more in 'the processes by which subjects are constituted as effects of power' (Sarup, 1988: 82), that is to say, how individuals in particular social settings and contexts are affected by power relations in terms of their self-identities, attitudes and their (psychological) predispositions.

Foucault's position on power and its close tie with knowledge was profoundly influenced by Nietzsche's philosophical writings. Nietzsche wrote of power in a general sense as the 'will to power' and not as a reflection of a particular theory of power. Such theories are found in Marx's work or that of liberal economists, wherein power is exercised from some central agency such as the state or as some constitutional apparatus such as the law, rights and sovereignty. Foucault picks up on this theme and fixes on the interdependence of power and knowledge as the pivot of his own discussion. The link between power and knowledge is in the creation of new capacities and types of activity for individuals. The docile bodies created by disciplinary routines or the normalised sexual practices and identities produced through the new discourses on sexuality represent such 'productive' effects of power. Modern power does not operate through the repression or limitation of existing capacities and forms of activity, but through the construction of new identities, knowledge and practices.

In this sense, it can be seen that discursive knowledge is very practical in its effects (hence the coupling of discourse/practice). Discourse in this sense is present not only in written texts 'but in definite institutional and organizational practices'. Moreover, it is practical in nature in that

> it disciplines the body, regulates the mind and orders the emotions in such a way that the ranking, hierarchy and stratification which ensues is not just the blind reproduction of a transcendent traditional order, as in feudalism. It produces a new basis for order in the productive worth of individuals, as they are defined by these new disciplinary practices of power. (Clegg, 1989: 153)

In general terms, Foucault understands power not as a commodity which may be acquired or seized, nor is it the property of an individual or class. 'Rather it has the character of a network; its threads extend everywhere' (Sarup, 1988). Resistance, too, exists everywhere and simply reinforces the need for discipline and subjugation in the first place. Thus Foucault views modern society as highly differentiated and fragmented. Within society power itself is variegated, draws upon many different resources and can be found in a diversity of sites and social relations. Foucault says of modernity that there have never existed more centres of power or more linkages and contacts between sites of power. Thus he views power as a multiple and mobile field of force relations where far-reaching, but never completely stable effects of domination are produced. Foucault's idea of power is as 'a more or less stable or shifting network of alliances' within which points of resistance will open up (Clegg, 1989: 153). Foucault himself suggests that the appropriate metaphor for understanding the operations of power is that of warfare in which one speaks of strategies, tactics, struggle and conflict (Foucault, 1980).

It is important to remember that, for Foucault, power mechanisms operate independently of people. This is quite in line with his insistence that the subject is 'dead' and should therefore be decentred. People (or subjects) are simply the conduits through which power operates whilst also being 'produced' by that power. That is, individual subjectivity (identity, psychological predispositions and energy) is an effect of power relations since, as we have already seen, the individual is already enveloped in forms of discourse and practice, and power is an essential component of both. Moreover, as Foucault says, power is everywhere (along with resistance to it), and thus it is impossible to step outside the net of power, to move out of its 'force field'.

It has been argued that in his later work Foucault moves away from this predominant concern with power and domination and its formative effects on subjectivity and self-formation. In this respect Foucault's work on ethics and 'technologies of the self' shifts attention to the self, subjectivity and the ability of individuals to define their own identities (Best and Kellner, 1991: 65). This is not to say that Foucault completely jettisons his ideas about the abolition of the humanist subject. He still retains the idea that people are conditioned by social discourse and practices but now the individual is seen as a creative agent who can overcome socially imposed limitations and attain self-mastery.

Unfortunately, as Best and Kellner point out, this is done largely at the expense of Foucault's former concern with power and domination. In this sense, I agree with Best and Kellner that Foucault 'never adequately theorizes both sides of the structure/agency problem' (1991: 69). This is a general problem with Foucault's approach and I shall come back to it. Nevertheless, it remains true that if we are to extract Foucault's positive contribution to the study of power then we have to accept his earlier emphasis on power as a 'structural' phenomenon which operates regardless of the intentions of individuals and their activities. Within the field of force relations that constitute forms of domination, the individual is a mere vessel through which the effects of power are passed. The person is a container whose self-identity and psychological interior is largely a product of the relations of power, discourse and practice in which he or she is enmeshed.

The Break With Marxism and Total or Grand Theory

The Plural and Fragmentary Nature of Power

From what we have already said it is possible to discern the elements in Foucault's approach that take him away from some of the classical concerns of Marxism. First, his insistence that power has no centre or source and that there are no subjects who 'possess' it places Foucault at odds with the Marxist emphasis on the class struggle and the state as the central foci of power. Furthermore, Foucault's suggestion that power is a variegated phenomenon existing in a plurality of social settings and locations, means that the Marxist emphasis on the mode of production and the work and industrial sphere in general is put into question.

Since the 1960s Marxists had become aware of the limitations of Marxism in understanding domination away from the factory and place of work. Groups such as women, children, students, minority groups and so on suffered domination, and this could not be grasped by exclusive reference to the workplace. In short, daily life beyond the workplace was not easily understandable in the categories of classical Marxism. Foucault gave voice to this inadequacy in Marxism by proposing that the new technologies of power 'emerge at multiple points in social space and are not located in the state' as Marxists (and liberals) think (Poster, 1984: 104). Any critical analysis of society had to be able to embrace this fact by concentrating attention on specific sets of practices involved in particular configurations of power and domination.

From Foucault's point of view, we can no longer rely on Marx's 'totalising' theory (what I have previously referred to as 'grand' theory – a theory which tries to explain everything in terms of a comprehensive framework of concepts).

Marxism views domination as the expression of an interdependent unity (the capitalist mode of production). All conflicts, struggles and forms of power are reducible to this central core. By viewing power as decentred and multiple, Foucault is able to view technologies of power (and forms of resistance) as distinct but interrelated phenomena. Thus, for Foucault, the regimes of power experienced by women, gays, prisoners, asylum inmates and racial minorities cannot be reduced to a single all-embracing explanatory concept such as the 'mode of production' (Poster, 1984: 104).

As an adjunct to this, Foucault's strategy is to 'conduct an ascending rather than descending analysis which sees power as circulating throughout a decentred field of institutional networks and is only subsequently taken up by larger structures such as class or the state' (Best and Kellner, 1991: 52). As Fraser (1989: 26) puts it, Foucault 'rules out' the crude Marxist critiques of ideology, and an overemphasis on the influence of the state and the economy, and instead rules in the 'politics of everyday life'. For if power circulates everywhere, even at the most mundane levels, then any effort to transform the regime must make an effort to address those everyday practices. Here we can see that, while breaking with totalising theories such as Marxism, Foucault retains his link with a critical theory of society. Foucault unpacks the presuppositions of grand theorising and addresses the plurality of forces, practices and regimes of power that exist within any society. As such, he subjects the micro politics of everyday life to scrutiny, often seeming to dissolve macro concerns into an analytic concentration on micro practices.

This is an almost complete reversal of the conventional Marxist tendency to think of macro structures as exerting an overwhelming influence on micro practices. Foucault's alternative, to posit diverse plural centres and regimes of power and discursive practices, is also to some extent characteristic of thinkers who have been labelled 'postmodern' such as Jean Baudrillard and Jean-François Lyotard. In this respect, the postmodern movement represents a break with grand theory or 'meta-narratives' which attempt to capture the whole movement of history in terms of some overriding theme such as emancipation of the working class or the progress of reason. In line with the fragmentary and local nature of power and resistance, smaller narratives which aim at partial and local analyses are the order of the day for these writers.

The Rejection of the Concept of Ideology

This anti-totalising impulse, this critique of grand theory and meta-narratives, derives from the influence of the work of Friedrich Nietzsche on Foucault and other (postmodern) writers. (Although it must be remembered here that Foucault cannot be completely assimilated into the postmodern fold.) Nietzsche's influence here is yet another reason for Foucault's drift away from the basic assumptions of Marxism. Nietzsche was suspicious of the notion of absolute truth and any philosophy which claimed to be based on universal principles. All discourses are merely perspectives or partial claims on truth, insofar as the perspective itself will always affect our interpretations of reality. The upshot of this is that there are many truths seen from different perspectives.

Foucault takes this as the cornerstone for his rejection of the notion of ideology, at least in the way it had become defined in the work of Althusser and other structural Marxists. The trouble with this notion of ideology was that it set up an opposition between the 'truth' on the one hand and ideology on the other. Thus, in Althusser's terms, the scientific analysis offered by Marxism was the truth while everything else was a reflection of the falsity of bourgeois ideology. Foucault rejects this on several grounds. First, influenced by Nietzsche's notion of perspectives and the partial truths that they enshrine, Foucault wants to avoid a debate about what is real and what is illusory. What interests him is the idea that different discourses (like medicine, psychiatry, the social sciences and so on) produce truth effects and truth claims within their own terms.

That is, each discourse claims to have some hold on the truth and validity of those things that fall within its area of competence (or its subject matter). This in itself is the key to understanding the link between knowledge and power (the ability to define and construct subjectivities and modes of behaviour and so on). Thus the focus of Foucault's interest is the link between regimes of power based on conjunctions of discourses, knowledge and practices. He is not interested in whether the truth claims of discourses stand up to scrutiny. He is interested in the power effects of discourses which in themselves are neither true nor false.

Secondly, the way Althusser uses the concept of ideology involves a notion of the individual subject who is constructed in ideology (that is, who internalises the social positions and activities assigned by the power structure of capitalist society). This produces a centred and unified subject in some ways similar to that which appears in humanism (in others, very different). This notion of the subject, as we have seen, is not congenial to Foucault. Finally, Foucault rejects the whole notion of economic base and an ideological 'superstructure' which rests upon, and is secondary to, the economic base. For Foucault, discourses are not tied to the mode of production in order to achieve their power effects. For these reasons, Foucault is inclined not to speak of ideology, since it has these connotations. However, there is a non-pejorative sense that can be given to the notion of ideology in which systems of ideas are employed in ways which attempt to justify or rationalise forms of domination and make them seem natural and eternal (such as sexism and racism). Insofar as discourses themselves function in this manner then there is a common focus between ideology and some discourses as Foucault would conceive of them.

Finally, Foucault's work cuts itself off from Marxism (and other evolutionary theories of society) by embracing a distinctive view of history and historical method. Again, the influence of Nietzsche is paramount. A guiding theme of Foucault's approach to history is the celebration of 'difference' in terms of under-lining the foreignness of past discourses and practices as a means of questioning the supposed rationality and legitimacy of the present. This is undergirded by the identification of 'discontinuity' in history rather than viewing society in terms of continuous evolutionary development. Instead of concentrating on great moments and individuals in history, Foucault prefers to concentrate on 'illegiti-mate' naive knowledge and local struggles which have been denied or neglected in conventional history and theories. Thus Foucault emphasises the history of marginal or stigmatised groups such as the mentally ill and criminals in order to make the point that institutions and social practices often have 'discreditable' beginnings.

Evaluating Foucault: The Problem of Power and Domination

Certainly there is much in Foucault's work that is commendable. He offers us a vision of a decentred society and a decentred individual. In this sense, he avoids many of the problems associated with structural and humanist approaches. It could be argued, therefore, that he manages to provide a bridge between the two approaches and 'overcome' the dualism. However, I do not believe that Foucault's work, in and of itself, is an adequate resolution of the problem of dualism. I believe that his reformulation (or 'deconstruction') of some structuralist princi-ples goes a long way towards a solution, but that ultimately he remains trapped at the structural level, or at least, at an intermediate level. He never manages to interweave the two levels and give a full account of both structure and human activity. Also, his account of subjectivity and activity is deficient insofar as it fails to take into account many features of 'everyday life', despite his concern with this dimension of social existence. However, let me first deal with Foucault's dismantling of structuralism, particularly the Marxist version.

Through his historical analyses Foucault demonstrates the weaknesses of grand overarching schemes which attempt to reduce the movement of history to core concepts (like the mode of production) or universal principles (like the class struggle). Although Marxism is the principal target here, any theory which tends to see power as emanating from a central source or essence is deemed to be misguided. In this sense, Foucault alerts us to the diversity of forms and locations of power. Power is something which reaches into the finest capillaries of society; it circulates around the whole social body producing and facilitating new discourses and practices rather than simply limiting or repressing existing ones. Regimes of power are mobile force fields. They are shifting networks of alliances, strategies and points of resistance. Power operates within people through internalised disciplines and normalised identities, routines and practices. Power is everywhere, as is resistance to it; it is not simply the province of privileged or 'legitimate' authorities. It is a feature of those who resist forms of domination as much as those who enforce or apply it.

Having said this, it is also true that Foucault's notion of power is rather elastic and defies any definite pinning down. As a result of the vagueness or fuzziness that surrounds his notion of power, Foucault is able to evade or fend off potential criticism by stretching his notion to cover all eventualities. Thus, it seems that his view of power is truly one which 'sews everything together'. However, this is more apparent than real because ultimately it is unclear what power is and where it lies. If there are multiple centres of power, how many are there? If power is everywhere does this mean that power is evenly spread throughout society? Presumably Foucault's answer to this is no, since he envisages more or less stable forms of domination. But if this is the case what is the basis of particular forms of domination?

Foucault seems reluctant to specify this in case he is accused of producing a 'totalising' (read 'generalising') theory. He seems to prefer to imply that any more detailed specifications must be the result of empirical research into specific historical circumstances. I think that Foucault veers away too much from making any general pronouncements whatsoever and, as a result, is in danger of lapsing into a form of relativism which prevents making any distinctions between forms of domination based on different resources. He is unable to say whether any forms and centres (institutional or sub-cultural sites) of power and domination are more important than others. If they were, we could ask interesting questions about how and why they were related to each other. Such questions are of empirical as well as theoretical import.

However, Foucault refrains from making any general analytic statements about power and domination except that it is ubiquitous and circulates at all levels of society. The effect of this is to create the image of modern power as relatively amorphous and spread throughout the social body in an arbitrary rather *ad hoc* manner. This gives the impression that power (and the forms of domination it gives rise to, do not have any organised basis within society as a whole. That is, beyond specific locations (such as prisons, factories, schools or asylums) power seems to have no systematic organisational form on a society-wide basis (for example, as the result of general economic and political factors).

This vision of power as amorphous, scattered and fragmented and local exists in uneasy tension with Foucault's statement that there are more or less stable forms of domination. This is because the stability of forms of domination is often (though not always) related to the degree to which it has a crystallised organisational basis such as governmental bureaucracy. In such instances there have to be enforceable domains of influence for domination to be effective. This means territorial connections on an organised basis as reflected in, for example, Weber's (1964) discussion of forms of domination (legal-rational, traditional and charismatic) and their organisational forms. In this sense, Foucault has been rightly criticised for under-emphasising the 'macro' features of power. For example, Poulantzas (1978) and Best and Kellner (1991) suggest that Foucault underestimates the importance of state power as reflected in oppressive laws, the monopoly over the use of physical violence (army, police) and increasingly effective techniques of surveillance. Poulantzas (1978) argues that in fact these are the preconditions for the modern disciplinary society envisaged by Foucault.

A related point is that Foucault pitches his analysis of power at a level which brackets the question of who controls and exercises power. As Foucault insists, power is not a commodity and it is not 'possessed' by individuals or classes. Best and Kellner (1991: 70) point out that, in this sense, Foucault's account of power 'is mostly treated as an impersonal and anonymous force which is exercised apart from the actions and intentions of human subjects'. They go on to say (and I am in complete agreement) that, whatever new light is brought to bear by Foucault's reworking of power, it nevertheless obscures crucial aspects. In particular it masks the

extent to which power is still controlled and administered by specific and identifiable agents in positions of economic and political power, such as members of corporate executive boards, bankers, the mass media, political lobbyists, land developers, or zealous outlaws in the Pentagon and White House. (1991: 70)

Power Discourses and Practices

The whole problem of the bracketing of the question of who controls and exercises power is compounded by Foucault's reluctance to define what power is exactly. His attempt to treat it as an impersonal and anonymous force is a convenient prop here since it allows a certain level of ambiguity to enter into the analysis. Specifically, although he distinguishes between disciplinary and bio-power, Foucault tends to focus on the channels through which power circulates. That is, he tends to talk of the discourses and practices that are the conduits of power rather than try to define the substance of power. As a result, questions concerning what power is, what it does and how it manages to do it, are bracketed along with the issues of control and who exercises it. Clearly, although they 'carry' power, in themselves discourses are not the same thing as power. Discourses have to be used and mobilised in certain ways by particular groups or individuals before their power effects can be experienced by others. This in turn requires some institutional or structural base which acts as a frame of reference, a focus and holding point for the dissemination of power. In short, there must be some resource basis which supports and facilitates the distribution of power, albeit in the form of discourse and practices.

Exactly the same considerations apply to practices. While it may be true that power effects and its traces are inscribed in practices, the two are not identical. To appreciate the power dimension of practices we have to distinguish between types of practice (some being less centrally involved in the mediation of power, such as brushing one's teeth). We also have to understand the practice in a wider social context or setting (such as education or industry) before we can pinpoint the effects of power. In both discourses and practices then, we need to specify contextual details before their power dimensions can be fully appreciated. Power, therefore, cannot be understood simply in terms of its carriers or conduits, just as knowledge of veins and capillaries in the human body does not furnish us with information about the constituents of our blood.

As Foucault does not define power, his analysis of domination lacks definition; it has no particular shape, no boundaries, no topography. As such it tends to flow or leak into everything else. Such a diffuse and amorphous notion of power makes it particularly difficult to understand its spheres of influence and the intensity of its effects. Conversely, it proves difficult to trace the areas in which its influence is significantly diminished, or transformed in some way. Clearly the absence of such finer details limits the subtlety and flexibility of the underlying conception of power. This is paradoxical in that Foucault's original intention was to produce a view of power which was more pliable than the traditional (sovereign) conception and thus more appropriate to the local and fragmentary nature of modernity.

In summary, Foucault's notion of power makes us more analytically sensitive to the variegated nature of power and its effects. However, it pays little attention to the structural conditions under which power effects are produced in people. Conversely, Foucault is little concerned with the exercise of power. This entrapment at some impersonal, intermediate level is both the strength and the ultimate weakness of Foucault's analysis. Therefore, if we take Foucault's formulations as a significant addition to the armoury of existing approaches to power analysis then they must be welcomed. However, to the extent that they are meant to completely displace other conceptions and types of analysis of power then we must be more guarded. Foucault has not revealed the 'true' face of modern power for the first time. Rather, he has revealed important new dimensions of power and proposed alternative ways of tracing its effects.

Does Foucault Overcome Dualism?

Does Foucault's approach overcome the dualisms of action and structure, and macro and micro analyses? It is apparent that this indeed is what he intends, and certainly some commentators believe that this is what he has achieved (see Silverman, 1985: 82–92). However, in my opinion Foucault does not manage to overcome the dualisms or provide an adequate synthesis. There is no doubt that his approach is an intriguing attempt to provide an analysis which avoids the excesses of those one-dimensional approaches from which he wishes to dissociate himself. That is, on the one hand he wishes to avoid the errors of humanism, which reduces social life and social analysis to the intentions of free-acting individuals. On the other hand he rejects the determinism of structuralist approaches which reduce social life to the effects of macro forces.

It is possible to argue that in these aims he is successful to a degree. However, by adopting Foucault's 'middle way' of joining together discourse, practice, power and knowledge into a synthetic unity we are forced to incur fairly high costs. Many of the insights of humanism and structural approaches are lost on the way. I have already indicated some of the structural features that are lost, or at least under-emphasised, as a result of Foucault's notion of power as a ceaselessly shifting network of alliances caught within the operational net of discursive practices. In this section I want to concentrate on the other side of the dualisms; the subject, activity and micro processes in general. By examining these in closer detail we shall see that there are many unplugged gaps in Foucault's overall approach. Let me deal with these issues in two distinguishable segments, which are closely interrelated and stem from Foucault's concern to eliminate the humanist subject.

Power and the Self

Best and Kellner (1991) have noted that there are opposing tendencies in Foucault's earlier work as compared with his later work. In the earlier work Foucault is completely preoccupied with the analysis of power and domination and tends to overlook the importance of the subject. As we have noted, this is in line with his attempt to break with the humanist notion of the subject as a unified, rational and autonomous being. In this sense, Foucault is continuing with the structuralist assault on the humanist subject and its tendency to ignore or neglect social-structural issues like power and the manner in which subjectivities are socially constituted.

On this Foucault is to be applauded for his intriguing attempt to provide a critique of both macro theorists who over-emphasise the role of factors like class and the state, and micro theorists who often neglect the role of power almost completely. The 'often' qualification is important here because an over-keenness (on behalf of structuralists and post-structuralists) to reject humanism completely can lead to convenient distortions of the facts of the matter. Therefore let me reiterate what I said in Chapter 4 on interactionism, where I noted that the point is not that it does not have a conception of power, but rather that it has an activity-centred view of power which underplays the structural elements. Notwithstanding this important qualification, Foucault does try to provide some alternate middle ground in which to locate the issues.

Unfortunately, as he seems to have realised later in his career, Foucault's concentration on the intertwining of discourses and practices has the effect of pitching the analysis at some impersonal realm beyond the reach of the productive activities of human beings. The human self is denied any constitutive role in the circulation of power and the production of social life in general. Instead, human subjectivities are constituted by, and in, the play of power, discourse and practice. In his later work, however, Foucault seems to over-compensate for this absence by concentrating on technologies of the self and decentring his prior emphasis on power and domination (Best and Kellner, 1991: 65).

It is not that power and domination are completely forgotten; in fact they reappear in his concern with the Greco-Roman project of self-mastery, with a concern with the care of the self and with the search for individual styles of existence. In short, in Foucault's later work the centrality of an impersonal realm of power and domination is displaced by a concern with how the subject constitutes him or herself in an active fashion. However, Foucault never adequately connects the two phases or emphases in his work. There is no attempt to connect the constituted and the constituting self, and there is no adequate account of how technologies of the self can proliferate in the modern era, which he claims is saturated with power relations (Best and Kellner, 1991: 67).

Situations, Activity and Intersubjective Meaning

In my opinion this rather odd and paradoxical 'individualistic' strain in Foucault's later work results directly from his initial over-reaction to, and critique of the humanist subject. In his zeal (so typical of post-structuralist thought) to oust the bourgeois myth of the free, rational subject, Foucault completely overlooks situated interaction (intersubjectivity) as a domain of decisive importance. Sure enough, Foucault is right to want to decentre the subject, if by that is meant that the individual should not be viewed as the source of meaning. Foucault is also right to emphasise the role of discourse in the production and establishment of meanings (for instance, the meanings of sexuality, its modes and types of sexual identity are produced through discourses such as the sexual liberation and psychoanalytic movements, and so on). In this sense, Foucault's analytic stance enables one to establish the general social parameters of meaning.

There is no doubt that such parameters of meaning underpin the more specific assumptions and premises enshrined in the discourses (and practices) associated with particular power groups and institutions such as medicine, psychiatry, social work and so on. However, if it is assumed that this is the only valid level of analysis, it simply ignores what I shall call the 'interactive dimension' of meaning. This I take to be the main contribution of interactive and phenomenological schools of thought and unless this contribution is acknowledged then the structuralist and post-structuralist analysis of meaning will remain forever incomplete. The situated dimension of meaning refers to that element of meaning that is produced through intersubjective processes of negotiation, definition and general forms of creativity that are brought into play whenever and wherever human beings mix socially.

The problem with the interactionist approaches is that they tend to view meaning solely as emergent from face-to-face situations and, as a consequence, overlook the socially constituted production of meaning at the level of discourses, practices and power relations. This, of course, is the converse of Foucault's position, in which the notion of interactive meaning is lost by its dissolution into discursive meaning. This raises a more general problem with Foucault's analysis. Although he is ostensibly concerned with everyday life, the local and the marginal in modern society, he remains strangely unconcerned with face-to-face encounters and behaviour which constitute by far the largest portion of 'everyday life'.

This level of situated behaviour or face-to-face encounters is almost entirely missing from Foucault's analysis, preoccupied as it is with the historical dimension. That is, the genealogy of discourses and regimes of power. Actual conduct as it unfolds between describable actors is not an aspect of social reality that proves to be of interest to Foucault. This is a very unfortunate omission and is perhaps one that, more than any other weakness, prevents Foucault from achieving a synthesis between the realms of action and structure or macro and micro. The neglect of the intersubjective dimension perhaps accounts for the alarming oscillation between the earlier emphasis on power, domination and the constitution of the self, and the later lapse into an 'individualistic' preoccupation with self-constitution.

An interest in the intersubjective realm as an important aspect of social constitution might have rescued Foucault from his later flirtation with a form of individualism. The ironic feature of all this is that Foucault's later preoccupation with self-constitution at the expense of power and domination only reaffirms that which he spent most of his time strenuously denying. In effect, the centrality of the human subject in social analysis is reborn, albeit in a different form. This inadequacy is an unfortunate one because, as we have seen, Foucault's approach is generally one which is innovative and suggestive, both theoretically and empirically. Perhaps the most important general empirical implication we can draw from it is that we must look for power at every level of society. In this sense the emphasis on discursive practices entices us to trace the amorphous character of power and the way it 'strays' into, or infiltrates every nook and cranny of social life, including everyday routines.

A Final Comment

Although Foucault manages to bring new perspectives to social analysis, the potential of his contribution is severely limited by his adherence to the view that 'totalising' theories must be resisted at all costs. Again, Foucault is right in suggesting that often all-embracing frameworks of theory tend to erode the value of alternate approaches. This they do by monopolising and colonising whole stretches of knowledge and by rejecting rival and partial theories that do not 'fit in' with the master theory. However, as with his critique of the subject, he takes it too far. The effect is for Foucault to resist systematic theorising completely. He feels that such an enterprise inherently excludes or overlooks the differences he so vehemently wants to preserve. This is not true. Systematic theory does not have to be exclusive or dogmatic. It can be open-ended, flexible and used to generate auxiliary and innovative forms of theorising (see Layder, 1993, 1997, 1998). The fact that Foucault does not envisage this possibility is perhaps one of the most important reasons why there are significant gaps in his overall approach.

SUMMARY

- Foucault's work is influenced by a number of disciplines, including, history, sociology, philosophy, psychology and psychiatry. His work has definite connections with post-structuralism and postmodernism although it cannot be understood entirely in these terms.

- To account for power, domination and resistance in modern societies Foucault found it necessary to break with phenomenological and/or existential versions of Marxism (as found in Sartre's work) because they were founded on the assumption of individual freedom of choice and the role of individuals as creators of meaning. Foucault wanted to decentre the individual subject from social analysis in order to properly grasp the socially constructed nature of 'the subject'. In this sense, social discourses position subjects in a field of power relations and social practices. Language itself is never 'innocent' since the discourses it reflects express power relations and the positions and practices associated with them.

- Foucault traces the emergence of a new form of 'disciplinary' power in the seventeenth and eighteenth centuries. Disciplinary power placed people under continuous surveillance and supplanted the sovereign or monarchical power (based on punishment by torture) that had previously held sway. Disciplinary power enabled the pacification and control of, large bodies of people in prisons, factories, schools, hospitals and so on. Another modern form of power identified by Foucault is 'bio-power', which focuses on the body and targets whole populations instead of particular groups. Bio-power is reflected in the emergence of discourses that seek to define sexuality – its range and normal forms and in the professional discourses of psychiatry, medicine, criminology and so on.

- The newer forms of power have a 'capillary' nature and operate within society in a continuous, dispersed and localised manner, as opposed to sovereign (monarchical, state or class) power which operates top-down from some central agency. Foucault is interested in the way subjects are constituted as effects of power – in terms of their self-identities, attitudes and perceptions. In modernity there are multiple (and linked) centres or sites of power. The threads of power (and resistance to it) extend everywhere in society.

- Foucault breaks with the Marxist emphasis on the centrality of the class struggle, the state, the mode of production, and the work and industrial sphere in general as the foci of power. The new technologies of power extend well beyond these restricted confines and affect multiple groups, including those that are marginal and stigmatised. Foucault adheres to an ascending, rather than a descending conception of power that circulates through a decentred field of institutional networks and is only subsequently absorbed into class and state structures. In principle, Foucault replaces the Marxist over-emphasis on ideological critique and the influence of class and the economy with an emphasis on the politics of everyday life. Foucault rejects the notion of ideology as found in the work of structural Marxists. He is not interested in whether truth claims stand up to scrutiny, or in the difference between reality and illusion; he is more interested in the power effects of discourses which, in themselves, are neither true nor false.

- A critical evaluation of Foucault's work must consider the vagueness and over-elasticity of his conception of power and his difficulty in explaining how relatively stable forms of domination arise. Foucault's rejection of 'totalising' theory renders him unable to make searching, general analytic statements about power and domination. His rejection of more conventional approaches and issues (particularly about who exercises power) means that he overlooks important dimensions of power.

- On the issue of whether Foucault's work overcomes, or goes beyond, dualism, we must be very circumspect. On the one hand, Foucault's emphasis on power as reflected in discursive practices means that he under-estimates the effects of many structural features of modern societies. On the other hand, his treatment of social activity is quite deficient. In the first place, his later views on the nature of the self are at odds with his earlier insistence on the discursively constructed nature of self-identity. Secondly, Foucault does not take account of the relatively independent characteristics of intersubjective meaning and situated activity.

7

Beyond Macro and Micro: Abandoning False Problems

PREVIEW

- Elias's theory of 'figurations' (or interdependency chains) as the constitutive features of society.

- The civilising process in European society since the Middle Ages. The emergence of the concept of the individual as a closed-off, self-contained entity (*homo clausus*) in fourteenth- and fifteenth-century Europe. Elias's alternative conception of socially interdependent individuals (*homines aperti*) and the concept of figuration.

- Evaluating Elias's claim to overcome false distinctions in social analysis and his notion of the individual–society split in sociology. The pitfalls of extrapolating from long-term historical trends and general personality structures to the behaviour of unique individuals. The absence of an analysis of situated conduct and interpersonal encounters in Elias's work.

- Finding a place for the individual – the limitations of social constructionism.

- Evaluating the usefulness of the concept of figuration in resolving or dealing with the individual–society, agency–structure and macro–micro dualisms.

- The nature of social ties and social relations. Do 'false' dualisms exist and does Elias move beyond them?

This chapter deals with the view that the very idea that there are distinct macro and micro levels of analysis (or of society), or that there is such a thing as the macro–micro 'problem' are simply wrong. They are misconceptions that have resulted from a 'false' line of reasoning in conventional sociology. I focus on some of the ideas of Norbert Elias who advocates the use of the notion of 'figuration', which refers to the interdependent chains of individuals who constitute society. This is backed up by, and linked to a historical analysis of the emergence of the modern idea of the person as *homo clausus* (closed individual). Elias claims that, as a result of this more adequate characterisation of social life, it becomes apparent that the so-called problems of the 'individual and society' and the 'macro–micro' problem are merely artificial constructs. They result from a faulty understanding of the nature of social reality and the inadequate descriptive language of conventional sociology.

The Civilising Process and the Concept of Figuration

In a number of works, but particularly in *What is Sociology?* (1978a), Elias has suggested that the concept of figuration helps us to go beyond the false dichotomies and dualisms that plague contemporary sociology. This does not involve the debilitating idea of 'suspending belief' in either macro or micro features of social life. Rather, it attempts to bring such features together and thus dispenses with the false oppositions that result from dualistic thinking (see Burkitt, 1991), although I later question this assumption. The concept of figuration is meant to express the interweaving nature of these different aspects of social life. It has been claimed that it represents a 'breakthrough' which will help social theory and research to be *'more* fruitful' in relation to the agency–structure issue (Dunning, 1992: 244). While Elias's notion of figuration is a useful tool it also possesses serious limitations in dealing with the relevant issues.

Elias's work has to be understood in the context of an empirical and historical study of the long-term development of European society since the Middle Ages which is set out in his two-volume work *The Civilising Process* (1978b, 1982). As a whole, Elias's work has grown out of the conviction that long-term developmental trends have given shape to the major features of society and our knowledge of it. This concentration on the empirical, socially emergent nature of our knowledge ensures that any theoretical ideas that may flow from such an analysis are firmly grounded in data. Seeing things in a developmental perspective keeps our eyes fixed on the socially grounded nature of much of our knowledge.

However, we should beware of over-generalising his analysis to areas of social life which are beyond its reach. This problem is particularly acute for the analysis of situated interaction, as I shall go on to show. More generally, the uncritical extension of Elias's ideas only hinders an accurate appreciation of the strengths and limitations of his work. This is particularly the case with the so-called problem of the 'individual and society'. Certainly, Elias's work has added a historical depth to our understanding of this problem by documenting the emergence of the modern notion of the 'individual' as a closed-off, self-contained entity (*homo clausus*).

Elias argues that this self-perception of individuals first developed between the fourteenth and fifteenth centuries in Europe (that is, from the late Middle Ages to the the early Renaissance). The conception of the individual as an entity separated from society has come to dominate our thinking in the modern age. Thus people generally 'feel' themselves to be divided from the rest of society. More importantly, sociologists have tended to reinforce this (false) idea. For example, role theory, which is said to represent a 'bridge' between the individual and society, simply endorses the false problem of the individual and society. The idea of a dividing line between the 'inner self' and the 'outside world' is false because no such dividing line exists (Elias, 1978b: 122).

With the notion of 'figuration' the false distinctions between individuals and society, subject and object, inner and outer and so on, are abandoned in favour of the idea of interdependent chains or social networks between acting human beings. In this conception individuals are viewed as *homines aperti*, bound together in mutual interdependence in the historical processes that give rise to specific figurations. According to Elias, the concept of figuration helps us to detach ourselves from the feeling that there is a person 'within' and that all other people exist 'outside'. There is no separate (or pre-social) individual: people are always intimately interwoven with others through the interdependency chains that form the fabric of society.

The idea of a split between the individual and society developed historically as part of the civilising process in which people become more subject to self-control rather than reliant on external discipline. In his study of the civilising process, Elias (1978b, 1982) traces the development of the nation-state and the changing patterns of social behaviour and personality structure as connected aspects of the development of European society since the Middle Ages. The idea of the individual as a separate unit was linked to the changing social relations between people in this period. Central to this was the gradual disappearance of the warring lords and factions that comprised feudal society.

Competition between neighbouring territorial units and fiefdoms led to a concentration of power in the hands of ever fewer warlords. This meant that they were more easily able to support larger and more efficient armed forces, and forms of administration which could levy taxes to support them. The monopolisation of the right of taxation went hand in hand with a monopoly over the right to wage war on external enemies and the internal use of force as a means of putting down rebellions. This internal use of force imposed a level of pacification on ever larger areas that were once characterised by high levels of arbitrary violence.

The monopolisation processes eventually culminated in the development of more organised and depersonalised forms of power with a distinct administrative level. Kings and princes began to dominate by playing off rival factions against each other. This eventually led to the absolute monarchies and their courts of the seventeenth and eighteenth centuries. Louis XIV's court at Versailles was a prime example of the consequences of stripping power away from the feudal lords and concentrating it in the hands of an absolute monarch. The power of the aristocrats was further limited by their participation in the court society of the King. These long-term changes at the macro level were accompanied by changes in the personality and behaviour patterns of people at the micro level.

In the Middle Ages people were freer and more spontaneous, and levels of violence and aggressiveness were higher. Also, the degree of tolerance and sensitivity to various social and biological functions such as eating, blowing one's nose, urinating and defecating were very different from those we find acceptable in modern society. With the onset of court society, people became much more restrained and influenced by codes of conduct that required levels of self-control. This came about, according to Elias, as a result of the fact that people within specific territories were forced to live in peace with each other. Elias contends that, over many years, people's personalities, and the form and expression of their emotions gradually changes to accommodate such changing social circumstances. The pressure of living together at court led to a greater regulation of impulses and greater restraint (Elias, 1978b: 137).

Elias illustrates this with evidence from 'manners books' which were published between the thirteenth and nineteenth centuries. Such books undertook to define what was appropriate and acceptable social behaviour, especially with regard to the upper classes. How to behave when eating (the gradual introduction of the use of the fork, for example), when and when not to spit or break wind, attitudes towards nudity, sexuality and so on were the routine subjects of manners books. This evidence suggests that there was a gradual move towards greater refinement in manners and social etiquette, and greater regulation and self-control. The external controls on people's behaviour, backed by the use of punishment which predominated in the Middle Ages, from the Renaissance onwards became replaced by the influence of internalised self-control based upon elaborate codes of conduct.

It is in the context of this overall set of processes, both macro and micro, that Elias's ideas on the nature of the individual–society relation have to be understood. The concentration on restraint and self-control that developed as a result of the civilising process from the Renaissance onwards came to be enshrined in the notion of an 'individual "ego" in its locked case, the self divided by an invisible wall from what happens outside' (Elias, 1978b; 257). This notion of the self as a separate (autonomous) individual – a primary reality – is reflected in the work of Renaissance philosophers like Descartes, Leibniz and Kant. Elias argued that this philosophical influence has been detrimental to an adequate understanding of the intrinsically social nature of people. It has also resulted in a misunderstanding of the social and developmental nature of knowledge (the rise of science, the transcendence of mystical forms of thinking and so on). Instead of understanding the growth of knowledge as a response to changing social circumstances, the Renaissance philosophers insisted on the priority of the individual as a producer of knowledge by the autonomous application of human thought and reason.

Such legacies have led directly into modern conceptions of the 'entirely self-sufficient individual' (Elias, 1978b: 252–3). This has led Elias and his followers (notably Mennel, 1980; Burkitt, 1991; Dunning and Rojek, 1992) to argue that modern sociology itself has been unduly (if not wholly) influenced by this view of the individual–society relation. Consequently, they have suggested that Elias's notion of 'figuration', or the chains of social interdependencies in which people are enmeshed, represents a more adequate understanding of social reality. Clearly, Elias's work has added to our understanding of the modern notion of the individual by placing it in the context of long-term developmental processes, but does it represent the profound advance in understanding that is often claimed by his followers? A related question concerns the concept of figuration itself. I believe that it is useful and represents *one dimension* of the macro–micro problem. However, many other equally important problems thrown up by the macro–micro issue remain neglected in Elias's work.

Finding a Place for the Individual: The Limits of Social Constructionism

To suggest, as Elias does, that there is a widespread view among sociologists that stresses an individual–society split (which his own concept of figuration overcomes) is misleading. All the major figures (and most of the minor ones) in the history of sociological thought have understood individuals and society to be intertwined and inextricably fused. Indeed, this is perhaps the founding assumption of sociological thought itself. However, these figures have produced very different ideas about the degree to which the enmeshment of people in social processes allows for levels of individual creativity and independence, particularly in instances of social transformation. Marx's famous dictum that people make their own history, but not in circumstances of their own choosing, indicates a viewpoint on this that is generally shared, I think, by most sociologists. The point is, however, how should this be interpreted? Much sociological thought has been concerned with this issue.

One of the most persistent problems arising from this basic issue has been how to understand the social connectedness of individuals. In what ways are they intertwined with the social processes of which they form a part? This is the real issue. That is, the real question concerns which of the several accounts is more adequate and useful to social analysis. The idea that some authors or schools of social theory are entrapped in a false notion of an individual–society split is therefore quite misleading. The important question is not whether some sociologists posit a solitary individual cut off from society. It would be odd indeed if any sociologists attempted to do this. The question is, which of the accounts most adequately expresses the fundamental connectedness of the individual and society?

Related to this problem is the fudging of the distinction between individuals and the social contexts in which they act. Suggesting that the individual–society split is false suppresses the fact that individuals have private inner states which are, in a specific sense, separated from an outer world. It is all too easy to jump from the idea that individuals are social beings in a very important and embracing sense to the conclusion that there are no barriers at all between the individual and the social world. In this sense, the 'person' as an individual with a unique psychobiography and self-identity is submerged in social processes virtually without a trace. Now this, of course, is not something that applies to one school of thought. As we have seen, the question of the 'decentring of the subject' has arisen both with structuralist (Althusser, Poulantzas) and post-structuralist thought (Foucault). In these cases, too, the individual subject is replaced by a focus on the social construction of subjectivity.

As with all attempts to banish the individual subject as a focus of social analysis, we have to separate out myth from fact. Certainly, it is important for social analysis not to be mired in an unhealthy concern with the individual, especially if it leads to a view of society as the creation of individuals. However, in seizing upon this 'myth' of the individual as the centre of meaning and action, we must not become prisoners of another myth – that of social exclusivity. According to this, an individual's subjectivity and identity (and his or her emotional and cognitive counterparts) are constructed exclusively by collective forces, developmental trends and configurations of power and knowledge. This myth has the effect of banishing the notion of the individual almost entirely. But this simply makes social theory deficient – it cannot deal with whole areas of everyday experience and reality that cut across the social and psychological domains.

It is quite in order to choose to focus on power–knowledge complexes or developmental trends in social control and the *general* psychological mechanisms that correspond to them. The fatal error is in viewing the social construction of subjectivity (via an analysis of social contexts) as the only (and thus the most efficacious) form of 'social' analysis. On this view, any reference to internal emotional or cognitive states as individual characteristics is deemed guilty of reducing social phenomena to psychological attributes and viewing the individual as a separate atom unconnected to larger social networks.

But it is perfectly feasible to talk of the relatively independent properties of individuals as long as they are understood to have an organic connection with social processes. In this respect, I believe that social theory needs to reclaim and reconstruct the individual for social analysis. What is needed more than anything else is a clear distinction between general and specific claims as they relate to the different levels of analysis mentioned above. For example, a concentration on the socially constructed nature of sexuality or self-identity, as they can be traced over long periods of development, must be distinguished from a specific individual's identity and sexual development. Although all people must to some degree be affected by the social contexts in which they are raised (including the general historical background such as changing attitudes to sexuality), this does not and cannot mean that they are simply reflections of these circumstances.

Individuals are capable of both creatively resisting and embracing the cultural and structural guidelines that surround them. Both of these strategies also imply different levels of creativity in dealing with them; conformity and deviance are not the stark alternatives. There are varieties of conformity, some of which appear to have more in common with deviance, but which nonetheless represent a reasoned acceptance of social constraints. The same is true of deviance and resistance; they have many shapes and can be deceptive in appearance. Furthermore, individuals are not only creative and transformative agents, they also possess a unique 'psychobiography' which they carry around in their heads. This is a storehouse as well as a generator of behaviour. Thus unique childhood experiences (as well as later ones) constitute a well of attitudes and behavioural dispositions built up over time.

The psychobiography that we each possess is an 'underlying' mechanism that prompts lines of action, response and reaction to our social circumstances which are not simply reflections of the social conditions themselves. Thus, for example, although the modern age may be in general an age of greater social restraint, this cannot stand as an explanation of individual behaviour. The partly independent properties of individuals must be registered in our theories. This is because a person's behaviour is filtered through an amalgam of several influences. Unique psychobiographical experiences will intersect with the dynamics of particular situations and the influence of wider social contexts to determine a person's behaviour.

All this is a call for greater awareness of individual capacities, and for us as sociologists to make room for them in our theories. It is clearly not a call for an individual-centred approach to social analysis. My arguments are directed against 'fashionable' attempts to banish the individual as well as more traditional sociological approaches that stress the primacy of the social. There must be a balance and recognition of the different levels at which various features of society operate (in this case, the reality of the individual as an independent agent). The same consideration applies to more 'structural' or 'macro' phenomena – they have to be understood as belonging to one of several levels of social reality which mutually influence each other.

Overcoming False Distinctions: Possibilities and Pitfalls

That individuals are seen as *homines aperti* would seem to be a basic assumption of *any* analysis that is sociologically informed. It is quite wrong to claim that authors like Parsons (or, for that matter, any of the authors I have dealt with) are simply caught up in some false line of reasoning based on a split between the individual and society. As I have said, the real differences between sociologists arise over the question of *how* human social activities (including the solo activities of individuals) are related to the social contexts in which they are embedded. The challenge for modern social theory is to decide which of the versions or 'models' of this relationship are most adequate. It is by no means obvious that Elias's is superior in this respect.

The idea that modern social theory is plagued by a split between the individual and society is simply a 'red-herring' as far as sociology is concerned. It shifts attention away from the problem of understanding the nature of social activity and issues relating to the nature of face-to-face behaviour, the role of meaning and so on. These are the sorts of questions concerning 'situated conduct' which have been tackled by interactionists and phenomenologists but are conspicuously absent from Elias's work. Moreover, Elias makes no proper distinctions between 'individuals' (and their activities) and 'situated conduct' in terms of meaning, reflexivity and so on. Such distinctions are needed in order to deal with the complex relations between activity and its social contexts.

The unique psychobiographies and distinct personalities of individuals play a very important role in their responses to social situations, and the way they 'construct' the local realities and situations in which they live. Consider, for instance, the range of possibilities here – happy or unhappy families, 'good', 'strange' or 'strained' relations with parents and others, contentment or frustration at work, the 'making' of potential killers and criminals. The fact that we are always and everywhere enmeshed in social relationships with others should not lead us to undervalue the levels of *independence* we exhibit from them at the same time. Such considerations, of course, are very much the stock in trade of Freudian or neo-Freudian approaches to personality development. In fact Elias uses Freudian concepts to buttress his views about the increasing levels of restraint and self-control in modern societies. In Freudian terms this can be expressed as an increase in the level of 'superego' control (internalised moral rules about appropriate social behaviour), as compared with the more instinctual aggressive and sexual impulses of the 'id'.

However, Elias tends to use Freudian ideas in terms of their connection with long-term social developments and their implications for collective behaviour and the *general* personality structures of individuals. But what occurs in a general social-structural (or collective) sense does not allow us to understand the unique set of social circumstances surrounding the psychological development of individuals. For example, we may argue that there is a general historical trend towards increasing restraint and self-control that produces a general potential (or general predisposition) in human beings. However, this tells us very little about why particular individuals choose to behave with little restraint or self-control in particular situations.

Why do certain situations in modern society make people angry, lose their emotional composure or erupt into violence? Why does a particular situation affect one person differently from another? The study of long-term processes can provide a wide-angled view on such behaviour by suggesting what range or type of emotional responses are usual or even probable at certain historical periods, but it cannot provide us with the reasons why different individuals respond to the same general circumstances in vastly different ways. Answers couched in terms of long-term shifts in general personality structures and behavioural patterns simply skirt the real substantive issues here.

History, Situated Behaviour and Social Analysis

An analysis of the wider historically formed contextual parameters of personality and typical modes of behaviour cannot 'stand in' for a close-up focus on the intertwining of self and situated activity (any more than a close-up focus on interpersonal encounters could furnish us with a historically informed developmental explanation). Some account is needed of the contribution of the unique psychobiographies of the real and describable human actors involved as they criss-cross and intertwine with the emergent and unfolding elements of the situation. Elias's work does not deal with the day-to-day routines of social existence as they are experienced by the social actors on the social scene, so to speak. There is no analysis of the way in which meaning emerges through interactive negotiation, no appreciation of the way in which collective definitions of the situation fashion the contours of interpersonal encounters. In short, there is no discernment of what Goffman (1983) calls the 'interaction order' existing in its own right with its own properties and partly separable from an institutional order (see Chapter 11).

Viewing people simply as members of interdependency chains overlooks the ceaseless flow of social activity as it successively builds, evaporates and rebuilds itself in situations which are sometimes routinely connected in time and place, sometimes disrupted or prematurely brought to an end. Other facets of social existence are lost too, for example, the sense in which face-to-face encounters often grow out of the foundations of previous encounters or spontaneously 'flower'. Sure enough, the interaction order is related to the wider institutional order, but this is a complex relationship which is not adequately expressed by the term 'networks of interdependence'.

Figuration and the Macro–Micro Problem

It is frequently suggested that Elias has made breakthroughs or produced more adequate work than has hitherto been on offer in sociology. The implication is that he has somehow 'gone beyond' the false and naive assumptions that are implicit in other versions (perspectives, frameworks, theories) of the sociological enterprise. For example, Mennel has argued that sociologists 'still lack the ability to link micro and macro levels of sociological theory and find it difficult to conceptualize the appearance of "emergent properties" of large-scale collectivities' (1980: 47). He goes on to say that in order to do this it is best to use Elias's approach, which encourages the sociologist to think of sprawling networks of people enmeshed in long chains of interdependence, rather than simply interacting directly with each other in face-to-face groups. This alerts us to the increasing impersonality of social relations as they move away from immediate encounters. For example, our relations with our immediate family are much 'closer' (in terms of distance) and more personalised than our relations with various heads of government or the effects of some international crisis. Nonetheless, we are, at varying distances and levels of intensity, just as dependent upon the larger more impersonal chains of connection as we are on the face-to-face encounters with our families.

On this basis Mennel argues that Elias's notion of interdependence 'is more widely serviceable for sociological purposes than that of interaction, because it can be used from the most "micro" to the most "macro" level of discussion' (Mennel, 1980: 48). He goes on to point out that other sociologists, notably Bott (1957), in her study of the social networks of families, have demonstrated the usefulness of thinking in terms of social networks. There is no doubt that network analysis has produced much interesting and useful work (see Scott, 1991, for an overview and appraisal). For example, Mitchell (1969) produced some pioneering work on urban networks and developed some important conceptual distinctions which help us identify different types of networks. Such features as the density of the network (to what extent the people are in touch with each other) and the level of connectedness (the number of relations each person has with others in the network) are important distinguishing criteria.

However, I disagree with Mennel's suggestion that, if we join network analysis to Elias's notion of interdependencies, we then have a more serviceable means of linking macro and micro than the concept of interaction. By suggesting that networks of interdependencies are the 'links' between macro and micro phenomena the distinctive characteristics of activities and structures are blurred. Thus, Elias and his followers are led to the conclusion that, for all intents and purposes, structures and activities are the same (networks of varying size and density and so on) and that they have similar properties. This deflects attention away from rather more important dissimilarities, which are, perhaps, most acute when we ask the simple question 'In what sense is face-to-face interaction the same or different from structural or macro (for example, institutional) phenomena?'. From an Eliasian point of view the answer would be that they are both networks of individuals distinguished simply by the greater length of the interdependency chains in macro phenomena and that face-to-face encounters are characterised by more immediate and personalised involvements. To an extent this is true, but it leaves out of account some important qualitative distinctions between face-to-face encounters and more distant (mediated) social relations.

For example, dealing with someone on a face-to-face basis (say in a family, or in a coffee bar) is very much influenced by the reality of the *presence* of other people. In this sense, the ongoing nature of relationships in these sorts of situations is a reflection of how well or badly we are getting on with the people involved. That is, in more technical terms, it depends upon how the reflexive monitoring of each other's conduct creates cohesion or disharmony in the situation. Also, the character of our relations depends on how well the aims and intentions of the participants are being catered for by the direction and momentum of the encounter.

For instance, one person may want emotional reassurance in a situation, while the other(s) simply want to 'pass the time of day'. Both sets of objectives may not be served by a particular encounter. Similarly, although people bring with them memories of previous encounters (their stored experience of others), it is the actual behaviour of others (that is, the consequences that flow from their immediate presence), that seals the fate of the encounter. For instance, an unhappy previous experience may be 'repaired' by the conciliatory messages and responses given off by the same participants in a current encounter.

The Nature of Social Ties and Relations

As social relations stretch away into the impersonal realm of institutional phenomena, say, our connection with some government agency, we find that our ties of interdependence are based primarily upon an absence rather than a presence. We do not experience the presence of the government as such; there is no face-to-face encounter with the institution. Sometimes we deal with such an institution in quite impersonal terms (such as when we engage in correspondence about matters involving taxation). At other times we deal in a face-to-face manner with a 'representative' who may in fact be not much 'closer' to the institution than ourselves in terms of formal authority (for example, a clerk in a tax office).

In this sense, our relationship with the institution is mediated by the presence of a representative.

However, what happens in the encounter with this representative (for example, whether our tax rebate claim is upheld or not and whether, subsequently, an argument ensues between us) does not depend entirely on the immediacy of our personal encounter. That is, the outcome of the encounter does not depend *primarily* on whether we gel as human beings, or the fact that we are neighbours or that we give each other emotional reassurance. Rather, it depends upon our legal obligations as citizens of a particular country and the rules and sanctions that the authorities have the power to put into operation should we disagree with, resist or otherwise disregard them. In this sense, in our dealings with the tax office clerk we are participating in two distinct forms of relationship which are embodied within the same encounter. First, we are dealing with a social relationship which is based upon an absent form of interdependence – our tie with the institution and its powers over us – which is mediated by the clerk. Secondly, we are enmeshed in a face-to-face relationship with someone with whom we have a relatively impersonal (official) relationship and an externally defined interest.

To say that our ties of interdependence with institutions (that is the link between macro and micro phenomena) are understandable simply in terms of networks of greater and lesser scope and impersonality is to radically misconstrue the nature of both situated activity and institutions. Although networks (in the sense of connections between people) are present in situated encounters, the defining properties of the latter are to be found in the reflexive monitoring of conduct and the situated definitions and meanings that influence the behaviour of the participants. Similarly, although it may be useful to express some aspects of structural (institutional) phenomena in terms of 'networks' of connections between people, we have to remember that these are often 'absent', potential or mediated connections. We must be aware that the defining characteristics of institutions are not to be found in the connectedness of people as such. Rather, they are defined in terms of the influence of reproduced practices on the behaviour of many people, many of whom have no connections with each other and are unlikely to have face-to-face contact.

Also, concentrating on the interdependencies in networks deflects attention away from significant differences between groups and forms of social organisation. In this sense, it is the *nature* of the ties between people (rather than the fact of ties *per se*, or the 'form' or pattern they exhibit) that is the crucial defining feature. For example, it is the nature and obligations of friendship ties that define networks of friendship in the first place, and distinguish them from the gossip and information networks found, say, in an occupation (like the acting profession for instance). Similarly, it is the nature of the ties (pecuniary, altruistic, contractual and so on) and the resources that underpin them (law, money, property) that are of crucial importance in understanding work relations, political involvements and power conflicts between groups.

Conclusion

It would be unwise to think of figurations as the most serviceable or effective way of linking macro and micro phenomena, as Mennel suggests. Important qualitative differences in the characteristics of social life would be masked in the process. It is also misleading to suggest that the only sociological alternative we have to Elias's concept of figuration is to think in terms of role theories which emphasise a bridge between individual and society and thus reproduce the traditional dualism (Mennel, 1980: 61). Similarly, claims to the effect that Elias's perspective is the only one to refuse to 'separate society and the individual' (Burkitt, 1991: 187) are vastly exaggerated. The idea of the interdependence of individual and society is a defining feature and basic assumption of sociology, and has been conspicuous in the work of many theorists, including Parsons and the classical founding fathers.

Elias's work on the civilising process highlights the effects of long-term unplanned social trends. Without doubt it represents *one way* in which objective and subjective dimensions of social life can be brought together. However, it represents but one aspect or dimension of a much more complicated process and is insufficient in itself to account in full for the complexities and subtleties of both face-to-face behaviour and other more impersonal forms of social organisation. In Elias's framework we do not have to suspend belief in the existence of macro or micro phenomena as with the phenomenologists discussed in Chapter 5. However, by being encouraged to think in terms of interdependencies (rather than in terms of the nature of situated activity or the nature of institutions), we are, at the same time, encouraged to overlook some of the most important characteristics and properties of these phenomena.

I have tried to indicate that by simply abandoning these dualisms and distinctions we do not make any advances in our understanding of social processes. In fact, we lose sight of some very real and important distinctions in social life which are essential to an understanding of macro–micro connections.

SUMMARY

- Elias proposes that the concept of figuration, which refers to interdependency chains of individuals, is the basic constituent feature of society. The concept is designed to overcome what Elias regards as false dualisms, such as agency–structure and macro–micro but particularly the individual–society split which, he claims, is pervasive in sociology.

- The concept of figuration is employed in close parallel with Elias's empirical and historical study of the long-term development of European society since the Middle Ages. Elias documents the development of the modern notion of the individual as a closed off, self-contained entity (*homo clausus*) in the fourteenth and fifteenth centuries in Europe – the late Middle Ages to the early Renaissance. According to Elias, this conception of the individual has come to dominate our thinking in the modern age. Elias argues that this false line of thinking is reflected in role theories (like Parsons's). He further argues that we should reject this mistaken line of thinking and replace it with the concept of 'figuration' which abandons false distinctions between individuals and society, subject and object, inner and outer, in favour of the interdependent chains or social networks between individuals. The idea of the split between the individual and society developed historically as part of the 'civilising process' in which people became more subject to self-control rather than reliant on external discipline.

- Elias's claim about the individual and society split in sociological analysis is largely misplaced. Most sociologists either see the individual as firmly embedded in social relationships or as entirely socially constructed.

- In fact the real problem for sociology (as well as for Elias's work) is its excessive emphasis on the social construction of the individual. This makes it hard for sociological analysis to grasp the uniqueness of individuals within a generalising frame of reference.

- As a means of overcoming the agency–structure and macro–micro problems, the concept of 'figurational processes' is limited by, among other things, its neglect of face-to-face interactive processes and the importance of intersubjective meaning in social behaviour.

- The suggestion that networks of interdependencies are the 'links' between macro and micro phenomena only blurs the distinctive characteristics of social activity and social structure, respectively. The quite different properties of situated activities and institutional structures are simply overlooked by treating them both as interdependency chains of greater or lesser length and scope. Such a strategy obscures the qualitative differences between face-to-face encounters and more distant (mediated) social relations. It is the nature of the socially constituted ties between individuals that is their crucial defining feature rather than the extent or scope of networks of interdependency chains.

- Elias's work on the civilising process highlights the effects of long-term unplanned social trends. Although the use of the notion of figurational networks represents one way in which objective and subjective dimensions of social life may be brought together, it is certainly not the only, or most important way. Figurational processes and social networks do not register the most important characteristics and properties that distinguish face-to-face encounters from the impersonal social relations of institutional phenomena that stretch away from them over time and space.

8

Giddens's Structuration Theory

PREVIEW

- Structuration theory represents Giddens's attempt to overcome the agency–structure and macro–micro dualisms. The key concept is 'the duality of structure'.

- The nature and influence of structuration theory.

- The methods and subject matter of sociology.

- Against traditional and scientific approaches.

- The 'practical' nature of social analysis.

- Against dualism in social analysis.

- The duality of structure.

- Social practices, knowledge and skills

- Levels of awareness and consciousness.

- Basic security, trust and routines.

- The importance of time and space.

- Power, agency and the dialectic of control.

- Giddens's conception of structure.

- Systems, institutions and types of integration.

- The problem with Giddens's definition of structure.

- The problem of the durability of social systems.

- Is the social landscape flat or contoured?

- Structure versus habitus.

- How much creativity and how much constraint?

- Self-identity and society.

- Structuration theory and empirical research.

- Balancing agency and structure.

- Critical problems in structuration theory.

This is the third and final chapter in the section I have labelled 'Breaking Free and Burning Bridges'. Let me first say why Giddens's work fits in with this characterisation. We have looked at the work of authors who have, in rather different ways and sometimes for very different reasons, rejected the dualisms that have characterised previous (more 'traditional') approaches. In Giddens's work we find a similar emphasis. He is strongly against the entrenched 'oppositions' between traditions of social theory which this entails. Giddens's work, then, is very much concerned with breaking down these divisions and concentrating on the convergences and overlaps between them. In this sense, his work as a whole can be summed up as an attempt to provide a framework of theoretical concepts which is 'synthetic' in spirit.

He tries to develop a wide-angled approach which draws from a range of ideas, sources and approaches. However, as Craib (1992) points out, unlike many other thinkers (Parsons, for instance), Giddens is not concerned with providing a tightly integrated framework which provides an overall theory of society. Such a project would be too rigid for Giddens's purposes, and in any case would not fit in easily with his ideas about how social life itself influences our attempts to explain it, or theorise about it. Instead, Giddens wants to offer a set of 'sensitising' concepts that might prove to be of use in social analysis generally, and social research in particular. In this manner, 'structuration theory', as it is called, can be drawn on as and when the sociologist feels that small bits, or whole chunks of it would prove illuminating or helpful for a particular analysis.

'Structuration theory' refers to an exceedingly wide range of topics and areas of interest: the nature of day-to-day interaction, the development of the nation-state and citizenship rights, class analysis, evolutionary theories of society, time-geography, the nature of modernity, surveillance, war and so on. Furthermore, Giddens draws on an immense variety of writers and schools of thought in social theory from the classical sociologists to contemporary theorists of many stripes and persuasions. I shall not give a complete overview of the totality of Giddens's ideas (for this see Cohen, 1989; Held and Thompson, 1989; Bryant and Jary, 1991; Craib, 1992; Kasperson, 2000). Instead, I concentrate on Giddens's notion of the 'duality of structure' as an attempt to overcome the action–structure and macro–micro dualisms. Of course, this necessitates that we stray into quite a few of the areas that Giddens has written on. However, I feel that the core of his ideas on this topic can be approached without going into the more traditionally conceived 'macro' concerns that he also covers (such as the emergence of the nation-state or the time–space constitution of social systems and so on).

Like Foucault, the ethnomethodologists and Elias, Giddens wants to 'break away' from the traditional dualistic approaches. However, unlike these others, Giddens seems very much more conscious of the contributions that more traditional approaches have made. Thus, while he is firmly against some forms of social theory (particularly those which emphasise the determination of social activity by structure), he has a much more receptive attitude to other strands of theory. In short, there is more of an attempt to enter into a *dialogue* with alternative approaches than we have seen so far in this section. This allows us to view his theory in the general context of social theory. It therefore makes it easier both to evaluate the fullness of its contribution to an ongoing debate and to identify some of its weaknesses. Both a strength and weakness of structuration theory is that it has a foot in both camps of the dualism debate. That is, while it clearly breaks new ground, it also retains definite links with the traditions from which it draws sustenance.

This is both a conscious effort on Giddens's part and the result of the 'internal dynamics' of the theory itself. By this I mean that some of the implications of the theory tend to work against its initial assumptions. For example, as the theory unfolds (especially during the period 1976–1984), various aspects of it begin to underscore the importance and indispensability of 'dualism' rather than to reinforce the idea that we should do without it altogether. However, this argument needs to be laid out in much more detail so I shall come back to it at various junctures.

The Influence of Structuration Theory

Giddens begins to outline structuration theory in his book *New Rules of Sociological Method* in 1976. Prior to this he had written two books, one on the classical theorists, Marx, Durkheim and Weber (*Capitalism and Modern Social*

Theory [1971]) and a book on social class (*The Class Structure of the Advanced Societies* [1973]). In neither of these is there any real intimation of the theory that was to subsequently emerge (although Giddens does use the term 'structuration' in the book on class). Up to this point, even though Giddens had taken a critical stand towards theories and theorists with which he disagreed, the criticism was such that it could be absorbed into the sociological mainstream without too much discomfort. However, the project that Giddens embarked upon with the publication of *New Rules of Sociological Method* could be said to represent a complete departure from accepted sociological orthodoxy. Since then, and with its maturation, increased complexity and sophistication, Giddens's project has attracted a great deal of attention.

I think that one of the main reasons for this is that, at the time it emerged, sociology itself was in need of some coherence and unity after a decade of self-questioning and factional splits. In the mid-1960s there was a growing dissatisfaction with the current orthodoxy (Parsonian inspired 'structural-functionalism') that had dominated academic sociology since the 1940s. Various schools of thought (notably 'conflict theory' and forms of radical Marxism, as well as phenomenological and interactionist schools of thought) had emerged as a counter to this orthodoxy. However, the effect of this was not to create a growing consensus about the aims, analytic procedures and methods of sociology. Rather, the situation began to look like a form of sectional warfare, with various groupings vying with each other to fill up the void created by the demise of Parsonian functionalism.

In this context Giddens began to define the contours of structuration theory. Insofar as the theory attempted to bring together a number of seemingly disparate strands into a 'synthesis' then it provided a coherent unity around which debates could revolve, instead of each group remaining committed to their own entrenched schools of thought. I am not suggesting that structuration theory has been adopted as a new orthodoxy or has replaced sectional rivalries; far from it. Also, much of sociology, particularly that concerned with empirical research, remains unaffected and uninfluenced by structuration theory. However, it did create a focal point around which much theoretical debate could centre. Furthermore, the compatibility of the theory with a spread of diverse approaches enhanced the range of its appeal. Apart from having a foot in both camps of the dualism debate (that is, retaining dualism or leaving it behind), it displays an honest eclecticism (that is, it deliberately borrows certain aspects of other theories and recycles them for its own purposes). Coupling these together means that it is almost guaranteed to be a 'user-friendly' tool to an extremely wide cross-section of practising sociologists.

The Methods and Subject Matter of Sociology

Giddens endorses a view of social analysis which has more in common with the humanist approaches (Chapters 4 and 5) than with the more traditional scientific' approaches (Chapters 2 and 3). Thus the title of Giddens's 1976 book refers back to Durkheim's classic work *The Rules of Sociological Method* (1982), first published in 1895. In this Durkheim lays out some methodological rules for sociological research which suggest that sociology should, as far as possible, model itself on the natural sciences. In essence, Durkheim argues that like physics, chemistry, biology and so on, sociology is concerned with an independent, objective subject matter. These 'social facts', as Durkheim described them, must be analysed in a detached way avoiding reference to subjective attitudes or commonsense assumptions.

Giddens's 'new' rules reverse Durkheim's emphases and offer a view of sociology which stresses that its 'subject matter' (that is, people and the products of their social activities), cannot be treated as independent and objective sets of pre-established facts. People are intrinsically involved with society and actively enter into its constitution; they construct, support and change it because it is the nature of human beings to be affected by, and to affect, their social environment. Unlike the molecules, atoms and force fields of the natural sciences, people do not remain unmoved by their own feelings and motivations. They are not simply compelled by forces outside of themselves (as are natural phenomena), they do not act mechanically and blindly as if compelled by laws of nature. By reflecting on their own behaviour and circumstances they always have some choice in the matter. They are always capable, to some degree, of resisting the constraints imposed on them by society and of influencing and transforming their social situations.

Thus, sociologists are encouraged to seek out the skilled ways in which people produce (create) and reproduce (re-enact) existing or established aspects of society (social practices) as they go about their daily business. Sociologists must attend to the everyday behaviour of people as an *important* aspect of their analyses. Giddens stresses that people are skilled and knowledgeable, and that they cannot therefore be considered to be dupes of the (social) system or mere reflections or 'bearers' of its demands and requirements. By emphasising this and reinstating the importance of the analysis of the minutiae of daily conduct ('everyday life'), Giddens aligns himself to a considerable extent with humanist and, in particular, ethnomethodological strands of thought. At the same time, this defines Giddens's project in opposition to more orthodox functionalist and structural-Marxist schools of thought.

Giddens's new rules point the sociologist away from 'pre-given' social facts in the Durkheimian sense and towards the people who are actually involved in producing social forms (or bounded areas of social life) through their very activities. Thus the analysis of social life is necessarily tied to the interpretation of behaviour and the social rules that 'contain' particular segments of the social world (such as a monastery, a school, a class situation, a neighbourhood). However, Giddens is careful to say that structuration theory is not simply a version of interpretative sociology (ethnomethodology, phenomenology), since he acknowledges that society is not a creation of individuals (1984: xxi). So, while social study involves some analysis of the meaningful worlds of the people who are being studied, it also recognises that social institutions pre-exist individuals.

Against Traditional Scientific Approaches

Giddens is trying to reconcile some elements of both the newer interpretative forms of sociology with the more traditional 'structural' forms (what Giddens calls 'institutional analysis'). However, in so doing he departs from the orthodox structural version in some considerable measure. There are three elements of traditional 'structural' forms which Giddens rejects. First, as we have seen, Giddens is quite against the idea that sociology should model itself on the natural sciences. For him there can be no universal 'laws' of social life. Human behaviour cannot be predicted with the precision that is possible in the natural sciences because it varies according to people's intentions, objectives and the historically changing meanings which give them sense and context. If it is possible to make any generalisations at all about social life then they will be limited to particular times, places and circumstances.

Secondly, Giddens rejects the idea of structural forces which 'externally' constrain and determine behaviour. This is what Giddens calls 'objectivism' and it takes a number of forms all of which Giddens rejects. First, the idea that there is an independent (objective) subject matter of social study such as Durkheim's 'social facts', 'structures' or 'systems' or even 'institutions' has to be dismissed and replaced by the idea that people's reasons and motivations are central to social analysis. Also, approaching social analysis in a detached impersonal way fails to take account of the 'give and take' between observer and observed. The sociologist is just as much part of social life as those she or he is observing. As a consequence, sociological knowledge 'interacts' with 'lay' knowledge (including 'common-sense' knowledge), and this must be taken into account. Finally, social behaviour must be 'interpreted' by the sociologist and this necessitates much more engagement with people than the notion of an objective observer implies. In order for the sociologist to include some reference to people's meanings and motivations she or he must be able to subjectively understand them.

Thirdly, Giddens rejects 'functionalism'. Although Parsons's work influenced much of sociology during the 1940s and 1950s, 'functionalism' was a general force and had many prominent adherents (for example, the highly influential Robert Merton). Giddens suggests that, as the dominant orthodoxy for over two decades, functionalism went hand in hand with both naturalism and objectivism. Not surprisingly, Giddens is very critical of it. His main objection is to the idea that societies as 'social systems' have properties of their own which can be analysed independently of actors' wants and reasons. For example, the idea that social systems have 'needs' (such as the need for integration or balance or adaptation) involves this kind of explanation. (For more technical details see Giddens, 1977.)

The 'Practical' Nature of Social Analysis

In his most systematic outline of structuration theory (1984), Giddens states that those working in social theory 'should be concerned first and foremost with reworking conceptions of human being and human doing, social reproduction and social transformation' (1984: xx). By this Giddens is suggesting that far too much time has been spent on epistemological issues (those concerning how we know what we claim to know), rather than on ontological questions (such as what is the nature of the things we know – what is their reality). Social theory should not concentrate on the question of the validity of knowledge, or on the kinds of evidence that would count for or against particular theories or explanations. Instead, it should produce theoretical accounts of actual behaviour and social experience, and the way humans rearrange their social circumstances.

Certainly Giddens has a point here. If social theory concerned itself solely with abstract matters, particularly problems of validity, then it would regress into an endless and sterile debate about appropriate procedures and how to 'assess' or evaluate each other's basic assumptions. However we cannot go too far with this line of reasoning. What appear to be 'neutral' descriptions or accounts often contain judgements concerning the validity of the descriptions we are presenting and we must be aware of these in our analyses. The implications of this can be seen in the following example. If we ask someone the way to a house in the suburbs, we assume that the person's answer is correct or valid – in that it gives us a good impression of the terrain and the signs by which we can measure our progress. However, if we repeatedly get lost while following the instructions, we would be led to the realisation that the description offered by the passer-by was, in fact, invalid. The original set of directions only *appeared* to be correct (valid). Alternative descriptions of the route might have made us realise that really it was just one among a number of possible descriptions (of more or less use for our purposes).

My general point is that we should be cautious about Giddens's idea that we should be concerned primarily with the reality (ontology) of human behaviour, its nature and its potential. Certainly, questions concerning the nature of behaviour or society, such as, 'What are the constituent elements of society or social processes?' are important. However, these questions cannot be answered in isolation from epistemological questions such as 'How do we know this?' 'What are our arguments and evidence in support of our claims?' It is always important to take note of the assumptions that underlie social theories since they are crucial to assessing their adequacy. For instance, for Giddens, human activity and people's reasons and motivations are of central importance because he believes that society does not exist apart from them. However, this focus moves attention away from the idea that society may be made up of a number of different elements many of which may be best understood as impersonal structural features rather than people's reasons and motivations.

However, by rejecting questions of epistemology and presenting his own version of social ontology in this way, Giddens seems to suggest that other models of society will be misleading if they do not follow this path. We are faced with a choice between either accepting Giddens's model or seemingly falling into the errors of the three 'isms' (naturalism, objectivism and functionalism). This has the effect of eliminating other lines of enquiry that may prove useful, such as the alternative suggested above: that is, that society is constituted by a number of different elements or building blocks (including activity) some of which are best understood as structural characteristics.

Against Dualism in Social Analysis

According to Giddens, supporters of different theoretical positions have attempted to defend their own space and this has has not helped in gaining a true

Structure	v	Action
Objectivism	v	Subjectivism
Macro	v	Micro
Society	v	Individual
Institutional analysis	v	Interpretative analysis

Figure 8.1   *Dualisms in Social Theory*

picture of the elements of social life. For example, supporters of functionalism and structuralism (as reflected in the work of Parsons, Althusser, Lévi-Strauss and so on) have tended to defend the idea that sociology should view social phenomena as independent of individuals. This has meant that they also tend to support versions of objectivism and naturalism. Their overall view of social analysis gives priority to the concept of 'structure' which is said to constrain or limit the forms of action and meaning in which people may engage.

On the other hand, what Giddens calls the 'interpretative' schools of thought (ethnomethodology and phenomenology) take the individual (subjectivity) as the centrepoint of analysis. They emphasise that the subjective experience of individuals and the meanings that their activities have for them are the most important things in the social world. Anything which lies outside subjective experience is thought to belong to an impersonal realm of little or no relevance to our understanding of social life. So adherents of these schools tend to support versions of subjectivism (action and meaning are the most important) and humanism (people rather than 'objective' things are the subject matter of sociology).

These two great blocks of social thought have created a yawning division in social analysis which must be overcome, otherwise the two 'empires' will simply continue to pull in opposite directions forever. In themselves these two camps represent a dualism – two sets of entrenched and opposing positions – but they also give rise to, or are associated with, the other 'unnecessary' dualisms in social theory (see Figure 8.1). Giddens wants to overcome these divisions and put an end to the empire-building that goes on under their names. The principal divisions tend to reflect the opposition between structure and action; they are seen as mutually exclusive domains and starting points for the analysis of society. This falsely assumes that structure and action are separate, or that one 'determines' the other in a quite exaggerated manner. Both draw attention away from the essential connectedness of structure and action (object and subject, macro and micro and so on).

The Duality of Structure

Instead of a dualism, Giddens suggests that we should think in terms of a *duality*, a 'duality of structure'. That is, rather than two separate and opposed phenomena, we should think of one, in this case structure, which has a dual nature. In this formulation, structure is intrinsically related to action and vice versa; they are two sides of the same coin. We shall see further on that the two are united through social practices – the things that people regularly do and which form part of the social fabric of their lives – which Giddens regards as the proper focus for social analysis. Practices are part of the 'duality of structure' in that they consist of both action and structure. In this way Giddens argues that structure is not 'external' to action; it is, in a sense, more 'internal' to the flow of action which constitutes the practices in question.

The duality of structure is the core of the theory and is the basis upon which the other dualisms in social theory may be overcome, resolved or somehow brought together. It enables us to tackle the twin issues of social production and reproduction. Social production has to do with the way in which social life is produced (or created) by people as they engage in the social practices which are the substance of their lives and social experiences. This is an insight that has derived primarily from the interpretative schools of social theory. For Giddens, human beings create meaning and social reality from within social settings, and therefore social forms such as institutions and structures have no existence apart from the activities they embody.

The problem of social reproduction, on the other hand, is concerned with the question of how it is that social life becomes patterned and routinised. How is it that forms of social order (including both harmonious co-operation and dissent and conflict) persist despite the creative and transformative capacities of individuals? How are institutions, organisations and cultural patterns reproduced over time (typically beyond the lifetimes of single individuals)? Social reproduction (or replication) has to do with the question of how social activity also provides continuity and pattern in social life.

Giddens points out that the interpretative sociologies have tended to concentrate on the problem of social production at the expense of social reproduction. That is, they have tended to concentrate on the human actor as a centre of meaning, a free agent who creates the social realities around him or her. As such, these schools of thought neglect the influence of institutions and other durable patterns in social life. Conversely, the structural (or institutional) forms of sociology have concentrated almost exclusively on the problem of social reproduction. In this sense, they have viewed the human actor solely as a product of the constraining influences of social structure. As ciphers of structural demands, people are condemned to repeat and reinforce the very conditions that restrict their freedom in the first place.

Social Practices, Knowledge and Skills

Giddens uses the concept of practices to show how production and reproduction are intertwined. We have seen how Foucault (Chapter 6) relies very heavily on the notion of practice (along with that of discourse) in his analyses. Giddens is keen to distance himself from Foucault's usage, which he argues is associated with the idea that practices are solely social constructs. This is something I pointed out in Chapter 6, when I suggested that Foucault's notion of discourse/practice seems to float at an impersonal level above the actual activities and face-to-face situations in which people are involved in daily life. Giddens does not see practices in this way. Practices can never simply be 'empty' expressions of the social community, they are inseparable from the direct and active involvement of people.

When they interact with others, people automatically draw upon resources which they have 'picked up' during their lives, either in formal settings (for example, education), or through informal means, via friends and family. These cover a vast range of knowledge and skills which, once learnt, tend to be taken for granted. These resources can generally be thought of as 'interactional skills', in that people regularly employ them in their ordinary routine dealings with others. Formal knowledge of language (speaking and reading skills) or of the local environment or setting, or getting on and dealing with others, or knowing what to do in dangerous or threatening circumstances, are all examples of resources.

We draw on these in order to be able to make things happen (to conduct conversations, to become friends, to deal with police or company representatives) in social life. But these things are not only part of our own personal repertoire of abilities, they belong and are available to others as part of the stock of socially shared knowledge and skills. However, our unique personalities, styles of behaviour and the experiences they reflect (as well as our moment-to-moment feelings and emotional responses) tend to imbue our actions with a distinctive flavour. We act 'creatively' in this sense by bringing to bear our unique characteristics upon socially shared knowledge. We interpret 'rules' about how to act in the presence of others (elders, 'authorities', children, parents and so on), just as we all have our own unique ways of dealing with situations (for example, through humour, manipulation, sympathy, aggression).

Thus, social practices reflect the ability of humans to modify the circumstances in which they find themselves, while simultaneously recreating the social conditions (practices, knowledge, resources) which they inherit from the past. This – what Giddens refers to as the 'recursive nature of social life' – is not simply a matter of intention on the part of human actors. Certainly, people do intend to do things in social situations (to win a game or a lover, to achieve understanding and so on), but by so doing we unintentionally reproduce the social fabric which underpins the rules of the game, the etiquette of courtship, the norm of co-operation and so forth. This interlacing of intended and unintended consequences of social activity plays a very important role in structuration theory in general and the duality of structure in particular.

By stressing this connection Giddens emphasises that what he means by 'structure' in social life has to be seen as both the *medium* and *outcome* of social activity (Giddens, 1976). The rules and resources we draw on are the medium of our activity in the sense that they enable us to do things and to have intentions. At the same time, they also represent the outcome or consequence (largely unintended) of our activities insofar as we endorse their value by using them, and therefore contribute to their further continuance.

Levels of Awareness and Consciousness

Giddens views human beings as possessing different levels of consciousness or awareness and these affect the way they actually engage in activity. First there is the unconscious motivational level, which represents the human being's deep-seated desires and emotions. While these provide a general 'background' influence on behaviour, a person is not 'compelled' to fulfil or gratify these desires. (In fact such desires may be 'repressed' from conscious awareness.) In this sense such motivations may only provide outlines or general plans for action. More important for Giddens are those elements of the actor's psychological disposition over which he or she has some control. These are *practical* and *discursive* consciousness.

I have touched upon practical consciousness in the discussion of the duality of structure. This refers to the practical skills and knowledge that people have and which they employ in their behaviour. Knowledge of 'how to go on' or what to do next in social situations involves an understanding of the social conditions in which people act. However, this sort of knowledge is not something which people are always able to put into words, because it is used in an 'automatic' way. That is, in the practical circumstances of everyday life people tend simply to *do* certain things rather than 'discuss' them. On the other hand, discursive consciousness refers to the ability to comment rationally on our activities – to describe and discuss the reasons for our behaviour. There is no absolute dividing line between these two forms of consciousness, but they do indicate the manner in which people often switch between them.

It is in the context of practical and discursive consciousness that we can understand another characteristic of human behaviour: the reflexive monitoring of activity. Such self-monitoring of the actor's own, and others' behaviour as it is 'played out' in various situations enables a person to respond flexibly to circumstances and unforeseen eventualities as they arise. Thus, activity is able to proceed on a continuous (although not always smooth) basis. The employment of knowledge and skills in both practical and discursive senses, along with reflexive self-monitoring, works to sustain the continuity and flow of activity.

Giddens counterposes this model of the human actor with that associated with 'structural' sociology. This latter typically discounts or minimises the importance of the knowledgeability of actors (particularly the practical aspects). Giddens is primarily concerned to show that whatever goes on in society and its institutions does not go on 'behind the backs' of people. For research purposes in particular, it is important to take note of the manner in which actors' reasons and intentions are centrally involved in the creation and recreation of social life.

Basic Security, Trust and Routines

In Giddens's theory an essential ingredient of human existence is 'ontological security', which refers to a person's elemental sense of safety in the world and includes a basic 'trust' of other people. This is necessary in order for a person to maintain a sense of psychological well-being. (In fact, Giddens borrows this concept from Laing's [1969] work which argues that mental illness – schizophrenia – results from the lack of such security.) This basic sense of security is developed early on in childhood and continues to play an important role in adult life, particularly as it is reinforced by the routines of social life. This is reflected in the fact that when the routines are broken or disrupted for some reason, people exhibit confusion, anxiety and anger. Giddens finds support for these ideas in Garfinkel's experiments with trust and Goffman's notion of 'mutual tact'. People deploy 'mutual tact' in everyday interaction to help maintain composure when their security is threatened. Ontological security seems to underlie all our activities and thus is 'present' at different levels of our awareness.

Giddens also draws on Goffman's work on encounters. Encounters are the coming together of people either in formal occasions (such as a party or a wedding), or more informally in gatherings (casual interactions, say in a coffee bar or on the street). Both kinds of encounter involve the co-presence of two or more people who monitor each other's behaviour. Also, encounters can be 'focused' (based on face-to-face monitoring and the accommodation of each other's intentions) or 'unfocused' where there is little deliberate co-ordination. The conversation or 'talk' in which people are engaged during such encounters is extremely important for Giddens and must be taken seriously. Goffman's work and that of the ethnomethodologists is important, according to Giddens, insofar as such mundane features of everyday encounters are intimately linked (through the duality of structure) to the more institutionalised features of social systems. In this sense, encounters and their study should not be written off or dismissed as irrelevant, trivial or fleeting (as Gouldner's 1971 critique suggests).

The Importance of Time and Space

Giddens is generally concerned with the way that social behaviour and encounters carve out paths through space and time. Different aspects or conceptions of time are important and intermingle with each other in our daily existence. There is the biographical time that attends our own ageing and lifespan. This intersects with the repetitive cycles of activity that surround our daily activities and routines (encounters). Finally, there is institutional or organisational time, in the sense that we all participate in social forms that preceded us, or will outlast us as individuals (educational and government institutions, industrial firms, hospitals and so on). These different aspects of time are interfused in our daily existences and intersect with the spatial patterns that represent our social lives.

One of the main concepts which refers to space in Giddens's work is that of 'locale'. This points to the use of space in the settings of interaction. A room in a house, a restaurant, a workshop or even some wider territorial area, are all examples of locales in that they link a physical location with the more institutionalised aspects of social life. That is, spaces are not only physical but social, involving typical rules of procedure, etiquette, forms of deference and authority and so on. Another crucial aspect of Giddens's schema is the 'stretching' of social relations in time and space. This is important because it refers to some of the distinctive features of modern societies.

In traditional societies much of daily social life was conducted on a face-to-face basis. In Giddens's terms, there was high 'presence availability'. As societies become much more complex in their historical development, large areas of social life are institutionalised and centralised – in short, removed from the here and now of interaction and displaced to other specialised regions and organisations. In this sense, there is an added dimension to social existence. Not only do people interact on a face-to-face daily basis, but they are influenced by much more diffuse social relations (class, ethnic, governmental, economic) which stretch away in time and space. In modern societies this stretching in time and space is of fundamental importance. Also, the development of electronic means of communication (telephones, computers) in modern societies has meant that people do not have to be physically present to each other in order to interact. The dispersion of populations and the specialisation and regionalisation that is an intrinsic feature of modernity has also meant an increase in the influence of mediated or indirect relations between people. For example, modern systems of power in these circumstances depend very much on techniques of surveillance to control and monitor the behaviour of large sectors of society. Thus, again there is an added component of social life in modernity based on the possibilities created by a decreased dependence on face-to-face interaction and general presence availability.

Power, Agency and the Dialectic of Control

Giddens is critical of the idea that we can define human action simply in terms of intentions. Sure enough, human beings have purposes and intend to do things, but this leaves out an essential feature: the capability of human beings to do things in the first place. All human action, in this sense, implies power – the capability of producing an effect. It is the ability to make a difference in and on the social world, of transforming (to some degree) the circumstances in which one finds oneself, that is perhaps the essential feature of human action.

Although all action involves power in this sense, it does not mean that people are unfettered in the things they can achieve and transform. The extent of one's influence is limited by the resources at one's disposal. Also power is relational – my power over you is to some extent dependent upon the power that you have over me – and this means that the wider context has to be taken into account.

I might have more formal authority over you and this requires that you obey my commands (as in relations in the armed forces, or a hierarchical work organisation). In other circumstances you may control my behaviour because you have a loaded gun pointed at my head.

Clearly the social context and the specific circumstances in question will tilt the power balance one way or the other. However, power is never an unlimited capacity, with one person or group holding absolute power over others who are totally powerless. Subordinates (be they individuals or groups) always have *some* resources at their disposal with which they can attempt to alter the balance of the power relationship. Babies can cry to attract the attention of their parents, prisoners can engage in 'dirty protests' or hunger strikes to put pressure on the authorities. This does not ensure that the power relation will be equalised or even turned around, but it does mean that people are never completely helpless when subject to the power and control of others. Giddens terms this phenomenon 'the dialectic of control' and suggests that it is always at work wherever power exists.

The 'dialectic' refers to the alterations in the balance of power over time and in changing circumstances as a result of the attempts by subordinate groups to use the (sometimes meagre) resources at their disposal. Giddens emphasises the importance of the dialectic of control at both the individual level (a prisoner's protest or hunger strike) as well as at the collective or group level (the development of workers' rights through protest, collective action and the evolution of citizenship rights). He does this seemingly in order to underline the fact that people are never simply the helpless playthings of social forces completely beyond their control. Giddens believes that both Parsons and Foucault are guilty of this erroneous assumption. However, for Giddens we must always remember that the relational nature of power means that it never simply flows from the wills and intentions of individuals.

Giddens's Conception of Structure

In Giddens's theory, structure does not mean anything like the same thing as it does in conventional approaches (like structural functionalism). In orthodox usage 'structure' tends to refer to the institutional features of society as opposed to the micro features of face-to-face interaction. Very often, this meaning is not distinguished from that which attaches to the term 'system', and thus the two are typically thought to refer to pretty much the same thing – the visible patterning of social relationships in society. For Giddens, 'system' refers to these latter aspects which have traditionally been thought of as institutionalised or 'macro' features (although there are still significant differences which I shall go on to mention).

Giddens defines 'structure' as rules and resources that actors draw upon as they produce and reproduce society in their activities. We have dealt with some aspects of this in talking more generally about the duality of structure and people's knowledgeability. Rules come in all shapes and sizes so to speak. Some are more explicit and codified than others (such as the rules of promotion in a bureaucratic organisation), others are unwritten and apply to the minutiae of behaviour in public settings (proper conversational distance, eye contact, mutual tact and so on). Such social rules are formulae which enable us to 'go on' in social situations even if we cannot explicitly state what the formulae are in any detail. Resources are of two main kinds. Allocative resources refer to material objects (like raw materials or land) which enable people to get things done (start a business, exert control over employees). Authoritative resources complement these and refer to non-material factors (such as status or hierarchical position) which enable command over other human beings. Resources generate power which underpins a person's ability to effect change in his or her social circumstances (their transformative capacity).

Taken together, rules and the different kinds of resources *enable* people to do things, to make a difference in the social world. Giddens argues that this aspect of structures has been down-played by conventional objectivist approaches which, instead, have focused on their *constraining* nature. Structures also generate behaviour by providing the rules and resources which fuel it. Social structures are not analogous to natural phenomena such as earthquakes or hurricanes, which may destroy towns and their inhabitants 'without their in any way being able to do anything about it' (Giddens, 1984: 181). Social structures do not 'act on' people like forces of nature to compel them to behave in any particular way. In short, 'structural constraints do not operate independently of the motives and reasons that agents have for what they do' (Giddens, 1984: 181). Human beings always have some choice in the matter, they are never absolutely compelled by social circumstances. As with the 'dialectic of control', Giddens feels that there are always *some* resources available to humans with which to act in ways that countervail social pressure.

We seem to have here a notion of structure which incorporates the good features of both humanist and structural approaches to sociology. However, closer inspection reveals that Giddens's notion of structure has much more in common with the humanist version. This is because he rejects all objectivist' notions which view structure as, in some part at least, external to activity and distinct from actors' reasons and motivations. Thus, in Giddens's sense, structure is 'internal' to activity – it has no existence beyond the situations in which people are acting. In this sense, structure does not have a continuous and tangible (real) existence. Rather, it has a 'virtual' existence, which can be understood first, as traces in the memories of the people who draw on the rules and resources that constitute it. Secondly, structure exists only at the instances in which the rules and resources are actually being employed in the activities of people. This is what Giddens means when he says that structure only exists in its 'instantiation' in human action.

Systems, Institutions and Types of Integration

By making structure something that only exists in memory traces and its actual use in behaviour, Giddens is left with the problem of accounting for the durability of social institutions over time. This is normally accounted for in the conventional notion of structure. However, Giddens makes a clear distinction here between structures and those aspects of society which have a more durable and 'observable' (real) existence. Thus, for Giddens, social systems and institutions refer to the visible patterns of social relations that have become a routine feature of society by being continually reproduced in people's behaviour. Social systems refer to reproduced practices while institutions refer to reproduced rules and resources. However, I think it is more useful to think of these as simply different aspects of the same thing – the structured pattern of social relationships (over time and space) that give societies their form and definition. This includes established practices and the power relations that underpin them.

Giddens's distinction between social and system integration helps us to understand in slightly more detail what he means by system. Social integration refers to the nature of actual encounters between people (co-presence), whereas system integration refers to relations between people (particularly collectivities) as they are stretched out over time and space and away from the immediate presence of others. This emphasis on collective aspects of society as they are 'removed' from immediate encounters seems to overlap with what is usually referred to as the institutional structure of society, that is, features such as the economy (including occupational structure), the polity, the educational system and various belief systems such as religion and morality.

A crucial difference is that, for Giddens, social structures, institutions and systems do not exist independently of the reasons, motivations and reflexive behaviour of actual people. They 'exist only insofar as they are continually produced and reproduced via the duality of structure' (Giddens, 1977: 134). As sociologists we may concentrate our attention on institutional phenomena or social systems at certain times to aid investigation (Giddens, 1984: 285) but we must never forget that institutions do not have a 'life of their own' – social life is 'made to happen' by social actors in the flow of their intentional conduct. Ontologically, then, institutions and systems only exist insofar as they are bound up with people's reasons and motivations. I think I have now covered enough of structuration theory in terms of a straightforward exposition of the main ideas. For the rest of this chapter I want to engage in a critical evaluation of the theory.

The Problem with Giddens's Definition of Structure

I think many of the problems with structuration theory stem from Giddens's novel idea of structure and the fact that he separates it from the idea of system. Basically, this seems to create more problems than it solves. The notion of structure is far too closely associated with the idea of a framework or scaffold, upon which social activity is hung and interwoven, for it to take on a radically different meaning (rules and resources). That is, it is too closely bound up with the conventional notion of social structure as the wider context of social behaviour for it to be totally redefined. This is where much confusion arises over Giddens's claims to be 'overcoming' the dualism between action and structure. If structure no longer means what it usually means, then the notion of a 'duality of structure' is confusing and misleading in that it appears to tackle the traditional problem of action and structure (as institutional context).

However, Giddens does not so much resolve the old problem as move it to one side by focusing on an entirely new problem and *its* solution. That is, Giddens abandons the conventional idea of an 'objective' social reality independent of the activities of people. Thus the problem becomes, 'How can structure be formulated as an aspect of activity itself?' The answer is that action and structure are different aspects of the same thing – social practices. In this sense, the 'old' problem is never tackled because it is no longer defined as the important issue. Now I appreciate that Giddens wants to reformulate the conventional issues entirely, but unresolved issues become hidden from view and forgotten about if one simply adopts new definitions and problems.

The Problem of the Durability of Social Systems

There is an uneasy tension between the idea that 'system' refers to the patterning of social relationships as they are stretched out over time and space, and the fact that they *only* exist in the instances in which they are created and recreated by actual people. Now there is nothing wrong with saying that social relationships and practices are produced and reproduced in the activities of people (their reasons and motivations). But there does seem to be something odd about the idea that they have no existence beyond these things. This seems to imply that reproduced practices are virtually the same thing as people's reasons and motivations. If this is so, it strongly suggests that social reality is dependent upon psychological phenomena – something which Giddens is otherwise strongly against.

There is further ambiguity in Giddens's view that the more 'institutions bite into time and space – the more resistant they are to manipulation or change by any individual agent' (1984: 171). In other words, the longer particular institutions (such as marriage) have existed in a society and the more steeped they are in the traditions, customs and laws of that society, the less easily can they be changed or disregarded by individual people. In this sense, it would appear that such institutions appear to confront individuals as pre-existing social circumstances which endure beyond the lifetimes of individuals. (We find the same emphasis in Giddens's notion of institutional time.) However, these emphases seem to pull in the direction of a more conventional notion of 'objective' structure – the idea that social systems are indeed something more than people's reasons and motivations.

It is not that people and their activities (including their reasons and motivations) are any less important than Giddens makes them out to be in the constitution of social systems. Rather, it is that social systems have more durability and independence than Giddens seems to want to admit. This tends to reduce the scope of his theory. The omission of the partly independent character of social systems means that his account of the nature of social activity tends to be skewed towards the subjective side in which people's reasons and motivations are central to the creation and replication of social systems. His account of the way in which social systems act back on people's activities is less convincing because he does not acknowledge that they have objective properties, partly independent of people's reasons and motivations.

Is the Social Landscape Flat or Contoured?

A related problem concerns the fact that Giddens distinguishes between 'structure' as rules and resources and 'system' as reproduced relations. This moves attention away from the distributive dimension of social systems which reflects a patterning of the allocation of resources. Thus, the unequal distribution of money, power, property and so on, is patterned in a specific and objectively observable manner reflecting the general power structure in society. As Eisenstadt (1985) has argued, this distributive dimension is associated with other features such as the division of labour (the occupational and organisational structure) and various integrative and regulative mechanisms (economic, political, bureaucratic, legal and cultural institutions).

Such organisational 'layers' of society become more autonomous as societies develop over time into more complex forms. This is not to deny that they are human constructions or that they can be transformed by human effort. As Eisenstadt (1985: 18) points out, although they are partly independent, such constructions are always both 'there' and fragile to varying degrees. In other words, these layers are more or less durable depending on the extent of pressure for change exerted by different groups in society. I have also made similar arguments (Layder, 1981, 1997). This approach insists there is a 'depth ontology' to society. That is, it suggests that social reality is stratified or layered according to different characteristics. Most importantly, aspects of society or social life have varying levels of distance and independence (although never complete independence) from the reasons and motivations of humans as they are employed in their behaviour.

Structuration theory, by its very nature, tends to flatten out social reality since it is only ever something which is directly and immediately implicated in the activities of human beings. It is not that Giddens does not speak of social relations over time and space, as we have seen, but he does not characterise them in terms of a depth ontology which allows for degrees of objectivity and removal from human activity. Structuration theory is thus 'thin' on the structure or institutional side of the action–structure problem. The account of social activity in structuration theory is far more dense and rounded (Giddens even speaks of a stratification model of the actor) than it is with regard to social structure.

Furthermore, 'dualism' tends to re-emerge in structuration theory in Giddens's distinction between social integration and system integration (which is intended to replace the macro–micro dualism). Clearly, the dualism between social and system integration deals with a real difference between face-to-face encounters and social relations which may never involve the mutual presence of the people involved (an ordinary citizen's relationship with a monarch or head of state, or a customer's relationship with the owner of their bank). It seems that the distinction between social and system integration reasserts a fundamental dualism inherent in social reality, rather than denies it.

A similar issue arises over what Giddens calls 'methodological bracketing'. This refers to the extent to which we can put to one side aspects of the duality of structure when it comes to empirical research. Thus, when we are analysing an institution or a type of society, we may 'bracket out', or leave to one side, the question of the way in which people produce and reproduce them in their daily activities. Conversely, when we are analysing the strategic activities of people in a particular setting, we may leave aside the analysis of the institutional context. Giddens insists that this is simply a methodological device that enables us to focus our attention on the topic at hand, and that 'in principle' each should be 'rounded-out with a concentration on the duality of structure' (1984: 288). However, the very fact that it is possible to concentrate attention on either 'institutional analysis' or 'the analysis of strategic conduct' seems to suggest that these represent rather different aspects of social reality, even though we might also accept that they are interdependent and interwoven.

Structure Versus Habitus

What Giddens means by 'structure' has a lot in common (although there are differences) with Bourdieu's (1977) notion of 'habitus' and I cannot help but think that greater clarity would be gained for structuration theory by adopting a similar term. This would clearly separate it from the conventional notion of structure (and system) and eliminate some of the confusion caused by the overlapping of the two terms. Bourdieu's conception of 'habitus' refers to the basic stock of knowledge that people carry around in their heads as a result of living in particular cultures or subcultures. Thus a person coming from a working-class background will carry the 'influence' of that environment into her or his behaviour (for example, in terms of local knowledge, type of speech pattern, type of attitude towards marriage and so on – see Bott, 1957; Bernstein, 1973).

Habitus is the set of 'dispositions' that feeds into a person's anticipations about what they want and what they can achieve in their interpersonal relations. For example, a middle-class person will typically feel more at ease than would a working-class person when dealing with authority figures such as teachers or lawyers, because of shared values, life experiences and educational background. In the same way, Giddens speaks of the rules and resources that people draw upon with his notion of structure. In Giddens's and Bourdieu's concepts there is a common reference to the fact that these dispositions are not consciously talked about, they are simply brought into a person's behaviour without them really being aware of their influence. Giddens refers to this as 'mutual knowledge' or, in other words, being able to, or knowing how to 'go on' in any particular encounter.

There is another similarity in that habitus is the means through which people produce and reproduce the social circumstances in which they live. This makes it similar to Giddens's idea about structures being both the medium and the outcome of activity. However, Bourdieu is much more inclined to view social circumstances in the more conventional 'objective' sense of structures and institutions than is the case in structuration theory. Correspondingly, Bourdieu views human behaviour in a more mechanical and 'determined' manner than Giddens, insofar as it is always conditioned by the habitus. This is where the comparison begins to break down. In Giddens's work the human actor is allowed much more freedom to be transformative and creative within the social environment. As we have seen, for Giddens, human beings are agents in the social world by virtue of their ability to make a difference; that is, their ability to exert power.

How Much Creativity and How Much Constraint?

Giddens often seems so concerned to break away from the deterministic implications of conventional theories of structure, that sometimes he seems to overstate the degree to which people are free and unfettered by social conditions. He constantly emphasises that structures *enable* as well as constrain behaviour. In this sense, structure is implicated in people's freedom of action as much as it is in the limitations that it imposes on their behaviour. Certainly, at specific points in his work, Giddens has emphasised the creative component of human action at the expense of the conforming aspects. However, Giddens has also shifted his position on this. For example in his *Sociology: A Brief but Critical Introduction* (1981a: 14), he states that 'we create society at the same time as we are created by it' (see also 1976: 123 for a similar statement), whereas in a later work he says 'it is not the case that actors create social systems; they reproduce and transform them, remaking what is already made' (1984: 171).

In the light of the shifting connotations that he associates with human creativity, it is no surprise that his notion of constraint has been subject to the criticism that it is rather weak and underdeveloped. (Layder, 1981, 1997; Archer, 1982, 1995; Craib, 1992). Very often, Giddens's concern to break away from objectivism leads him to overstate the case against it. He believes that all forms of objectivism are tainted with the same flaws as are associated with both functionalism and the idea that the social sciences are exactly like the natural sciences. However, we do not have to accept these latter ideas (flawed as they are) in order to accept that society has more or less objective components, and that these influence activity in both an internal and external way (Layder, 1987, 1989, 1997). In this sense, there is a case to be made that Giddens underplays the objective force of structural constraints insofar as he suggests that they only exist in the reasons and motivations of actors.

This notion of constraint does not adequately capture the sense in which we are 'compelled' to do things by external social forces at the same time as we may consciously decide that we want to do them. For example, in order to become a university lecturer a person has to study to obtain a first degree, then a doctorate, pass an interview to demonstrate competence and so on. Such requirements are 'external' social requirements and, as such, anyone who wishes to become a university lecturer is 'compelled' to take them into account. In this case, the person decides to conform because they value the attainment of this particular goal. He or she is not 'compelled' to become a university lecturer, but in order to become one the person is 'compelled' to conform to certain requirements. With Giddens's vehement rejection of objectivism there is a certain sense in which structuration theory seriously underplays the compulsion inherent in social life. Giddens attempts to stave off criticism that his theory over-emphasises freedom of action and people's ability to transform their circumstances by suggesting two things. One is that the extent of people's freedom and 'transformative capacities' depends on the particular circumstances in question. The greater the entrenchment of forms of domination the less possibility there will be of changing things. Secondly, at various points in the vast body of work on structuration theory, Giddens simply emphasises the idea that people do not create society, they only reproduce what is already there.

However, this seems to run counter to the idea that people are inherently creative and transformative in their activities. If people are not 'producing' or constructing social reality but merely following conventional patterns, then surely their behaviour cannot be said to be particularly creative and certainly not transformative. Much rides on what is meant exactly by the term 'creative', and one can accept that even the following of conventional routines and patterns of behaviour involves the application of knowledge, skills and resources in a 'creative' fashion. However, this is a far cry from the idea that the routines and patterns of social relations are being transformed in the process.

Self-Identity and Society

In his later work (1990, 1991), Giddens has begun to concentrate on the problem of self-identity in the late modern world, tackling an area which was rather underplayed in the earlier work. In this sense, there seems to be a movement into a new agenda of problems in Giddens's work as a whole. Of course there is also continuity and the foray into the nature of self-identity can be seen as a filling-in of some blank spots in structuration theory. Giddens notes what he calls 'the reflexive nature of self-identity', which refers to the fact that in the modern world the self is constantly revisable in the light of circumstances (for example, after a divorce the parting couple will each try to develop more 'independent' selves). This produces a 'narrative' and theme for the individual's sense of self which follows their biographical story-line.

As Craib (1992) notes, structuration theory offers a view of the person as lacking emotional responses and a healthy disregard for the routines of social life. It is true that Giddens does tend to emphasise the trusting and altruistic side of social life as a basis for ontological security and the building of routines. In this sense, his borrowing from Goffman's work has a rather one-sided concentration on the importance of basic trust in social relations, rather than the darker side of manipulation and self-interest (which, incidentally, can also be glimpsed in Goffman's work).

But even greater problems attend the more general synthesis of activity and structure that is proposed by structuration theory – as I have tried to indicate in the previous section. Specifically, Giddens's flattening of the ontological terrain of society – his one-dimensional vision of social reality – poses far greater difficulties for the theory in its effort to grasp the complexity of social phenomena. By way of reinforcing this view, it is interesting to note that

Giddens puts forward a 'stratification model' of the human agent (that is, different levels of emotion, understanding and awareness) but is unwilling to do the same in relation to society. In my view, structuration theory's grasp of the complexity of human activity is not matched by an equivalent appreciation of social-structural depth.

Structuration Theory and Empirical Research

Despite certain problems with Giddens's theory, I feel that it represents an immensely positive contribution to the debate about action and structure and the macro–micro link. One of its great strengths in this regard is its potential for empirical application. Some critics have suggested that structuration theory is a 'typical' piece of abstract theorising that has no particular relevance to real world issues. As a consequence, it has been implied that it does not help in the construction of empirical research problems. In my opinion this kind of criticism is misplaced and ill-founded. We have to appreciate that general theories like this relate to the empirical world in rather different ways from those that are more closely focused on empirical problems. Thus, applying this kind of theory to empirical research will, perhaps, involve extra effort or ingenuity – at least initially – than is usual in such circumstances.

It is certainly wrong to imply or state that structuration theory is not suggestive of empirical research problems or that it does not lend itself to applied research since many pieces of empirical research have used it or called upon it (or various aspects of it). Giddens's own views in this regard are instructive insofar as he does not envisage its wholesale application to research problems (1983). Rather, he sees the theory as a set of 'sensitising' concepts which may aid in the initial formulation of research or in illuminating the findings in some way.

However, it is important to bear in mind that the use of any single concept from the theory in a research project must be done with at least one eye on the wider context of structuration theory as a whole. Otherwise, particular ideas may be misused or 'forced' to play an alien role in projects that have little bearing on the theoretical issues. It is to Giddens's credit that he has construed structuration theory in a non-dogmatic and flexible manner, since it aids incorporation into research and does not impose a 'total world view' which is, unfortunately, often the case with general theories.

Balancing Agency and Structure

Apart from its empirical viability and openness, structuration theory is undoubtedly correct about certain theoretical issues. Giddens is right to emphasise that we must move away from the idea that action and structure are separate and unrelated mutually opposing entities, and towards the understanding that they are deeply implicated in each other. In this respect, I endorse Giddens's argument against the 'phoney war' between adherents of interpretative versus structural schools of thought within sociology and the entrenched dogmas that they defend. There has to be some way of bringing the two together which enables us to capitalise on the strengths of both approaches and to jettison their weaknesses. Giddens must be credited with attempting to do this while withstanding the temptation to abandon the 'traditional' terms of reference altogether. As we have seen with Foucault and Elias, this strategy is not without its costs in terms of lack of continuity and incompleteness.

One of the most compelling features of structuration theory as compared with those of Foucault and Elias, is its refusal to abandon a concern with the notion of human agency. In Foucault's work, one effect of a radical decentring of the subject is to create an image of social forces as seeming to 'float in space', without anchorage in human activity. This is too great a price to pay for an escape from subjectivism and psychological reductionism. Giddens's work demonstrates the weaknesses involved in Foucault's dissolution and absorption of the individual into the play of general social forces. Also, Giddens's rather more rounded characterisation of social activities (drawing on the work of Goffman, Garfinkel and Wittgenstein in the process) underlines the lack of subtlety and precision of Elias's notion of figuration.

It could be argued that the main strength of structuration theory is its concern with the individual in social analysis. In their zeal to break free and burn bridges, other authors have neglected fundamental problems of human agency. The agency–structure dualism, more than anything else, animates structuration theory. Of course, it must be appreciated that the agency–structure problem shades into, and overlaps, the individual–society problem. By talking of human agency we are highlighting the degree to which individuals are capable of changing the circumstances in which they find themselves and of responding creatively to social constraints. By contrasting it with structure we are attending to the way in which the social context moulds and shapes activity and behaviour. (It must be remembered that these are the definitions I have focused on, and that some theorists have spoken of agency in relation to collective phenomena and structure as referring to micro phenomena.)

The very notion of agency draws attention to the fact that human beings are not simply hapless victims of social circumstance. The agency–structure problem is concerned with their interdependence. Giddens's work represents the view that agency and structure are mutually constituted, that they cannot be understood as separate entities in any sense. In this respect his work has many affinities with that of other sociologists whose work falls within the same synthetic tradition: Bourdieu (1977), Bauman (1973), even Berger and Luckmann (1967). Giddens is strong on highlighting those aspects of human agency which express the powers of human beings to transform their social circumstances. Whether understood in the minor sense of changing the course of a conversation in a casual encounter, or in a more spectacular manner as revolutionary action, this ability reflects the intrinsic powers of human beings as social agents.

Giddens is careful to suggest that human agency is always conditioned by a dialectic of control. That is, power is always embedded in reciprocal social relations and this implies the formation of compromises and balances restricting the ability to impose one's will. This is, perhaps, the greatest strength of structuration theory – its attempt to incorporate the full force of the human ability to make a difference in the social world while recognising the limitations imposed by the social context. There are problems with Giddens's construal of this, particularly the idea that people's reasons and motivations play such a prominent role in our understanding of society in general. But I shall come back to this in a moment. In another way, structuration theory is an advance on post-structuralist and post-modernist thought. Giddens does give human beings some 'depth' while preserving their individuality, and this is evidenced in his 'stratification model' of the human agent (the unconscious, and practical and discursive awareness).

Compared with Foucault and Elias, Giddens's work affords greater continuity between the problems of orthodox sociology and his proposed alternative – structuration theory. Despite the vast differences in their work, Foucault, Elias and the ethnomethodologists (Hilbert in particular) all tend to break with orthodox theories without advancing adequate reasons for ignoring the problems that traditional approaches tried to resolve. These anti-dualists seem to assume an almost magical synthesis of the middle ground without actually explaining the mechanics of bringing agency and structure together. First, the slate is wiped clean by rejecting existing approaches, and then, in the vacuum so created, they offer their alternative visions which are designed to replace the rejected orthodoxy. Giddens does not proceed in this manner. He carefully picks over the bones of both structural (institutional) and interpretative theories, saving what he can to incorporate into his alternate vision.

Of course, what he produces by way of a synthesis 'goes beyond' what has gone before, and in this sense his work competes with others to sustain a certain vision of society and social activity. More than anything else, this central image is enshrined in the notion of the 'duality of structure' which expresses the mutual constitution of activity and institutions – their inherent inseparability. As I said earlier, this is the point at which certain critical questions arise. Giddens seems to have provided a way out of the dilemma of choosing agency or structure as the more important focus of analysis. This takes us beyond the phoney war between proponents who insist on the priority of one or the other side of the dualism. He insists that both sides are seamlessly bound together and that social analysis must acknowledge this 'reality' (this is the point of his claim to be describing the ontological features of social life). However, the contentious issues arise over what we make of this claim. How do we interpret it?

In one sense the idea of the mutual implication of action and structure provides us with a powerful and adequate grasp of the continuous interrelations of agency and structure in social life. Institutions cannot be understood entirely independently of the social activities that brought them into existence in the first place. Similarly, social activity is the lifeblood of institutions – it ensures their continuity in time. The opposite is equally true. Face-to-face behaviour is always to some degree stamped by the wider institutional backdrop against which it takes place. It is not just a question of what is happening in the here and now, as if social encounters could be divorced from wider institutional influences. It is on the question of exactly how this 'mutual implication' can be understood, not only as a theoretical model but also as an adequate account of empirical reality, that my differences with Giddens are based.

Critical Problems in Structuration Theory

First, agency and structure in structuration theory tend to be merged in a rather 'biased' manner. In Giddens's terms, the idea that agency and structure have distinct identities is the result of 'false' dualistic thinking. In reality, action and structure merge imperceptibly into one another. One of the apparent advantages of this model is that it seems to provide a 'balance' between the mutual influences of agency and structure. However, Giddens's insistence that structure can never be separated from people's reasons and motivations reveals a tendency to emphasise agency rather than structure. While there are other places in which he seems to suggest that structures are something more, he nevertheless predominantly insists that structures have no existence apart from actor's reasons and motivations and their employment in particular instances of activity. This heavy weighting of motives and activity means generally that structural elements become rather understated in his theory.

Secondly, Giddens over-emphasises impermanence and continuous process in social life and thus understates the relative durability of structural patterns and elements. A corollary of Giddens's overwhelming concern to incorporate agency, reasons and motivations and the transformative capacities of people is a concern with process and impermanence as a basic fact of social life. For Giddens, people are not helpless victims of ineluctable social forces. It is a mistake to think of social forces as if they were natural phenomena in the face of which people have no choice. For Giddens, social forces are quite unlike earthquakes, for example, whose effects compel people to act in certain ways – they cannot act otherwise. In the social world, people do make choices based on their reasons and motives, and are continually involved in changing and moulding the social circumstances in which they find themselves. This is his point about there being no structure (or system) in social life apart from the social activities of the people who constitute them. Thus there is nothing static about the forms of social life; they are constantly changing and being rearranged through the productive activities of people.

This motif of impermanence relies heavily on the ethnomethodological idea (and is consistent with some symbolic interactionist ideas) that society is a continual accomplishment of individuals. Now Giddens does not want to suggest, as some ethnomethodologists do, that structures and systems do not have an important role to play in social analysis. However, he does insist that structures do not have any independent characteristics and that they are in no sense external to people. Thus it is difficult within the terms of structuration theory, to capture the sense in which structural characteristics endure over time. While it is important to stress that social institutions are not permanent in any absolute sense, because they are, after all, human constructs, it is equally important not to go to the other extreme by suggesting that they are in a constant state of flux. Giddens comes dangerously close to this conclusion by offering us an image of modern society as less than solid and in a state of constant reconstruction.

The motif of impermanence arises, I think, from two sources. First, Giddens's uncompromising rejection of functionalism, with its implication that social systems are beyond the reach of people in their everyday lives – that they have lives of their own, so to speak. Secondly, the image derives from an empirical observation based on Giddens's experience in California in the 1960s. Scott (1992) suggests that Giddens's experience and perception of California around the time of the hippie movement led him to be struck by the theatricality of modernity. He quotes Giddens to the effect that these observations led to the conclusion that 'the world was nothing like as solid as it appeared'. Scott then goes on to comment that 'very many subtle thoughts have flowed from that single observation'.

I think this is a very revealing insight into the basic assumptions and imagery that underlie structuration theory. It correctly underscores the gap that Giddens sees between his own work and the objectivist traditions (functionalism and orthodox structuralist sociology) which he so vehemently rejects. These latter approaches to social analysis have stressed the overarching hold that objective structures (be they of domination or mechanisms of integration) have over the lives of seemingly hapless members of society. In my view, the conviction that this 'model' of society must be resisted at all costs has led Giddens to over-emphasise the weaknesses of objectivism and to neglect its potentially useful aspects. Giddens's work is thus driven away from the notion of society as a coherent and relatively enduring structural pattern, somewhat independent of the reasons and motives of most people. The idea that there is a structural domain that has varying degrees of independence from the routine everyday lives of people is lost in structuration theory. As a result, the idea that creativity and change produced in face-to-face conduct is contoured and bounded by definite structural parameters is somewhat compromised by Giddens's insistence on the inherently transformative capabilities of human beings.

This takes us into a third problem area in structuration theory – its inability to allow for the assessment of the impact of different social orders. Insofar as action and structure are mutually constitutive, it is difficult to prise them apart in order to understand the nature of their interplay and the contribution that each makes in different circumstances. In short, it is difficult to analyse the way in which structural features may predominate in certain areas at certain times, while the creative and transformative activities of people may come to the fore at certain other times and places. The notion of the simultaneous constitution of action and structure hinders one's ability to assess the relative impact or influence of the different social orders.

It also tends to compact their effects into one time frame (instances of ongoing conduct), rather than seeing structural conditions as constructed orders that exist prior to the ongoing activities and which are the immediate focus of activity. It is not that activity has no organic link with institutional structure. Certainly, activity reproduces these structures in an ongoing manner, but the time frame involved in face-to-face encounters is rather different from that involved in institutions, which often continue over many generations. Now Giddens is aware of such differences in time scale and indeed distinguishes between the lifetime of individuals, the *durée* of daily conduct and the *longue durée* of institutions (Giddens, 1987). However, the point is that to really appreciate the difference created by these time frames we have to prise apart structural conditions and ongoing conduct in a way that creates the very dualism that Giddens seeks to avoid.

Finally, structuration theory has a certain absorbency and flexibility that allows it to accommodate seemingly contradictory elements (as in the case of different time frames compacted into one through the mutual constitution idea, and reinforced by the notion that structure only exists insofar as it is instantiated in conduct). In this respect, the overriding problem for Giddens is to keep the mutuality of action and structure together while at the same time reserving the right to talk about them separately in a conventional sense. This is no more apparent than in his notion of 'methodological bracketing', whereby it is possible to concentrate on either 'strategic activity' or 'institutional analysis' in social research. This caveat is inserted into the research implications of structuration theory in order to overcome the difficulty of concentrating on both at the same time.

However, the notion of methodological bracketing has two principal effects. First, it ensures that structuration theory is compatible with both interactionist and structural theories (including those objectivist versions that Giddens otherwise rejects). Secondly, it preserves a link with the dualism that structuration theory appears so strongly to eschew. This is because the methodological 'holding apart' of structure and action simply reaffirms the importance of preserving a substantive distinction between them (Layder, 1987, 1989). It seems to underline the efficacy of talking about different social orders while set within the context of a theory that endeavours to rid social analysis of the pernicious effects of dualism. Of course, to preserve the dominant logic of the theory, Giddens can only tinker with the possibilities of dualism through a methodological backdoor. In the final analysis, the principle of duality has to be preserved. In this sense, the theory of structuration misses out on some of the more interesting features of dualistic thinking which allow for the coupling of different orders.

SUMMARY

- In structuration theory, Giddens uses the concept of 'the duality of structure' in an attempt to overcome the agency–structure and macro–micro dualisms. Although he wants to break free of dualistic approaches, his ideas represent more of a dialogue with alternative 'conventional' approaches than do those of Elias or Foucault.

- According to Giddens, the subject matter of sociology cannot be treated as independent and objective 'facts'. People are instrinsically involved in society – they are skilled and knowledgeable and actively enter into the constitution of social life.

- Giddens rejects the idea that sociology should model itself on the natural sciences (naturalism). He also rejects the 'objectivism' associated with naturalism as well as 'functionalist' theories (as in Parsons's work) which suggest that social systems have properties of their own independently of actors' wants and reasons.

- Giddens claims that sociology should be more concerned with ontological questions, such as what is the nature of social activity or social life, rather than epistemological questions concerning the validity of our knowledge. Although, seemingly, this a practical suggestion, Giddens does not sufficiently take into account the fact that questions about the nature of reality always involve epistemological concerns about the validity and adequacy of social theories.

- Giddens wants to overcome the phoney war between institutional analysis and interpretative analysis which represent many associated and 'unnecessary' dualisms in social theory.

- Instead of dualism we should think in terms of a 'duality of structure'. In this formulation, structure and action are intrinsically related to each other (two sides of the same coin) through social practices.

- Social practices reflect the ability of humans to modify their circumstances while simultaneously recreating the social conditions (practices, knowledge, resources) inherited from the past. This is what Giddens terms the 'recursive' nature of social life, in which structure is understood as both the *medium* and *outcome* of social activity.

- Humans have different levels of awareness and consciousness – unconscious, practical consciousness and discursive consciousness. They are connected to skillfulness and knowledgeability in humans and their ability to reflexively monitor their own conduct.

- Basic ontological security (a person's elemental sense of safety and his or her trust in others) is secured through social routines. In different types of society different dimensions of time and space are involved in routine encounters and daily existence. In traditional societies there is 'high presence availability' – social life is conducted on a face-to-face basis – whereas in modern societies social relations are stretched over time and space and involve technologies of surveillance.

- All human action implies power – the capability of making a difference in the world. Giddens often refers to this as the 'transformative capacity' of human agency. In any power relationship there is a 'dialectic of control', in which subordinates always have *some* resources at their disposal.

- Giddens defines 'structure' as 'rules and resources' that actors draw upon to shape their conduct. Structures *enable* people to do things as much as they constrain behaviour. Structure is internal to activity (Giddens rejects the idea of an objective external structure). Structures are not 'real', they have a 'virtual' existence as people's memory traces and thus they only exist insofar as they are instantiated in human action.

- 'Social systems' refer to reproduced practices, but like structures they only exist insofar as they are continually produced and reproduced through the duality of structure.

- Because Giddens proposes a radically different conception of structure from the traditional one, he really doesn't solve the existing agency–structure problem. Rather, he moves the problem to one side and focuses on a newly conceived problem – 'How can structure be understood as an aspect of activity?' Giddens's concept of structure seems to have more in common with Bourdieu's notion of 'habitus' than it has with the traditional concept of structure.

- Giddens tends to over-emphasise the importance of reasons, motives and activity – the subjective side of social life – and thus under-emphasises the durability and independence of social systems. Giddens rejects a layered view of society – a depth ontology – by rejecting objectivism out of hand. Paradoxically, however, his notion of 'methodological bracketing' seems to endorse a major distinction in social reality between 'institutional analysis' and the analysis of 'strategic activity'.

- Structuration theory also tends to underplay the degree of compulsion and constraint in social life.

- In later work, Giddens begins to concentrate on the problem of self-identity but adopts a rather 'rational' view of the actor underplaying important emotional aspects.

- Giddens regards structuration theory as a set of 'sensitizing concepts' to aid in the initial formulation of research or in illuminating the findings of research.

- Giddens's refusal to abandon a concern with human agency is to his credit, but he doesn't achieve a satisfactory balance between the mutual influence of agency and structure – structural elements become rather understated in structuration theory. Within the terms of the theory it is difficult to understand the interplay between agency and structure and to assess their relative contributions in particular instances.

- Giddens's theory misses out on some of the interesting and productive features of dualistic thinking and more moderate forms of objectivism. Thus his theory doesn't envisage multiple domains of social reality and the important connections between them.

part four

only connect:
forging links

Introduction

In this last part of the book I examine the work of a number of authors who have developed their theories in the context of a distinction between two orders (or levels) of society. These are (loosely, because I do not mean to imply that there is definite agreement on terms) an 'interaction order' (including the world of everyday life, or interpersonal encounters, in short, the micro world) and an 'institutional order' (including 'social systems' and structures – general features of the macro world). In this sense they could be said to be working *within* the tradition of dualism rather than *against* it (as was the case with the authors in Part 3). This should not be taken to imply that these authors see no problems with dualism. Rather, it means that whatever problems do exist are thought to be fundamentally about how to connect the two orders. So, unlike those in Part 3, these authors wish to establish links between the two orders rather than to break them down and reconstitute social analysis in a radically different form.

As I hinted at the end of the previous chapter, although this broad, common objective serves to group these writers together, it is merely the starting point and basis upon which many differences of opinion begin to emerge about the exact means of bringing the two orders together, and the links that are forged as a consequence. The strategies and solutions to these problems proposed by this group are many and extremely varied. I have tried to bring some order to this material by identifying what I take to be the most important and distinctive approaches on offer. In Chapter 9 I have taken as a theme the diversity of views that are possible regarding the linkages between macro and micro levels of analysis. While some authors appear to be rather ambiguous about the exact linkage, they nonetheless stress the importance of interweaving the two levels. Others, while recognising the existence of both macro and micro orders, have a definite preference for one or the other. This is born out of basic theoretical assumptions held by the authors concerned such that they believe (for what they take to be sound theoretical reasons) that one or the other order has priority in terms of explanatory importance.

In the first section of Chapter 9 I briefly review Pierre Bourdieu's theory of practice and Dorothy Smith's feminist approach to the analysis of everyday life. These two are what I call 'intermediate cases' in that they have definite affinities with those who wish to break free and burn bridges with dualism while at the same time they operate with a distinction between external structures and situated conduct. In the same chapter I discuss some of the ideas of Jeffrey Alexander and Richard Munch. Although they have produced quite distinct bodies of work they are both associated with neofunctionalism. This up-dated version of Parsons's systems theory attempts to plug the gaps and resolve some of the problems implicit in the original work. Both Alexander and Munch emphasise the necessity for bringing together what Munch (1987) calls action theory and systems theory. They also recognise the importance of the contributions that action theory has made (and must continue to make) towards this project. However, their work gives a central place to macro, collective phenomena as setting the conditions and terms under which social action (the interaction order) takes place.

In the final section of Chapter 9 I discuss Randall Collins's work, especially his notion of 'interaction-ritual chains', which is quite opposed to the 'macro-downwards' approach to social interaction evident in Alexander and Munch's neofunctionalism. Collins takes a quite contrary position which gives priority to the micro world of interpersonal encounters as a basis for a general understanding of society and our experiences of social life. Collins believes that there are very few things in social life that could be said to possess a 'macro' existence. Those things which are generally described by sociologists as macro features (power structures, money, property, class and so on) are, according to Collins, simply aggregations or clusterings of micro interactions. Thus, all macro 'variables' are capable of translation into micro terms.

In this sense, the micro world is seen to be the primary 'reality' to which the sociologist must attend. There are many other authors who adopt a similar position believing that interactionist and phenomenological schools of thought have substantiated the primacy of the micro beyond all doubt. (For example, see the selection of arguments in Knorr-Cetina and Cicourel, 1981.) However, I believe that Collins's work is the most sophisticated and original in this respect and thus is the strongest exemplar of this position. Of course, I have fundamental disagreements with Collins's position in general, but there are aspects of it that I find useful and suggestive.

Chapter 10 considers the work of Jürgen Habermas in relation to the macro–micro issue. Habermas's output has been prodigious but my discussion is selective, focusing in particular on his massive two-volume work *The Theory of Communicative Action* (1986, 1987). In this, Habermas elaborates on a distinction which first appeared in his earlier work, that of the 'lifeworld' and the 'system'. Again, this represents a distinction between different orders of social reality although Habermas's formulation departs somewhat from the macro–micro distinction as used by the other authors mentioned in this part of the book. Furthermore, Habermas does not just see this as a generic distinction applicable to the analysis of contemporary society. The distinction between lifeworld and system has to be understood in the context of his wider views on social evolutionary development. The emergence and uncoupling of the system from the lifeworld is a decisive moment in social development and sets the scene for the subsequent 'colonisation' of the lifeworld by the demands imposed by the social system.

Habermas's theory is an intriguing attempt to marry systems theory with action theory (notably aspects of symbolic interactionism). Insofar as it is an attempt to develop a comprehensive general theory it can be compared with Giddens's work on structuration. Of course there are profound differences, not the least of which is Habermas's recognition of the central importance of distinguishing between the intersubjective world of everyday life and the objective world of systems revolving around the partly independent workings of money and power. There are certain rigidities and over-elaborations in the theory of communicative action and a ready grasp of the work as a whole is not helped by Habermas's general stylistic inaccessibility. Nevertheless, it does provide some essential ingredients for a full and adequate understanding of the macro–micro connection.

In Chapter 11, I deal with the work of four authors who, in rather different ways, defend versions of dualism. They believe that the distinctions between agency and structure and macro and micro should be preserved and acknowledged with a view to achieving a better understanding of their different properties and how, precisely, they are linked with and reciprocally influence each other. However, each of the authors (Erving Goffman, Jonathan Turner, Nicos Mouzelis and Margaret Archer) hold very different views on the exact nature of the links between agency and structure and macro and micro levels of analysis, even though they are all broadly committed to dualism as a general principle.

In the final chapter I discuss my own 'theory of social domains', which has certain affinities with the work of several of the authors already discussed in Part 4. However, domain theory also charts its own course in dealing with the individual–society, agency–structure and macro–micro dualisms and the problems they pose for social analysis. In particular, the theory of social domains attempts to go beyond 'analytic dualism'. It does so by recognising that social reality is multidimensional and constituted by four principal domains that are interlinked and reciprocally influential. By understanding agency–structure links against this background of 'ontological variety', many of the theoretical problems associated with dualism can be tackled on a firmer basis.

9

Linking Agency and Structure and Macro and Micro

PREVIEW

- This chapter reviews the work of a number of authors who, in rather different ways, try to link the agency–structure and macro–micro dualisms instead of 'breaking free and burning bridges'.

- Pierre Bourdieu's 'theory of practice' attempts to link the analysis of objective social relations with that of social agency through the concept of 'habitus'.

- The feminist theory of Dorothy Smith explores women's experience from the standpoint of women.

- Jeffrey Alexander's work on the reality of collective phenomena and the neofunctionalist (Parsonian) approach represented by the work of Richard Munch.

- Randall Collins's notion of the 'micro-translation' of macro phenomena.

As I have suggested there is a wide diversity of writing that tries to link macro and micro levels in rather different ways. This means that at the margins there are theorists who represent intermediate positions between those who wish to burn bridges and break free of dualism, and those who unequivocally adopt a strategy of linkage rather than dissolution. In the opening sections of this chapter I discuss the work of two such authors who otherwise have little in common in terms of the substance and intentions behind their work. The first is Pierre Bourdieu, whose work I briefly mentioned in the previous chapter on Giddens. Here I expand a little on his theory of practice. I suggest that his work has a great deal in common with Giddens's but that there are important differences. It is these differences which endow Bourdieu's work with its ambiguous relation to the dualism debate.

The same applies to Dorothy Smith's work. In one sense she is definitely against dualism, but in another she employs a distinction between levels of social reality. Next I discuss the work of two neofunctionalist writers who are clearly more attuned to identifying and accounting for the links between micro and macro phenomena. Both Jeffrey Alexander and Richard Munch owe much to the work of Parsons and, perhaps not surprisingly, their work tends to underscore the importance of the macro world of social systems. After this I examine the opposing position which is reflected in the work of Randall Collins who suggests that we should give theoretical priority to the micro world. There are problems with positions which emphasise the priority of either macro or micro orders; nevertheless, this work illuminates various aspects of the relationship between the two orders.

Bourdieu's Theory of Practice

In exactly the same sense as Giddens (and Elias) Bourdieu is against the false oppositions which have shaped theoretical thinking about the social world. Oppositions such as objectivism–subjectivism, freedom–determinism (and many others) must be broken down in order to understand how the reality of people's activities (he prefers the term practice) is an amalgam of many influences. Again, like Giddens, he stresses that structural theories (like those of Parsons and Althusser) seem to operate with a view of social processes as if they were detached from, and independent of people's activities. This simply leads to a view of social behaviour (as in role theory) whereby it is treated as a mechanical outcome of objective social relations. On the other hand, interactionist and phenomenological theories seem to treat social activity as if it emanated from within social situations untouched by any more encompassing social relations.

Both approaches are flawed because they reduce behaviour to one or other of these extremes and thus miss the truth of the overlapping middle way. Bourdieu suggests that the two orders are tied together through actual social practices, wherein objective social relations are produced and reproduced within particular situations. In this respect Bourdieu is fairly similar to Giddens. However, there is a sense in which Bourdieu's theory is less confusing than Giddens's. This is because Bourdieu retains the idea that there is such a thing as an objective world which is different from the world of situated behaviour, whereas Giddens insists that they are simply different aspects of the same thing (the duality of structure). Also, Bourdieu retains in this sense the traditional definition of structure as the external social context of behaviour. Thus he tries to theoretically account for the links between action and structure by introducing the notion of 'habitus' which I discussed in the chapter on Giddens.

Habitus refers to the durable set of dispositions which we carry around in our heads as social actors as a result of our social experience in certain kinds of backgrounds and circumstances (class, language, ethnicity, gender and so on). Our experience in certain social settings and circumstances predisposes us to approach the world with the knowledge and interactional resources that we have acquired in those circumstances. Thus habitus is a cognitive and motivating mechanism which incorporates the influence of a person's social context and provides a conduit or medium through which information and resources are transmitted to the activities that they inform. Thus the mutual influences of objective context and the immediate situations of activity are translated back and forth through the medium of the habitus. While the habitus sets the wider parameters of a person's activities, people have also to be understood as creative beings. In particular situations people have to 'improvise' on background resources (of the habitus) in order to be able to deal with the unpredictable situations that are a constant feature of everyday life.

The habitus plays much the same role as the notion of structure in Giddens's work, as I pointed out in the previous chapter. It represents the resources that people draw on to make activity happen, but at the same time limits its potential. Thus it is the key mechanism which interweaves the creativity of individuals with their direct involvement in the reproduction of structural resources. Bourdieu's notion of habitus does have a definite advantage over Giddens's notion of structure, because Bourdieu makes clear distinctions between the external context of activity, the immediate situational circumstances, and habitus which acts as a conduit between them. In Giddens's theory the notion of an external context is not properly defined because of his insistence that there is no level of reality in social life beyond people's reasons and motivations.

It is interesting here to see how the different dualisms of agency–structure and macro–micro play slightly different roles in Bourdieu's work. Habitus refers very definitely to the agency–structure dualism since it is the pivot around which the production and reproduction of society is accomplished. In this sense, the opposition between agency and structure is abandoned (as it is in Giddens), and seemingly transcended. However, because Bourdieu makes a clear distinction between the context and the situational circumstances of social practices, the distinction between macro and micro as different levels of social reality is upheld. This is a more satisfactory position than Giddens's, since it does not entirely rule out the value of objectivism as a form of social analysis. It only rules out those versions which insist on the complete autonomy of objective social relations.

Having said this, however, there are a number of drawbacks to Bourdieu's proposals, some of which are similar to those associated with structuration theory. First, Bourdieu does not give enough attention to the emergent properties of particular situations, since these cannot be read off from structural resources nor from the unique abilities of individuals to be creative. As we have already seen (Chapters 4 and 5), they emerge from the dynamics of encounters which draw together the inputs of several actors, producing an unanticipated outcome. This 'webbing' of behavioural strategies is a result of the situational circumstances of the activities in question as well as the influences of what Goffman calls the 'interaction order' (see Chapter 11). In this sense, Bourdieu overlooks the independent contribution of the interaction order as a domain in its own right.

This omission results from Bourdieu's over-emphasis on the way in which habitus ties together the influences and effects of agency and structure. While, as we have noted, Bourdieu takes objective structures more seriously, ultimately their fate is pretty much the same as in structuration theory. They tend to be dissolved into activity since they cannot exist except in the actual practices that reproduce them. This makes it very difficult to understand social systems as patterns of domination which endure and have effects beyond the situations of their actual implication in practice. Thus, wide-ranging and variegated fields of influence such as gender, class, power and organisation, existing at different levels of closeness to activity and producing variable effects on practice, tend to be compacted into a flattened-out social terrain. Agency and structure are intrinsically linked through habitus and expressed in practice. Thus it becomes difficult to unpack and assess the relative impact of structures on action and action on structures in different historical and empirical circumstances.

Feminist Theory: The Work of Dorothy Smith

Smith's work suggests that women have been largely excluded from positions of influence in sociology and so have not been able, until very recently, 'to give themes and topics to the general sociological discourse' (Smith, 1988: 61). She wants to develop a theory which takes account of women s experience and this means stepping outside the male-dominated discourse that prevails within sociology. One aspect of this male discourse is the idea of the impersonal, objective social scientist who is detached from the particularities of experience and who speaks in terms of a supposedly universal, generalising frame of reference. This impersonal and 'universal' stance simply masks the fact that sociology, like other professions academic or otherwise, is dominated by males and reflects and expresses their experience.

This has to be understood in terms of what Smith calls the 'relations of ruling' and the problematic of everyday life. However, before focusing on the components of her theory as such, let me try to situate her work in relation to the general concerns of this book. I regard Smith's work, like Bourdieu's, as somewhat ambiguous on the dualism question. Certainly, in one sense she is very much against the oppositions between agency–structure and macro–micro insofar as adherents simply assert their own position at the expense of those in opposing camps. In this sense, she is of the opinion that macro and micro and agency and structure are intertwined and mutually implicated.

Nevertheless, this does not mean that she believes in some seamless synthetic unity whereby objective and subjective aspects of social life are entirely dissolved into each other. In fact, she operates with a distinction between external social relations and the local circumstances of everyday life which is, in many respects, very much like the dualism inherent in the macro–micro distinction. Clearly her work can be interpreted as upholding the dualism in terms of different orders of social reality. However, there are, in other respects, indications that Smith also holds to a view which gives priority to the world of immediate experience as the true point of reference for understanding the totality of the social world. From this point of view the notion of an external observer is precluded from her analysis and she is unwilling to speak of social system properties independently of the experience of the involved observer. I feel that this places an unnecessary restriction on the range and depth of her analysis. As we shall see in Chapter 10 the critical theory of Jürgen Habermas endeavours to incorporate the standpoints of both external and internal observers.

Smith points out that her own theoretical endeavours have been influenced by the work of Mead, Garfinkel and Marx, and in this sense, her work, like Giddens's, is eclectic. From Marx she has derived an interest in what she calls the 'relations of ruling' in modern capitalist societies. This refers to the structured forms of power, organisation, direction and regulation that exist in modern societies and through which ruling groups maintain and reproduce their dominant positions. In this sense Smith's work is a blend of orthodox Marxism and feminist theory, for she sees the relations of ruling as expressing the interests of the capitalist middle classes which are also those of white males. Thus the form of domination in modern society is a mixture of economically determined class position and patriarchal rule and women are a subordinated group along with the working classes and ethnic minorities. It is important to understand the relations of ruling as intersecting and co-ordinating forms of social relations; they are not disparate and diverse as they are in Foucault's writing. At the same time, Smith's schema is more elaborate than the conventional Marxist position in that it allows for the interweaving presence of patriarchal power in the ruling apparatus.

Moreover, for Smith, power exists at multiple sites (although it is definitely not ubiquitous as Foucault suggests). It inheres in 'a complex of organised practices, including government, law, business and financial management, professional organisation, and educational institutions as well as the discourses in texts that interpenetrate the multiple sites of power' (Smith, 1988: 3). 'Texts' are another important feature of Smith's overall theory. It is through texts and documents (medical records, tax records, certificates, contracts, police reports and so on) that the relations of ruling intersect with the local actualities of lived experience. Thus everyday life is influenced by the relations of ruling which are embodied in the authority and generality of these texts. Buying a house, renting a car, applying for a job, paying taxes and so forth, require that the person deal with such texts and conform to their demands in a manner acceptable to the ruling groups. These texts provide the link between lived experience in a local setting and the organisation of rule which is constituted externally to individuals and their friends and relations, as well as local practices and circumstances. Thus texts mediate the forms of power and domination in modern societies. They translate power and control into acceptable practices.

While Smith can be seen to borrow heavily from Marxist and critical theory traditions (as well as feminism) in her conception of the relations of ruling and the role of texts and documents in them, in other respects she draws on phenomenological sociology to inform her view of everyday life. This is reflected in her central project, which is to understand the 'problematic of the everyday world' particularly as this applies to the experience of women. Put simply, Smith is interested in the way in which the everyday world that is the centre of our experience is organised by and tied to larger social processes as well as locally organised practices. She points out that a feminist approach would start with women's experience from women's standpoint 'and explore how it is shaped in the extended relations of larger social and political relations' (1988: 10).

It is because women have been largely excluded from the relations of ruling that they experience a fault-line in their consciousness of everyday life. Contrary to many traditional forms of sociological analysis which seem to posit a unified consciousness, women experience a disjuncture between their own personal, lived experience and that of the official, impersonal male-dominated organisations and culture that 'invade' much of daily life through the media of texts and documents. Women, as subordinates, also experience themselves and the world in ways that are foreign to conventional sociological analyses. In particular, women do not necessarily experience their life worlds as something to be mastered and controlled according to their own interests. This purposive notion of human agency, in which the ability to make a difference in the world is the defining feature, is really only applicable to the experience of males involved in the relations of ruling.

By contrast women often suppress their own interests in order to cater for those of their children, husbands, partners or parents and so on. Women are thus primarily engaged in balancing the interests and projects of others and may therefore be said to be engaged in a much more co-operative venture than that implied in the typical male quest for control. Similarly, women, who are for large periods of the day located in households, work in isolation from face-to-face interactions. This contradicts the implicit assumption of micro sociology that such interaction is equally available to everyone (Lengermann and Niebrugge-Brantley, 1992). Women's experience of face-to-face interaction is much more intermittent and is often responsive rather than purposive. This is related to the fact that women are more often than not treated as subordinates rather than equals. In this sense, patriarchal power invades the details of daily existence and produces rather different experiences for women. They are much more concerned with learning the expectations and meanings of the dominant group of males in order to get by, thus suppressing their own interests.

All in all, social theory neglects to take into account the way in which structural inequalities of gender are played out in the arena of everyday life. These elements then define the particularities of women's experience and provide the starting point for the development of a theory which may account for them. However, in attempting to understand the lived experience of women, Smith does not adopt a phenomenological perspective wholesale. In fact it is here that the influence of Marx becomes paramount. Smith's central contention is that the local world of practices (everyday life) cannot be understood entirely within its own terms. The everyday world is organised by social relations (relations of ruling) which are not fully apparent in it or contained in it. These social relations are external to the local practices of everyday life and inhere in the organisational forms of corporate capitalism. In this respect, Smith leans on the analysis found in the

Grundrisse and *Capital* where Marx locates the conditions of people's activities outside the local settings where they confront each other. These conditions are 'organised by relations external to the everyday world and beyond the power of individuals to control' (Smith, 1988: 95).

Smith understands these external relations (which are based around the capitalist marketplace) as central aspects of complex societies that emerge through a historical process of development. Thus, in simpler social forms, society does not have this double character because the determining social relations are fully present to the experience of its members. It is only when societies become structurally more complex, with more and more organisational forms having emerged to tackle specialist functions and operations, that the determining social relations become hidden from view. Furthermore, as the external relations of domination and control become more evolved, they increasingly and extensively penetrate the directly experienced local worlds and practices. For example, the relations between men hanging around on streetcorners and the relations of women to them 'are organised by the development of capitalism to the level at which work for labourers is strictly casual and at which a segregated labour force organises an urban pool of undifferentiated workers who are on call' (Smith, 1988: 96).

We shall see in Chapter 10 that Habermas has proposed a similar model in which the influences of a social system begin to penetrate and colonise the lifeworld, spreading the logic of the system at the expense of the original texture of the lifeworld. However, we shall also see that this is where the similarity ends, because Smith rejects the viewpoint of an external independent observer which Habermas's model of the system entails. At this point, we can begin to see the full contours of Smith's vision of the problematic of everyday life. She is against dualism in the form in which macro and micro analyses are viewed as mutually exclusive and opposing approaches. However, she is definitely a dualist in the sense that she distinguishes between two levels or orders of social reality: local practices and the external social relations which penetrate and determine them. Thus macro and micro are interfused.

Evaluation

However, Smith goes on to insist that this macro–micro linkage has to be approached exclusively from the direction of micro to macro and back again. That is, the starting point *must always* be from the point of view of the lived experience of actual people (in this case women). It can never begin from a macro vantage point since this would be (for Smith) to deny the reality of the subject and to actively eliminate her presence. As she says 'the fulcrum of a sociology for women is the standpoint of the subject. A sociology for women preserves the presence of subjects as knowers and actors' (1988: 105). The analysis must always begin with the lived experience of local practices and then move on to an analysis of the social relations that extend beyond them and determine them.

In this respect, Smith adheres to the ethnomethodological critique of conventional sociology. This insists that by taking an objective standpoint, conventional sociology eliminates active subjects by viewing them as mere ciphers of system influences. On this view, theorists like Parsons, for example, invent objectified conceptual frameworks which bear little relation to the realities, lived experiences and local practices of actual subjects. These theories are ideological forms which represent the relations of ruling (capitalist and patriarchal domination) as if they were natural and universal features of social life. Smith (1988: 153) points out that 'as subjects, as knowers, women are located in their actual everyday worlds rather than in an imaginary space constituted by the objectified forms of sociological knowledge built upon the relations of the ruling apparatus and into its practices'.

On this view, methods of macrosociological thinking create accounts of social processes as if they were 'wholly external' to the individuals who bring them into being, and in so doing they sever any connections with a world of active subjects. Smith evidently has no faith in the vast corpus of macrosociological work on the grounds that it automatically suppresses the notion of the active subject. Now I am in full agreement that the active subject must not be obliterated in sociological analysis, but I cannot agree that such a denial is a *necessary* accompaniment of macrosociological thinking or any variant of conventional (male) sociological discourse which attempts to view social relations from some kind of objective viewpoint. This is far too harsh a judgement of a vast array of sociological approaches.

I disagree with Smith about this issue on several grounds. First I believe that much macrosociological theorising is a useful complement to micro analyses. Thus, while it may not be possible to recover actual social practices in the form of lived experience, by beginning analysis from a macro point of view, this does not automatically mean that the analysis is worthless, or that the theoretical framework is inherently unsympathetic to the notion of an active subject. There is nothing mutually exclusive about macro analysis and active subjects even though Smith and ethnomethodologists would have us believe so. Such things can only be settled by recourse to the actual facts in particular circumstances. Sometimes it is a matter of interpretation. For example, Parsons's work is usually the butt of this kind of criticism, but as I made clear in Chapter 2, while there are serious inadequacies associated with Parsons's analysis of social behaviour, it is misleading to say that he tries to deny or suppress the active subject.

Secondly, while Smith believes that beginning from a macro direction is inherently flawed, there is a sense in which her own theory endorses a certain kind of macro analysis as a prior starting point. For example, Smith's analysis is based on the (macro) premise of the organised nature of capitalist society and patriarchal domination. It is only in terms of the logic of these macro relations which extend to the furthest reaches of everyday life that we can, in the final analysis, understand local practices. This, indeed, is the logic of Smith's own position. If we cannot understand the everyday world on its own terms and (following Smith) we are forced to examine the social relations which stretch away from it and determine it externally, then we are automatically forced to invoke some prior notion of an external macro structure in order to make sense of the local practices. What does this external macro structure turn out to be but capitalist patriarchal relations of ruling!

The hidden agenda here is that Smith is not against certain forms of macro analysis, only those that seemingly threaten the premises of her own argument. Of course, if the rest of conventional sociology is infused by male ideology and inextricably linked with the relations of ruling (through sociological texts), then of course all conventional macro analyses will be understood as a threat. I think this is a pity because it simply places obstacles in the way of potential dialogue between macro analyses which do not necessarily share the same premises as Smith, but which are, nonetheless, not hostile to the notion of active subjects. In fact, it could be argued that such analyses focus on institutional analysis and bracket out the analysis of strategic activity primarily for reasons of analytic and methodological convenience (see Giddens, 1984) rather than out of a need to deny active subjects.

More generally, I believe it is possible to study social relations from an objective viewpoint without losing sight of the active subject. In this sense it is possible to talk about properties of the social system or social organisation (or, indeed, the interaction order) without reference to individuals or activity as such, while in no way denying the reality of subjects and their active implication in the production and reproduction of social relations and processes. Such a premise underlies the work of several of the authors I shall go on to examine in this and later chapters.

In conclusion, I would like to suggest that Smith's work is provocative and insightful, but that it unnecessarily restricts its purview by insisting on a micro starting point. Also, and somewhat ironically, despite this starting point Smith has little to say about interaction as such; she is more interested in consciousness and experience from the standpoint of women. This is an interesting and important topic, but it does rather neglect the importance of the interaction order itself, or at least the implications for face-to-face conduct in general that flow from a sociology of women. Certainly there is much to admire in Smith's work. She raises issues about subjectivity, gender inequalities, consciousness and the problems attendant on women's participation in a patriarchal society which have been consistently overlooked in sociological discourse.

It is clear that some aspects of women's social experience are specific to women and this must be recognised in social theories. However, there are other aspects which are related solely to the subordinate role that women are forced to play in modern society. In this sense, many features of women's experience are generalisable to other subordinate groups in society – including males who are excluded from the relations of ruling – and this has been acknowledged to some extent (for instance, by Smith, and by Lengermann and Niebrugge-Brantley, 1992). Smith's work also raises again the question of power. The idea of a dual system of domination based on class and gender encourages us to think of power and control in ever more complex terms and raises the question of the extent to which power in general is linked to patriarchy.

The addition of a gender element gives the whole notion of power an extra dimension which is often lacking in conventional Marxist analyses. However it is important to note that although Smith talks about multiple sites of power this is nothing like the capillary form of power of which Foucault speaks. In this sense, power is not everywhere and it is not productive and enabling in the ways that Foucault's analyses imply. For Smith, power is understood more as a conventional notion of structured domination emanating from the organisational forms of the relations of ruling, and playing primarily a prohibitive and constraining role. Surely a comprehensive account of power in modern society would require something of both Smith's and Foucault's conceptions.

Finally, I think a great strength of Smith's theory is that it refrains from reducing everyday life to an unrestrained celebration of the primacy of lived experience and local practices. She does not make the mistake of ethnomethodology and phenomenology of suggesting that local realities are understandable in their own terms. Her insistence that, in order to understand everyday experience we must trace the external social relations that provide its conditions of existence, is an essential precondition for theoretical advance in understanding macro–micro linkages. It is unfortunate, in the light of this, that Smith severs links with many conventional forms of sociological analysis that could help in the teasing out of such linkages. It is also unfortunate that the emphasis on the importance of external relations is somewhat compromised by her over-rigid insistence that the correct approach is one that starts exclusively from the micro world of lived experience. Again, this simply works to create unnecessary and unwarranted barriers between potentially complementary forms of analysis.

Recognising the Reality of Collective Phenomena

The work of Jeffrey Alexander (1985a, b) in many respects takes an opposing view to Smith. Alexander is very critical of theories which begin at the micro-level (as in symbolic interactionism) and assume that macro-phenomena are simple expressions of more complicated networks of interaction (see the discussion of Blumer's notion of 'joint activity' in Chapter 4). Alexander's objection is quite simple and derives from his sympathetic reading of Durkheim's work. This suggests that, although strong on the question of human freedom, such a position cannot properly account for the unique character of what Alexander terms 'collective phenomena' – or in other words group and institutional aspects of society. Durkheim's claim that such aspects constitute a reality *sui generis* (of its own unique kind) is exactly what Alexander means here. Alexander is also harking back to Parsons's concern with what he called the 'emergent properties' of social systems (see Chapter 2).

I find this a very compelling argument, as I have tried to make clear throughout this book. It may be that we do not want to take Durkheim's work or Parsons's at face value, without important amendments and modifications, but the basics of the argument still hold. If we do not regard collective (macro) aspects of society as significantly different from the micro aspects (interpersonal encounters), then they are simply dissolved into the micro world and, as a result, the institutional (macro) world ceases to have any distinctive shape or pattern. Consequently, any analysis that proceeds on this basis is always in danger of wrongly reducing social phenomena to psychological or individualistic terms. (Incidentally, although Giddens argues strongly against such 'methodological individualism', it is also true that it is difficult for structuration theory to resolve this issue because Giddens rejects the idea of a social realm independent of actors' reasons and motivations).

Alexander is right to suggest that it is extremely important to recognise the unique characteristics of collective phenomena as against other kinds of social patterns, as evidenced in interpersonal encounters, for instance. This does not automatically mean that one is committed to some kind of deterministic theory that denies the freedom and creativity of people. It is important to recognise that the two realms or orders are parallel and interwoven with each other at the same time. Approaches such as symbolic interactionism and ethnomethodology reject the notion of a collective and objective realm as a basic assumption, and thus cannot grasp the conditions which underpin face-to-face interaction (see also Goldthorpe, 1973). However, it is possible to give an adequate account of human freedom and creativity if one includes a notion of a uniquely constituted social realm. This is the nub of Alexander's position. Clearly, the collectivist starting point has the advantage of being able to incorporate a wider range of social processes.

Further, Alexander suggests that it is only by employing some collectivist notion (such as Parsons's idea of a social system held together by the internalised value commitments of people) that one can properly account for social order. If we begin with the interpersonal domain as the basis for an account of society as a whole, we produce a picture of randomness and unpredictability rather than social order (Alexander, 1985b: 27). Thus the precondition for integrating both macro and micro theories is to begin from the collectivist position. It is only by starting from the assumption of a relatively independent collective (macro) world that one can begin to approach the problem of how individual personalities are enmeshed in larger patterns of interaction, social institutions and cultural forms. This takes us back to Parsons's notion of the social system and the different system levels (see Chapter 2). This is obviously a result of Alexander's great sympathy with Parsonian functionalism. While this emphasis on the importance of a macro starting point tends to over-stress its determining properties (as it does in Parsons's work), elsewhere Alexander et al. (1987) adopt a position which insists that macro and micro are on more of an equal footing in the sense that they mutually constitute each other.

Neofunctionalism

The continuing influence of Parsons in Alexander's work brings us to the recent movement in social theory known as neofunctionalism. Alexander has been associated with this, as has Richard Munch (1987) on whose work I shall focus here. Neofunctionalism is an updated version of functionalist theory and is heavily dependent on Parsons's social system framework. However, its distinctiveness lies in its attempt to go beyond the limitations inherent in Parsons's work and to take account of newer developments in social analysis. Thus issues such as the nature of 'scientific' social analysis, the role of conflict and processes of change, and the influence of phenomenological schools of thought have all become important problem areas to be included in the neofunctionalist fold. The aim is to use Parsons's framework as a starting point to explore other avenues that have been opened up by alternative points of view. In particular, neofunctionalists consider themselves to be advocating a position which asserts the 'mutual inter-relations between macro and micro levels' (Munch and Smelser, 1987: 385).

Munch's work is a good example of the explicit use of Parsons's framework to establish the ground for the mutual interweaving of action and systems theory. In many respects Munch directly appropriates Parsons's analysis, adding his own refinements and elaborations along the way. If we remember that Parsons's frame-work was already fairly complicated and cluttered up with rather too many analytic distinctions, one can imagine that Munch's analysis tends to take this to its extreme. However, in essence the basic assumptions remain the same as in Parsons's work. There is a concern for a 'voluntaristic' notion of action which is, nonetheless, directed towards goals, which are in turn shaped by social norms. Also, social activity takes place in the context of various system levels (organismic, personality, cultural and social) and society is divided into four sub-systems (see Chapter 2).

The intentions of neofunctionalists like Alexander and Munch are quite clear: to attempt to bring macro and micro analysis together by viewing them as inter-weaving aspects of the whole. Similarly, other divisions such as 'individualism versus collectivism' and 'action theory versus systems theory' must be overcome and integrated into a comprehensive analysis (Munch, 1987: 138–50). In this wish to overcome the divisiveness of those who perpetuate an 'either or' debate, neofunctionalists share a lot in common with many of the writers mentioned in Part 3. However, a crucial difference is that authors such as Alexander and Munch wish to see an integration of approaches rather than a wholesale aban-donment of traditional theorising.

Such is the intention. The only question is whether it is possible in the context of a full commitment to Parsons's ideas especially, as I have said, when there is a tendency to focus on institutionalised aspects of behaviour rather than the nego-tiated and situated elements. Another feature which highlights the problems standing in the way of a full incorporation of the micro dimension into neofunc-tionalism is that it operates with a 'high level' view of action. From this stand-point, activity is understood as directly implicated in processes of social change viewed as the outcome of collective action in complex historical circumstances. This involves tracing typical behavioural patterns implicated in significant social changes and has a definite and important role to play in social analysis in general.

Indeed, it can be traced back to the classical sociologists – for example, Weber's (1967) analysis of the relation between the protestant ethic and the economic activity of early capitalists.

However, the disadvantage of viewing the micro world solely or largely in these terms is that it moves attention away from the practical level of everyday life. Thus, such an approach neglects those dimensions of face-to-face conduct which are best understood as the outcome of complex negotiations and definitions of actual (rather than 'typical') social actors. In sum, the neofunctionalist position has difficulty in 'reaching down' into lived experience and everyday life to comprehend people's behaviour from their own point of view and the situation in which they find themselves. Therefore the neofunctionalist claim to be attempting to incorporate an action approach has to be understood in this context and in terms of the limitations it imposes on our understanding of human activity in general. This kind of approach and its limitations are reflected in Munch's analysis of the emergence of modern law (1987: 145–9).

The purpose of Munch's analysis is to draw attention to the fact that any revamped functionalist approach must move away from the notion that social developments are uniform and follow an inner logic. In this sense, modern law is thought to develop as a response to the increasing complexity of the social system in general. Munch points out that systems theory suggests that there is a 'system logic' which 'predetermines' the course of social development. In the case of modern law this simply ignores the variety of pressures and processes that result from people acting in terms of certain interests and with varying degrees of collective power. As Munch says,

> to adopt an action-theoretical orientation, one would have to understand the development of certain characteristics of the law (rationality, binding authority, uniform enforcement, and change dependent on interests) as the results of how certain actors carry out their actions according to certain principles, thus influencing how the law is shaped. (Munch, 1987: 148)

There is no doubt that this is an important point. Any systems approach that hopes to integrate action theory must accept the view that all aspects of society are, at root, human constructions which operate via human agency and which are capable of transformation through the application of human effort or struggle. In this sense, there is much to be learned from tracing the effects of collective activity and the resultant shaping of the social environment. However, this does not automatically provide us with information about everyday life and the way in which an individual's behaviour emerges from a complex of situated processes.

It is a focus on the dynamics of situated conduct – on the social- psychological dimension of ongoing human activity – that struggles for recognition in the neo-functionalist framework. As I have said, this follows from adopting an approach to micro phenomena starting from the level of collective activity and working down toward the micro level. Unfortunately, such analyses generally do not dig deep enough and therefore remain at a level above the interaction order and the dynamics of interpersonal encounters.

Collins and the Micro-translation of Macro Phenomena

At first glance, Collins's work is quite unlike that of Alexander and Munch and others working to forge a link between systems theory and forms of microsociology. Collins, in this respect, shares much in common with a radical micro stance (as in ethnomethodology) insofar as he rejects macro concepts like 'system' and 'state' 'as abstractions without causal reality'. At best they are 'living forms of rhetoric which have misled sociological theorists into taking them as literally true' (Collins, 1981). This provides us with an outright rejection of much macro theory which is quite unacceptable if we are to build theories which do full justice to the complexity and (ontological) depth of social reality. Collins's position is in line with a number of writers who believe that the micro world of interaction is the only social reality because it is observable and directly accessible in empirical terms (see discussion of Garfinkel and Hilbert in Chapter 5).

As I have said in previous chapters, the importance of forms of social organisation (such as labour markets, bureaucratic organisations, financial institutions, power, gender and class hierarchies) are seriously overlooked by taking the micro world as the paramount reality. Although the world of direct social experience (the intersubjective world) is of great importance, distortions in our overall view of society occur by looking down only 'one end of the telescope' so to speak. There is much in Collins's work which suggests that he is of the opinion that the micro world is of primary importance, both theoretically and empirically (see Cicourel, 1981; Knorr-Cetina, 1981). However, Collins's position is rather more original than most in this area. Interestingly, he does not completely reject the idea of macro phenomena. Instead he believes that so-called macro phenomena are simple 'aggregations' (groupings or collections) of micro encounters. What we call social structure is only a collection of repeated micro situations. All structural or macro concepts and ideas in sociology can, therefore, be translated back into the micro terms upon which they were originally built. Thus, for example, ideas about the structure of power in organisations can be translated into detailed empirical descriptions of the ways in which particular people actually exert authority in those settings. The notion of social class can be translated into descriptions of the ways in which people use various kinds of speech code in certain situations.

While it is true that such concepts and ideas can be 'redescribed' in this way (although not 'translated' as Collins claims), he seems unaware that such a redescription does not reflect the lack of a true macro reality, it simply means that macro level phenomena also have micro level implications. For example, the macro reality of social class understood as an unequal distribution of resources (money, property and power) does not disappear if we focus on one of its micro-level counterparts – the use of language and forms of speech by people in specific situations. That is, the way people from different social classes talk (see Bernstein, 1973) is not equivalent to the 'class structure' as a macro pattern of social inequality. They are two entirely different orders of social reality which intersect at particular points in time and geography.

Micro-translation involves the mistake of assuming that macro analysis and concepts are trying to describe the same thing as micro analysis – the everyday world of interpersonal encounters. This misses the point that macro analysis is dealing with 'parallel' but quite distinct aspects of society which are, as Giddens has rightly observed, 'deeply implicated' in each other. Thus, while it may be that they are so tightly interwoven that they may not be easily prised apart, this most definitely does not mean that they, or their effects, can be reduced to either macro or micro terms or levels of analysis. Now Collins wants to avoid the charge that he is merely engaging in micro-reduction by saying that he is only proposing a form of 'micro-translation' (Collins, 1983). However, it is difficult for Collins to dodge this charge when it is accepted that translation between macro and micro is impossible since they refer to different things. We cannot translate macro into micro (or vice versa); we can only say that macro and micro phenomena have their counterparts in different levels of analysis, or that their mutual effects are reflected in their intertwined forms.

Collins (1983: 187) insists that macro structures such as 'states, business organizations, historical processes, the world system' do exist, and this sets him apart from the more radical of micro sociologists. However, he believes that they are simply large collections of micro situations and that therefore they can be 'boiled-down' to their constituent micro elements. For Collins there are only three 'pure macro variables': time, space and number. In these terms, there is the sheer number of encounters that make up a macrostructure, the way in which they are spread out in physical space and their duration in time. However, Collins points out that, as such, these variables do not do anything in and of themselves.

We must look to human beings acting in situations in order to isolate the 'real causal forces' and the 'glue that holds together the social structure' (by which Collins means the repeated pattern of encounters).

The Dynamics of Interpersonal Encounters

Collins's strategy of theory-building does not sufficiently come to terms with the issue of different levels of social reality (and the associated problem of how we analyse them). However, Collins does make some interesting observations about the dynamics of interpersonal encounters which, if lifted away from the wider 'micro-translation' context of his work, would be of use to those seeking to bring together macro and micro analyses. Collins's comments concerning the basic micro mechanisms which constitute the stuff of everyday social life could be used to fill out the kind of analyses favoured by the neofunctionalists and Parsonians. Similarly, approaches such as Giddens's, which depend on a rule-following and largely 'rationalistic' model of human action (even though Giddens does allow for unconscious elements), could well be balanced by Collins's emphasis on the emotional side of social encounters.

In making the social encounter the basic unit of analysis, Collins moves away from the idea that the individual is the focus of the macro–micro connection. According to Collins each individual comes to every encounter with three kinds of social resources acquired in previous encounters. These resources are: a certain amount of emotional energy; conversational or cultural capital; and a social reputation. That is, each person enters the encounter with feelings of enthusiasm, depression, self-confidence and so on, and this is what Collins refers to as the level of 'emotional energy'. Secondly, conversational or cultural capital refers to the ways in which people talk, the kinds of speech codes they use and the things that they talk about – the topics and subjects they know about and are interested in. Finally, a person's social reputation consists of what other people know and believe about this person. An encounter of several people represents a meeting and matching up of a number of different resources. The length of the encounter will depend upon how engrossing the conversation is and whether the individuals concerned like and are impressed with each other and so on.

People tend to see encounters in a pragmatic fashion by implicitly comparing what they are getting from particular encounters in terms of interesting conversation, emotional uplift and ego enhancement, with other encounters that are available. Thus people bring with them certain combinations and levels of resources with which to negotiate the next encounter. In this sense, chains of encounters are created whereby resources are reaffirmed, created or depleted. For example, the use of speech codes by members of particular social classes may be reaffirmed in some encounters. Also, new conversational topics or items of interest may be picked up during others. Collins particularly emphasises the flow of emotions in such situations. When the people involved are social equals and the encounter is successful then a certain 'ritual bondedness' takes place between those involved. The individual who has successfully negotiated this solidarity 'gets a little positive jolt of emotional energy' (Collins, 1983: 192).

Collins argues further that, if a person links up and bonds with another with higher power or status, then the original person picks up more emotional energy. Being rejected reduces one's energy, especially if it happens often. In unequal encounters, Collins suggests that the person who dominates the encounter picks up a surplus of self-confidence and energy, whereas the one who is dominated loses emotional energy. This analysis is a perceptive and suggestive starting point for understanding the dynamics of encounters which could be linked to other conceptual frameworks (say Goffman's or Turner's, see Chapter 11). It certainly suggests a number of interesting hypotheses that could be tested by empirical research on interaction processes. It also promises to link up with the more psychodynamic theories of emotion (such as those of Freud and Giddens). Perhaps even more important than this, such a theory of ritual chains of interaction connects with behaviourist and exchange theories. These have postulated that individuals relate to each other in market-like terms on the basis of the gains and losses made from various 'investments' (involvements) in particular relations with others.

Having said this, however, I have to repeat that such possible links with other theories have to be seen in the context of a dissociation from the wider implications of Collins's views. In particular, I would strongly resist Collins's argument that it is the making of chains of encounters that distributes and redistributes the resources and emotional energies in such a way as to create the macrostructures of power and stratification in society (Collins, 1983: 192). Society-wide systems of class, gender and ethnic stratification are quite different orders of phenomena from their behavioural counterparts that can be observed in specific situations. Such things as forms of talk, types of racial or sexual harassment on the street and so on are intimately related to the unequal macro distribution of resources, but it is a mistake to assume that they are simply repetitions of micro encounters. To do so is to ignore vast tracts of social reality. I share with a number of other writers the view that the integration of macro and micro analyses can only come about by recognising the different levels at which social reality manifests itself (Duster, 1981; Layder, 1981, 1993, 1997; Goffman, 1983; Turner, 1987; Ritzer, 1992).

SUMMARY

- This chapter has reviewed the work of Bourdieu, Smith, Alexander, Munch and Collins, who all endorse the reality of the agency–structure and macro–micro relationships. However, the authors envisage their interconnection and relative importance in different ways.

- In his theory of practice, Bourdieu attempts to unite objective structural approaches with interactionist and phenomenological approaches through his concept of 'habitus' (people's durable dispositions deriving from their background experience). Habitus translates the mutual influences of objective context and the immediate situations of activity. Bourdieu thus incorporates a notion of objective social relations (absent from, and thus a weakness of, structuration theory), but also tends to overstate their influence at the expense of the creative possibilities of situated activity as well as individual creativity.

- Dorothy Smith, with her feminist standpoint sociology, is somewhat ambivalent on the relationships between agency–structure and macro–micro orders. On the one hand, she insists on the micro starting point of women's experience and consequently rejects much macro theorising which, for her, seems to negate this experiential starting point. On the other hand, she does not make the phenomenological mistake of suggesting that local practices/realities are understandable in their own terms. For Smith, gender inequalities, power, domination and 'relations of ruling' are external to, and stretch beyond, the local circumstances of everyday life.

- Jeffrey Alexander insists on the importance of the reality of collective phenomena in understanding the links between institutions and interpersonal life. This must be an initial assumption of social analysis otherwise there would be randomness and unpredictability rather than social order.

- Alexander's position is closely associated with 'neofunctionalism', which rests on a solid foundation inspired by Parsons's writing. Richard Munch's work on the emergence of modern law exemplifies the strengths of neofunctionalism. However, the dynamics of situated conduct and the psychological aspects of individual behaviour struggle for recognition in neofunctionalism.

- Randall Collins believes that 'so-called' macro phenomena are simple 'aggregations' of micro encounters and that all structural and macro concepts can be translated back into micro terms. But macro and micro refer to radically different, parallel and emergent levels of social reality and are not reducible to each other. Thus macro or structural phenomena cannot be translated back into micro encounters. Nevertheless, Collins's work does contain some perceptive insights into interpersonal encounters that are not found in other approaches.

10

Habermas's Lifeworld and System

PREVIEW

- Habermas's general theoretical project.

- The nature of communicative action.

- The lifeworld.

- The development and uncoupling of the system.

- The colonisation of the lifeworld by the system.

- Appraisal: self, emotion and motivation; over-emphasis on shared understanding; over-refinement of concepts; the lifeworld–system distinction; the macro–micro problem; the nature of power; social interaction and the lifeworld; Habermas's contribution.

Habermas's General Theoretical Project

The work of Jürgen Habermas is voluminous and complex. It is a sustained attempt to provide a comprehensive theory of society in the 'grand' manner of the classical thinkers. Indeed, Habermas draws on the work of Marx, Durkheim, Weber and Mead among others, extracting what is of value in their work while rejecting those aspects which do not serve his efforts at theoretical synthesis. So, while indebted to the classical thinkers – particularly Marx and Weber – Habermas subjects their work to a rigorous critique and attempts to refashion it according to the demands of his own project. Habermas's attempt at synthesis also embraces the work of later authors such as Parsons, to provide a quite unique approach to the study of society. The incorporation of systems theory into his work has been the butt of criticism from 'critical' theorists, who detect more than a hint of regression to a conservative and outmoded form of theory. However, Habermas is insistent that the only way to advance a critical theory is to incorporate systems theory into an overall framework which attempts to marry both systems and action theories.

Having mentioned the 'critical' component of Habermas's thinking let me elaborate on this by pointing to the connections between his work and that of the Marxist thinkers mentioned in Chapter 3, and the critique of Marxism that was offered by post-structuralist writers like Foucault (Chapter 6). Habermas is associated with the 'Frankfurt School' of critical theory and is, in fact, the best known of the second generation of writers who are connected with this institute. The Frankfurt School was set up in 1923 as an institute for Marxist studies and, in the period after the Second World War, a number of important research topics were investigated there such as the nature and emergence of fascism, authority and the family, and art and popular culture (Pusey, 1987). The three most prominent and influential authors at the school were Theodor Adorno, Max Horkheimer and Herbert Marcuse.

What linked the representatives of the Frankfurt institute was a concern with human freedom and the way it had been curtailed through forms of domination and social repression in the modern world. The 'critical theory' which emerged from the institute was aimed at diagnosing the ills of modern society (the things that prevented people's fulfilment) and identifying the nature of the social changes that were necessary in order to produce a just and democratic society. Born in 1929, Habermas is still actively engaged in developing his ideas and continues with the Frankfurt tradition insofar as his work is also 'critical' in intent. However, it is important to realise that Habermas does not build on the work of Horkheimer, Adorno and Marcuse. Instead he sets out to 'reconstitute the whole paradigm of critical theory' (Pusey, 1987: 33) and, as such, he is more concerned with reconstructing the work of classical writers.

As compared with Foucault and post-structuralist writers, Habermas can be seen as rather more committed to traditional ideas, including Marxism. Most importantly, Habermas deals in systematic theory – the grand and 'totalising' theory that was rejected by Foucault (and other post-structuralist and postmodernist thinkers). Habermas believes vehemently in the usefulness and necessity of such a general theory as a means of identifying social trends and developmental processes that are of immense significance for a critical theory. While severely critical of various aspects of Marxism, Habermas does not reject it all. He uses aspects of it to construct his own synthetic model, drawing on many other sources in the process. Similarly, Habermas does not reject out of hand the Enlightenment project of reason, as do post-structuralism and postmodernism. He believes in the efficacy of reason (the growth of certain forms of 'rational' thinking) and its potential for enlightenment and social emancipation.

Of course, Habermas is wary of the exploitative and dominative effects associated with the spread of technical and bureaucratic rationality in modern society. Similarly, he is aware of the limitations of conventional scientific (positivistic) forms of reasoning in social analysis and the dangers of a subject or individual-centred mode of analysis. Habermas's own thought grapples with these problems and tries to work out viable solutions without rejecting altogether the Enlightenment project of the search for rational understanding. In this and other respects he moves away from postmodern thought which rejects all aspects of modernity and forms of reason (including general social theory).

Habermas believes that there are unfulfilled potentials in modern society which have to be rescued from the pathological tendencies which continually undermine them. In this respect he is very much of an optimist about modernity and its future as regards the elimination of the grosser forms of inequality and domination, the securing of an enhanced quality of life and the safeguarding of the natural environment. Habermas also moves away from the prevailing notions of the Frankfurt School which fail to identify some of the redeeming features of capitalist 'bourgeois' society. So, as compared with both the original Frankfurt critical theorists and with the 'critical analyses' of Foucault and other post-structuralist thinkers, Habermas is something of an independent voice. It is this originality which makes his work so distinctive and worthwhile.

Certainly, in relation to the macro–micro problem, Habermas presents us with a fully-fledged theory which has much to offer in terms of a possible resolution. This is not to say that I believe that he has, in fact, provided the definitive solution. Rather, I believe that he has provided us with insights which are not present in much of the other work I have discussed in this book. It is Habermas's bold attempt to weld together aspects of action theory with systems theory that provides the most interesting focus of attention here. Unlike Giddens, Habermas does not reject the 'objectivism' of systems theory, as found say in Parsons's work. Rather, he suggests that there should be a balance between systems theory and those approaches which emphasise the importance of language and meaning in social interaction.

In this sense Habermas provides a very useful counterpoint to Giddens's work as well as that of Foucault. His notion of a fundamental division in social reality (both methodological and real, as I shall go on to show) challenges the assumptions of those writers who insist that such distinctions are false or misplaced (Chapters 6, 7 and 8). Of course, it is precisely this attempt to reconcile two apparently incompatible approaches that attracts much criticism as well as praise. My discussion of Habermas's work will centre around the extent to which he has been successful in 'stitching together' these two important strands in social theory. For this purpose my discussion will concentrate on the two volume work entitled *The Theory of Communicative Action* (Habermas, 1986, 1987). In this massive work Habermas summarises much of his prior work in the context of a fully worked out theory of the connection between what he terms the lifeworld and system.

The Nature of Communicative Action

Before plunging into a precise definition of the lifeworld in Habermas's terms, let me detail some of the essential ingredients that provide its background context. First, Habermas draws on the work of Max Weber, who elaborated an account of the process of 'rationalisation' in the modern world. This involved several elements including the growth of scientific knowledge and its application to modern technology. The development of 'rational' knowledge led to the decreasing importance of magic and religion as ways of interpreting the physical phenomena of the world. Weber regards this as part of the demystification and disenchantment of the modern world. Also, Weber emphasised the growing influence of bureaucratic organisation in modern society, especially as this was part of the development of capitalist forms of economic activity. These developments could be characterised as an increasing rationalisation of the world and society in which technological mastery was dependent upon the application of reason and scientific knowledge.

Weber argues that, as a consequence, there is a loss of meaning because of the breakdown of metaphysical and religious world views (Brand, 1990) and a loss of freedom because of the effects of the 'iron cage' of bureaucracy. The dominance of instrumental reason and instrumental action were the characteristically 'rational' features of modernity in Weber's analysis, and this view was shared by the early Frankfurt writers. To an extent, Marx was also entrapped in this view of action and reason, as reflected in his emphasis on the role of human labour in social development. In all these views there is a tendency to assert the dominance of instrumental reason as human beings act in and upon the world of physical objects. Habermas calls this a 'philosophy of consciousness' because it tends to view the operation of reason in one-dimensional terms – as in the example of a person applying knowledge to achieve particular goals.

According to Habermas, such a view of rationality and reason is unduly limited. It simply ignores what Habermas calls 'communicative rationality', which is concerned with the way in which people in interaction are preoccupied with reaching an understanding. Any adequate theory of society must take into account the fact that action is also based on the achievement of shared understanding. Thus, for example, Marx's conception of the importance of human labour as informed and guided by instrumental and technical reason must be supplemented by a notion of 'interaction' which refers to mutual understanding and normative consensus between communicating individuals (Habermas, 1971). In simple terms Habermas is drawing attention to the fact that when people come together in encounters, they are engaged primarily in achieving some understanding on the basis of which further interaction may proceed. Language plays a vital role in this and is the distinctive characteristic of humans as opposed to animals. Humans use language as a communicative device with which to achieve consensus

> in a situation in which all participants are free to have their say and have equal chances to express their views. Thus there is in language an in-built thrust for the achievement of what Habermas calls the 'ideal speech situation' in which discourse can fully unfold its potential for rationality. (Brand 1990: 11)

Here Habermas draws on the work of Mead, who pointed to the importance of language and meaning in the achievement of co-operation in social encounters (see Chapter 4). In that Habermas stresses the importance of communicative action, he also rescues a wider conception of rationality from that imposed by the work of Weber and the early Frankfurt School. On the one hand, in Habermas's terms we can and must speak of action as informed by an instrumental purpose in which a person persuades another by 'sanctions or gratifications, force or money' (Habermas, 1982: 269). This Habermas calls 'strategic action' and it is motivated by practical (or as Habermas puts it 'empirical') concerns. On the other hand, 'communicative action' refers to the co-ordination of the activities of two or more people on the basis of a shared understanding such that each person tries to convince the other(s) with the effect that the resulting action is motivated through reason.

Communication and Validity Claims

In communicative action people try to influence each other by putting forward claims which are such that they can be criticised and subject to debate. The meshing of action is not based on some pre-established consensus about appropriate ways of acting, as in Parsons's framework. Rather it depends on the give and take of encounters and the way in which those involved can make their claims influence the understanding that is eventually reached. People do this by putting forward 'validity claims'. This means that they try to persuade each other of the appropriateness of their own views by backing them up in various recognised ways.

Habermas suggests that there are three sorts of validity claims which, in turn, refer to three 'worlds'. First we have the objective, external and factual world and this corresponds to validity claims based on the best way of achieving some desired state of affairs. Secondly, there is the social world of interpersonal relations regulated by social norms and so on, and these correspond to validity claims based on the normative rightness of what is being argued. Thirdly, we have the world of subjective experience according to which validity claims are based on the sincerity and authenticity of a person's advice to another. In distinguishing between these different claims and the worlds to which they correspond, Habermas is not suggesting that this is the way they are in the practical circumstances of everyday life. In the 'messy' contexts of our real-life social behaviour, the claims are often mixed up with each other such that there are no neat boundaries between them. The purpose of Habermas's 'classification' of claims and worlds is to enable us to analyse the constituent elements involved in particular instances of communicative action.

The point is that in encounters with others we are automatically engaged in reaching some shared understanding. This may be something quickly reached and briefly experienced – such as a few words exchanged between two people in a queue, say about the length of the queue, the location of the coffee, or even the fact that they had not seen each other for a long time. On the other hand, we may be involved in a lengthy debate with others about some issue or other – such as how to resolve an argument that threatens to break our relationship, or whether one person should move out of a particular neighbourhood. In any case the encounter would encompass the making of claims and counter-claims on the part of those present with a view to coming to some understanding about the next step. This may, in fact, be an agreement that we suspend the discussion until some future date, or alternatively it could require one of us to change our minds and views on a particular issue and submit to the other's wishes. Any outcome is possible but it will be preceded by an attempt by those involved to sort out the correctness and validity of each other's opinions and perspectives with a view to reaching some sort of understanding about what the 'next step' should be.

For instance, a daughter may take it upon herself to convince her aged, widowed mother, who lives on her own in what has become a red light district in a city centre, to move out of this neighbourhood (this is a modified example originally derived from Brand, 1990). The daughter may suggest a number of things to back this up which draw upon the three worlds and types of claims that Habermas identifies. For example, she may suggest that it is a dangerous area for an aged person to live and that her mother therefore runs a great risk of being attacked or burgled (reference to external facts of the matter). Secondly, she may suggest that a senior citizen cannot lead a dignified existence in such an area because people who live there are 'looked down upon' by others living in more 'respectable' neighbourhoods (reference to social norms). Finally, the daughter may try to convince her aged parent by saying that she feels unhappy about the situation and that this could be considerably alleviated if her mother moved to a safer and more respectable area.

Now the mother may counter all these arguments with her own (it's not really dangerous, other people are snobs, your feelings are not my problem) and win the argument against moving. On the other hand, the parent may be convinced and ask her daughter for help to move away. In either case, shared understanding and eventual agreement has been reached through the mutual give and take of discussion involving various claims to validity. Habermas feels that in such instances of communicative action there is a natural push towards a shared understanding based on the free exchange of arguments founded upon genuine information (rather than on deceit, lies or manipulation – that is, being 'economical' with the truth).

Of course, people do try to manipulate and deceive others as well, depending on the circumstances. Various ploys are used in these cases to disguise intentions such as attempts to gain a person's confidence by appearing sincere and genuine when, in fact, the real motive is manipulation or exploitation. In such cases language itself is not the only 'tool' that is used to achieve particular ends. All manner of non-verbal means (facial expressions, gestures, manipulation of personal space), may be used by unscrupulous characters to attain selfish objectives (money, goods, dominance and so on). Although the question of whether a person's intentions are honourable or not is an important one in real life, it does not alter the fact that action proceeds on the basis of shared understandings fashioned out of the relative merits of various kinds of validity claims.

The Lifeworld

This is the general picture of social interaction that Habermas presents us with in his depiction of the 'lifeworld'. What then is the lifeworld? Habermas suggests that the lifeworld is the general background context in which these validity claims (informed by different kinds of 'rationality' or reasoning) take place. That is, while claim-making and the everyday stuff of conversational exchanges goes on in the foreground, this all depends on a background of assumptions. The two together form what Habermas means by the lifeworld.

In this sense it refers to the way in which our activities and ideas are related to the institutional, economic and cultural structure of the society in which we live. Through our experience of living in particular societies we acquire views and perspectives on the world which colour our attitudes and influence our actions. We draw on cultural knowledge and language forms that we share with other members of society or our own social group. These 'stocks of knowledge' and cultural 'recipes' for action provide us with information about how to deal with specific situations and generally shape our perceptions and understandings of the world. In short, these are basically much the same as those described by phenomenological writers (see Chapter 5) and provide a background consensus of assumptions for everyday conduct – a kind of storehouse of knowledge that is passed on from generation to generation. This represents one way in which Habermas's general theoretical framework links up with a number of other traditions of thought.

However, Habermas conceives of the lifeworld in rather broader terms than is the case with phenomenological strands of thought. The differing validity claims as they relate to the different 'worlds' described by Habermas make his theory much more inclusive in scope than most types of action theory. Habermas is suggesting that there are ontological domains (levels or aspects of reality) which expand the general subject matter (and thus, the scope) of his theory. For instance, the idea of an objective world as distinguishable from a social world which is, in turn, distinct from a subjective world is something which is denied in many, if not most, action theories. Habermas is not claiming that these worlds are separate and unrelated to each other. On the contrary, he sees them as interfused, but at the same time it is important to distinguish them as constituent features of a seemingly unitary whole.

It is also important to understand that these features of reality do not simply refer to methodological distinctions. That is, they are not simply constructed by theorists to make it easier to deal with a complex subject matter. These are *real* distinctions as well as analytic ones. This fact is often confused by commentators with the idea that they must therefore refer to discrete and opposed entities. It is crucial to be aware that, although these are distinctions that point to actual differences in reality, this does not mean that they are separate and unrelated to each other. The same goes for other aspects of the lifeworld. The background of common assumptions that people draw on in their everyday conduct also includes reference to different social domains such as personality, and structural, institutional and cultural aspects of society. The lifeworld represents the patchwork which, through communicative action, draws together the different strands of social life, such as the assertion and maintenance of self-identity, the regulative effects of social norms and the stock of knowledge that informs shared understanding.

This model has definite affinities with Parsons's ideas about different system levels (personality system, social system, cultural system and so on – see Chapter 2), and to some extent Habermas recognises the influence of Parsons's work. However, he is critical of Parsons's notion of the 'interpenetration' of the systems. Habermas argues that it is difficult to see how personality, culture and society hang together in the context of Parsons's view of action as purposive and regulated by values. Habermas points out that Parsons has no conception of an 'intersubjectively shared world' and goes on to say that 'without the brackets of a lifeworld centred on communicative action, culture, society and personality fall apart' (Habermas, 1987: 225). Thus it is that Habermas's conception of the lifeworld binds the various elements of social reality together.

On this view, the lifeworld appears as a smooth web of communicative action. However, it must also be recognised that it represents the intersection of social action and social structure. As such, we can see here the stitching together of the lifeworld and system in Habermas's theory. The essential point, however, is not to think of these two spheres of social reality as if they were simply different aspects of the same thing. This would obscure certain social processes and produce a confused analysis. Moreover, such a strategy would make it impossible to analyse the core social problems that manifest themselves in modern societies.

In relation to this, Habermas argues that one way of thinking about the distinction between lifeworld and system is in terms of different kinds of social integration. Social integration is produced through the intertwining of the activities of two or more people in face-to-face interaction. On the other hand, system integration derives from the consequences of various activities for the functioning of the social system in general. This takes us back to Lockwood's distinction between the integration of actors and their actions as compared with the fitting together (or otherwise) of various parts (institutions) of the social system. I shall come back to the issue of social integration presently; let me here pursue the question of how lifeworld and system are related to each other.

The Development and Uncoupling of the System

Habermas conceives of the development of society in evolutionary terms whereby there is a progressive increase in social complexity. The history of social development is the history of the emergence of ever more complicated social arrangements in order to co-ordinate populations on an increasingly large scale. In the earliest types, the functional requirements of society (that is the things that are necessary for the society to continue as a going concern), such as the production and distribution of goods and services and the passing on of cultural knowledge, are all handled within the kinship system. In these types of tribal society, marriage relations provide a principal means of social integration. There is no distinction between social and system integration in such egalitarian tribal societies. As Durkheim (1964) pointed out, the binding force of collective beliefs, both mythical and religious, also provide an important aspect of social integration in these segmental societies.

Over large tracts of historical time societies have become ever more complicated through internal specialisation and differentiation and population increase. Various forms of inequality emerge, in particular through the development of political authority based on the power to sanction others. In short, state institutions emerge which are disconnected from kinship systems and thus provide the conditions under which systemic mechanisms can begin to separate themselves from the institutions which provide general social integration. This is also reinforced by a gradual switch from the authority of religion and myth as an integrating force, to a greater reliance on language and linguistic communication as a means of achieving understanding and consensus on social goals.

The next stage of evolutionary development witnesses the emergence of markets for goods, co-ordinated through the use of money. Eventually, with the parallel development of the legal system, the economy detaches itself from political institutions and becomes a sub-system in its own right. Habermas argues that the new systemic mechanisms are contained or 'anchored' within the lifeworld. However, in the context of increasing rationalisation of the world, that is, the development of expert areas of knowledge concerned with the newly formed sectors of society (new occupational groups, the rise of scientific knowledge, development of new skills and expertise), the lifeworld becomes 'overloaded' so to speak. The complexity of validity claims in the context of growing specialisation in society (political, economic, occupational) makes it more and more difficult to reach shared understanding. There is pressure for sub-systems such as government and markets to become detached from the lifeworld and to operate on the basis of codified law.

The development of expert systems (such as politics, economics and the natural sciences) means that whole areas of knowledge are removed from the control and manipulation of people in their everyday lives, although, of course, this knowledge enters into the fabric of social life. These areas of knowledge become the province of skilled experts. In this sense, great pressure is exerted on communicative action insofar as the sorting through of validity claims becomes so much more complicated. This creates the need for mechanisms which will relieve the pressure on communication as a means of routinely dealing with competing validity claims. Money and power are the media that come to perform this task in the areas of government bureaucracy and economic markets. They provide standardised solutions to the problems of deciding between validity claims. The operation of market forces allows for the distribution of goods and services in terms of a standardised medium of exchange – money – and thus dispenses with the need to bargain, negotiate and eventually agree on the price or value of a commodity. Power is a rather more diffuse medium but, nonetheless, operates by cutting through the need to achieve understanding through linguistic means.

Power and money, operating in terms of political and economic forces and institutions, are the main systemic mechanisms that eventually uncouple themselves from the lifeworld. As such, leadership and goal-setting are related to money and power in society and thus they become its main 'steering mechanisms'. In this respect, they take over the functions that the influence and prestige of particular people performed in previous times. In effect, money and power are more generalised aspects of influence and prestige. The new steering mechanisms attain a good deal of independence from the lifeworld and this is made possible by the development of law as a systematic and codified body of principles and statutes. In this fashion, Habermas links the general process of rationalisation in society to the development of codified law and thus to the eventual independence of system features like political and economic institutions.

The uncoupling of systemic elements enables rather more complicated social networks and forms of interaction to take place 'behind the backs' of individuals. In these circumstances people feel that they no longer have an overall grasp of social processes and cannot directly affect the events that surround them. However, at the same time integration is made possible through the meshing of systemic elements. In large areas of society, social integration based on communicative understanding is replaced by system integration through the operation of markets and power. The state and the market are no longer subject to the domain of communicative action whereby language is employed to criticise validity claims. The adjudication of validity claims via language and interaction has been short-circuited. The co-ordination of action in the system is primarily attained through the 'empirical' rather than rational motivations of people. That is, self-interest, rather than more rounded considerations such as what is right or appropriate in the circumstances, tends to hold sway. In this sense, as these areas become detached from the necessity of reaching shared understanding through linguistic communication, they also become neutralised in normative and moral terms.

As the uncoupling of lifeworld and system progresses, the systemic aspects move out of the orbit of control of the lifeworld. This is why Habermas insists that it is necessary to understand society not only from the perspective of individuals as actors in the everyday lifeworld, but from an external observer's perspective on the operation of the system. Habermas suggests that phenomenological and ethnomethodological approaches (see Chapter 5), which view society entirely in terms of the lifeworld, are often restricted to describing 'trivial everyday knowledge' because of the inherent limitations of their perspective. They focus simply on problems of social integration and neglect the functional forms of integration (those institutions and mechanisms which ensure the continuance of society as a totality). They ignore the systemic elements which come to play such a crucial role in modern society as they uncouple from the lifeworld.

The Colonisation of the Lifeworld

Habermas argues that, after having uncoupled itself from the lifeworld, the system re-enters it and interferes with its operation. Habermas refers to this as the 'colonisation' of the lifeworld by the system, because it resembles the way in which colonial overlords penetrate and dominate the indigenous societies they come to rule over. In this manner, Habermas is able to develop a fully critical perspective on modern society. His combination of action and systems perspectives allows him to create a unique analysis of some of the 'pathological' features of modernity which had been first identified and commented on by the classical theorists. Durkheim pointed to pockets of 'anomie' which indicated a lack of moral guidelines resulting from social disorganisation. These resulted from the social disruptions entailed in the transition to modern industrial societies. Weber identified the lack of meaning and loss of freedom associated with increasing rationalisation, while Marx, in his early work at least, saw 'alienation' in the form of powerlessness and estrangement (particularly of industrial workers) as a characteristic feature of modern capitalism.

Habermas's theory of the colonisation of the lifeworld allows him to draw different conclusions about the nature of modernity from those of the classical theorists. Unlike Weber, Habermas does not view bureaucratic domination as an inevitable 'iron cage' which holds society in a malevolent and vice-like grip. Habermas dispenses with the pessimistic emphasis on the inevitability of meaninglessness and loss of freedom in Weber's work. Instead he stresses the fact that the system elements could be forced out of the lifeworld to create a just, free and egalitarian society. There is nothing inevitable about these social processes. Protest movements and pressure for social change should be directed at the potential for free debate and consensus on goals and the distribution of resources which Habermas feels is inherent in communicative rationality. In this sense, he believes in rescuing this aspect of Enlightenment reason, which has come under siege by the colonising imperatives of the system – in the form of power and money.

This critical component makes a parallel with the work of Marx. However, Marx unduly stressed the role of labour (strategic and instrumental action) in history and social development. According to Habermas, Marx did not sufficiently stress the role of interaction as a communicative attempt at shared understanding. Thus Marx did not grasp the fact that, through the penetration of money and power into the lifeworld, communicative reason was markedly displaced by instrumental reason. Similarly, the early Marxist scholars of the Frankfurt institute were unable to deal with the problem in the way that Habermas is able to because of their reluctance to adopt a systems perspective. In Habermas's view, it is always possible for social resistance to be marshalled against the colonising tendencies of the system. In this way the critical potential of new social movements such as feminism, green politics, and anti-nuclear lobbies can be maintained without discarding altogether the project of modernity. This, of course, puts Habermas at some odds with both 'anti-' and postmodernists.

The notion of the colonisation of the lifeworld indicates the fact that the steering media of money and power begin to penetrate into areas of everyday life and practice which require communicative action. The economy and the state destroy communicative processes in areas where they remain necessary such as cultural activities, education and socialisation in general. Also, the system elements are disruptive of activities which are essential integrating elements in society, such as moral and normative rules and idea and value systems like religion. All these areas become subject to the demands and dictates of the economic and administrative system. Thus the moral and practical elements of communicative action in these areas are forced into the background while technical and utilitarian values predominate. This is most noticeable in modern societies, with their emphasis on consumerism, the accumulation of property and possessions, competitive individualism and the goal of economic achievement.

Habermas argues that this colonisation of the lifeworld is not always apparent to people, because of the fragmentation of everyday consciousness brought about by rationalisation. That is, with the explosion of technical knowledge and the specialist expert sub-cultures that arise as a result, everyday consciousness loses its unity and fragments. For Habermas, it is not, as Marx argued, that people are prevented from understanding the true nature of their subjection by the distorting influence of ideology. Rather, it is because everyday consciousness is severed from expert sub-cultures, and thus fragmented, that the need to understand or interpret the overall nature of social existence is removed.

Habermas's theory of colonisation also moves away from Marx's analysis insofar as the protests against colonisation come from what he terms the 'new politics'. In this sense, Habermas's diagnosis of the ills of modernity requires us to abandon Marx's notion of a labour-driven politics of dissent which centres around class conflict, the production and distribution of goods and services and conventional political party divisions. Instead, Habermas conceives of the new politics as concerned with a reclaiming of those areas of the lifeworld which have so far succumbed to incursions from the system. In this sense, the process of colonisation is indifferent to the traditional Marxian lines of conflict.

The new politics (the peace and women's movements, ecological groups, gay rights, affirmative action and so on) is not concerned with distribution problems as such. Rather, it is concerned with 'problems of the quality of life, equal rights, individual self-realisation, political participation' (Brand, 1990: 115). In Habermas's terms, such critical theory feeds into political action in the sense that it underscores the idea that the colonisation of the lifeworld is not an inevitability. In principle, through political action, the goal rationality that derives from the system and is injected into the lifeworld can be made to submit to the normative and moral demands imposed upon it from the lifeworld.

An Appraisal of the Theory

Self, Emotion and Motivation

Although Habermas is interested in the psychological interior of individuals (their 'subjectivity'), he has been taken to task for his lack of depth in this regard. Habermas's position, in brief, is that the penetration of bureaucratic logic into the everyday lifeworld 'threatens and destroys the cultural foundations of communicative action' (Elliot, 1992: 105). Organisational rationality drives emotionality and artistic sensitivity from the realm of the self and thus leads to a repression of inner nature. We are no longer able to understand our motivations, the elements that push us to behave in certain ways. Habermas does draw on Freud's work in this regard, particularly his notion of the unconscious. However, as Whitebook (1985) has pointed out, Habermas tends to view the unconscious in linguistic terms, since this fits in with his emphasis on the importance of language in communicative action. Accordingly, Habermas understates the importance of the unconscious understood as prior to, and independent of, language – as an aspect of bodily drives and needs.

As a result, Habermas is unable to adequately account for the interplay between language, 'unconscious drives, reason and desire' (Elliot, 1992: 112). In Whitebook's terms, Habermas 'fails to capture the sense of an "inner foreign territory" which is a hallmark of Freudian thought' (1985: 157). In principle, the inner reaches of the self are visible and accessible via language both to the individual and to others. So, on these terms, Habermas fails to give a rounded view of the person as possessing bodily drives and an emotional inner core which is often beyond the level of conscious awareness. I think that this criticism is correct up to a point. The lack of emotional depth accorded to human beings is, however, a very common feature of social theories. It is true that Habermas's tendency to insist on the 'linguistic nature of everything' waters down his view of human beings and social activity. In this respect, Habermas seems to be overly fond of the power of reason (as it is expressed in language), and thus provides too formal a view of desire and emotion in humans.

On the other hand, such a criticism can be taken to an extreme which suggests that all human behaviour is the result of unconscious drives and desires. However, this would be to disregard those aspects of behaviour that are consciously monitored and controlled. Furthermore, as Giddens has underlined, there are wide areas of social behaviour which operate below the level of conscious awareness (what he calls practical consciousness). Taking these into account, it is obvious that the 'emotional depth' or 'roundedness' that any one theorist accords to human beings is very much to do with the relative importance they give to different facets of social behaviour in their overall approach. In this context, Habermas's view of human agency is certainly in need of amendment but is not irretrievably flawed.

Over-emphasis on Shared Understanding

Another facet of Habermas's work that has come in for critical attention is his central idea that human activity is somehow driven towards shared understanding (communicative consensus). There are those who suggest that in his drive for a 'formal' model of interaction he confuses understanding with agreement and does not sufficiently attend to the fact that often communication leads nowhere in particular. In fact it may lead to a profound lack of substantive agreement rather than to shared understanding as such. There is no reason why people should yield to 'the better argument' as Habermas seems to think. In fact there are countless reasons why someone should resist such an eventuality, even if they can appreciate the force of another's reasoning. There is in all this a tendency for Habermas to idealise 'communicative action' by insisting that, in circumstances of equal access and equal information, there is a push towards shared understanding or consensus. In this sense his notion of an 'ideal speech situation' is truly an invention. As Turner (1988) puts it, there is in much of Habermas's work a utopian idealism which overlooks the fact that all communication (and interaction) is inherently distorted.

Over-refinement of Concepts

The idea that Habermas is too eager to make conceptual distinctions and elaborations which, on closer scrutiny, do not hold up, is also a common theme in the critical literature and there is some substance to this. I think this is often related to the above-mentioned predilection for making contrasts between an idealised future state of affairs and a current and insufficient one. This perhaps reflects the vision of a theorist who is committed to a critical theory which must identify what is wrong and indicate what can be done to put it right. However, this can lead to confusions, or at least ambiguities in conceptualisation. One of these concerns the distinction between 'labour' and 'interaction'. Habermas introduced this distinction in his earlier work (1971), but later (1987) he tends to use the distinction between strategic and communicative action. Clearly there is some point to this kind of distinction, which refers on the one hand to instrumental goal-directed action motivated by money or threat of sanctions, and on the other to shared understanding through reasoned discussion.

There is no doubt that, on a general level, such a distinction usefully characterises different elements of action. However, Habermas often uses this, and other distinctions, on an 'either or' basis, implying that activity can be understood in terms of 'pure' types. However, in many, if not all cases, human activity reflects a mixture of influences. To say that human labour, for example in the context of a factory, is completely saturated by instrumental motives, would be to ignore the human dimension of workers' relations with both colleagues and authority figures. Shared understanding resulting from the give and take of reasoned discussion is just as much a feature of socially organised labour as are instrumental or strategic motives (Giddens, 1976: 68). Conversely, interaction itself is often hedged in by selfish or manipulative intentions.

Another example of Habermas's penchant for 'pure' distinctions which turn out to be a lot more muddy than he anticipates, relates to his distinction between social and system integration. Habermas insists that social integration is founded on a normative consensus achieved through communication, while system integration is founded on regulation based on forms of control extending beyond the immediate situation. However, as Mouzelis points out, 'the participant's perspective is perfectly compatible with forms of integration based on coercion' (1992: 269). As Mouzelis says, concentration camps and prisons provide examples in which the inmate's perspective does not rely on mutual agreements with the guards, but neither does 'integration' take place behind their backs. The two forms of integration are not as discrete as Habermas thinks, nor are they exclusively associated with either systems or action.

Also, in those formal organisations such as government bureaucracies where system imperatives are supposed to dominate, it is wrong to suppose, as Habermas does, that lifeworld elements are excluded. Mouzelis draws our attention to the fact that many scholars who have studied bureaucracies have concluded on the basis of empirical studies that bureaucratic rules are never exhaustive and thus can never provide ready-made solutions to problems confronted by organisational members. Thus Mouzelis takes exception to Habermas's view that members of such organisations have no need to achieve consensus by communicative means. Empirical research has revealed that this assumption is quite wrong and thus, again, Habermas's pure distinction between different types of integration is an oversimplification. The same also applies to capitalist economies. It is just not true, as the cases of Switzerland and the Scandinavian countries show, that they are 'exclusively or even predominantly integrated via steering media' (Mouzelis, 1992: 276).

The Lifeworld–System Distinction

One of the crucial criticisms of the theory of communicative action concerns the distinction between lifeworld and system. Several authors have pointed out that it is not always clear exactly what Habermas means by this and whether this sort of distinction has any validity. For instance, McCarthy (quoted in Brand, 1990: 131) believes that there is no real need for the systems theory that Habermas so readily employs. Instead, says McCarthy, most of this could be described in terms of action theory. Habermas, however, is adamant that such micro-reduction is inadequate to explain system features such as institutions. We have covered this sort of ground in previous chapters so I will not dwell on it here, except to register my broad agreement with Habermas. There are, however, various points of disagreement that arise over the nature of the system, and the connection with social activity that I shall come back to in due course.

However, on the other hand Mouzelis and Giddens (1987) have also complained that Habermas's analysis of the system does not readily incorporate references to 'macro actors' strategies and their struggles'. How is it that political movements and group pressure and protest lead to modifications in system elements? There is a definite understatement of collective action in Habermas's work even though he consistently mentions the new political movements such as ecological and feminist groups. As Mouzelis says, Habermas does not really demonstrate the connection between the new social movements and the other elements in his model of modern societies. As with the question of the 'lack of depth' of the human personality in Habermas's work, I think that the issue of collective action and its consequences is something that could be expanded upon by Habermas. It is a question of the need for elaboration rather than an irredeemable flaw in his theory.

Another aspect of the distinction between lifeworld and system concerns the question of whether it is methodological or a substantive. Mouzelis (1992) insists that Habermas has confused a methodological distinction (deriving from Lockwood's initial definition of social and system integration) with a substantive one. Giddens (1987: 250) also suggests that the distinction between lifeworld and system cannot be both methodological and substantive. This is not simply an abstract matter of little significance. It goes right to the heart of one of the most basic issues of social theory. So let us consider it in rather more detail. Lockwood

(1964) initially proposed this distinction simply as an analytic one which aids analysis rather than one that points to differences in actual reality. For Lockwood the point was that there was no corresponding distinction in social reality – the circumstances of social life are such that they are an untidy amalgam of different influences and phenomena.

However, in order to analyse society we need some method of holding the various elements 'apart' so to speak in order to be able to make statements about how they operate in reality. So, for convenience, we can imagine social and system integration as separate phenomena referring to different aspects of society. However, when it comes to the study of actual societies or aspects of them, we have to be careful not to make such clear-cut separations. This is because the distinction is artificial – it is simply a methodological ploy or procedure which allows us to examine one aspect of reality at a time. This is what both Giddens and Mouzelis focus on. They suggest that there is some ambiguity in Habermas's use of system and lifeworld. It is not clear whether he believes the distinction to be methodological (a construct) or real – a substantive distinction. Moreover, they suggest that it cannot be both, and that Habermas has confused an artificial construct with an empirical reality.

I agree that Habermas often seems to view these as 'pure' distinctions and that it is misleading to view lifeworld and system as separate from each other in the way that Habermas sometimes seems to indicate. However, I do not think it is correct to suggest that the distinction must be either one thing or the other – methodological or real. Surely this is much the same sort of error as imagining that lifeworld and system are entirely separate! I am arguing that there can be no such thing as a purely methodological (or analytic) distinction – that is one which does not correspond to some actual reality. If it was not a substantive matter at all then the distinction itself would be, at worst, totally useless or at best very misleading. In this sense, I believe the lifeworld–system distinction to be both methodological and real. It serves as a way of theoretically understanding some aspects of society and thereby provides us with a (methodological) means of analysing various kinds of empirical data.

In short, lifeworld and system are both analytic and real aspects of society. However, it does not follow that these refer to separate or unrelated aspects of society. In my view, lifeworld and system are completely interrelated, although I admit that Habermas is often unclear and ambiguous on this. He sometimes speaks of them *as if* they referred to clearly separated and unrelated aspects of integration. In this sense, Habermas is guilty of over-formalising or unduly 'purifying' the distinction. However, Mouzelis and Giddens (and others) seem to overlook Habermas's great achievement in this respect. That is, he draws attention to a distinction in social reality which can only be grasped by some combination of action theory which emphasises and captures the participant's perspective with a version of objective institutional theory which understands society as a functioning whole from an external (observer's) perspective.

A Reformulation of the Macro–Micro Problem?

The above mentioned insight and achievement must not be undervalued in the clamour to criticise the weaknesses of the theory of communicative action. Habermas's overall viewpoint on the relation between macro and micro levels of social analysis is thus highly fruitful and suggestive. It bears no small relation to the work of Alexander, Munch, Goffman, Turner and Archer (see Chapters 9 and 11) all of whom conceive of different orders of social reality even if they do not view them in exactly the same terms as Habermas. Of course, there are other differences and sometimes profound ones at that, but nonetheless the continuities should not be ignored or overlooked.

One of the main differences concerns the exact relation between the different orders. As we have seen in the two previous chapters there is substantial disagreement among these same authors about this matter. With regard to Habermas, perhaps the main point of divergence concerns the very fact of the 'gap' that appears between lifeworld and system in terms of social activity. It seems that in a very real sense for Habermas, the lifeworld is synonymous with social activity and that system has to do with things that are entirely different from activity such as money and power. Of course, this is the point of the criticism that Habermas tends to reify system elements (that is, to speak of them as if they were 'things' rather than social constructions). In this respect I would agree more with Giddens, insofar as we must always view social institutions and activities as inextricably linked with each other. On the other hand, the advantage of Habermas's theory is that, because it clearly distinguishes between the domains of system and lifeworld, it becomes possible get a clearer indication of the contribution that each domain makes in different circumstances.

In this respect Habermas's theory underlines the different characteristics of activities and social systems rather more than Giddens's. Structuration theory tends to push the two domains together as if they were a single entity. This has the effect of under-emphasising the already established character of systems (or social structures). Habermas's theory manages to capture this difference, but is rather less successful at indicating the intertwining of the different social orders. However, even though Habermas does manage to pick out significant differences in the two domains, it is also true that he does not sufficiently trace through the empirical dimensions of this problem. With his idea of the colonisation of the lifeworld by the system, Habermas seems to envisage an even spread of penetration of system elements into the lifeworld.

Now, while the thesis of colonisation is intriguing and suggestive of testable propositions, it does need more specification in an empirical sense. It needs to be able to specify which areas of the lifeworld are more susceptible to colonisation and which are more resistant. These questions cannot simply be settled on a priori theoretical grounds, they must be connected to empirical research. In this sense there should be a close link between empirical research and general theorising – something which has been conspicuously absent from both theoretical scholarship and empirical research hitherto (see Chapter 12). Certainly the question of the extent of penetration of the lifeworld cannot be finally solved in entirely empirical terms. Theoretical issues of power, domination and resistance (among others) need to be worked out as well. However, it has to be recognised that the variable nature of colonisation has an irreducible empirical dimension to it; thus co-operation between theorists and researchers is essential.

The Nature of Power

The issue of power is also something of a weak spot in the theory of communicative action. Habermas tends to view power as if it was a single type of phenomenon rather than something which takes on different forms and functions at many different locations in society. Habermas tends to view power as a steering medium, something which is attached to political institutions in the service of societal goals. In this sense, Habermas does not understand power in the way that Foucault does, as a circulatory medium which operates through the whole social body at even the most microscopic levels. Foucault manages to capture something of the way in which power enters into the domain of everyday life in a more convincing manner. Furthermore, Foucault's vision of power extends to those who resist its influence rather than understanding it as something which solely operates from the 'top down' so to speak. In this sense, Habermas's framework does not adequately deal with the multiplicity of sites and levels at which power is found in society and its association with marginal and excluded groups as well as those at the centre.

Similarly, Habermas does not really view power as a medium of interaction in everyday life irrespective of the incursions of system influences. Giddens's view of power as an intrinsic aspect of being a social agent – the ability 'to make a difference' – more clearly registers the pervasiveness of power and power relations in modern society. My own work on power and control in interpersonal relations (Layder, 2004b) also draws attention to the importance of power as a generic feature of everyday life – even the most fleeting of encounters. However, although it is necessary to accept a wider view of power, we should not go to the other extreme and see it as so diffuse that it has no boundaries or specific forms. The danger of adopting an exclusively Foucauldian perspective and viewing it in such generalised terms would be that we lose hold of the notion of power as an effective instrument of analysis. Being able to discriminate between types, levels and degrees of power relations is absolutely essential and again requires empirical research to help to make this possible.

Social Interaction and the Lifeworld

Having underlined the necessity of viewing the connections and mutual influences between lifeworld and system in more flexible terms than Habermas, let me now turn to the lifeworld itself. Habermas understands the lifeworld as an exchange of validity claims centring around the most efficient way of achieving objectives, the appropriateness of proposed actions and the sincerity with which they are proposed. These efforts at reaching understanding go on against the backdrop of shared cultural resources (background assumptions built into language and culture). Now this, as Habermas claims, is an advance on those theories, particularly of the structural or systems variety, which tend to stress the 'private' tie between the individual and the social world of which they are a part. The notion of the lifeworld introduces the idea of a patchwork of interactions between people who share a background of linguistic and cultural resources. Thus individuals are caught up in social interdependencies which provide the medium through which conflictual or harmonious interaction may occur in social encounters.

Sure enough, this provides us with a much richer account which borrows from phenomenological strands of thought. The notion of interactive dynamics gives a more adequate impression of the nature of everyday social life. Also, Habermas's ideas about ideal speech situations alert us to the kinds of inequalities that can occur in interactions and the sorts of distortions that may result. Notwithstanding the criticism (Turner, 1988) that Habermas may be underestimating the extent to which communication is always distorted, his account does bring in issues of power, inequality and system influences. As such, he manages to counter-balance the phenomenological influence with an objective or structural strand. Moreover, the stress on negotiation and bargaining over validity claims ensures that Habermas does not make Parsons's mistake of viewing consensus as the result of conformity to pre-established cultural norms and expectations.

In all these respects Habermas's theory has great virtues. However, as with Giddens (and to some extent, but in rather different ways, with Elias and Foucault), Habermas tends to compact the world of everyday interaction into the wider social context. In Habermas's case, this is done through the notion of the lifeworld itself. However, such 'drawing together' has the effect of eliminating the 'interaction order' in Goffman's terms as a domain in its own right. There is no distinction between the constraints and enablements that emerge from the preservation and reproduction of social identities in the immediate circumstances of encounters, and those of the wider social and cultural milieu. Nor is there any provision for the analysis of meanings and definitions of reality which are embedded in local circumstances and which cannot be simply read off from an analysis of system elements.

Unfortunately, there is, in the theory of communicative action, no understanding of the relative independence of the interactional and structural domains of social life. As such, it lacks an appreciation of the subtlety and complexity of the couplings that exist between the two orders. This is perhaps because of Habermas's tendency to group Goffman's work with that of phenomenological writers who, in his view, do not readily go beyond the more superficial aspects of common sense. As the discussion of Goffman's work in Chapter 11 makes clear, he is a dualist in the sense that he believes in the relative independence of the structural and the interactional domains of social life. Had Habermas been more appreciative of this aspect of Goffman's work, he might have taken advantage of a unique opportunity to marry a critical theory of society with a theory of the interaction order. This would have combined an important emphasis of the colonisation of system elements with an understanding of how the interaction order both succumbs to, and resists, the incursions of systemic influences.

Habermas's Contribution

Habermas provides a carefully worked out theoretical marriage between action and systems theory. In particular, he provides a much needed emphasis on system properties as they intersect with what he calls the lifeworld of everyday interaction. Habermas's theory also establishes an important connection between the analysis of linguistic communication (which is central to phenomenological and interactionist theories) and objectivist theories of structures and systems. In this sense, Habermas taps into the more robust features of objectivism without incorporating its more pernicious aspects, such as a simplistic theory of knowledge and a deterministic account of action. Habermas's theory allows for a creative account of human agency while embracing an objectivist frame of reference with respect to macro structures. This is the option that Giddens unfortunately rules out, and this detracts from the explanatory power of structuration theory. In this particular respect, Habermas has produced a more embracing theory. On the other hand, Giddens's account of action and its productive and reproductive effects seems rather more intricate and rounded than Habermas's. The latter's notion of communicative action is overly bound up with the question of consensus and reaching shared understanding and thus overlooks other, rather more dissonant features of social interaction.

Furthermore, Habermas provides an analysis of power and domination in his account of the colonisation of the lifeworld by the system. In this he incorporates Marx's emphasis on the nature of political economy and the sources of power that underpin forms of domination and structural inequality. Again, this is an important ingredient that is missing from those theories that concentrate almost entirely on micro events. But such a concern is also missing from poststructuralist and postmodernist theories that are formed around a critique of Marxism, a denial of general theory and an emphasis on the fragmentary and dispersed nature of power (Foucault), or even the purported 'disappearance' of power (Baudrillard). Habermas's account of system steering media (money and power) is an important corrective to the nihilistic and relativist strands in much postmodern theory.

However, Habermas does not use Marx in an uncritical and dogmatic manner. He subjects Marx's work to a swingeing critique and uses only those aspects that are essential to an adequate account of modernity. Also, Habermas reformulates Weber's work at the same time as he draws on his theory of rationalisation to provide a means of understanding the uncoupling of the system from the lifeworld. In accounting for the eventual colonisation of the lifeworld by the system, Habermas is able to fuse together elements of Marx, Durkheim and Weber in the guise of their diagnosis of the ills of modernity. Also, in identifying the pathological incursion of system elements into the lifeworld, Habermas is continuing the tradition of critical theory (begun by the Frankfurt Institute) by carrying forward elements of the Marxist tradition which the post-structuralist and postmodernist writers seem to have abandoned.

SUMMARY

- Drawing on the classical writings of Marx, Durkheim and Weber, as well as contemporary strands of social theory, Jürgen Habermas develops his own critical theory which attempts to marry action and systems theories. He is associated with the 'Frankfurt School' of critical theory but has also developed independently of it to diagnose the 'ills' of modern society. Unlike in post-structuralism and postmodernism, Habermas does not reject the Enlightenment project of reason and its potential for social emancipation.

- Habermas stresses the importance of 'communicative action', in which people act together on the basis of shared understanding motivated by reason as against 'instrumental or strategic action' based on sanctions, gratifications, force or money.

- In communicative action, people try to persuade each other of the appropriateness of their own views by putting forward 'validity claims', of which there are three types. The first is based on objective claims about the facts of the matter, the second draws on social claims about 'normative' rightness or appropriateness, and the third appeals to subjective claims like sincerity and feelings.

- The lifeworld is the general context in which validity claims are put forward and refers to a background of common assumptions that people draw upon in their everyday lives. The link between the lifeworld and system represents the drawing together of agency–structure and macro–micro issues in Habermas's terms.

- Social system elements emerge from the lifeworld progressively over time in tandem with social development and the increasing complexity of societies. The development of leadership institutions and expert systems creates pressure for subsystems such as government and markets to become detached from the lifeworld and operate on the basis of codified law. The steering mechanisms of money and power cut through the need to achieve understanding through linguistic means. In large areas of society, social integration based on communicative understanding is replaced by system integration brought about through the operation of markets and power.

- The system re-enters the lifeworld and colonises it. Everyday consciousness is fragmented by expert sub-cultures. A new politics replaces Marx's labour-driven politics of dissent and class conflict. The new politics is concerned with reclaiming those colonised areas of the lifeworld.

- Habermas has been criticised for his emphasis on language, rational communication and reason, and neglecting the (pre-linguistic) unconscious and the role of emotion. Similarly, his idealised view of communicative action (and his notion of 'the ideal speech situation') overlooks the fact that all communication is, to some degree, inherently distorted. Habermas often over-refines concepts and employs them in black and white, 'either or' terms.

- While there are problems with his lifeworld–system distinction, Habermas identifies a fault line in social reality that can only be grasped by a combination of action theory and some version of objective institutional theory. He manages to capture the difference between these two major orders of social reality but is less successful in indicating how they combine and interrelate. Habermas has a view of power as a steering mechanism and an element of domination, but he overlooks its important presence in everyday social interaction. Generally, Habermas underplays the influence of what Goffman calls the 'interaction order' and its relation with institutional or systemic phenomena. Habermas manages to fuse aspects of the work of Marx, Durkheim and Weber in diagnosing the 'ills' of modernity and furthers a strong tradition of critical theory.

11

Varieties of Dualism

PREVIEW

- This chapter reviews the work of Erving Goffman, Jonathan Turner, Nicos Mouzelis and Margaret Archer, who emphasise the distinctive, but mutually constitutive, relation between agency–structure and macro–micro orders.

- Goffman's notion of the 'interaction order' and its loose coupling with the institutional order. Rawls's and Giddens's different interpretations of Goffman's ideas. The distinctiveness of Goffman's theoretical position.

- Jonathan Turner's theory of interaction and his view of macro and micro analyses as a 'division of labour'.

- Nicos Mouzelis's ideas about why sociological theory has 'gone wrong', his 'tentative remedies' and their problems.

- Margaret Archer's 'morphogenetic approach' and some critical comments on her 'analytical dualism'.

In this chapter I deal with the work of four authors who, in different ways, emphasise the distinctiveness of the agency and structure and macro and micro worlds as well as their equal importance in understanding how the social world is constituted. While the four authors dealt with here – Goffman, Turner, Mouzelis and Archer – all share this general commitment, they each have different understandings of the nature of dualism and of the way forward for social theory.

Erving Goffman regards the relation between the two orders as one of a 'loose coupling'. I shall say more about this in due course, but briefly it suggests that the relationship between the two orders varies according to empirical circumstances.

I think that there are drawbacks in viewing the relationship in quite the way that Goffman suggests, although he does make out a convincing case for the distinctiveness of what he calls the 'interaction order' and the 'institutional order' and the fact of their connectedness. I argue that Goffman's work must be 'rescued' from interpreters who insist that it should be understood as overcoming or dissolving the macro–micro dualism. Instead, Goffman's work should be taken on its own terms as a statement of the usefulness of distinguishing between different social orders.

Jonathan Turner who has written extensively on theories of interaction, has a very different view of the macro–micro relation, although he is in agreement with Goffman that the two orders cannot be simply assimilated into one comprehensive concept or framework. Furthermore, as compared with the writers dealt with in the previous chapter, both Goffman and Turner hold a rather more 'egalitarian' view of the relation between the two orders. Neither author feels that one order has priority over the other as a theoretical assumption or starting point. Any 'priority' that occurs is due to the variations produced by empirical circumstances. In theoretical terms, both orders are of equal importance. This makes Turner's and Goffman's work quite different from the authors discussed in Chapter 9.

Goffman and Turner are undoubtedly committed to dualism. However, as compared with the work of Mouzelis and Archer, they are rather lukewarm versions of dualism. Goffman approaches dualism from the point of view of his interest in the interaction order and how it is coupled with the institutional order. He did not work out the connection between the two in any rigorous theoretical manner, nor did he imply that it was urgent to do so in the face of the more pressing issues and problems of social theory. Although Turner is more conscious of the wider context and problems of social theory, he is indifferent to working out the connections between macro and micro orders. This is because he believes that macro and micro refer to different levels of social reality that operate largely independently of each other and hence can be dealt with separately as part of an academic division of labour.

In contrast, both Mouzelis and Archer have much stronger, positive views on the importance of working out the connections between agency–structure and macro–micro. Furthermore, their views have been worked out against the wider backdrop of theoretical debate about agency and structure. They both believe (as I do) that theories that give undue primacy to either structure (Parsons, Marx, functionalism, structuralism) or agency (symbolic interactionism, ethnomethodology, phenomenology) are flawed. But so also are the theories of those who attempt to abandon dualism and replace it with a purportedly synthetic alternative, such as Giddens's 'duality of structure' or Foucault's 'discursive practices' or Elias's 'figurational processes'.

Goffman and the Interaction Order

Goffman's work is mainly concerned with the nature and dynamics of interpersonal encounters, especially as seen from the point of view of the actors involved. Despite this seemingly limited focus, Goffman's work draws to our attention the fact that the world of everyday encounters is varied, fascinating and highly complex. These topics are undoubtedly connected to the rather more formal issue of the relation between macro and micro phenomena, although Goffman's comments on this are scattered throughout his more detailed and empirically engaged writings (see Burns, 1992; Manning, 1992, for recent overviews of Goffman's work). However, in his presidential address to the American Sociological Association in 1982, Goffman explicitly focuses on this question. He actually entitles this talk 'The Interaction Order' and it is on this that I shall concentrate.

Goffman begins by saying that his concern is with social interaction, that is social situations in which 'two or more individuals are physically in one another's response presence' (Goffman, 1983: 2). Phone conversations and letters provide other 'reduced versions' of the real thing. Such interaction goes on in city and rural settings, public and private life, 'in intimate longstanding relations and fleeting impersonal ones'. It can be observed in crowded streets, at breakfast tables, in courtrooms and bedrooms and in supermarkets. Goffman points out that this domain of face-to-face relations – 'the interaction order' – is 'a substantive domain in its own right'. Goffman means by this not only that situated or face-to-face interaction is a valid area of study with definite boundaries, but that it possesses its own inner workings and mechanisms which are derived from, and give shape to this domain itself. That is, the interaction order is not a simple reflection, outcome or consequence of the wider institutional orders on which sociologists have traditionally concentrated, from Durkheim to Parsons. Goffman does not want to say that the interaction order is completely cut off from the institutional order, but that it has its own distinctive characteristics and that it operates relatively independently. In this respect it warrants special study.

What is this 'interaction order'? Rawls (1987) has usefully summarised four main elements of the interaction order as she has drawn them from Goffman's work as a whole. First, there are the needs of the social self. Each individual's self-identity is dependent upon the responses of others in order for it to be sustained.

In particular, the way the individual presents him or herself (the image they convey, the strategies they use to obtain what they want) creates constraints on the interaction order. For Goffman, the interaction order protects itself from the self-interests of those involved by placing moral obligations on them to adhere to the ground rules of the interaction. However, the interaction order itself provides a protective membrane for the self. Since interaction and the social self are by nature fragile, the individual is never completely secure in an encounter. There is always the possibility that a discrepancy between the image or 'front' that a person is attempting to convey and their real self will be revealed to those assembled. With this possibility always in view, people implicitly agree not to violate or exploit the working consensus of encounters not only to 'save face' on behalf of others, but for fear that they too might be placed in a similar situation at some future time.

Thus, the interaction order is primarily defined as a set of ground rules and moral obligations which provide constraints on interaction (as well as enablements and motivations) organised around the care and maintenance of social selves. The second constituent element has to do with the durability and capacity for resistance of the interaction order in the face of external threats to its existence. Even total institutions like prisons, monasteries, mental asylums and so on, find it difficult to eradicate the workings of the interaction order among their inmates. As Goffman's own work on mental asylums demonstrates, the preservation of self-identity in the face of processes which work to undermine its stability attests to the vigour and endurance of the mutual obligations and moral resources of the interaction order. Thirdly, the interaction order is a domain in which meaning is produced. That is, meanings arise from the mutual involvements of participants in particular situations and their definitions and negotiations. Such meanings are distinct from those that can be extracted from institutional objectives or role expectations. (This aspect of the interaction order is very much in line with interactionist and phenomenological thought, see Chapters 4 and 5.)

Finally, commentators have often criticised Goffman for stressing the exploitative side of human nature, whereby people tend to put on a front or image in order to manipulate the feelings and impressions of the 'audience' to whom they are playing. In this sense, people get what they want through ruses and the subtle manipulation of others. However, as both Rawls (1987) and Giddens (1987) in their different ways show, Goffman's work strongly emphasises a moral dimension to social interaction in which trust, tact and a willingness to take on the responsibilities of involvement with others play a central part. The very notion of an interaction order is a moral one insofar as it depends upon the moral commitment of people to its continuance.

This is not just a matter of altruism (although this undoubtedly plays a role). It is more a matter of being aware that most of the transactions of social life occur at the face-to-face level and therefore collaboration is essential (Giddens, 1987: 113). Morality is thus born out of an understanding of the general need to bring off, or successfully manage, the great majority of encounters in order that social business is able to proceed. It is for these reasons, as Giddens has correctly noted, that 'people shore-up or repair the moral fabric of interaction, by displaying tact in what they say and do, by engaging in "remedial practices", and helping others to save face' (Giddens, 1987: 113). Above all else, these are the emphases we find in Goffman's work as a whole.

The Loose Coupling of Micro and Macro

These, then, are some of the basic features of the interaction order as portrayed in Goffman's work. As I have already said, although Goffman views the interaction order as a domain in its own right, it also intersects with other social orders. This is the basis of his notion of a loose coupling with the institutional (macro) order, so let us now examine some of the examples that Goffman gives of this loose coupling. In this respect, Goffman distinguishes between two aspects of social order which are 'external' to the domain of face-to-face interaction. First there are general resources such as language and shared cultural knowledge which people draw upon as a means of managing encounters with others. This enables Goffman to distance his own work from those who espouse what he calls a 'rampant situationalism' (Goffman, 1983: 4).

To every situation we enter we always bring elements of language, speech styles and cultural knowledge that we share with others, and without which it would be impossible for us to organise our behavioural and verbal activity. Although such given 'resources' may be modified during a social contact, the 'knowledge base' itself reaches beyond particular situations. Here we see an example of the loose coupling that Goffman envisages. Clearly, people create meaning in face-to-face encounters in the sense that local agreements, definitions and understandings hold sway during their course (and sometimes after – depending upon whether the same people come together again). In skilfully applying their knowledge in encounters people actually refashion and create meanings in relation to the important things or topics that encounters centre around. Nonetheless, Goffman is quite clear that this only takes place against the backdrop of wider 'extra-situational' resources of a cognitive and cultural kind.

Furthermore, one does not determine the other in any strict sense although they significantly influence each other.

Another source of such extra-situational influence comes from the baggage of prior dealings one has had with the other participants. In this sense, we carry around an established biography (or history) of previous encounters which automatically affects how those currently brought together in an encounter relate to each other. Again, this reflects a loosely coupled relationship between the interaction order and other domains of shared experience beyond the immediate situation. Goffman distinguishes between these proximate resources that people draw into their activities to 'make it happen' in an immediate sense, from the wider distribution of power resources which underpin various hierarchically arranged groupings such as those based on class, gender and ethnic divisions. These are also subject to the loose coupling idea, and Goffman gives a number of examples to illustrate the diversity, complexity and subtlety of the forms to which this coupling may give rise.

Before moving on to these examples it would be well to dwell on some of the more formal ideas that Goffman proposes about the coupling. It is necessary to be very clear about what Goffman actually does say, so as to be able to compare it with commentators' interpretations of his work, and thus to be able to identify any discrepancies between them. At one point in his presidential address Goffman directly asks the question, how will 'features of the interaction order be geared or linked into, connected up with, tied into social structures?' (Goffman, 1983: 11). He answers this by saying that they are not expressions *of* structural arrangements. At best they are 'expressions advanced *in regard* to these arrangements'. He goes on to claim that 'social structures don't "determine" culturally standard displays, merely help select from an available repertoire of them' (Goffman, 1983: 11).

For example, such 'displays' as priority in being served, precedence through a door, interruption rights in talk, are only loosely coupled to any social structures that might be associated with them. These displays are significantly stamped by the situations in which they occur and the people who display them. As Goffman puts it – they 'are interactional in substance and character'. The link between interactional practices and structures is one which Goffman characterises as 'a set of transformation rules, or a membrane selecting how various externally relevant social distinctions will be managed within the interaction' (Goffman, 1983: 11). An example of this is the way in which women in general do not interrupt when engaged in conversations with men, since men often dominate and 'talk down' to women. This represents an expression advanced in regard to structural patterns. However, Goffman points out that there are certain men, particularly junior executives, who 'similarly have to wait and hang on others' words' – that is, their bosses or superiors in authority. This suggests that there is a role category that women and junior executives share 'and that this will be a role that belongs analytically to the interaction order, which the categories women and junior executives do not' (Goffman, 1983: 12).

This amply demonstrates the idea of a lack of direct coincidence between the interactional and structural orders. This allows for a form of analysis that is sensitive to the mutual influences of both orders and the fact that the balance of the influence – its strength and direction – will vary according to particular circumstances. Sometimes what starts out merely as an expression of interactional life, such as a Bank holiday social affair or block party (as in the case of London's West Indian community in Notting Hill) can end up as an expression of a politically self-conscious group. As Goffman observes 'the carnival was more the cause of a social movement and its group formative effects than an expression thereof' (Goffman, 1983: 10). On the other hand, interactional incursions into structurally influenced political spheres may have little effect on the structural arrangements that are being questioned. Goffman here gives the example of blacks and women who in recent times have breached segregated public places, sometimes with lasting consequences for access arrangements, but with little change in the place of blacks and women in the social structure.

In other cases, fads and fashions in interactional practices stem from the influence of wider social movements but do not correspond to structural changes. Here Goffman cites the increased informality in dress and forms of greeting in the business world as a result of the hippie movement which nevertheless did not alter the wider structural influence of status, hierarchy and the dominance of economic power. All in all, Goffman's image of the interface between the structural and interactional orders as a membrane which selects which influences are allowed through and which are not, and whether they are transformed in the process, is a very suggestive and telling one. We cannot say which influence will be stronger and which will spread beyond its point of origin in advance of the exact empirical circumstances. However, we can be sure that there will be a mutual interchange of effects.

Goffman is clear that, while the interaction order produces its own domain of social constraints and motivations which derive from the needs and consequences of selves in interaction with others, it is never a completely independent order. In some circumstances, the effects of structural arrangements are, for all intents and purposes, 'blocked' by the membrane around the interaction order, but never entirely – there is always the possibility that something will get through. Goffman highlights this by looking at the phenomenon of queuing – waiting in line for a bus, at an airport check-in or at a supermarket check-out. For Goffman, the queue is perhaps the purest example of the workings of the interaction order because, on the face of it, the influence of external organisation is almost entirely blocked out. There is an understanding that all those in line will be treated the same or 'equally' without favour or prejudice and that this is expressed in the idea that people will be dealt with on a first come first served basis. This has the effect of blocking the influence of social status and class and a whole host of 'attributes which are of massive significance outside the situation' (1983: 14).

Queues are organised in terms of immediate considerations (such as procedures for joining an already established queue), rather than in terms of the external objectives of those in line (such as where they are going and why). Regardless also of their external statuses (occupational rank, seniority, gender, ethnic background), people make a commitment to the orderliness of the line and its maintenance. In this sense, it is the purest example of commitment to the interaction order because the influence of external factors is seemingly minimal. However, Goffman is careful to point out that this state of affairs has more of an assumptive quality about it. People tend to feel that queuing is organised around egalitarian principles, but this does not always correspond to what is actually going on.

Goffman notes that there are some unstated qualifying rules (regarding external factors) that have to be satisfied before people are allowed to 'follow through' a service transaction. For example, there are age qualifications for purchasing some goods like alcoholic drinks. Also, people have to demonstrate sobriety, language ability and solvency before being allowed service. As Goffman says 'the order "Cup of coffee to go" might not receive the laconic reply "cream or sugar?" if it is a street bum who places the order' (1983: 15). Also, all manner of informal discriminations may occur in a way that does not disturb the apparent orderliness and fairness of the system. People may in fact be discriminated against or unfairly favoured by preferential treatment (better seats, more courteous handling, quicker or more thorough service), while the acts themselves may be done in such a way as to make them deniable if challenged.

In sum, the sense of fairness that prevails in queues is often more apparent or 'imagined' than real. In fact, says Goffman, 'externally based attributes are ... given routine, systematic "recognition"'. Furthermore [equal treatment] in no way is sustained by what in fact goes on – officially or unofficially – during service transactions. What can be sustained and routinely is sustained is the blocking of certain externally based influences at certain structural points in the service framework. Out of this we generate a sense that equal treatment prevails. (1983: 16).

So even in the example of queuing for service transactions – the purest instance of local determinism – the interaction order is not untouched by the other social orders which intersect with it at various points.

Some Comments on Goffman's Ideas

The Importance of the Interaction Order

It seems to me, from the examples he gives, that Goffman was fairly clear and consistent in his account of the interaction order itself and its relations with other social orders, in particular social structure and institutions. However, in his earlier work Goffman did not explicitly address these issues, and moreover much of this work centred on what appear at first sight to be rather lightweight matters – the details of everyday life, the presentation of self and so on. In this context it has sometimes been all too easy for Goffman to be dismissed by commentators as dealing with a 'folksy' insubstantial subject matter (Gouldner, 1971) or as espousing an incautious individualism or subjectivism (Alexander, 1985b). Both these views are based on misinterpretations of Goffman's work, as other commentators have pointed out (Giddens, 1987; Rawls, 1987).

I agree with Rawls that Goffman cannot be viewed as a theorist whose work is based on an individualist assumption – the idea that social order rests upon individuals and their motivations. Goffman himself is as clear as crystal about this: the self is a social product and can only be understood in relation to its social context. (In this sense it is also incorrect to suggest that interactionist approaches are 'subjectivist', see Chapters 4 and 5.) Furthermore, even though Goffman's primary interest is in face-to-face behaviour, he rejects the idea that the 'situation' is the only or the primary level of social reality that is of importance to sociologists. Rawls (1987) is also right to underline Goffman's argument that the interaction order is a domain in its own right, as a new and important insight. In particular, the idea that the interaction order contains a different order of constraint (and enablement) than that provided by institutions is of fundamental importance for a sociology that can properly integrate macro and micro features.

I agree in the main with Rawls's (1987) argument that Goffman should be credited with challenging our theoretical understanding of social organisation, as opposed to simply enriching our understanding of the details of interaction. Having said this, however, at various points in Rawls's interpretation I detect a tendency to elevate the importance of the interaction order beyond that which is consistent with Goffman's own ideas. For instance, Rawls says that Goffman argues that the 'needs of interaction and social self are a source of consistent social constraint which does not originate in social structure' (Rawls, 1987: 138). While this does not rule out *any* connection between the two orders it does rather heavily suggest that there is little in the way of a reciprocal relation between them. This I would reject, first on the grounds that it presents a distorted picture of the nature of the social self. Self-identity as part of general personality formation is intimately related to the wider structural and historical context as several authors have demonstrated (Elias, 1978b, 1982; Giddens, 1991). Secondly, such an interpretation does not square with Goffman's own views as they are presented in his 1983 paper.

Another example of Rawls over-stressing the independence of the interaction order is her insistence that the constraints that derive from 'involvement obligations' 'do not arise from the social structure, class relations, the division of labor, or cultural ideas, but rather from the requirements of self and sociality' (1987: 140). Such a pronouncement seems entirely foreign to Goffman's explicit attempt to move away from any absolute notion of local determinism (as we have seen above). It is surely more accurate to understand the moral dimension of social life in Goffman's terms as deriving from both institutional and interactional sources. Just as people bring with them the 'cognitive relation' that Goffman speaks of, formed from shared cultural resources, so too they are members of a moral community which stretches beyond immediate encounters and which undoubtedly leaves its imprint on them in some form or the other.

Giddens's Critique of Goffman

Giddens (1987) takes an opposite tack to Rawls. He is against the idea of an interaction order in its own right and thus is critical of what he takes to be Goffman's modesty and the self-imposed limitations on his work. Giddens suggests that Goffman falls into the dualistic trap of assuming that interactional and institutional orders are separate and unrelated. Furthermore, as a result of this false separation Goffman seems to view the workings of the interaction order as being inevitably limited to that order. In Giddens's view, Goffman does not see the far-reaching implications of his own work, especially for the reproduction of the structural or institutional order. From the review above, I think it is clear that, while Goffman does not necessarily draw out these implications in any extended sense, his framework as a whole is capable of dealing with system reproduction in the way that Giddens suggests. In any case, Goffman's stress on extra-situational resources, the loose but complex coupling of orders and the mutual filtering of influence and so on, seems entirely consistent with what Giddens envisages in this respect.

However, an advantage that Goffman's 'model' (albeit not fully elaborated) of the macro–micro relation has over Giddens's is contained in the notion of the interaction order itself. Giddens eliminates this intermediary element of social life as a partly independent domain of its own. Thus structuration theory suffers from an inability to conceive of creativity and constraint in social life as filtered through this 'extra' domain which has important consequences for both activity and structure. Giddens's critique tends to overlook the importance of the inter-action order as Goffman envisaged it, while in Rawls's work we get an over-statement of its importance. It is important to rectify both of these assumptions in order to return to the spirit of Goffman's original ideas and draw from them what we can in the way of an adequate model of the macro–micro relation.

The Distinctiveness of Goffman's Position

Since I believe that both Rawls and Giddens in their differing ways have departed from Goffman's original line of argument, it is worth restating the main contours of Goffman's model. His main point is that there is a distinctive social realm which he calls the interaction order. This contains constraints (and enablements) which are geared to the preservation of selves and the generation of commitment to responsibilities and obligations during encounters. These constraints, commitments and obligations have a different form and do rather different things from those associated with the institutional order, although at the same time they are directly implicated in each other.

That is, it is not that institutional factors are removed from analytic concern by recognising the influence of the interaction order. Rather, they exist alongside and are interrelated with each other. Both orders possess their own characteristics and therefore they have to be understood as different, but interwoven aspects of society. There is a filtering upwards and downwards between the two orders; they perpetually give rise to the conditions under which they both operate. This is Goffman's 'loose coupling' idea which allows for operating variations in accordance with empirical circumstances. Sometimes the interaction order will succeed in blocking or filtering out the majority of structural influences, at other times structural constraints may predominate (as in extreme coercion or confinement). However, neither of the orders is ever entirely free of the influence of the other; they are utterly dependent on each other.

This, of course, is only a sketch, but I believe that it represents an accurate account of the workings of the interaction order as indicated in Goffman's work. If this is the case, then it is plain that Goffman's writing cannot be 'recruited' in support of theoretical positions which insist on the primacy of action or subjective understanding any more than he can be said to have rejected or resolved the notion of a macro–micro dualism. Goffman clearly believed in the fundamental importance of distinguishing between different kinds of social order (one of which was the interaction order). He happened to have been most interested in the interaction order and devoted most of his time to its description and analysis, but he was never of the opinion that it was the only, or the most important realm. It also follows that the implications of his work are not confined to the realm of the interaction order. In this respect, his theoretical model is 'open' to the informative influence of others who have concentrated their attention on other social orders.

Goffman's Contribution

Goffman's notion of an 'interaction order', constituting a social domain in its own right, represents nothing less than a 'continuation' of the classical project instigated by Marx, Weber, Durkheim and Simmel, of defining the contours of social reality more generally. These classical authors pointed to the twin spheres of social action on the one hand, and the historically formed social conditions under which it is enacted on the other. They all pointed, albeit in their different ways, to the manner in which the subjective realm of social action is both formed and constrained by the reproduced practices that constitute the institutional domain of modernity.

What the classical authors tended to neglect (although Weber and Simmel are less guilty in this regard) was the constructive dimension of human action itself. As we have seen, modern theorists like Parsons and the structural Marxists have tended to reinforce this neglect by stressing that individual subjectivity and action are reflections of structural conditions. It has been the phenomenological tradition (through Schutz and eventually into ethnomethodology, Wittgenstein's philosophy, and interactionist schools of thought) that have centred on the idea of human action as socially constitutive – that is, the view that people are active creators of social reality rather than simply the playthings of structural forces. Moreover, this notion of the creativity of human behaviour was extended into the realms of everyday life and routine activity. The productive and creative effects of human activity were seen to be diffuse and generalised, and thus not the exclusive preserve of political action, class struggle and revolutionary transformation as they are in Marx and his later interpreters.

This was a theoretical advance insofar as it identified a social domain which had hitherto been obscured. Unfortunately, this advance was made at the expense of those structural issues of power and domination that defined Marx's work and the wider issues of social integration that characterised Durkheim's. Now I would not claim that Goffman provides us with a complete solution to this dilemma. For instance, he provides us with no analysis of power and domination, and no extensive analysis of institutions except insofar as they impinge on situated interaction. Nonetheless, I do feel that his notion of the interaction order provides a link between these modern action theories and the classical sociological concerns with macro-structural features of modernity. There are several reasons for this.

First and foremost, Goffman does not see the interaction order as completely independent of the institutional order; he sees them as 'loosely coupled'. Again, I think I would want to quibble with the idea that they are always loosely coupled, but nevertheless, the vision of an intersection between the structural and interactional domains provides a promising starting point that is inclusive of an objective structural realm. This furnishes a key link with the classical projects of Marx, Durkheim and Weber. Moreover, the inclusion of an objectivist element provides an advantage that is lacking for the anti-dualists (Giddens, Foucault and Elias) – it enables us to talk about the external conditions of activity. Secondly, and most crucially, Goffman proposes that there are constraints and enablements that derive from the interaction order itself and which cannot be deduced from, and must not be confused with, those that derive from the institutional order. In this sense Goffman is adding to Durkheim's work on institutional constraint by pointing to other sorts of constraints (Rawls, 1987: 146).

However, having made this point, it is all too easy to forget that Goffman does not use this as a platform from which to eschew the importance of institutional constraint. Goffman's notion of the loose coupling between the two orders and the examples he gives in his presidential address clearly point to the fact that he thought both orders were equally important although the influence of each would vary according to empirical circumstances. In this sense, Goffman was at least able to sketch some of the connections between macro and micro phenomena. As Giddens says, perhaps modesty forced him to downplay the scope and general implications of his writing. But it is not true that his notion of an interaction order hampered his efforts in this regard by limiting the applicability of his analysis to this order. On the contrary, it is because he was so intimately aware of the properties of the interaction order that he did not confuse its emergent characteristics with those of the institutional environment.

Without doubt Goffman was aware of the intimate tie between interaction and institutional orders and it is precisely because of this that his detailed analyses of everyday encounters have gained so much credibility outside the sociological community. However, his presidential address and other scattered comments make it clear that that he never lost sight of the complicated and delicate mediations that the interaction order interposes between human agency and the wider social fabric. It is only by making such distinctions between social orders that we can depict the 'layering' of social reality. Such 'stratified' views of social reality are lost to analysis in the 'flat' ontologies proposed by those who attack dualism. For example, Giddens's 'duality of structure', Foucault's 'discursive practices', Elias's 'figurations', the ethnomethodologist's 'concrete activities' (or local practices) and so on, all presuppose a flat social terrain.

Turner's Theory of Interaction

Let me now turn to the work of Jonathan Turner, who believes that any integration or resolution of the macro–micro problem will come only after rather more detailed and painstaking work has been done at both macro and micro levels. Turner (1988) believes that attempts to link the two are premature. It is only after sociologists have developed 'precise micro theories of interaction, on the one side, and macro theories of social structure on the other' that they will be able to determine whether there are points of reconciliation. However, he says that if pressed he believes 'that micro and macro analysis will always remain theoretically disconnected. Neither is more important; each simply provides a different kind of insight into human affairs' (1988: vii).

Despite Turner's seeming reluctance to bridge the gap between macro and micro analyses, at several points in his work he does give us a sustained consideration of what would be involved. I shall return to his views on this after a brief discussion of his work on the theory of interaction. By giving us a fairly detailed account of the dynamics of interaction, Turner provides some necessary ingredients for a comprehensive and integrated view of the macro–micro problem. Turner engages in a fine-tuned review of existing theories past and present on interaction, extracts those aspects that he finds useful and then synthesises them into a model of the general principles of interaction. For detailed accounts of these see Turner (1987, 1988), here, I shall simply provide an overview of this work.

One of the fundamental processes in what Turner calls 'micro-dynamics' concerns the importance of the self. As with Collins's work in Chapter 9, Turner stresses the importance of the emotional side of the self as a balance to the interactionist idea (see Chapter 4) that the self is basically a cognitive entity. That is, Turner wants to move away from the idea of the self as an information processing unit which emerges from, and is constructed out of, language and communication. Although these are of fundamental importance, an undue emphasis on them obscures the fact that the self is a 'feeling construct' and consists of 'a configuration of self-feelings about oneself as an object' (Turner, 1988: 200). Also, unlike many interactionists (like Goffman), Turner suggests that there is a 'core self' which people carry with them 'from context to context as part of their emotional baggage' (1988: 201).

Although a person is not always aware of the deep emotional feelings that are bound up with their core self, they are usually more aware of the 'situational or peripheral' selves that they present or project in particular situations. The interrelation between these different aspects of self is the focus of the dynamics of the self in interaction with others and the energy levels that fuel a person's vitality and sense of self-esteem. Much of a person's social energy is directed at avoiding anxiety involved with low esteem and any felt inconsistencies between their core and peripheral selves. The need for confirmation of self lends emotional intensity to encounters.

People with low self-esteem will tend to work harder to sustain their sense of self, especially in situations where the other people involved seem to be disconfirming or undermining it. Also, unless social situations are structured to some degree by minor rituals and standardised procedures (for opening and closing encounters, for example), a person will seek to change or leave the situation. The lack of a stable context in which to sustain a sense of self-worth and well-being will be undermined and anxiety will predominate. Of course, the opposite is also the case. To the extent to which the situation stabilises and confirms self-feelings and self-worth then the encounter will be prolonged and is more likely to be repeated.

Another essential aspect of micro-dynamics is to do with the fact that people want to feel 'that they are part of events'. This desire can range from a need to be closely 'bonded' with others in an encounter, to the requirement that they at least feel and perceive themselves to be 'loosely in touch with the flow of events' (1988: 204). Here Collins's work is important insofar as his theory of interaction rituals points to the way in which people in encounters generate solidarity by matching up their common interests, speech styles, reputations and so on (see Chapter 9). However, for Turner, the ritual use of words and gestures will only produce feelings of solidarity when a person's needs for inclusion are strong. The need for inclusion in this sense also revolves around the need to trust others and to sense that their responses are predictable. This makes the general need to feel included quite pervasive, because even in the most perfunctory and uninvolving social encounters people like to feel that they are 'in touch with' and 'a part of' what is going on.

This then moves us into areas which directly connect the self with the social encounters in which they are embedded. People need to feel a sense of security, a sense of the predictability and trustworthiness of others. Without these under-lying 'props' people may feel that social interaction is awkward and anxiety-provoking. As Turner says, it is important for people to 'feel right about' their dealings with each other in terms of 'sensing a rhythm, flow and predictability' (1988: 206). Turner suggests that the work of Garfinkel (1967) is important here in highlighting the idea that people share a similar factual world, because this helps to create the generalised sense of 'feeling right' in encounters. Garfinkel's experiments (see Chapter 5), in which normal agreements and expectations about situations were deliberately disrupted, revealed the extent to which people work hard to 'repair' a 'sense that they share, experience and participate in a common world' (Turner, 1987: 171). To the extent that a sense of this common factual world is sustained then anxiety is reduced. Thus the need for facticity (a sense of the factual nature of a shared social world) is 'a powerful motivational force in human interaction' (1987: 173).

In drawing on Garfinkel's work, Turner is careful to distance himself from the extreme ethnomethodological position which denies the importance of real social structures. Turner's point is that not only do such 'ethnomethods' as 'accounting', 'filling in' and 'interpreting' serve to create a *sense* of social structure, they actu-ally serve to create real social structures in the process. Thus, even if a person's feeling is to some extent illusory, it would give them the confidence to continue, resume or reproduce the interaction in which they are involved. Thus the sense of a shared factual world is directly connected to the problem of the reproduction of real social structures, and Turner is scathing of those ethnomethodologists who believe that social structures themselves are illusory.

Similarly, Turner draws upon Habermas's notion that during the course of interaction people make (validity) claims about the best way of achieving things, about the sincerity of their own and others' actions, and about the social appropriateness of various activities and attitudes. Both Habermas's notion of claim-making and the ethnomethodological stress on 'accounting' are seen by Turner to be essential components of a mainstream sociological analysis of activity. That is, Turner strips these ideas of their 'exclusive' association with, on the one hand, the radical critique of mainstream sociology (from ethnomethodology) and, on the other, their implication in a critical theory of society (Habermas).

Macro and Micro Analyses: A Sensible Division of Labour?

I have a great deal of sympathy with Turner's approach because it is eclectic in the sense that he realises that no one school of thought or framework of ideas can provide us with a comprehensive picture of the macro–micro link. He therefore draws selectively from different sources and pulls them together to provide an overall model. I would go along with this strategy for a number of reasons, but perhaps the most important is that it moves away from excessive theoretical parochialism. Also it prevents 'preferred' theories from becoming entrenched in inflexible positions which simply serve to mask inadequacies in the theories that are being defended. As Turner says

> for too long sociologists have argued from doctrinaire positions associated with this or that intellectual camp. No one approach has captured all of the micro dynamics of the social world; we need to be more tolerant of, and receptive to, ideas in what are usually considered incompatible approaches. (1988: 213)

I would endorse Turner's basic position here, although I would not restrict my comments to theories of micro-dynamics as Turner tends to; such comments also apply to structural and macro theories.

In Turner's case this strategy has been especially fruitful, providing us with complex and detailed models against which we can measure empirical studies of social encounters. I find his models of interaction to be perceptive and stimulating; they fill out our knowledge of both interactional processes and the macro structural conditions under which they occur. In this respect, much of what Turner says can be usefully integrated with other theories and frameworks, even where he has not already done this. At this point it is instructive to look at what Turner says in relation to potential linkages between macro and micro analyses. As I suggested earlier, Turner is sometimes rather ambiguous about the potentiality for combining macro and micro analyses. In one sense I think this reflects a certain degree of modesty about his work. He feels that he is simply working on one part of the whole problem – micro dynamics, or basic processes of interaction – and that this is in accord with the intellectual division of labour between macro and micro analysis that is required by the situation.

However, I think that this underestimates the extent to which a concentration on macro features automatically involves reference to the micro world and vice versa. In this sense I think that Giddens is absolutely right to argue that both action and structure and macro and micro levels are intrinsically implicated in each other. For research purposes we may find it easier to 'bracket out' one half of the analysis while we concentrate our attention on the other, but in reality the two are inseparable. However I would depart from Giddens's framework insofar as I assume that, although macro and micro features are tightly interwoven, they also represent distinct orders of social reality. This is a position which Turner also seems to endorse, for at certain junctures he seems to be happy to abandon the separatist implications of a macro–micro division of intellectual labour. It is at this point that I find myself in closest agreement with Turner's overall position.

Turner rejects the reductionism of micro sociologists who argue for the primacy and exclusivity of the domain of social interaction. He also rejects Collins's strategy of the micro-translation of macro concepts. Such ideas are not only vague according to Turner, but they also completely ignore the problem of emergent properties. He argues that we cannot fully understand the micro world without knowledge of the macro structural parameters that order micro encounters. As he says 'the symbolic and material resources available to individuals, the placement of people in space, the amount of time people have, the options that are realistically available, and just about everything that is possible in a micro encounter are all dictated by macrostructure' (1988: 211). Moreover, Turner is of the opinion that, instead of trying to decompose the macro world into aggregated micro events 'we should conceptualize both macro and micro in terms of their own *distinctive properties*'. In this way it 'becomes possible to reconcile the two, not by blending them together but by seeing certain variable states of one influencing the variable states of the other' (1988: 212).

This formulation (albeit a rather sketchy one), is consistent with Goffman's view of the relations between the interaction order and the macro structural orders. Both authors emphasise the distinctiveness of the macro and micro orders, even though they recognise their intrinsic interdependence. Most crucially they recognise the importance of resisting the blending together of the two orders in analytic terms. This would destroy the empirical integrity of the two orders – that is, it would give us an inadequate picture of their real nature – and thus hinder our understanding of them.

Mouzelis: Why Did Sociological Theory Go Wong?

Mouzelis believes that sociological theory has taken a number of wrong turns and is keen to get it back on track. This discussion will examine Mouzelis's arguments about why sociological theory has managed to get itself into trouble – what he terms the 'diagnosis' of its problems – and will then go on to look at some of the 'remedies' he proposes. Although I agree with some of Mouzelis's suggestions about remedies, I think there are also some weaknesses and problems with them, as will be evident in the discussion. I am in much greater agreement with Mouzelis's diagnosis of what went wrong with social theory. Indeed, it connects with many of the issues already raised in this book.

Mouzelis believes that what he calls 'micro sociological theorising' (in the guise of symbolic interactionism, ethnomethodology, and phenomenology) are basically over-reactions to Parsons (and some Marxists), who tend to exclude people – social actors – from their analyses while emphasising the role of the social system. But by replacing this with a concern with actors and their point of view, they neglect the influence of hierarchies that exist at different levels of social reality – micro, meso and macro – on the capacities of individuals. In particular, the neglect of power – the fact that some people are more powerfully placed in terms of their command of resources – biases the analysis exclusively towards the micro dimension and away from important micro–macro, and agency–structure linkages. Mouzelis also rejects the idea that macro phenomena are basically aggregations of micro episodes (as exemplified in Collins work – see Chapter 9).

Another target of Mouzelis's criticism of the current state of sociological theory are 'rational choice theories' which try to show that 'at the basis of all social phenomena are real, purposive actors pursuing their interests in a more or less rational manner' (Mouzelis, 1995: 28). Mouzelis mentions the more 'standard' (though nonetheless trenchant) criticism that in the 'messy' real world people do not operate on the basis of a rational calculus with cleanly defined goals and objectives solely geared to the maximisation of their satisfaction. But he also points out that rational choice theories fail to examine emergent configurations, hierarchical relations and power struggles between competing groups. He also pinpoints their neglect of the importance of historical and cultural contexts which influence the behaviour of actors and groups. Thus, says Mouzelis, like all generalisations lacking in context, the propositions of rational choice theorists tend to be merely trivial or wrong. Thus such theories are as unsuccessful as the interpretative micro sociologies 'in establishing effective linkages between micro and macro levels of analysis' (Mouzelis, 1995: 40).

Post-structuralism and postmodernism are also regarded as responsible for taking social theory along some false routes and culs-de-sac, according to Mouzelis. The idea of decentring the subject (at the heart of both post-structuralism and postmodernism) means that these approaches are unable to deal with the problem of how and why certain discourses (and the discursive practices they organise) are more powerful than others. As Mouzelis points out, unless individual and collective actors are put at the centre of analysis, the social world is 'reduced to a non-hierarchical "flat" place, and as such it can neither be described nor explained properly' (1995: 48). Similarly, the postmodernist attack on the notion of an empirical world beyond language, texts or other symbolic constructions leads to an extreme relativism that hinders empirical research.

Overall, Mouzelis is scathing of post-structuralism and postmodernism as reflected in the work of Foucault, Derrida, Baudrillard and Lyotard. Their rejection of boundaries between disciplines means that these approaches operate with an indiscriminate mixture of concepts derived from philosophy, literature, sociology, psychoanalysis and semiotics. Along with their neglect of social hierarchies and the agency–structure distinction, this produces an ill-thought-out, hotchpotch of ideas. Complex macro phenomena are simplistically explained by reduction to signs, texts, discourses and so on. As a result, postmodern theorising

> is marked by a relativism that tries to persuade us that any theoretical construction, however bizarre or crude, is just as true or false as any other. It is also not surprising that postmodernist theory tends to adopt a style where the lack of depth and of substantive analysis is concealed by a quasi-poetical language glorying in the obscure, the ambivalent, in plays on words and similar gimmicks. (Mouzelis, 1995: 54–5)

I agree wholeheartedly with what Mouzelis objects to in rational choice theory, post-structuralism and postmodernism. I also agree, in the main, with what he says about micro sociology, although I would take issue with his view of Goffman, whom he characterises as 'just another' microsociologist. I think it is clear from my previous comments on Goffman that it is unwise to see his work as solely restricted to issues in microsociology without any concern for the macro or structural side of the equation. Certainly, his loose coupling idea would give the lie to this interpretation. But apart from this, Mouzelis pinpoints the basic flaws in these approaches and indicates what they lack. Most importantly, they lack a concern with agency–structure linkages and social hierarchies, as they exist at different levels of social structure and social analysis.

Moreover, in my view, Mouzelis's general aim of reappropriating sociological theory as a means of generating a set of conceptual tools that will help sociologists build bridges between different paradigms and approaches by removing the obstacles to open-ended communication is highly desirable (and has always been a central aim of my own work [Layder, 1990, 1993, 1998]). I agree that the only way of achieving this state of affairs is to oppose the dismissal of the agency–structure distinction as misleading and as creating more problems than it solves. Any attempt to reject or 'transcend' the distinction leads to a theoretical impasse. The way out is to show how various paradigms use the agency–structure distinction and to examine the complex linkages between them.

Problems with Mouzelis's Remedies

Via critical encounters with major figures such as Parsons, Elias, Bourdieu and Giddens, Mouzelis outlines what he describes as some tentative remedies for the parlous state of sociological theory. Mouzelis's comments on Elias are very much in accord with those found in Chapter 7. In this respect, Mouzelis agrees that 'figurational sociology claims to overcome the conventional distinction between agency and structure since the concept of figuration entails both' (1995: 75), but concludes that the concept cannot displace that of 'institutional structure' and that both concepts are necessary for viewing social arrangements in a multi-dimensional manner. Boudieu, with his notion of 'habitus', and Giddens, with his concept of the 'duality of structure', also try to synthesise or transcend structural and interpretative sociologies. Mouzelis insists that they both fail in this regard, but that if they are 'restructured' they can 'help us understand better the way in which participants relate to social wholes'.

Mouzelis points out that Bourdieu's notion of habitus does not transcend the subjectivism–objectivism distinction (as Bourdieu thinks it does) for reasons already covered in this book (see also final chapter). That is, the notion of habitus (as actors' predispositions) is still trapped at an objective structural level and does not take account of what Mouzelis calls the interactive–situational dimension of 'social games'. Bourdieu believes that the notion of habitus goes beyond both interpretative sociology (symbolic interactionism, ethnomethodology and so on), as well as the institutional (structural, system) theories of Parsons and various Marxists. Mouzelis, however, points out that it does not. Rather, habitus sits comfortably alongside, and complements, both Parsonian role theory and the interpretative sociologies as another general (universal) dimension of social action.

I agree with Mouzelis's general assessment of the notion of habitus – that it simply complements other approaches (both subjectivist and objectivist) rather than transcends them or replaces them. However, unlike Mouzelis, I believe that although habitus adds to the conceptual armoury available for researchers to *describe* various aspects of social behaviour, it does not add anything substantial – *of an explanatory nature* – to the debate about the nature of the linkages between agency and structure or macro and micro. To say that habitus serves as part of the description of social action doesn't help in the explanatory understanding of agency–structure links – how we account for their nature or how they are formed.

Mouzelis also has a rather puzzling construal of Giddens's structuration theory, particularly his notion of the duality of structure. On the one hand, Mouzelis says that the concepts of structuration theory lead to a 'dead end as far as the integration of subjectivist and objectivist sociologies is concerned' (1995: 119). The duality of structure notion leads to the conflation of agency and structure (1995: 12) and, as a result, like Bourdieu, Giddens does not transcend the dualism inherent in it. On the other hand, Mouzelis claims that the duality of structure can be seen as complementary to subject–object dualism and thus can become part of a useful and legitimate approach to understanding agency–structure linkages.

But this is a contradictory position to hold. If, indeed, the duality of structure principle conflates agency and structure, as Mouzelis says it does, then *ipso facto*, it cannot register the discrete connections between these two orders of reality. Conflation means to blend or fuse together, and this would have the effect of dissolving any distinct (or partly independent) characteristics possessed by agency and structure. The consequence of such blending or fusing is that the duality of structure principle cannot be of use in teasing out the links between agency and structure. This can only be achieved in the context of a conceptual framework that is able to register the distinct (and partly independent) characteristics of agency and structure. Put another way, it is not possible to argue that the duality of structure principle conflates agency and structure while also claiming that it is complementary to dualism.

The reason why Mouzelis attempts to hold these incompatible views is because he operates with rather idiosyncratic definitions of 'duality' (as in the duality of structure) and dualism. Mouzelis understands duality and dualism (quite wrongly in my view) as different cognitive capacities of actors with respect to social rules. Thus, for Mouzelis, a 'duality' (of structure) refers to circumstances in which people are unable to distance themselves from social rules and resources, whereas 'dualism' refers to circumstances in which they can distance themselves from such rules. Mouzelis moves from these (erroneous) definitions to the claim that duality and dualism are compatible. Thus, he argues, because in some situations actors do not distance themselves from rules and resources while in other situations they do, both duality and dualism exist in social life. Thus Giddens's 'duality of structure' simply needs to be extended to embrace dualism as well, in order to link agency and structure into a more encompassing framework.

The basic flaw in this strategy is that the duality of structure is not about the inability of actors to distance themselves from rules any more than dualism is about their ability to do so. There is a fundamental ontological confusion here. The ability (or otherwise) of actors to distance themselves from social rules concerns their mental capacities in dealing with and orienting to the social environment. But actors' rule-distancing abilities and skills are not relevant to the 'duality versus dualism' problem which is primarily about whether or not social structures (or systems) are real. In this respect, Giddens's notion of 'duality' is about structures having a virtual existence (as memory traces) and as being understood as internal to agency, whereas dualism is about structures having a real existence (beyond the minds of individuals) and which must be understood as both internal and external to agency.

The problem or dilemma is also about whether agency and structure should be regarded as relatively autonomous (as in dualism) or whether their distinctive characteristics should be conflated and dissolved (as in duality). Regardless, it is of paramount importance that these issues should not be confused with the analytically separate issue of the rule-distancing skills of individuals. Rather than strengthening structuration theory, the strategy of trying to incorporate actors' rule-distancing skills into Giddens's notion of the duality of structure merely adds to its weaknesses. In any case, it does little to further the understanding of agency–structure linkages that Mouzelis is otherwise so keen to achieve.

Mouzelis's emphasis on the importance of power hierarchies, collective actors, institutional and figurational structures and different levels of social organisation has merit, especially when employed as a critique of conceptual frameworks in which such emphases are missing. However, his general view of power has some fundamental limitations. The primary drawback is that it is couched solely at the structural or systemic level. This is a common error in sociological analysis and fails to take account of the (variable) subjective powers of individuals as a result of their psychobiographical experiences. Also it does not register the different but intimately connected, mediating roles of 'situated activity' and 'social settings' (understood as relatively autonomous social domains), wherein both objective and subjective powers are modified and transformed (Layder, 1997; see also Chapter 12 for a more detailed discussion).

This restricted notion of power feeds into Mouzelis's failure to appreciate the more positive aspects of Goffman's work on the interaction order. It also leads him to a misconceived rendering of the distinction between micro and macro orders. Mouzelis castigates Goffman's wholly orthodox view of the interaction order as equated with 'micro' and the institutional order as 'macro'. Instead, says Mouzelis,

> both orders can be micro and macro. When face-to-face interactions have consequences which stretch widely in time/space, they are macro. On the other hand, when institutions are embodied into role positions which entail low levels of power (or games whose outcomes do not stretch so widely), then they are micro. (1995: 158)

This redefinition of micro and macro is based on a misunderstanding of the respective natures of 'institutions' on the one hand, and 'face-to-face conduct' on the other, and further compounded by a lack of distinction between forms of power and the consequences of power games played by powerful actors. In the first place, 'micro' in its conventional sense is about the analysis of face-to-face relations (variously referred to as encounters, situated activity, interaction). That is, it is about the immediacy and personalised quality of actual interpersonal relations in encounters. In this sense, the 'micro' world is quite different from what is referred to by the term 'institutions', which refers to impersonal, reproduced relations, which are typically stretched widely in time and space. Thus the term 'micro' can never be equated with the institutional order, just as the term 'macro' can never be equated with the interaction order. Mouzelis confuses radically different aspects of social reality (different kinds of thing), which are, nonetheless, closely intertwined with each other in the social world. Thus it is possible to speak of micro interactions as occurring within institutions, and of them being influenced by institutions, as well as institutions being 'given life' by cohorts of actors and their micro interactions.

Certainly, as Mouzelis says, some micro interactions can have implications for institutional and other phenomena if they involve powerful games between powerful actors and if their consequences stretch widely in time and space. But in itself, 'micro' (as face-to-face conduct) is quite neutral with regard to outcomes and the power of those involved. Here, Mouzelis's restricted notion of power comes into play. He makes no distinctions between individual power, interactional power, the power derived from organisational setting, and wider command over resources, and this is, perhaps, a reason why he wrongly equates the micro world with low power and macro with high power. In this respect, Mouzelis's habit of speaking of 'mega' or 'macro' actors is also quite misleading. It is more accurate to say that some actors have more power than others in some situations and settings. As a consequence, it is sometimes the case that the actions of such powerful actors may (or may not) have far-reaching consequences for macro phenomena like institutions.

Emphatically, though, this is not the case all the time, as for example when such actors deal with their spouse or friends with regard to some personal issue, or when their actions are part of some routine pattern of behaviour (for a more detailed examination of these issues see Sibeon, 2004). Powerful as well as powerless actors engage in (micro) face-to-face conduct all the time, but the consequences of such behaviour are not necessarily of far-reaching import. Much situated behaviour, regardless of whether it involves very powerful, moderately powerful or relatively powerless individuals, have consequences that are very limited and local.

In this respect, Mouzelis does not recognise the usefulness of Goffman's notion of the interaction order for grasping the important role of situated interaction (micro, face-to-face conduct) and its loosely coupled relationship with the institutional order. In Chapter 12, I argue in more detail that while Goffman's views are in need of amendment, they contain some useful theoretical ideas consistent with the essential and positive aspects of dualism. Most importantly, they resist the conflationary tendencies to be found in Giddens's, Elias's and Bourdieu's work, as well as the pure 'abandonment' (of the agency–structure distinction) posturing of post-structuralism and postmodernism.

Archer's Morphogenetic Approach

Archer's work (1982, 1988, 1995) is a rigorous defence of what she terms 'analytical dualism'. As such, it is the strongest advocate of the necessity for understanding the interplay between agency and structure than the other three authors considered in this chapter. Although there is more in common between her work and Mouzelis's (than with Goffman's or Turner's), there are also substantial differences, as we shall see. I think these differences arise mainly because Archer takes more care over ontological, epistemological and methodological issues associated with the establishment of agency–structure linkages. In this respect, some of her work is very akin to my own (Layder, 1981, 1982, 1990) and both bodies of work have developed in parallel at roughly the same time, although there are aspects of my own work (Layder, 1993, 1997, 1998, 2004a, b) that take a quite different direction and I discuss these in the concluding chapter.

By calling her social theory 'morphogenetic', Archer is drawing attention to the fact that the ordered forms (the 'morpho' part of the term) that society takes have their genesis (the 'genetic' part of the term) in human agency, just as social beings have their genesis in social forms (Archer, 1995: 167). This formulation attempts to capture something of the interplay between agency and structure (understood as distinctive realms of social reality), a consistent theme in her work. Her main complaint about the current state of social theory is that it is 'conflationary'. That is to say, different social theories, perspectives or frameworks tend to collapse together what, in fact, should be regarded as different levels of social reality. Thus agency and structure are collapsed together, dissolving their distinctive properties and obscuring the interplay between them. Much of what she says about the conflationary tendencies of social theories is consistent with what has been said so far in this book, although I have not used the term 'conflation'. However, Archer's discussion of different kinds of conflationary theorising serves as a useful summary of some of the overall themes covered so far.

Archer distinguishes between 'downwards' conflation, 'upwards' conflation and 'central' conflation. By 'downwards conflation' she is referring to those theories that understand social activity as the determinate resultants of social factors. Thus, as we have seen, Parsons and other functionalists (and neofunctionalists) as well as Marxist and structuralist theories in general, tend to emphasise the importance of 'social structure' or the 'social system' in setting the terms under which human beings play out their social lives. In this sense they over-stress or exaggerate the causal influence of social structural or systemic factors on human behaviour and social activity. Conversely, by 'upwards conflation' Archer points to theoretical perspectives like symbolic interactionism, ethnomethodology and phenomenology, which tend to view society as free creations of social agency. Thus, whereas in downwards conflation the relatively independent role of agency is denied in the face of the overwhelming influence of structural forces, upwards conflation entails the denial of the relatively independent role of structural or systemic factors in the face of the overriding influence of human agency.

Archer reserves the term 'central conflation' for those theories dealt with in Part 3 of this book, in which there is a conscious attempt to transcend the agency–structure problem. As I have expressed it, authors like Foucault, Elias and Giddens have attempted to break free of the orthodox agency–structure debate and to 'burn bridges' by adopting a vantage point which, they think, goes beyond it. By acknowledging that agency and structure are mutually constitutive, these theorists feel that this somehow resolves the debate. But as I have pointed out, this is very far from the truth. In the main, what they have succeeded in doing is turning their backs on the complex problems involved in adequately understanding agency–structure links. Arguably, Giddens's theory of structuration and Bourdieu's theory of practice are more sensitive to the complexities of the problem than Elias or Foucault, but even they fall down on the issue of what Archer calls central conflation. The idea that agency and structure are mutually constitutive artificially 'flattens' the social world into a single dimension (such as 'a duality of structure' or 'habitus'). The stratification of the social world is lost to analysis and thus it is impossible to examine the different, but linked, contributions of agency and structure to the formation (and reproduction) of social processes.

The advantage of what Archer calls 'analytical dualism' and 'the morphogenetic approach are precisely those that are denied to 'central conflation'. Instead of 'sinking one into the other', Archer insists that 'structure and agency can only properly be linked by examining the *interplay between them over time* and that without the proper incorporation of time the problem of agency and structure can never be satisfactorily resolved' (1995: 65). Apart from the temporal dimension, the notion of 'emergence' is an important component of 'analytical dualism', as it is in my own work (Layder, 1981, 1990). In this respect, agency and structure possess their own *emergent properties,* and thus it is impossible to treat them as if they are in any way equivalent to each other, or as if they can account for one another in an explanatory sense. But acknowledging these different properties and characteristics doesn't mean that the search for linkages between agency and structure is thereby compromised.

In fact, this leads to a recognition of one of the most important differences between approaches like Archer's and my own, that stress the distinctive emergent properties of different parts of social reality ('domains' in my terms, [Layder, 1997]) from those that emphasise the relationship between agency and structure as a duality rather than a dualism. Duality or 'central conflation' theorists make the mistake of assuming that dualism must entail separation and opposition between agency and structure and that it must, therefore, be a 'false distinction'. But, in fact, the dualism endorsed by both Archer and myself assumes that there are *real* differences between agency and structure (so that the distinction between them cannot be false). At the same time, they are closely interwoven aspects of social reality rather than separate and opposed. By pointing to real, substantial differences in the characteristics of agency and structure, their emergent properties are preserved, while at the same time the interconnections between them are also acknowledged.

By understanding agency and structure as *different but connected* in this manner, we are better able to grasp their respective contributions to social processes as well as the links between objective and subjective aspects of social reality. This is precisely what is needed when social researchers attempt to account for the historical emergence of divisions of labour, social hierarchies, forms of domination and exclusion and so on. Clearly, these refer to what are conventionally referred to as macro features of society and it is necessary to understand that they operate relatively independently of the routine activities of those who are influenced by them. Such structures, systems and the values and discourses enshrined in them, endure and outlive the generations that brought them into being in the first place. And, while successive generations (and individuals) have been responsible for changing or transforming various aspects of them, their fundamental structure precedes and post-dates particular individuals and groups (Layder, 1981, 1990).

Archer uses her empirical research on the development of educational systems to provide examples of the sometimes very complex elaborations of structure and agency (including collective agency) that occur over time. She is keen to stress that structures can be said to pre-exist successive cohorts or generations of actors (underpinning their emergent properties and relative autonomy) as a counter to the 'conflationist' idea that they can be reduced to patterns of social interaction or practices. But this does not mean that such structures are 'reified' because Archer stresses that structural elaborations can only occur through the medium of social activity.

Archer is also very concerned with what she calls the 'over-social view of the person' in sociological analysis. This is a problem common to many forms of sociological analysis, including that of Giddens and other 'central conflationists'. Effectively, this view suggests that self-identity is entirely social in origin and form. We have no private lives or inner passions, or unique personalities that shape our thoughts and behaviour, independently of, or at odds with, the social forces that also undeniably shape our behaviour. Archer takes issue with these mistaken assumptions that are typically found in social analysis and her critique of the over-social view of the person chimes with both Craib's (1998) and my own work (Layder, 1997, 2004a, b).

Critical Reflections on Analytical Dualism

I agree strongly with Sibeon (2004) when he points out that Archer has an unusual conception of micro and macro that should be resisted in favour of retaining more conventional definitions (indeed, as they have been employed in this book). Sibeon is critical of Archer's contention that the 'societal properties of Britain' may be 'macro' when viewed in terms of a study that is focused on Britain, but 'micro' when Britain is looked at in the context of Europe (Archer, 1995: 10). Sibeon suggests that switching to such a terminology is potentially confusing when say, France is, for some purposes, described as a micro entity and a small group of friends is described as a macro entity (Sibeon, 2004: 46–7). He goes on to say that a reason for 'Archer's wish to abandon conventional distinctions between micro and macro is her contention that "micro–macro" and "agency–structure" are simply different versions of exactly the same debate'. I side with Sibeon on this, and my previous comments on Mouzelis's attempt to redefine these terms are also pertinent here. Without repeating them, let me approvingly quote Sibeon once more: 'micro is not the same thing as agency and macro is not the same thing as structure'. Sibeon goes on to reinforce the point that the micro–macro distinction is a useful conceptual tool for marking out variations in the properties and temporal and spatial scale of social phenomena (Sibeon, 2004: 48).

Another problematic aspect of Archer's work concerns her general view of the micro world. She makes two assumptions about 'small-scale interpersonal encounters' that indicate limitations in her overall approach. The first is contained in her statement that the existence of such small-scale encounters 'does not make them into a sociological category'. The second assumption is apparent when she continues that 'much less if this is on the presumption that they are somehow immune to factors belonging to other strata of social reality' (Archer, 1995: 10). Both of these assumptions betray a downgrading of the theoretical and empirical importance of interpersonal encounters. As a consequence, Archer misses out on what I term the 'domain of situated activity' as mediating the effects of individual psychological factors, including emotion, desire, spirituality, personality (which she otherwise endorses), as well as various kinds of structural or systemic element.

By pointing to this mediating role I am referring to the relatively independent influence of situated activity but, at the same time, by no means suggesting that it is immune from influence by other factors. Quite the contrary, 'mediation', by its very nature, involves multiple reciprocal influences. In this respect, Archer overlooks the fact that the domain of situated activity possesses emergent properties in its own right, despite her own very stringent emphasis on the importance of emergent properties as underpinning the stratified nature of social reality. Oddly, this is a stratum with its own emergent properties that Archer refuses to acknowledge.

This leads us into an even more fundamental problem with Archer's 'analytical dualism'. Now I am in complete agreement with the idea that agency and structure, as integral, distinctive, emergent entities, must not be conflated, dissolved or defined out of existence as they are in structuration theory and others based on 'flat' ontologies of practice. This requires that such theories must be rejected *in toto* (and not tinkered with, or added to, as Mouzelis suggests). Furthermore, they must be replaced with more adequate conceptual frameworks that preserve and accommodate the distinctive properties of agency and structure while simultaneously attempting to tease out their linkages and reciprocal influences. But 'analytic dualism' still tends to oversimplify what are hugely complex aspects of social ontology and hence leads to restrictions in explanatory scope and power. A truly adequate explanatory framework must be grounded in a more complex and expanded notion of social reality – one that recognises the interconnections between *multiple social domains* and hence moves beyond the rather confined terms of analytic dualism.

SUMMARY

- The work of Erving Goffman, Jonathan Turner, Nicos Mouzelis and Margaret Archer shares the view that the agency–structure and macro–micro dualisms refer to real, non-reducible orders of social reality. However, they have very different understandings of the nature of these dualism(s) and the manner in which their constituent elements are tied together.

- Erving Goffman's work has mainly concentrated on the unique characteristics of what he calls the 'interaction order'. However, he distinguishes between this and the institutional order and suggests that their relationship can be characterised as a 'loose coupling'. The interaction order brings together the needs of the self, a morality of trust and give and take, a concern with interactive meaning and resistance to institutional influences. Goffman is definitely against what he refers to as 'rampant situationalism' and therefore cannot be regarded as just another interactionist or phenomenologist. He characterises the interface between interactional and structural (institutional) orders as a 'membrane' that selects which influences are allowed through and which are not, and whether they are transformed in the process.

- Anne Rawls misinterprets Goffman by suggesting that he viewed the interaction order as self-contained and independent of social structure. Giddens over-stresses the directness of the links between interaction and institutions by empha-sising the idea that the interaction order performs distinctive functions and possesses distinctive characteristics. Goffman's actual (theoretical) position on the interaction order needs to be rescued from these misleading interpretations.

- Jonathan Turner's theory of interaction suggests that attempts to resolve or inte-grate macro and micro-analyses are premature and can only be achieved after sociologists have developed precise micro theories of interaction and precise macro theories of social structure. Turner's view of 'micro-dynamics' involves the importance of the self and its emotional underpinnings. Sustaining self-esteem, security, predictability and trustworthiness are pivotal to 'feeling right' in encoun-ters. Turner's view that micro and macro analyses will always remain disconnected seems to undercut his own suggestion that agency–structure and micro–macro are mutually constitutive. It is also at odds with other emphases in his work, in which he rejects Collins's strategy of micro-translation of macro concepts and emphasises the importance of emergent properties.

- Nicos Mouzelis diagnoses the problems of sociological theory in an attempt to pinpoint why it has gone wrong. He believes that the microsociologies are overreactions to structural and systemic theories (like Parsons's and Marx's). The propositions of 'rational choice' theorists are either trivial or wrong. As far as post-structuralism and postmodernism are concerned, their rejection of individual and collective agency and their attack on the notion of an empirical world beyond lan-guage and texts leads to an extreme relativism that hinders research. Although Mouzelis is critical of many aspects of their work, he feels that Bourdieu's notion of 'habitus' and Giddens's 'duality of structure' are important for the establishment of agency–structure links. However, Mouzelis's attempt to appropriate or 'extend' these concepts and to integrate them with dualism runs into major theoretical and substantive problems.

- Margaret Archer's 'morphogenetic approach' relies heavily on what she terms 'analytical dualism'. Importantly, this approach counters what she describes as the 'conflationary' tendencies of current social theories and, as an alternative to them, it emphasises the distinctive emergent properties of agency and structure as well as their interplay over time. Archer also argues against the idea that the self is entirely socially constructed, a theme found in much sociological analysis. However, like Mouzelis, Archer wishes to redefine conventional ideas of macro and micro, but again, like Mouzelis, her proposed changes are rather idiosyncratic and inappropriate, producing greater confusion rather than clarity. Archer's views on the nature of small-scale encounters and their role in social analysis lead her to undervalue the emergent properties of situated activity. Overall, 'analytic dualism' underplays the complexity of social reality by failing to grasp its multi-dimensional nature.

12

New Directions: The Theory of Social Domains

PREVIEW

- What is in the social universe? What does social reality look like?

- The domain of psychobiography.

- Personal identity, emotion and agency.

- Problems with the concept of agency.

- The domain of situated activity.

- Situated activity and meaning.

- Power, control and emotion.

- The domain of social settings.

- The domain of contextual resources.

- Connecting agency and structure.

- The duality of social relations.

- Power and social domains.

- Constraints and enablements: agency and structure.

- Social production and reproduction.

- Goffman's interaction order and social domains.

- Habermas: lifeworld, systems and power.

- Bourdieu, power and agency.

- Self, psychobiography and disposition.

- The dialectic of separateness and relatedness.

- Connecting theory and research: adaptive theory.

- Adaptive theory, social domains and agency–structure links.

- Adaptive theory compared with other approaches.

- Conclusion: core dualisms and social theory.

This chapter pursues the issue raised at the end of the last chapter concerning the possibility of going beyond dualism and understanding social reality as multiple interrelated domains. The chapter is organised mainly around a discussion of my own work (Layder, 1981, 1990, 1993, 1997, 1998, 2004a, b), which involves two closely related emphases in social analysis. First, what I call the 'theory of social domains' (otherwise referred to as 'domain theory') deals with the problems surrounding the individual–society, agency–structure and macro–micro dualisms. The discussion naturally covers different facets of many of the issues and authors that have already figured prominently in this book. In particular, the discussion elaborates on various themes found in the work of Giddens, Bourdieu, Habermas and Goffman, among others.

The second emphasis is on creating practical social research strategies related to the development of social theory – what I term 'adaptive theory' – and which focuses on more empirical dimensions of agency–structure (macro–micro) connections. This raises issues that, so far, have only been considered briefly in passing. The chapter ends with some concluding comments that place the discussion in this chapter in the wider context of the book as a whole. They also serve to summarise the overarching themes about core dualisms and various theoretical responses to them that have informed the organisation of the book.

What is in the Social Universe? What Does Social Reality Look Like?

The theory of social domains rejects the idea that social reality can be properly understood in terms of theories or perspectives that attempt to reconcile or synthesise agency and structure but only succeed in merging or dissolving their

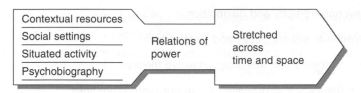

Figure 12.1 *The layering of social domains and power in time and space*

distinct characteristics, as is the case with Foucault (and postmodernists in general), symbolic interactionists, phenomenologists, Elias, Bourdieu, Berger and Luckmann, and Giddens. Domain theory suggests that instead of a simple dualism (of agency and structure) we should think of the social universe as multi-dimensional – as four interconnected domains. Such a perspective acknowledges the richness, complexity and depth of the social universe, qualities that are denied or obscured by the reductive tendencies of the above theories.

As we have seen in Parts 2 and 3, theories that reject the dualism of agency and structure substitute for it with some singular process or phenomenon. Thus Foucault speaks of 'discursive practices', Bourdieu of 'social practices', Giddens of 'the duality of structure' and/or reproduced 'social practices', Elias of 'figurations' or 'process analysis', while symbolic interactionists talk of 'joint activity' and phenomenologists of 'intersubjectivity' of 'local practices'. However, describing social reality in terms of such singular 'unifying' processes artificially compacts the nature and scope of social reality. Any sense of its depth, richness and complexity is thereby lost.

But by itself dualism is not enough. What is meant by the concepts of agency and structure (system) must be unpacked to restore the subtlety and complexity obscured by the terms themselves. In short, we need a multi-dimensional approach that takes into account the variegated nature of social reality.

On the left of Figure 12.1 the four social domains are represented vertically as layers of social reality 'frozen in time', so to speak. The lower layers represent more immediate, personalised aspects of social reality, while the higher ones are relatively more remote and impersonal. This vertical dimension indicates 'ontological depth' and directly conflicts with those theories that collapse together agency and structure to present a 'flattened' image of social reality. But this purely vertical representation does not capture the dynamics of social activity and social processes. Social processes are never static, they constantly move through time and space. In this sense the layers or domains are stretched out along a horizontal axis depicting the ever-flowing nature of social processes and human activities. Thus the domains exist in both vertical (depth ontology) and horizontal (space and time) dimensions. The centre of Figure 12.1 indicates that the domains are interconnected through social relations of power which are also stretched out over time and space.

The Domain of Psychobiography

The psychobiographical domain highlights an individual's existence as it follows a career trajectory through time and space in the social world. It maps a person's unique experiences as they have unfolded from birth to the present. As such it indicates how their interactions with primary caretakers (and other early experiences) have coloured their attitudes, ideas, values and dispositions. It also traces the impact of critical experiences (like illnesses or psychological traumas) on the manner in which they psychologically manage their personal and social lives. Every individual's trajectory is unique because his or her life develops in the context of a unique configuration of relationships with others. Even if a person shares a great deal with siblings, the smallest differences may be of great importance to his or her own psychosocial development. Furthermore, every person responds differently to social experiences (even shared ones).

These two facets are strongly interlocked. Each person's experiences and social relationships are unique in themselves and this fact reinforces the individuality of the person's social and psychological responses to them. For most of us these twin pressures towards individuation continue throughout our lifetime and become even stronger as we explore our autonomy and independence in ever-wider social contexts. A stress on our uniqueness is of the utmost importance for a refined understanding of social experience and social interaction. Most social theories either deny or suppress and devalue this fact by exaggerating the extent to which the 'individual' (or 'subject') is a socially constructed effect of the influence of social forces such as discourses, rule following, socialisation and so on. Social constructionism obliterates individual characteristics and unique subjective responses, producing a defective understanding of the relationship between the individual and society.

Personal Identity, Emotion and Agency

The theory of social domains suggests that individuals exist both 'inside' and 'outside' society. We can never escape from social influences entirely, but as individuals we also retain a significant measure of independence from them (Layder, 2004a, b). We are, albeit in a minor sense, asocial and anti-social beings who have private desires, wishes and needs that often conflict with social expectations and values. We are emotionally unique beings, not simply rationally self-reflexive agents choosing the most appropriate way of maximising our satisfaction (as suggested, for example, in rational choice theories). Emotions such as jealousy, anger and hatred are capable of disrupting the smooth veneer of social situations and relationships. Motivations associated with these emotions drive us to behave in ways contrary to custom, ritual and routine, although this behaviour is also shaped by important social components. Such emotions and motivations ensure that we are never entirely the creatures of society. We are distinct individuals whose psychological requirements are often antithetical to the social order.

Because we are unique, the fit between the individual and society is imprecise, imperfect and much more tenuous than most sociologists would allow. Processes of socialisation by parents, peers, institutions and the values and mores they seek to inculcate, cannot create individuals who are completely held within their grip. As self-reflexive beings we choose to adhere (with varying degrees of commitment) to some values, expectations, ideas and objectives rather than others. Emotional uniqueness also means that the fit between society and the person is precarious with respect to mental well-being. We must resist the idea that society is a well-oiled machine in which social routines and rituals automatically produce ontological security (inner psychological security), which is precisely the picture Giddens (1991) paints. Craib (1994) rightly points out that all adults feel contradictory fears associated with intimacy such as abandonment, or of being engulfed by others. The experience of social life is as likely to be one of disappointment and anxiety as it is of security and trust.

Indeed, from the point of view of domain theory, anxiety and insecurity are never completely allayed, conquered or successfully 'inoculated' against. Every situation must be regarded as a potential threat to inner security for even the most calm and mentally stable of us. What distinguishes those who are (or seem to be) unfazed by ordinary social existence and those who are socially disabled by chronic fear and anxiety is that the former are able to manage and deal with the uncertainties and threats (to self-esteem and security) that are inherent features of everyday existence. In this sense security and trust are forever 'unfinished' and incomplete. They are best understood as temporary, personal (although social as well as psychological in nature) 'accomplishments' generated within everyday encounters. Thus, trust and security vary from situation to situation depending on the level of threat they pose as well as the individual's personal level of tolerance

(Layder, 1997). But the capacity for trust and security also varies in relation to critical life events and their effects on psychological resilience.

Problems with the Concept of Agency

Psychobiographical factors underline the limitations of the concept of agency in the work of theorists tackling the agency–structure problem. The concept of agency does not capture the accretive nature of personal identity as it develops over time or the way the psychobiographical process produces emotionally unique individuals. In short, it fails to register the variability of personal powers, capacities, resources and skills that each individual uniquely possesses. Thus a major problem with the concept of social agency is that it is an over-general depiction of human beings – it does not capture the crucial (individual) details. For example, Giddens speaks of social agents as possessing what he calls a 'transformative capacity', by which he means that human beings are capable of altering their social circumstances. In this sense we are never simply the hapless victims of social forces; we always have some means at our disposal to deal with or counteract our circumstances, no matter how oppressive they happen to be. This is true insofar as we are all responsible, to some extent, for our own destiny. Rather than acquiesce we can choose to resist oppressive circumstances (say poverty or chronic illness) and carve out areas of independence, no matter how modest they may be.

However, the idea that we are all equally endowed with the same generic transformative capacity fails to grasp the great variations in the strength of such personal capacities. Only a notion such as psychobiography can begin to tap into these variations by tracing personal experience (through social life) over time. Each person is formed as a unique bundle of subjective powers, emotions, skills and resources that are liable to alter in response to changing circumstances. Actually, human beings do not have generic skills or qualities – real individuals possess uniquely variable powers. It is true that some people are more than capable of managing their own emotional needs as well as dealing with others and challenging situations. But for many others their 'inner power' is less pronounced and robust. Thus they are much less effective in dealing with challenging circumstances or even dealing with the routine problems and misfortunes of life. The notion of a generic transformative capacity does not register individual variation in emotional intelligence, resilience and subjective power. The lack of equivalent powers of control means that it is misleading to speak of the transformative power of social agency as a generic capacity of human beings.

The Domain of Situated Activity

Ironically, while the concept of agency is misleadingly general with reference to the subjective powers of individuals, when we turn to the main area in which the business of social life is conducted – social interaction – it tends to be too 'individualising'. Although personal powers vary, other social domains influence the extent to which this power prevails in particular circumstances. The concept of social agency does not capture the influence of situated activity – the intersubjective dimension of social life – and differs from psychobiography in a number of respects.

First, situated activity is governed by a rather different notion of time. Whereas psychobiography frames the lifetimes and personal identities of individuals as they are traced by personal and social careers, situated activity frames the beginning and ending of encounters. This directly highlights the episodic nature of situated activity which, in Goffman's (1967) phraseology, is punctuated by the 'arrivals and departures' of those involved. Episodes of situated activity are evanescent in nature – from the moment they are initiated, time is running down until the natural business of the encounter is completed. This may be a fleeting exchange between two people (a greeting or a comment on the weather) or it might last several hours (a committee meeting or a night out) but, generally, episodes are relatively short and limited by whether those involved are 'physically in one another's response presence' (Goffman, 1983). Often, there are chains of mini-episodes as people break off and come together during more prolonged business.

Situated Activity and Meaning

The episodic and evanescent quality of situated activity feeds into another distinctive characteristic of this domain – it is an arena in which meaning is created. As we saw in Part 2, symbolic interactionists, phenomenologists and ethnomethodologists have all emphasised that social interaction is the primary arena for the creation of meaning. Blumer (1969) suggested that meaning arises from the mutual responses of those present in the interaction as opposed to social structural or systemic factors such as role, status and class. Garfinkel (1967) and his followers have stressed the indexicality of meaning – that is, it is internal to the (unique) situations in which it arises. As such, indexical meaning cannot be understood outside the context of its use.

While interaction is one important source of meaning, as these writers have shown, domain theory departs substantially from symbolic interactionism and phenomenology over the broader question of meaning. The creation of meaning is not limited to the domain of situated activity – it is an amalgam of the influences of different domains. In the first place, meanings are partly products of psychobiography and therefore possess a personal, private component. Blumer explicitly rejects this idea, as do Goffman and Garfinkel, by suggesting that personal (psychological) predispositions tell us nothing about how meaning is perceived in face-to-face encounters. Only internally organised local (situational) practices can reveal this. For example, according to these authors, the meaning of a kiss has nothing to do with the prior subjective attitudes and feelings of those involved. Meaning resides entirely within the interactive situation in which it occurs.

But this denial of subjectivity, or of an 'inner' human psychology, will not do. Clearly, if you have a general aversion to kissing because of embarrassment or because you find the exchange of bodily fluids repellent or because of anxiety about sexual intimacy, then this will undoubtedly colour the meaning that you and the other person will attribute to the act itself. Of course, it won't wholly determine the meaning. The interpersonal dynamics and the emergent nature of the interaction will play a significant part, but crucially the personal, subjective aspects of meaning cannot be dismissed as irrelevant.

These same authors also reject the view that 'external' factors, such as class and gender or general social ideas about sexuality and friendship, significantly influence the creation and emergence of meaning. They argue that such factors only become 'significant' in the context of the unfolding nature of interaction and that this is not inevitable. Even if they do become significant, they only do so as 'topics' raised by the participants. They do not influence proceedings irrespective of the purposes and intentions of those involved. This is tantamount to dismissing the relevance of stored cultural phenomena ('third world' phenomena in Popper's [1972] terms) in the formation of meaning. This is as unsatisfactory as the prohibition on personalised aspects of meaning.

In the theory of domains, the influence of reproduced, 'stored' cultural meanings (as found, say, in dictionary definitions) on situated activity is emphasised rather than denied. Meaning within activity must be understood as an amalgam of subjective, external and situated influences. This view of situated activity, however, does endorse the phenomenological idea that encounters themselves also create emergent, shared aspects of meaning and behaviour which are 'internally' generated (Malone, 1997).

Power, Control and Emotion

Situated activity, then, is a subtle and complex amalgam of the powers, emotions and mutual influences of multiple individuals that unfolds in the real time of the encounter. While its outward appearance may be apparently smooth and untoward, it is likely that rather more is taking place beneath the surface of the encounter. This is particularly so with the mutual exchange of emotion and feeling, much of which goes on below the conscious awareness of the participants. Individuals approach encounters not only with their apparent intentions, objectives and purposes, but also with diffuse emotional needs that must, in part, be catered for within the encounter. Each participant requires minimal levels of recognition, acceptance, inclusion, approval and other psychological reassurances in order that personal identity, security, self-esteem and self-value are affirmed and reaffirmed.

These are obtained via the attention, care and deference given by others. Such 'underground' emotion work accounts for constantly shifting feelings of alignment and attunement (or conversely of estrangement and awkwardness) that are typically experienced in encounters. The relative success of such a vast amount of everyday, face-to-face behaviour is due to the hugely skilled nature of human beings in social life. At the same time, difficulties and feelings of being out of kilter are never far from the scene. As Scheff has observed, much of routine interaction is 'a fast moving blur of misunderstanding, error, folly, alienation, with only rare and all too brief moments of attunement' (Scheff, 1990: 50).

Given that this is so often the case, it is perhaps strange that more people do not opt out of, or in various ways avoid, everyday encounters on a more regular basis. Clearly, 'avoidance' occurs to some extent, and with some individuals rather more than with others. However, the compelling enticement of situated activity is that it is the principal means of fulfilling desire for social recognition, acceptance, inclusion and approval. At the same time (and again, largely beyond conscious awareness), each person engages in power and control strategies in the unfolding activity (Layder, 2004b). Individual powers (skills and capacities) are conditioned, modified, reined-in or enhanced by the emergent nature of encounters.

Individuals control and influence encounters in three distinct senses. First, there is the question of self-control and the general need to maintain self-composure during social interaction. Lapses of self-control and composure in public are only sanctioned or encouraged in very specific and 'appropriate' circumstances. Unpredictable, unscheduled breakdowns threaten the smoothness and 'organised' character of encounters. Secondly, recognition, approval and so on, have to some extent to be engineered through mutual emotional exchange. Each person must both give and obtain emotional satisfaction from their social exchanges. This is mainly achieved by mutual benign control and influence, a process in which each person acknowledges and honours the interests, rights and needs of others (Layder, 2004a, b). Of course, altruism often takes back seat to self-interest and manipulation. Much routine social interaction is a mixture of altruism and 'softer' forms of manipulation and self-interest.

Thirdly, situated activity is the most 'at hand' means that people have for dealing with their broader life situation. An individual's life situation is, in part, an objective network of social relationships with those who are most closely implicated in their personal circumstances. But 'life situation' is also deeply psychological in nature. It is a sensitive reflection of an individual's general feeling, tone and state of mind. It registers how well or badly a person is coping with circumstances and events, be they positive (as in marriage, a windfall, the birth of a child) or negative (such as family misfortune, ill-health and so forth).

The Domain of Social Settings

Situated activity represents the practical focus of transactions between people in lived time and, as such, mediates between subjective and objective elements of social reality. It filters and conditions the influences of both psychobiographical and structural (or systemic) domains. As system elements, social settings form the immediate environment of situated activity. Settings vary in their organisational form. In some, relationships are formal and tightly structured, such as schools, universities, hospitals, industrial/commercial firms, government bureaucracies and so on. Others are based on informal, loosely patterned relationships such as friendships, partnerships and family networks. Although their form is variable, social settings are clearly distinguishable from other domains in that they are local aggregations of *reproduced* social relations, positions and practices. As such, social settings embody systemic (structural) aspects of social life – the reproduced outcomes of past social activities that influence behaviour in the present.

In more formal settings, social relationships are clearly defined and typically hierarchical in nature – usually a graded sequence of positions and statuses. Interaction is defined through these positions and the practices associated with them, and commitment is generated by career inducements and penalties. In more informal settings, positions and practices are less crystallised and precisely defined, and commitment is not organisationally 'enforced'. Nevertheless, the influence of these elements is equally real and engaging as far as the minds and behaviour of participants are concerned. For example, the position-practices associated with friendship or parental behaviour are drawn from a diversity of sources, including tradition, best practice, neighbourhood, class position, ethnicity, personality and experience. As such, they call for strong commitment and adherence, but are policed and sanctioned by wider communal influences. Furthermore, there is greater leeway for individual interpretation of position-practices. In this sense, how you behave as a parent has a great deal more to do with your personal identity and experience than with strict custom and practice. How you behave 'in private', as a friend, as a supporter of a sports team or as a hedonistic pleasure seeker, is to a great extent a question of personal beliefs and personal style. But in the final analysis there are strict limits on the kind of behaviour regarded as socially acceptable.

The Domain of Contextual Resources

From the point of view of an individual's experience the outermost social domain of contextual resources represents the most encompassing feature of the social environment. There are two constituent elements. First, a distributional aspect in which material resources are unevenly allocated and aligned with groupings such as those based on class, ethnicity, age, gender, status and so on. These furnish the immediate socio-economic context of particular social settings (educational, occupational, domestic/familial, neighbourhood and so on) and their effects are felt and experienced in social activities and the inner mental lives of individuals.

The other element of contextual resources derives from the historical accumulation of cultural resources such as knowledge, mores, artifacts, media representations, sub-cultural styles, fashion and popular culture. This is also the ultimate source of societal values (dominant, sub-cultural or counter cultural), which not only shape the cultural context of social settings, but also the consciousness of those individuals who are influenced by them. In part at least, this bears some resemblance to Parsons's (1951) notion of a 'cultural system' except that Parsons only really included legitimate (central) values and therefore excluded ideology and oppositional values. But such cultural items also reflect what Popper (1972) describes as 'knowledge without a knowing subject'. The most vivid examples of such knowledge are the libraries of books that constitute a store of cultural documents and exist independently of their use by particular individuals or groups.

Contextual resources, then, embrace both material and cultural dimensions. We can understand the relationship between them in a broadly Marxian sense, in which the distributional elements provide the infrastructural foundation on which the cultural or ideological elements rest. By this I do not mean that the material infrastructure *determines* the ideological, cultural and discursive super-structure, but rather that it influences it in a diffuse manner. There is a wide array of discursive forms and not all of them are direct ideological reflections of the economic infrastructure.

Connecting Agency and Structure

Although social domains are clearly distinguishable from each other, it is impor-tant not to lose sight of the links and continuities between them. While the domains have their own distinct characteristics and properties, they do not oper-ate separately or autonomously. Although as domains of social reality, psychobi-ography and situated activity primarily embody subjective and intersubjective components, they are greatly influenced (constructed and informed by) the more objective system domains of social settings and contextual resources.

Likewise, settings and contextual resources are not, in themselves, subjective or intersubjective phenomena, but they are only 'brought to life', so to speak, by individuals and their intermeshing activities. However, while they do not exist independently of activity, system elements cannot be reduced to, or understood as identical with, subjective or intersubjective phenomena. They have been reproduced in time and space through regular usage by successive generations of individuals. Historically they have become 'relatively independent' of current activity and this characteristic distinguishes them from the real, present time of unfolding situ-ated activities (encounters). In this sense, elements of agency and system interfuse and influence each other but without destroying their distinctive characteristics and generative power.

The Duality of Social Relations

The duality of social relations refers to the tension between their 'free-form' and 'reproduced' aspects or between their 'personally' and 'socially' defined character-istics. Friendship is a good example. In a practical sense, being someone's friend means something like 'getting on with them' and doing things with them in a way that provides satisfaction for both parties. We like each other's company, we get on well and are keen to ensure the survival of the relationship. As long as things remain like this it is unlikely that we would question the friendship. But if we have a row or strongly disagree about something, our taken-for-granted assumptions about 'friendship' may suddenly be thrown into question. We may ask 'Can he or she really be a friend?' – if, for example, she or he revealed a confidential matter to someone else or reneged on an agreement. All the hidden assumptions about friendship, its obligations, rights and responsibilities are suddenly revealed.

The socially defined character of friendship can be seen not only when it breaks down, but also when it transmutes into, or from, some other kind of bond such as romantic or sexual love. What starts out as a platonic friendship may develop into a more intimate romantic or sexual relationship. And while the underlying friendship may remain as part of the newly established sexual relationship, the type of intimacy will have changed. Similarly, a once passionate love affair may peter out and end up as friendship. In both cases, a qualitative change in the relationship takes place.

The duality of reproduced and free-form elements is inherent in all social relations. On the one hand, there are the socially defined and sanctioned aspects of social relations and the practices associated with them. On the other, situated activities involve the creative interpretation and modification of them. In some relations the reproduced aspects are dominant and exert a high level of constraint over behaviour. In others, the free-form aspects are more prominent and capable of tolerating a wider range of discretion for individual interpretation and enactment. But this is simply a matter of degree. The influence of either reproduced or free-form elements may be minimised in different settings and circumstances but can never be driven out entirely. There are always residual elements of both in all situated activity and individual behaviour.

Power and Social Domains

Each domain embodies a different form of power. Although individual and intersubjective forms of power belong to the domains of psychobiography and situated activity, we need to consider how they relate to the powers that derive from settings and contextual resources. Since the latter are reproduced features of social life, they represent power that has become historically entrenched in institutions and organisations. Such powers have endured over varying spans of history and represent established asymmetries structured around social relations, positions and practices. In varying degrees they are resistant to attempts to transform, modify or side-step their influence. Individual behaviour and situated activity exist within this envelope of more encompassing power relations. Thus episodes of social activity are a blend of individual, intersubjective and systemic (organisational or structural) forms of power. It is important to grasp the objective character of these reproduced relations of power and that the duality of social relations ensures that all social behaviour contains some imprint of them, no matter how faint, in the form of objective enablements and constraints.

In this sense, power must be understood as a multi-dimensional intermingling of forces. It should not be conceived as a uni-dimensional process as in Foucault's 'discursive practices', Giddens's 'dialectic of control', Elias's 'figurational' power, or Mouzelis's 'formal hierarchies'. A truly adequate and comprehensive notion of power must include genuinely objective and subjective elements as well as intersubjective ones. Only in this manner can the binding of agency and structure be fully understood.

Constraints and Enablements: Agency and Structure

To counter successfully the slide towards subjectivism that haunts structuration theories (including not only Giddens's but also Bourdieu's, Berger and Luckmann's, Blumer's and Glaser and Strauss's), it is important to preserve some notion of the objective aspects of social constraint. For example, Giddens claims that constraint cannot be understood independently of 'people's reasons and motivations' and are not external or objective in any sense. Thus they do not 'compel' people without their being able to do anything about it. Giddens is forced into this radically intersubjectivist position because he flatly rejects what he calls objectivism and determinism (see Chapter 9), which, he argues, automatically exclude people's choices, reasons and motivations. But Giddens overlooks the fact that some form of moderate objectivism is required to account for key aspects of institutional and cultural phenomena. He also fails to appreciate that a moderate objectivism need not undervalue the importance of reasons and motives.

An adequate explanation of constraint must focus on far more than reasons and motives. The mediating influences of situated activity, settings and contextual resources are crucial in enabling and constraining behaviour externally, as well as internally. Phenomena like norms, expectations, discourses and so on are trans-situational in that they exist and exert influence well beyond the situations of their use (Durkheim, 1982). The theory of social domains suggests that subjective, intersubjective and objective phenomena are different facets of a common social reality. They are not mutually exclusive, and hence competing, conceptions of social reality. From this perspective constraints do not operate independently of people, but neither are they reducible to people's motives and reasons.

In this sense, we are only 'compelled' by social forces when we are psychologically engaged with them, either voluntarily or through coercion. But when we freely decide to pursue goals or ambitions, such as becoming 'successful' or escaping from deprivation, the compelling character of constraint is plainly evident. In order to achieve such goals we must overcome social obstacles to their achievement, such as acquiring credentials or specialist knowledge or material resources. Simultaneously we have to adopt socially defined (rather then individually desired) pathways to their fulfilment. This is the same for both legitimate and illegitimate activities. For instance, material success may be achieved through hard work and perseverance, but it may also be 'acquired' by criminal activity. However, both routes highlight the compelling 'external' character of social constraints.

Social Production and Reproduction

Structuration theories propose that people are actively involved in *producing* or *creating* society while at the same time being centrally involved in its *reproduction*. This account has a number of unfortunate consequences. It vastly exaggerates the creative and transformative capacities of individuals by failing to appreciate that in their everyday activities people primarily reproduce rather than create social structural or system elements. For instance, in conversation we continually reproduce the rules of language use by drawing on these rules to make ourselves understood. If we were routinely innovative in our use of language, we would make little sense to others. Coining new idioms in language and conversation are not inherent features of routine social life. They cannot be, otherwise reciprocity, co-operation and orderliness in social life would be severely hampered. On the other hand, in everyday life social reproduction is essential for the continuity and flow of social processes.

Secondly, and somewhat ironically, structurationists underplay the level of creativity involved in situated activity by over-stressing the immediacy of the link between institutional factors and social behaviour. Thus in their terms, human creativity is limited to individual interpretation and innovation with respect to the enactment of institutional directives (values, discourses and so forth). In this sense the structurationist schema does not grasp the creativity involved in localised constructions of social reality. As a result, structurationists miss the creative aspects associated with the mediating influence between individuals and social systems.

Goffman's Interaction Order and Social Domains

How do Goffman's ideas about the interaction order (Chapter 11), relate to the theory of social domains? Goffman's work usefully draws attention to the relatively independent role of social interaction in relation to wider institutional aspects of society. However, there are important respects in which domain theory parts company with Goffman's ideas. For example, the theory of domains acknowledges the importance of individual psychobiography in shaping and influencing social behaviour, while Goffman, rather dogmatically, rejects the importance of 'the individual and his psychology'. Instead, he restricts his attention to 'the syntactical relations among the acts of different persons mutually present' (1967: 2). Another crucial difference is that Goffman conflates and confuses emergent interactive behaviour with the wider institutionalised values that inform such behaviour. This can be observed in Goffman's discussion of 'involvement obligations' as an example of the workings of the interaction order. Goffman fails to distinguish between involvement obligations as *general rules* that require people to display interest and involvement during face-to-face encounters and *how they actually behave* in specific situations.

As Garfinkel (1967) and Cicourel (1973) have pointed out, real sequences of interaction rarely correspond to general social rules about behaviour. Actual interactive behaviour cannot be described or analysed by invoking 'extra-situational' rules that are assumed (by the analyst) to organise proceedings. Only 'inside' knowledge of what is going on within the encounter from the participants' viewpoint can provide this. As general social rules (or expectations), involvement obligations themselves tell us little about how people express their involvement or how they feel when they do so. Depending on the unfolding circumstances they may even decide to ignore, get round or 'reinvent' such rules, such as pretending to be involved or giving less than full involvement. Therefore, Goffman's vision of the interaction order confuses and conflates the respective influences of very different (although deeply connected) aspects of social reality.

Habermas: Lifeworld, Systems and Power

As noted in Chapter 10, Habermas's theory of communicative action is firmly based on an ontological distinction between lifeworld and system phenomena. The theory of social domains suggests a similar fault line running through social reality and signifying the link between the reproduced character of system phenomena and the emergent characteristics of agency and action. Unlike the human beings (individuals and groups) who act within them and upon them, systems and their elements are non-acting phenomena. However, they are always in the process of being elaborated, restructured or transformed to varying degrees by specific individuals or groups. There is nothing in this conception of systems that involves reification. In themselves systems cannot act, nor are they capable of change independently of human intervention.

In domain theory the most striking difference from Habermas's usage of the lifeworld–system distinction is that the ontological dualism becomes part of a multi-dimensional perspective. While in Habermas's own schema dualism is seen as central (as it also is in Lockwood's 'social and system integration' and Archer's 'analytic dualism' of agency and structure), the theory of social domains understands it as part of a wider, more encompassing picture. Instead of a dualism we have a multi-dimensional framework of interlocking domains that represent qualitatively different aspects of social reality.

Another major difference concerns Habermas's restriction of the notion of power to the operation of the system elements of markets and bureaucracy. Power, for Habermas, is an alien intrusion into the lifeworld, an impurity resulting from its colonisation by system elements. This view of power underscores the undoubted importance of structural or systemic power as domination, but fails to account for subjective and interactive dimensions of power that cushion and condition the effects of systemic power.

Bourdieu, Power and Agency

Like Habermas, Bourdieu views power in an objective sense, but he conceptualises it in terms of class position and collective interests. Again, this is a one-dimensional view of power that effectively obscures other sources and forms, particularly psychobiographical and intersubjective powers which counter-balance the effects of systemic power. This skews Bourdieu's analysis towards objective factors as the major structuring principles of society and severely hampers his efforts to unite agency and structure through the notion of social practice.

Bourdieu's notion of 'fields' – such as economy, art, politics, intellectual or educational attainment – are defined as sets of objective positions within which individuals and groups struggle for advantage in the distribution of resources and the pursuit of interests deriving from them. In this sense, Bourdieu's framework avoids slipping into subjectivism by defining away objective aspects of structures and systems. There is also some advantage to be gained from viewing these objective aspects as integrally tied to the 'creativity' of human activity or practice.

But there are also problems with this analysis. Bourdieu's schema veers towards a view of human agency and practice as exclusively shaped by interests and dispositions defined in structural or systemic terms. Because Bourdieu does not acknowledge that 'fields' of practice are themselves an amalgam of two distinct (but related) domains – social settings and contextual resources (which are, in turn, different from psychobiography and situated activity) – his schema assumes a direct (unmediated) 'fit' between collective, group interests and individuals' dispositions. But this apparent tie between agency and structure is illusory. Bourdieu's framework does not take into account the mediating effects of social settings on the influence of contextual resources, in particular their fissuring and fragmenting effects.

In large part this structural bias results from Bourdieu's rather restricted view of social reality, which conflates several different sources and sites of power. As a consequence, his analysis does not register the important combined effects of these power sources. A case in point is Bourdieu's concept of practice, which fails to distinguish between the power deriving from psychobiographical agency and that stemming from situated activity. As already noted, an individual's subjective powers are variable and not simply the uniform effects of some generic notion of agency. Similarly, the emergent behavioural properties of situated activity must be taken into account in conditioning and mediating the influence of both subjective and objective forms of power.

Understanding power as multi-dimensional also means abandoning the idea of a uni-directional flow of power from one (higher) source – in Bourdieu's case from collective interests to social behaviour. Instead, power effects must be viewed as the combined effects of different domain sources of power. Some of these may, in certain circumstances, oppose each other in subtle and complex ways, while in others they may be relatively supportive. There are varying degrees of opposition and resistance to any currently dominant flow of power, which result in adjustments and counter-balances to it.

Of course, relatively durable forms of domination do exist but can only be formed from a multiplicity of factors in tension with each other. The exact nature of shifting power flows and alignments are issues to be decided by empirical investigation in varying substantive circumstances (and taking into account the role of chance [see Sibeon, 2004]). The answers to such questions cannot be decided by theoretical fiat, including a one-dimensional view of power.

Self, Psychobiography and Disposition

If we scrutinise Bourdieu's ideas about agency and 'habitus' in relation to practice and the reproduction of structure, it is obvious that, for him, the human self is an entirely social creation. There are no areas or capacities of the self that are not touched and influenced by the impress of social forces. Thus there is no notion of a unique, private aspect of the self in tension with the social order. In this respect Bourdieu operates with an over-socialised and 'over-constructed' vision of social agency. Not only is the self completely social in nature, but it is also geared to the pursuance of group (mainly class) interests. As a consequence of their social positioning, individuals and groups struggle with each other to gain competitive advantage in whatever field of activity they are engaged. Within these fields they seek to acquire various kinds of economic, political, social and cultural (or symbolic) capital in an effort to gain superiority. The self is thus 'oriented to certain interests' and 'motivated to compete and pursue strategies to enhance its power' (Parker, 2000: 48).

For Bourdieu such an apparent straitjacketing of individual capacities is analytically necessary to avoid the fallacy of endowing people with illusory freedoms. In effect, Bourdieu argues that individual subjectivity is only important in the context of the pursuit of collective, group interests. The mechanism that ensures the correspondence between individual and collective interest is the 'habitus' (see Chapter 9), which emerges from the dialectical relationship between social position and actors' dispositions. But this account of the self and the motivations and dispositions of actors is unsatisfactory because of its highly constricted view of the relationship between individuals and the social order. It denies the fact that individuals have a relative autonomy from the social order insofar as they are free to choose to behave however they wish within the context of the social choices available to them. Thus, although there is, in modern societies, a strong emphasis on the drive to achieve competitive advantage over others, this is neither the only option nor the one that many prefer, irrespective of their class and cultural positioning, or their field of activity.

An emphasis on a morality of competitive individualism and the exploitative manipulation of others may be strong in society, but it is not inevitably or mechanically incorporated into individual behaviour. As both Schelling and Goffman have observed, a great deal of social behaviour contains a muddy mixture of motives. These range from selfish (exploitative and manipulative) behaviour on the one hand, through to altruistic (caring, benign, supportive, co-operative) forms on the other. To suggest that people are generally predisposed to compete with others is to endorse an outmoded structural determinism. People are not simply 'lead by the nose' to pursue collectively defined interests since these may, and often do, clash with their situational interests and/or their psychological interests.

The notion of habitus does not allow for the uniqueness of individuals' responses to their own circumstances, or for the way in which emergent situational factors influence behaviour. It does not cater for the real possibility that people may choose to behave in ways that are counter to dominant discourses or social expectations. Also missing in Bourdieu's account is an appreciation of the spread of commitments and involvements that people sustain in relation to a diversity of settings in everyday life. In fact, people are influenced by multiple sources as far as their motivations and predispositions are concerned. People's motives are complex, ambiguous and many-sided – their predispositions are not a simple and direct outcome of social positioning and group interests.

The Dialectic of Separateness and Relatedness

The problems with social constructionism in general are succinctly summarised in Bourdieu's vision of a dialectic between position and practice, finessed by his notion of habitus. This allows no room for the influence of individual psychobiography (or even situated activity) on social behaviour. Because habitus predisposes people exclusively towards the pursuance of their collective interests, a simple (and rather mechanical) correspondence is fashioned between objective social position and practice. The unique skills, capacities, emotions and attitudes of individuals are completely squeezed out of the picture. In the theory of social domains this view of the individual is rejected. While being irreducibly social in nature, the person is also, in some measure, *apart* from society in the form of an interior psychic unity. This unity of personhood (self-identity) is not simply an outcome of social conditioning. Moreover, it contains elements that are antithetical and resistant to the shaping influence of social forces. Situated activity reinforces this tendency insofar as it produces emergent 'solutions' to problems faced by co-present individuals that are frequently at variance with social mores and established expectations.

Most importantly, the tension between social influences and low-key antisocial or asocial tendencies is generally reflected in social relationships by what I term the dialectic of separateness and relatedness. Individuals are caught up in this dialectic during their normal everyday behaviour. Otherwise expressed, the dialectic represents the pushes and pulls of involvement versus independence in social relationships (Tannen, 1987, 1992). Whereas Tannen has stressed how this duality manifests itself in different conversational styles, domain theory emphasises its more generic role in social interaction.

Social interaction is founded upon and draws together psychological and social realities. As such it 'finesses' the intersection between an individual's desires for independence and the equally pressing requirement for social involvement that social membership creates. The creation and maintenance of a stable self-identity requires both. On the one hand, during childhood an individual must develop a clear feeling of autonomy from parents or caretakers. A felt sense of a robust and separate identity must be carried over into adult life otherwise problems of insecurity and weak self-esteem will arise. On the other hand, as individuals, we need to preserve some social contact and close bonding with others in order to underpin a sense of self-worth, significance and the feeling of being loved and loveable which are minimum requirements for general security and self-esteem. Although the need for autonomy is very strong, it can only be achieved in early infancy through a firm basis of dependence on caretakers. In later life, of course, these dependencies take on a more 'voluntary' character as is reflected in the volatility as well as the stability of bonds of friendship, companionship and love.

The tensions and opposing pulls of these somewhat conflicting demands can be seen at work in social relationships and face-to-face encounters. Individuals often assert their independence (sometimes rather abruptly), because they feel that they are being swamped by the demands of others or unduly 'harassed' by the pressure for social conformity. On the other hand, too much independence may be perceived by others not only as threatening the continuity of a relationship, but as a direct attack on their own self-esteem and self-worth. Therefore, there is pressure on individuals not to send out too many messages of independence lest their own need-dependencies on others (for love and self-esteem and so on) are undermined.

The dialectic of separateness and relatedness is multi-faceted having diverse ramifications for personal relationships in particular (see Layder, 2004a). However, it is clear that the relationship between the individual and society can only be properly grasped in the context of a general appreciation of the role of this dialectic. It may be of some preliminary use to assert, as Bourdieu does, a dialectic between position and practice but, in itself, it does not begin to tap into the profoundly important intersection between personal and social reality. Indeed, unless the more fundamental and underlying role of separateness and relatedness is properly understood, practice itself cannot be adequately accounted for theoretically or substantively.

Connecting Theory and Research:
Adaptive Theory

Social theorists tend to regard themselves as specialists in theory and thus view issues about practical, empirical research as belonging to other specialist areas, including that referred to as 'research methods and techniques'. On the one hand, this specialisation has led to the development of theory that is little concerned with practical research and, on the other, to research that bears no organic connection with social theory. As a result both general social theory and social research are impoverished. For instance, the individual–society, agency–structure and macro–micro problems can never be resolved entirely in theoretical terms. Theory (propositions, ideas and frameworks) must be organically connected with research strategies that contribute to some test of their robustness and explanatory adequacy (Layder, 1990, 1993). Similarly, empirical research is limited unless it engages with important theoretical issues. In what follows I address these issues in relation to what I call 'adaptive theory' (Layder, 1998). First, I outline what adaptive theory is, and then compare it with other approaches.

Adaptive Theory, Social Domains
and Agency–Structure Links

The adaptive theory approach stresses that *to some extent* social research should concern itself with investigating agency–structure linkages understood against the background of multiple social domains. Secondly, again *to some extent*, social research should be concerned with generating theory that throws light on different aspects of agency–structure and social domain linkages. Of course the exact extent of either of these emphases will vary in relation to the nature and purposes of the research.

On the other hand, general theories (including frameworks and perspectives) must also be concerned with the development of theory about agency–structure links as they are embedded in multiple social domains. Furthermore, they should also attempt to translate theoretical depictions into researchable propositions. General theories should never be imposed on research data as total systems of explanation. Rather, they should be suggestive, sensitising and informative as regards possible lines of enquiry and explanation. They should be treated as open and flexible frameworks of ideas that may be revised in the light of argument and debate or fresh evidence.

These ideas must be understood in the context of a wider view of social science that embraces *ontological variety* in the social world by recognising its multiple domains. Such a view avoids conflating or compacting elements of agency and structure into a one-dimensional view of social reality. This must be accompanied by a *disciplined epistemological inclusiveness* that is able to incorporate and reconcile the equally valid insights of objectivism and subjectivism. Dogmatic or narrow epistemological assumptions cannot embrace the ontological diversity of the social world.

Adaptive Theory Compared with Other Approaches

In-depth research aims to gather as much information on a given area or topic (suicide, family networks, social policy, professional ethics, teacher–pupil relationships and so forth). However, its lack of focus on wider, more general theoretical issues means that it yields little in the way of theoretical interest. But genuinely cumulative social scientific knowledge can only be produced through systematic comparison of a wide range of empirical examples against a background of more general theoretical issues – especially agency–structure and social domain linkages.

Grounded theory (Glaser and Strauss, 1967) addresses some of these problems. It emphasises the generation of theory from research data using a range of comparative examples. However, many useful types of more general theory and theorising are regarded as invalid and rejected by the grounded theory approach because of its insistence that emergent theory must be grounded in the data of ongoing research (for more detail on this and the other issues raised in this section, see Layder, 1993, 1998). Furthermore, the grounded theory approach restricts its focus to intersubjective phenomena and thus only to one domain – situated activity – neglecting the influence of other domains.

General theory, more often than not, tends to be inward-looking, and not about establishing researchable propositions (about agency–structure and domain linkages). All too frequently perspectives like Marxism or symbolic interactionism are used as 'total' explanatory frameworks by more or less 'forcing' data into preconceived categories and concepts. Occasionally, empirical social researchers borrow from general theories to help them conceptualise research data or to provide a theoretical framework for it. But these tendencies rarely lead to theoretical innovation. Neither do they do anything to advance the cumulative development of knowledge, particularly about agency–structure and social domain links. Thus, in the main, general social theory lacks organic connections with either social research or theory generation.

Theory-testing approaches to research (Rose, 1985) have a different emphasis but are also limited. In the grounded theory approach, theory is tested against the emerging data of the research project and nothing else. In Merton's (1967b) 'middle range theory' approach a preconceived hypothesis is tested against research evidence. It is crucial to understand 'theory testing' in a broader way to accommodate more general theorising. In this sense empirical data must be validated in relation to propositions and theoretical parameters that are wider than the substantive topic under investigation, although they must not be allowed to dictate how data are explained. Thus, adaptive theories are not dictated or imposed by preconceived concepts and frameworks, but neither are they exclusively 'grounded' in the data of a research project.

An example of adaptive theory is the 'theory of emotion and interpersonal control' (Layder, 2004b) which endeavours to illuminate *specific aspects* of such phenomena as intimacy, romantic love, sexuality, emotions and work relations, crime, women abuse and serial murder. Although wide-ranging and seemingly diverse, these topics have a common link with power, control and emotion. In order to reveal the way in which this theory emerged and how it displays the characteristics of adaptive theory, it is best to think of it in terms of a four-stage sequence.

1 To inform this analysis I drew on domain theory as a general background to agency–structure issues and questions of emotion and interpersonal control. These were then integrated with theoretical/conceptual issues about the psychology of control and the sociological analysis of interpersonal encounters.

2 This cluster of theoretical issues was then interwoven with the empirical analysis of secondary (already published) data drawn from a wide range of areas such as

love, friendship, intimacy, sexuality, work relationships, women abuse, serial murder and so on.

3 My objective was to generate new theory about interpersonal power and emotion. This also involved teasing out the practical, concrete features of agency–structure links as they are embedded in, and meshed with, (a) different types of interpersonal control (from benign to malign), (b) different control strategies (manipulation, emotional blackmail, enrolment, coercion and so on), (c) different social settings (work, family, romantic partnerships, crime), and (d) typical emotions and feelings states (love, anger, pain, self-affirmation).

4 Finally, I wanted to produce a set of concrete propositions about the way in which human behaviour is shaped and influenced by interpersonal control. These propositions would concern such issues as how different types and strategies of control play a role in (a) establishing basic security and self-esteem for individuals, while at the same time (b) cementing or dissolving emotional bonds. They would also cover questions about how people's competence and capacity for control – of social interaction, their lives, themselves, other people – or indeed whether, or how, their failure to control these areas affects their mental health.

This sequence of analytic phases brings together all the elements of adaptive theory. First, the research was concerned with agency–structure links and their 'translation' into concrete issues about emotion and interpersonal control. Also, it was concerned with generating theory by engaging with a wide array of comparative examples of interpersonal control and by relating/connecting empirical data to theory of different levels of generality. The research was also influenced by general theory (the theory of social domains principally) blended with issues and concepts drawn from other psychological and sociological perspectives. But these general theoretical elements were not imposed on the data. They were used in a directive manner to suggest fruitful ways of generating theory – in this case, an emergent theory of emotion and interpersonal control. Finally, at every phase the analysis was engaged in a two-way process. At the same time as translating general theoretical concepts/ideas into researchable propositions, the analysis demonstrated how concrete examples of interpersonal control throw light on theoretical and conceptual issues about agency–structure links.

Conclusion: Core Dualisms and Social Theory

By way of a general conclusion let us return to the core themes of this book: the three main dualisms that have played such a prominent role in its organisation.

Individual ..... Society
Agency ..... Structure
Micro ..... Macro

In the later sections of the book I have tended to refer to the 'agency – structure problem' (or 'agency–structure links') rather more frequently than the other two dualisms. In part this is due to the fact that all three dualisms are closely related. Partly, also it is because mentioning all three in every instance is too cumbersome, and in that sense the agency–structure dualism serves to 'represent' them all. At the same time it is important not to lose sight of the different emphases and nuances to be found in each, as I pointed out in the introductory chapter. In this respect the individual–society and agency–structure dualisms have a closer affinity with each other than they have with the micro–macro dualism which stands slightly apart from them.

The former two are drawn together by a concern with how human behaviour is related to and connects with social reality. Thus the agency–structure dualism is probably best regarded as a more recent and slightly reformulated version of what has been traditionally referred to as the individual–society problem – except for the fact that the term 'agency' may apply to either individual or collective agents (such as social groups). Both dualisms are concerned with the intersection of human agency (individual or collective) and more encompassing features of the social landscape (social structures or systems or even 'society' itself).

It is this focus on human activity and its influence in changing, transforming, creating or reproducing social forms that produces the slightly different emphases between the individual–society and agency–structure dualisms on the one hand and the macro–micro dualism on the other. With the latter there is more emphasis on 'analytic focus' or level of analysis in the contrast between face-to-face behaviour studied at the 'micro' level as opposed to the larger-scale 'macro' level structures, systems, discourses and so on, which are also more extensive in space and time. Of course, there are significant overlaps and commonalities. The very nature of micro analysis means that it is more closely connected to social activity viewed as a creative process – a characteristic that is also implicit in the term 'agency'. Similarly, macro analysis is automatically concerned with the reproductive effects of social activity, which are precisely those referred to by the phrase 'structural phenomena'. So we are talking about a subtle difference in emphasis at the same time as a significant overlapping of reference and meaning.

Let us now briefly review the way in which the theories discussed in Parts 1–4 of this book have dealt with the problems posed by these dualisms. This will position the arguments presented in this chapter in a more embracing perspective. In Part 1, I discussed the work of Parsons (and to a lesser extent Merton) as functionalist theorists along with several varieties of Marxism (including humanist and structuralist versions). Despite their many political and theoretical differences, these perspectives share a commitment to a dualism of action (or agency) and structure (or system) in which the structural or systemic features have predominant influence over the action or agency side of the equation. Thus, while they are strong on the role of structural or systemic aspects of social reality, they underplay the autonomy and influence of activity and the creativity of human agency.

Those perspectives considered in Part 2 – symbolic interactionism, phenomenology and ethnomethodology – provide a sharp contrast to functionalism and Marxism insofar as they deny a dualism of agency and structure by rejecting outright the validity of concepts such as structure and system. These perspectives steadfastly cling to the notion that the intersubjective world is the only world that exists, and that there are, therefore, no emergent features of social reality beyond it. By rejecting the idea of structural or systemic elements they are unable to provide an adequate account of phenomena like institutions, divisions of labour (or occupational specialisation), bureaucratic organisations, cultural resources, structural or discursive power and so on. They are thus unable to account for, or even envisage, the dynamic interplay between agency and structure in social life.

In this respect the authors and perspectives considered in Part 3 – Foucault and postmodernism, Giddens and Elias – provide interesting attempts to at least grapple with the problem of overcoming or transcending the agency–structure dualism, even though in the end they all fail to do so. In very different ways, these authors manage to conflate, dissolve or merge elements of both agency and structure and thereby lose a grasp on their distinctive characteristics and influences. In the case of Foucault this eventuates in a view of social reality in which discursive practices reign supreme. He offers a postmodern vision in which agency is discounted and absorbed into the objectivity of discourses. On the other hand, Elias and Giddens, albeit in their very contrasting ways, reject the idea that relatively independent objective social forms exist, and are thus unable to reconcile the very real, objective elements of social reality with subjective (or intersubjective) aspects.

What the authors and perspectives examined in Parts 2 and 3 fail to consider is the possibility that the solution to the problems raised by the individual–society, agency–structure and macro–micro dualisms does not lie in transcending or abandoning dualism, but rather lies in understanding how agency and structure are interdependent and interlinked. The theories and authors examined in Part 4 – Habermas, Goffman, Turner, Alexander, Munch, Mouzelis and Archer, among them – all entail important contributions to exactly this issue. In particular, they stress that the agency–structure dualism expresses the interconnections between subjective, intersubjective and objective (structural or systemic) features of social reality. Further, they insist that, in fact, only by recognising this can the constitutive elements of agency and structure be properly identified and their interrelatedness adequately understood.

However, my own work on the theory of domains outlined in this final chapter suggests that we need to examine the ontological differences that are concealed within the notions of 'agency' on the one hand and 'structure' (or systems) on the other. By thinking of social reality in terms of the different but related domains of psychobiography, situated activity, social settings and contextual resources, we are tapping into profoundly different aspects of social reality that constitute what we call society. Thus the theory of social domains suggests that we must understand agency–structure links as embedded within an ontologically differentiated latticework of social reality. It is not simply a question of moving between different levels of analysis. It is not a question of analysis or analytic devices at all. It is question of grasping the overall nature of social reality as constituted by differentiated domains, each with its own properties and dimensions (of time and space, among other things). The radically different ontological characteristics, properties and dimensions of each of these domains needs to be registered and grasped before an adequate understanding of the interconnections between elements of agency and structure (individual–society, macro–micro) can be achieved.

SUMMARY

- The theory of social domains and the methodology of adaptive theory together provide a social analytic framework with which to understand agency–structure links.

- The social universe (or social reality) is made up of four social domains: psychobiography, situated activity, social settings and contextual resources. The domains can be understood as existing in a 'vertical' dimension, representing the ontological depth of social reality, as well as a 'horizontal' dimension, indicating how social processes are stretched over time and space.

- The domain of psychobiography highlights an individual's existence as a 'career' trajectory through time and space in the social world. It traces the uniqueness of an individual's self-identity in the context of his or her social involvements.

- Individuals are not entirely socially constructed, they exist both 'inside' and 'outside' society (the influence of social forces). Personal identity and emotion underpin social agency. Individuals are not simply rational, self-reflexive social agents, they are emotionally unique human beings whose ontological security is inherently precarious.

- Transformative capacity or power cannot be the generic or defining characteristic of social agency. Asserting generic properties of social agency produces a stereo-type which simply overlooks the immense individual variation in human capacities and competencies such as security and self-confidence, emotional intelligence, resilience and subjective power.

- The domain of situated activity is defined by the arrivals and departures of partic-ipants in face-to-face encounters and their social (intersubjective) exchanges. So defined, situated activity has a formative influence on meaning, but meaning is also created and influenced by psychobiography and wider contextual factors.

- In situated activity, power, emotion and control are intimately related and manifest themselves in three modalities: self-control; emotional exchanges associated with benign control; and a person's ability to manage his or her own current life situation.

- The domain of social settings forms the immediate environment of situated activ-ity. Social settings are local aggregations of *reproduced* social relations, positions and practices.

- The domain of contextual resources represents the most encompassing feature of society (social reality) and is comprised of two related elements. First, there is a distributional aspect concerned with the unequal allocation of resources and the social groupings affected by them, such as class, ethnicity, gender, age, status and so on. The second element represents the historical accumulation of cultural resources, such as knowledge, social mores, values, artifacts, media representations, sub-cultural styles, fashion and popular culture.

- The four social domains are intimately interlinked and bring together objective and subjective aspects of social reality to form a complex multi-dimensional unity.

- The 'duality of social relations' refers to the fact that any social relationship has both reproduced and free-form elements – or socially defined and personally defined aspects. The balance of influence between these elements is variable. In some kinds of settings social relations are more influenced by reproduced aspects, in other settings relations are more responsive to free-form interpersonal influences.

- Each domain embodies a different form of power. Social analysis in general should move away from uniform, uni-dimensional conceptions of power.

- Social constraints have an 'internal' (psychobiographical) dimension as well as an intersubjective and an 'external' objective character. Constraints cannot be simply defined in terms of people's motives and reasons.

- Although routine everyday social behaviour is highly creative and productive, its consequences are usually restricted to defined localities. In terms of wider social influence, routine behaviour is mainly reproductive (of institutions, values, discourses and so on). This is quite contrary to the view that society is simultaneously created and reproduced in every encounter.

- Goffman's notion of 'the interaction order' stresses the importance of social interaction as a relatively independent social order. However, Goffman fails to distinguish between *general rules* about interpersonal conduct and *how people actually behave* in encounters.

- Habermas identifies an ontological fault line between lifeworld and system phenomena (see Chapter 10). In some ways this is similar to the distinction in domain theory between reproduced system phenomena (settings and contextual resources) and the emergent characteristics of agency and action. However, domain theory is set within an elaborate, multi-dimensional view of social ontology and has a more subtle and complex view of power.

- Bourdieu's attempt to link agency and structure rests on a one-dimensional view of (mainly class) power which, in effect, influences social behaviour in a rather mechanical and deterministic fashion, despite Bourdieu's claims to the contrary. By contrast, domain theory stresses that power must be understood in terms of the combined effects of different domain power sources. The complex nature of these effects means that 'power flows' move in many different directions simultaneously and have varying 'weightings' of influence.

- Bourdieu's concept of 'habitus' does not allow for individuals' unique responses to their own life situations, or the way in which emergent situational factors sometimes have the effect of overriding collectively defined interests.

- The 'dialectic of separateness and relatedness' in social life represents the tension-fraught intersection between psychological and social realities. Being involved with others while also maintaining one's independence as an individual is, perhaps, the core existential problem of social life. The dialectic is also multi-faceted, having many diverse ramifications for both personal and social relationships (Layder, 2004a).

- The theory of social domains is also concerned with problems of empirical research as they relate to the many different facets of the agency–structure problem, particularly the nature of the linkages between them. In this respect, 'adaptive theory' methodology complements domain theory by developing research strategies designed to encourage the generation of theory about agency–structure links that are firmly grounded in research data.

- The adaptive theory approach draws upon the strengths of other methodologies and research styles such as in-depth research, grounded theory, general theory and theory-testing approaches. However, the adaptive theory approach also attempts to avoid the weaknesses and limitations of these approaches. How the principles of adaptive theory can be applied in social analysis is exemplified in 'the theory of emotion and interpersonal control' (Layder, 2004b).

- The core dualisms of individual–society, agency–structure and macro–micro have furnished the organising themes of Parts 1–4 of this book. As a contribution to Part 4, domain theory and adaptive theory suggest that we must go beyond what Archer calls 'analytic dualism'. We must understand the social world as ontologically multi-dimensional. The links between the constituent elements of agency and structure can only be adequately understood against such a backdrop.

Glossary

ADAPTIVE THEORY   An approach to social research that emphasises the dual influence of general theory and theory grounded in research data. Adaptive theory (Layder 1998) is closely linked with the theory of social domains (Layder 1997).

ALIENATION   Karl Marx uses this term to refer to the psychological effects that result from workers' loss of control over the things they produce and the nature of their work.

ANOMIE   Emile Durkheim uses the concept of anomie to refer to states of normless-ness or lack of social regulation. These can occur either in society in general (in disruptive periods of transition such as the early stages of industrialisation), or in particular sectors of society (for example, because of a relative lack of communal bonds). In such situations people lack firm guidelines for their behaviour and may become confused or depressed.

BEHAVIOURISM   An attempt to found a science of human behaviour modelled on the natural sciences, which avoids all references to 'inner' mental faculties like 'mind' and 'self', or to subjective phenomena like 'meaning'. Associated with the work of Skinner and Watson in psychology and Homans in sociology.

COMMUNICATIVE ACTION   Jürgen Habermas's 'theory of communicative action' traces the processes that have resulted in large areas of everyday life being overtaken by the influence of the social system elements of power and money.

CONTEXTUAL RESOURCES   The most far-reaching of the four principal domains in 'the theory of social domains'. It refers to distributional inequality as well as accumulated cultural resources.

CURRENT LIFE SITUATION   A person's network of social and personal relationships and the surrounding social circumstances. The concept also refers to how the individual feels about, and responds to, these factors.

DECENTRING THE SUBJECT   An attempt by some schools of social theory (notably structuralism, post-structuralism and postmodernism) to reject the idea that the individual should be a central focus of social analysis. Thus, these schools speak of 'abandoning the subject' or the 'death of the subject'.

DEPTH ONTOLOGY   A view which understands society as a series of 'layers' (or 'domains') that have rather different characteristics and properties but which are also tightly interwoven. It opposes the view that society is a 'flat' terrain composed of a single major element (such as 'discursive practices' or 'figurations'). It is also associated with the idea of a 'variegated ontology', in which society is understood to be composed of several different kinds of domain of social reality.

DIALECTIC   Two forces in conflict or tension which eventually give way to a newly formed amalgam of the two.

DIALECTIC OF CONTROL   Giddens's term to express the balance of power between individuals or groups. It stresses that subordinates always have *some* power resources at their disposal.

DIALECTIC OF SEPARATENESS AND RELATEDNESS   The tension between being involved with others socially and also maintaining one's independence as an individual. It marks the intersection of social and psychological reality.

DISCOURSE   Forms of talk or writing on a particular area or topic. Discourse involves the use of reason and argument based on a defined area of expertise, knowledge, or simply a body of opinion. It is intimately related to power and what becomes defined as the 'truth'. Thus we have 'medical discourse', or the discourses of 'racism' or 'sexism'.

DISCURSIVE   To proceed by argument or some form of reasoning with regard to a particular body of knowledge, opinion or prejudice.

DISCURSIVE CONSCIOUSNESS   Giddens's term for the things that people are able to express verbally about the social circumstances in which they live and how these affect their behaviour.

DISCURSIVE PRACTICES   This phrase points to the fact that talk, writing and bodies of ideas in general are associated with specific social practices and forms of power. Michel Foucault stresses these connections in his writings. Thus, for example, the doctor–patient relationship involves the employment of medical discourse and a power relation in which the patient defers to the doctor's advice and expertise.

DOMAIN THEORY   Or 'the theory of social domains' holds that social reality (society) is composed of four fundamental domains (psychobiography, situated activity, social settings and contextual recourses). Each domain has distinct properties and characteristics which are not reducible to each other but which are, nevertheless, closely interrelated and mutually influential.

DUALITY OF SOCIAL RELATIONS   Refers to the fact that any social relationship has both 'reproduced' and 'free form' (or socially defined and personally defined) aspects.

DUALITY OF STRUCTURE   Giddens uses this term to express his view that agency (action) and structure are simply different aspects of the same thing. Giddens believes that agency and structure must not be understood as separate and opposed to each other.

EMPIRICISM   The view that our knowledge of the world is gained exclusively by perception and the use of our senses. Thus, observation, experience and empirical testing of various kinds are seen as the only valid ways of gaining true knowledge. It is an opposing view to that of 'rationalism'.

EPISTEMOLOGY   A branch of philosophy concerned with the nature of knowledge. It poses the question 'How do we know what we claim to know?' In a practical sense it deals with the assumptions that underlie various claims to knowledge. Thus, it is generally concerned with questions of validity and verification – the reasons why knowledge is accepted or rejected.

ETHNOMETHODOLOGY   A sociological perspective based on the work of Harold Garfinkel. It focuses on how people create and maintain the orderliness of much of everyday interaction. It highlights the 'ethnomethods' that people use to make sense of what others say and do.

EXISTENTIALISM   A school of philosophy this is concerned with the nature of being and human existence and is associated with the work of Martin Heidegger and Jean-Paul Sartre. Existentialism is a human-centred philosophy which post-structural and post-modern writers oppose. *See* 'decentring the subject'.

FIGURATIONS   Elias's term for the ever-changing interdependencies formed by people in their social relationships. Thus 'figurational sociology' is a general approach to sociology based on Elias's ideas.

FUNCTIONALISM   A theoretical framework which focuses on the functions that social institutions and patterns of behaviour perform for society as a whole. It is associated with the work of Talcott Parsons and Robert Merton, among others. It is sometimes referred to as 'structural-functionalism'.

GENERAL THEORY   Theory expressed in an abstract manner which relates to the empirical world (of evidence and facts) in a rather general way, instead of being linked to a particular area or topic of study. Examples are the theory of structuration, the theory of communicative action and the theory of social domains.

GRAND THEORY   Theory which attempts to explain a great many phenomena within its own terms of reference. Often it is of a highly abstract nature like Parsons's social system theory.

HISTORICAL MATERIALISM   A view of human history, found in the work of Marx and Engels, which stresses the role of human labour in meeting material needs such as food, clothing and shelter.

HOMINES APERTI   Norbert Elias's term which expresses the idea that individuals are interdependent with others in human figurations.

HOMO CLAUSUS   Elias's term for a view of the individual as closed-off from social influences.

HUMANISM   A term that refers to theoretical perspectives which reject the idea that social life can be studied in the same manner that scientists study physical or natural phenomena. Humanism stresses the importance of meaning in social life and the interpretative skills of sociologists.

ID   Freud's term for the elemental drives (of a sexual and aggressive nature) that seek expression in our everyday behaviour. These drives are generally barred or repressed from our conscious minds.

IDEOLOGY   Ideas and beliefs which serve to support and justify the power and interests of dominant groups. Ideologies attempt to legitimise forms of social inequality.

INDEXICAL NATURE OF MEANING   This refers to the fact that often the 'meaning' of an episode of interaction, or a word, or even a whole conversation, cannot be understood without reference to the actual context in which it occurs. For example, words like 'he', and 'she', or 'there' and 'here', only make sense when we know to what, or to whom, they refer.

INSTITUTIONAL ANALYSIS   Giddens uses this term to indicate an analytic concentration on institutions while 'holding apart' the analysis of actual conduct.

INTERACTION ORDER   Erving Goffman's term for the analysis of face to-face-behaviour as 'an order of social reality' in its own right, that is, it has characteristics somewhat different from other social orders like those of structure, culture and institutions.

INTERPRETATIVE ANALYSIS   A phrase often used by Giddens to refer to a concentration on the strategic activities of people in their everyday lives while 'bracketing out' (or placing to one side) the analysis of social institutions.

INTERSUBJECTIVE WORLD   A level of analysis that concentrates on people's relations with others and the way in which they actively construct and reconstruct the social world.

LIFE SITUATION   *See* 'current life situation'.

LIFEWORLD   Habermas's term for the day-to-day world of interaction in which people attempt to arrive at communicative agreements. In Habermas's theory, this is distinct from the social system world, which operates according to different principles.

LOOSE COUPLING   A term used by Erving Goffman to describe the relationship between the interaction order and other social orders (such as the structural or institutional order). The looseness of the connection indicates the variety of ways in which the different orders may be related.

MUTUAL BENIGN CONTROL   The way in which people reciprocally control and influence each other in order to achieve mutual benefits by taking each other's rights, interests and feelings into account. This contrasts with competitive and exploitative control where one or both parties seek to gain advantage over the other either by manipulating or ignoring the other's rights, interests and feelings (see Layder, 2004a and b).

NATURALISM   The application of the framework of the natural sciences (physics, chemistry, and so on) to the social sciences. Thus it is very close in meaning to 'positivism'. Confusingly, however, the term 'naturalism' is also used to denote the necessity of studying social phenomena in their 'natural' settings (instead of in artificial conditions such as experiments). In this latter sense, naturalism has a close affinity with humanism.

NEOFUNCTIONALISM   Refers to the work of a group of sociologists who have elaborated and refined the work of earlier functionalist writers, particularly Parsons.

OBJECTIVISM   The tendency to view social phenomena as if they had an objective, 'external' existence independent of members of society. This contrasts with 'moderate objectivism', which only requires the relative independence of objective social phenomena, such as institutions, culture and knowledge.

ONTOLOGY   A branch of philosophy traditionally concerned with the nature of reality as we experience it. However, there is a broader sense in which it refers to what exists more generally – including things that are not within the realm of personal experience. In sociology, ontological questions concern the basic nature of society and social life. They ask 'What is society composed of?' 'What are its constituent elements?'

PASTICHE   A mixture of styles old and new which produce a collage or patchwork effect. It is associated with postmodernism as a cultural style.

PATTERN VARIABLES Parsons suggests that 'pattern variables' express 'dilemmas of action' for people in their everyday lives which have to be resolved in order for them to proceed. Parsons also uses the term to indicate the general patterning of social roles in different kinds of society.

PHENOMENOLOGY A strand of theory that focuses on people's perceptions of others and how their sense of normality and security depend on the quality of their relationships.

POSITION PRACTICES The socially reproduced positions and the practices associated with them that form the 'social settings' of situated activity. *See* 'social settings'.

POSITIVISM A vision of the social sciences modelled along the lines of the natural sciences. It stresses an objective (rather than an interpretative) method and the search for generalisations (laws) about human behaviour.

POSTMODERNISM There are three dimensions of postmodernism. First, the idea that there has been a move away from modern (advanced capitalist) societies to a new 'postmodern' form based on radically different principles of organisation. Secondly, the term also refers to a definite cultural style relying on pastiche or a mixture of many different styles. Finally, the term may refer to a set of ideas which includes the rejection of the following: science, objective knowledge and truth claims, 'the subject' (*see* 'decentring the subject') and so on.

POST-STRUCTURALISM The writings of a group of authors dissatisfied with structuralist theories that relate everything in social life to a unified structure which also determines people's behaviour. Thus, post-structuralists attempt to breakdown (decompose or deconstruct) the analysis of social life into its smaller constituent elements. Foucault's objection to Marxism reflects this view.

POWER The ability of individuals or groups to achieve objectives and to serve their own interests despite the resistance of others. Power can be based on a wide variety of resources (money, property, knowledge) which can be used to control and manipulate others.

PRACTICAL CONSCIOUSNESS Giddens's term for the practical, everyday knowledgeability of human beings – their basic knowledge of how to operate skilfully in social situations. This usually operates below the level of conscious awareness – that is, we normally just do the things that are required of us in social situations, we do not express them verbally.

PRACTICES The actual forms of conduct that exist in society, or some sector of it. Practices can be formal or informal, legitimate or illegitimate.

PRESENCE AVAILABILITY Giddens's term to characterise societies where social relations are conducted on a face-to-face basis. Thus, they exhibit a high degree of presence availability. In more complex (capitalist) societies, many social relationships are indirect and mediated by telephones, fax machines and so on, because of the dispersion of the population, sometimes over vast distances.

PSYCHOBIOGRAPHY The psychological profile of the individual that traces shifts and transformations in self-identity as they emerge from social involvements and experience over a person's lifespan. In the theory of social domains, psychobiography is one of the four principal domains of social reality.

PSYCHODYNAMIC The flux of emotionally-charged mental elements that influence and motivate us. Both childhood memories of interaction with parents as well as later adult experiences influence our attitudes and reactions (or responses) to others in social life.

RATIONALISM A view of knowledge that stresses its a priori nature, that is, its independence from our personal experience, observations and the evidence of our senses in general. Thus, it is the opposite of empiricism. Rationalism highlights the role of reason, argument and logical deduction from 'self-evident', or at least agreed upon, assumptions.

REALISM Recently, this term has been used to express an alternative view of social analysis to those of positivism and humanism. It attempts to combine a scientific view of society with a concern with interpretation and the analysis of meaning in social life.

REDUCTIONISM This term characterises forms of explanation which are inappropriate to the things they attempt to explain. For example, explaining institutions as individual rather than social creations.

REIFICATION At one extreme, reification is associated with the idea that society and social arrangements in general are produced by non-human entities such as Gods, or mystical or mysterious forces, rather than human beings. In turn, this is associated with the view that social arrangements are eternal and cannot be altered by human endeavour. A more moderate version of reification simply insists that societies or social forms are capable of acting and operating independently of human intervention.

ROLE The socially expected behaviour associated with a particular position in society or a sub-group. For example, the roles of 'parent', 'police officer', 'friend', 'leader', and so on.

SITUATED ACTIVITY Situated activity occurs between participants in face-to-face encounters and centres on the intersubjective (meaningful) exchanges that take place between them. It has a dynamic and emergent nature resulting from the collective inputs of those involved. Situated activity constitutes one of the four principal domains of social reality in the theory of social domains.

SITUATIONAL OR PERIPHERAL SELVES These refer to the images and behaviour that we exhibit in the presence of particular people, audiences or groups in order to create and sustain a certain impression of ourselves. These aspects of our identities are rather different from what we take to be our 'core' or main self-identities.

SOCIAL INTEGRATION The extent to which social relationships (between individuals or groups) are either smooth and harmonious, or exhibit conflict and tension.

SOCIAL PRODUCTION This refers to the (unresolved) problem of how society and its institutions are produced and created by people. This is the other side of the problem of social reproduction.

SOCIAL REPRODUCTION The way in which social practices and institutions are reproduced (and, as a result, continue to persist) over time through human activities. Reproduction represents the other side of the problem of social production.

SOCIAL SETTINGS One of the four principal domains of social reality in the theory of social domains. Social settings constitute the immediate environment of situated activity and are formed through local aggregations of reproduced social relations, positions and practices.

STRATEGIC ACTION Habermas uses this term to refer to action that is geared to the achievement of some material or instrumental goal, such as to sell a service or goods. This is distinguishable from 'communicative action', which is primarily aimed at arriving at shared understanding without any underlying material motive.

STRATIFICATION MODEL OF SOCIETY A view of society as composed of different layers. *See also* 'depth ontology'.

STRUCTURAL MARXISM The work of Marxists like Louis Althusser and Nicos Poulantzas who stressed the importance of the analysis of social relationships as objective structures which largely determine the behaviour of people. This kind of objective approach went hand in hand with a vehement rejection of humanism.

STRUCTURATION THEORY Giddens's theory which provides a general account of the way in which society is constituted through the activities and practices of human beings.

SUBJECTIVISM Understanding and explaining social phenomena in terms of the psychological dispositions of individuals. Often sociologists claim that subjectivism is 'reductionist'. *See* 'reductionism'.

SUPEREGO   Freud's term for the area of mental life responsible for the inhibition of anti-social behaviour. The superego is a storehouse of moral values and models of 'appropriate' behaviour which are first learned in childhood through parental control.

SYMBOLIC INTERACTIONISM   A theoretical perspective which derives primarily from the work of George Herbert Mead. It emphasises the role of the self, symbolic communication, language and meaning in everyday life.

SYSTEM INTEGRATION   The extent to which parts of society (the main institutions and the power relations that support them) either fit together into a coherent whole or exist in conflict and tension with each other.

THE THEORY OF SOCIAL DOMAINS   *See* 'domain theory'.

TOTALISING THEORY   Similar to 'grand' theory in that it attempts to explain an extremely wide range of phenomena within its own terms of reference. However, a characteristic feature of totalising theory is its rejection of other points of view. Post-structuralists and postmodernists often regard Marxism as a totalising theory.

UNCONSCIOUS   The unconscious refers to wishes and impulses that are hidden from everyday conscious awareness. Freud suggested that many such motives are developed during early childhood but are subsequently repressed from normal awareness even though they continue to play a key role in adult behaviour.

References

Alexander, J. (ed.) (1985a) *Neofunctionalism.* London: Sage.

Alexander, J. (1985b) 'The individualist dilemma in phenomenology and interaction-ism', in S. Eisenstadt and H. Helle (eds), *Macro-Sociological Theory: Perspectives on Sociological Theory, Volume 1.* London: Sage. 25–57.

Alexander, J., Giesen, B., Munch, R. and Smelser, N. (eds) (1987) *The Macro–Micro Link.* Berkeley: University of California Press.

Althusser, L. (1969) *For Marx.* London: Allen Lane.

Althusser, L. (1971) 'Ideology and ideological state apparatuses', in *Lenin and Philosophy.* London: New Left Books.

Althusser, L. and Balibar, E. (1970) *Reading Capital.* London: New Left Books.

Archer, M. (1982) 'Morphogenesis vs. structuration', *British Journal of Sociology,* 33: 455–83.

Archer, M. (1988) *Culture and Agency.* Cambridge: Cambridge University Press.

Archer, M. (1995) *Realist Social Theory: The Morphogenetic Approach.* Cambridge: Cambridge University Press.

Baudrillard, J. (1987) *Forget Foucault.* New York: Semiotext(e).

Bauman, Z. (1973) *Culture as Praxis.* London: Routledge.

Bauman, Z. (1982) *Memories of Class: The Pre-history and After-life of Class.* London: Routledge.

Becker, H. (1953) 'Becoming a marihuana user', *American Journal of Sociology,* 59: 235–42.

Becker, H. (1960) 'Notes on the concept of commitment', *American Journal of Sociology,* 66: 32–40.

Becker, H. (1970) *Sociological Work.* Chicago: Aldine.

Benton, T. (1984) *The Rise and Fall of Structural Marxism.* London: Macmillan.

Berger, P. and Luckmann, T. (1967) *The Social Construction of Reality.* London: Allen Lane.

Bernstein, B. (1973) *Class, Codes and Control, Volume 1.* London: Paladin.

Best, S. and Kellner, D. (1991) *Postmodern Theory: Critical Interrogations.* London: Macmillan.

Bhaskar, R. (1979) *The Possibility of Naturalism*. Brighton: Harvester.

Bittner, E. (1967) 'The police on skid row: a study of peace keeping', *American Sociological Review*, 32: 669–715.

Blauner, R. (1964) *Alienation and Freedom*. Chicago: University of Chicago Press.

Blumer, H. (1969) *Symbolic Interactionism: Perspectives and Methods*. New Jersey: Prentice-Hall.

Bohman, J. (1991) *New Philosophy of Social Science*. Cambridge: Polity Press.

Bott, E. (1957) *Family and Social Network*. London: Tavistock.

Bottomore, T. and Rubel, M. (eds) (1963) *Karl Marx: Selected Writings in Sociology and Social Philosophy*. Harmondsworth: Pelican.

Bourdieu, P. (1977) *Outline of a Theory of Practice*. Cambridge: Cambridge University Press.

Brand, A. (1990) *The Force of Reason*. Sydney: Allen & Unwin.

Brittan, A. (1973) *Meaning and Situations*. London: Routledge.

Bryant, C. and Jary, D. (eds) (1991) *Giddens' Theory of Structuration: A Critical Appreciation*. London: Routledge.

Burkitt, I. (1991) *Social Selves*. London: Sage.

Burns, T. (1992) *Erving Goffman*. London: Routledge.

Cicourel, A. (1973) *Cognitive Sociology*. Harmondsworth: Penguin.

Cicourel, A. (1981) 'Notes on the integration of micro and macro levels of analysis', in K. Knorr-Cetina and A. Cicourel (eds), *Advances in Social Theory and Methodology*. London: Routledge.

Clegg, S. (1989) *Frameworks of Power*. London: Sage.

Cohen, I. (1989) *Structuration Theory: Anthony Giddens and the Constitution of Social Life*. New York: St Martin's Press.

Collins, R. (1981) 'Micro-translation as a theory – building strategy', in K. Knorr-Cetina and A. Cicourel (eds), *Advances in Social Theory and Methodology*. London: Routledge.

Collins, R. (1983) 'Micromethods as a basis for macrosociology', *Urban Life*, 12: 184–202.

Cooley, C. (1902) *Human Nature and the Social Order*. New York: Charles Scribner's Sons.

Craib, I. (1984) *Modern Social Theory*. Brighton: Harvester Wheatsheaf.

Craib, I. (1992) *Anthony Giddens*. London: Routledge.

Craib, I. (1994) *The Importance of Disappointment*. London: Routledge.

Craib, I. (1998) *Experiencing Identity*. London: Sage.

Dahrendorf, R. (1959) *Class and Class Conflict in Industrial Society*. London: Routledge.

Douglas, B. (1970) *The Social Meanings of Suicide*. New Jersey: Princeton University Press.

Dunning, E. and Rojek, C. (eds) (1992) *Sport and Leisure in the Civilizing Process. Critique and Counter-Critique*. London: Routledge.

Durkheim, E. (1964) *The Division of Labour in Society*. New York: Free Press.

Durkheim, E. (1982) *The Rules of Sociological Method.* London: Macmillan.

Duster, T. (1981) 'Intermediate steps between micro and macro – integration: the case of screening for inherited disorders', in K. Knorr-Cetina and A. Cicourel (eds), *Advances in Social Theory and Methodology.* London: Routledge.

Eisenstadt, S. (1985) 'Macro-societal analysis – background, development and indications', in S. Eisenstadt and H. Helle (eds), *Macro-sociological Theory: Perspectives on Sociological Theory, Volume 1.* London: Sage. pp. 7–24.

Elias, N. (1978a) *What is Sociology?* London: Hutchinson.

Elias, N. (1978b) *The History of Manners: The Civilising Process, Volume I.* Oxford: Basil Blackwell.

Elias, N. (1982) *State Formation and Civilization. The Civilising Process, Volume II.* Oxford: Basil Blackwell.

Elliott, A. (1992) *Social Theory and Psychoanalysis in Transition.* Oxford: Blackwell.

Foucault, M. (1977) *Discipline and Punish: The Birth of the Prison.* Harmondsworth: Penguin.

Foucault, M. (1980) *Power/Knowledge: Selected Interviews and other Writings 1972–1977,* edited by C. Gordon. Brighton: Harvester.

Foucault, M. (1984) *The History of Sexuality: An Introduction.* Harmondsworth: Penguin.

Fraser, N. (1989) *Unruly Practices.* Cambridge: Polity Press.

Garfinkel, H. (1967) *Studies in Ethnomethodology.* Englewood Cliffs: Prentice-Hall.

Giddens, A. (1971) *Capitalism and Modern Social Theory.* Cambridge: Cambridge University Press.

Giddens, A. (1973) *The Class Structure of the Advanced Societies.* London: Hutchinson.

Giddens, A. (1976) *New Rules of Sociological Method.* London: Hutchinson.

Giddens, A. (1977) *Studies in Social and Political Theory.* London: Hutchinson.

Giddens, A. (1979) *Central Problems in Social Theory.* London: Macmillan.

Giddens, A. (1981a) *Sociology: A Brief but Critical Introduction.* London: Macmillan.

Giddens, A. (1981b) *A Contemporary Critique of Historical Materialism, Volume 1.* London: Macmillan.

Giddens, A. (1983) 'Comments on the theory of structuration', *Journal for the Theory of Social Behaviour.* 13: 75–80.

Giddens, A. (1984) *The Constitution of Society.* Cambridge: Polity Press.

Giddens, A. (1987) *Social Theory and Modern Sociology.* Stanford: Stanford University Press.

Giddens, A. (1990) *Consequences of Modernity.* Cambridge: Polity Press.

Giddens, A. (1991) *Modernity and Self-Identity.* Cambridge: Polity Press.

Giddens, A. (1992) *The Transformation of Intimacy.* Cambridge: Polity Press.

Glaser, B. and Strauss, A. (1965) *Awareness of Dying.* Chicago: Aldine.

Glaser, B. and Strauss, A. (1967) *The Discovery of Grounded Theory.* Chicago: Aldine.

Glaser, B. and Strauss, A. (1968) *Time for Dying.* Chicago: Aldine.

Glaser, B. and Strauss, A. (1971) *Status Passage*. London: Routledge.

Goffman, E. (1961) *Encounters*. New York: Bobbs–Merrill.

Goffman, E. (1967) *Interaction Ritual*. New York: Anchor.

Goffman, E. (1971) *The Presentation of Self in Everyday Life*. Harmondsworth: Penguin.

Goffman, E. (1983) 'The interaction order', *American Sociological Review,* 48: 1–17.

Gold, R. (1952) 'Janitors versus tenants: a status–income dilemma', *American Journal of Sociology,* 57: 486–93.

Goldthorpe, J. (1973) 'A revolution in sociology?' *Sociology*, 7: 449–62.

Goldthorpe, J., Lockwood, D. and Platt, J. (1968) *The Affluent Worker: Industrial Attitudes and Behaviour*. Cambridge: Cambridge University Press.

Goldthorpe, J., Lockwood, D. and Platt, J. (1969) *The Affluent Worker in the Class Structure*. Cambridge: Cambridge University Press.

Gouldner, A. (1971) *The Coming Crisis in Western Sociology*. London: Heinemann.

Gross, N., Mason, W. and McEachern, A. (1958) *Explorations in Role Analysis*. New York: Wiley.

Habermas, J. (1971) *Towards a Rational Society*. London: Heinemann.

Habermas, J. (1982) 'Reply to my critics', in J. Thompson and D. Held (eds), *Habermas: Critical Debates*. Basingstoke: Macmillan.

Habermas, J. (1986) *The Theory of Communicative Action, Volume I: Reason and the Rationalization of Society*. Cambridge: Polity Press.

Habermas, J. (1987) *The Theory of Communicative Action, Volume II: The Critique of Functionalist Reason*. Cambridge: Polity Press.

Hearn, H. and Stoll, P. (1975) 'Continuance commitment in low-status occupations: the cocktail waitress', *Sociological Quarterly,* 16: 105–14.

Held, D. and Thompson, J. (1989) *Social Theory of Modern Societies: Anthony Giddens and His Critics*. Cambridge: Cambridge University Press.

Hilbert, R. (1990) 'Ethnomethodology and the micro–macro order', *American Sociological Review,* 55: 794–808.

Hindess, B. (1973) *The Use of Official Statistics in Sociology*. London: Macmillan.

Hindess, B. (1977) *Philosophy and Methodology in the Social Sciences*. Brighton: Harvester Press.

Hindess, B. and Hirst, P. (1975) *Pre-capitalist Modes of Production*. Basingstoke: Macmillan.

Hindess, B. and Hirst, P. (1977) *Mode of Production and Social Formation: An Auto-critique of Pre-capitalist Modes of Production*. Basingstoke: Macmillan.

Hochschild, A. (1983) *The Managed Heart*. Berkeley: University of California Press.

Hughes, E. (1937) 'Institutional office and the person', *American Journal of Sociology* 43: 404–13.

Kasperson, L.B. (2000) *Anthony Giddens: An Introduction to a Social Theorist*. Oxford: Blackwell.

Keat, R. and Urry, J. (1975) *Social Theory as Science*. London: Routledge.

Knorr-Cetina, K. (1981) 'The micro-sociological challenge of macro-sociology: towards a reconstruction of social theory and methodology', in K. Knorr-Cetina and A. Cicourel (eds), *Advances in Social Theory and Methodology*. London: Routledge.

Knorr-Cetina, K. and Cicourel, A. (eds) (1981) *Advances in Social Theory and Methodology*. London: Routledge.

Laing, R. (1969) *The Divided Self*. Harmondsworth: Pelican.

Laing, R. and Esterson, A. (1964) *Sanity, Madness and the Family*. London: Tavistock.

Layder, D. (1981) *Structure, Interaction and Social Theory*. London: Routledge.

Layder, D. (1982) 'Grounded theory: a constructive critique', *Journal for the Theory of Social Behaviour*, 12: 103–23.

Layder, D. (1987) 'Key issues in structuration theory', *Current Perspectives in Social Theory*, 8: 25–46.

Layder, D. (1989) 'The macro–micro distinction, social relations and methodological bracketing', *Current Perspectives in Social Theory*, 9: 123–41.

Layder, D. (1990) *The Realist Image in Social Science*. London: Macmillan.

Layder, D. (1993) *New Strategies in Social Research*. Cambridge: Polity Press.

Layder, D. (1997) *Modern Social Theory: Key Debates and New Directions*. London: University College London Press (Taylor and Francis).

Layder, D. (1998) *Sociological Practice: Linking Theory and Social Research*. London: Sage.

Layder, D. (2004a) *Social and Personal Identity: Understanding Yourself*. London: Sage.

Layder, D. (2004b) *Emotion in Social Life: The Lost Heart of Society*. London: Sage.

Lengermann, P. and Niebrugge-Brantley, J. (1992) 'Contemporary feminist theory', in G. Ritzer (ed.), *Sociological Theory*. New York: McGraw-Hill.

Leonard, P. (1984) *Personality and Ideology*. London: Macmillan.

Lockwood, D. (1956) 'Some remarks on the social system', *British Journal of Sociology*, 7: 134–46.

Lockwood, D. (1964) 'Social integration and system integration', in G.K. Zollschan and W. Hirsch (eds), *Explorations in Social Change*. London: Routledge. pp. 244–57.

Luckenbill, D. (1979) 'Power: a conceptual framework', *Symbolic Interaction*, 2: 97–114.

McLellan, D. (1973) *Marx's Grundrisse*. London: Paladin.

Malone, M. (1997) *Worlds of Talk: The Presentation of Self in Everyday Conversation*. Cambridge: Polity Press.

Manning, P. (1992) *Erving Goffman and Modern Sociology*. Cambridge: Polity Press.

Marx, K. and Engels, F. (1968) *Selected Works*. London: Lawrence & Wishart.

Mead, G.H. (1967) *Mind, Self and Society*. Chicago: Chicago University Press.

Meltzer, B., Petras, J. and Reynolds, L. (1975) *Symbolic Interactionism*. London: Routledge.

Mennel, S. (1980) *Sociological Theory: Uses and Unities*, 2nd edn. Surrey: Nelson.

Merton, R. (1967a) 'The role set', in L. Coser and B. Rosenberg (eds), *Sociological Theory: A Book of Readings*. London: Collier Macmillan.

Merton, R. (1967b) *On Theoretical Sociology*. New York: Free Press.

Merton, R. (1968) *Social Theory and Social Structure*. New York: Free Press.

Miliband, R. (1987) 'Class analysis', in A. Giddens and J. Turner (eds), *Social Theory Today*. Cambridge: Polity Press.

Mills, C. (1940) 'Situated actions and vocabularies of motive', *American Sociological Review* 5: 904–13.

Mitchell, J. (ed.) (1969) *Social Networks in Urban Situations*. Manchester: Manchester University Press.

Mouzelis, N. (1992) 'Social and system integration: Habermas' view', *British Journal of Sociology*, 43: 267–88.

Mouzelis, N. (1995) *Sociological Theory: What Went Wrong?* London: Routledge.

Munch, R. (1987) 'Parsonian theory today: in search of a new synthesis', in A. Giddens and J. Turner (eds), *Social Theory Today*. Cambridge: Polity Press. pp. 116–55.

Munch, R. and Smelser, N. (1987) 'Relating the micro and macro', in J. Alexander, B. Giesen, R. Munch, and J. Smelser (eds), *The Micro–Macro Link*. Berkeley: University of California Press. pp. 356–87.

Parker, J. (2000) *Structuration*. Buckingham: Open University Press.

Parsons, T. (1937) *The Structure of Social Action*. New York: McGraw-Hill.

Parsons, T. (1951) *The Social System*. London: Routledge.

Parsons, T. (1966) *Societies: Evolutionary and Comparative Perspectives*. Englewood Cliffs: Prentice-Hall.

Popper, K. (1972) *Objective Knowledge: An Evolutionary Approach*. Oxford: Oxford University Press.

Poster, M. (1984) *Foucault, Marxism and History*. Cambridge: Polity Press.

Poulantzas, N. (1975) *Classes in Contemporary Capitalism*. London: New Left Books.

Poulantzas, N. (1976) 'The capitalist state: a reply to Miliband and Laclau', *New Left Review*, 93: 63–83.

Poulantzas, N. (1978) *State, Power, Socialism*. London: New Left Books.

Preiss, J. and Ehrlich H. (eds) (1966) *An Examination of Role Theory: The Case of the State Police*. Lincoln: University of Nebraska Press.

Pusey, M. (1987) *Jürgen Habermas*. Chichester: Ellis Harwood & Tavistock.

Rawls, A. (1987) 'The interaction order *sui generis:* Goffman's contribution to social theory', *Sociological Theory,* 5: 136–49.

Rex, J. (1961) *Key Problems in Sociological Theory*. London: Routledge.

Ritzer, G. (1992) *Sociological Theory*. New York: McGraw-Hill.

Roche, M. (1973) *Phenomenology, Language and the Social Sciences*. London: Routledge.

Rock, P. (1979) *The Making of Symbolic Interactionism*. London: Macmillan.

Rose, G. (1985) *Deciphering Sociological Research*. London: Macmillan.

Rosenau, P. (1992) *Post-Modernism and the Social Sciences.* New Jersey: Princeton University Press.

Roth, J. (1963) *Timetables.* New York: Bobbs-Merrill.

Sartre, J.-P. (1966) *Being and Nothingness.* London: Methuen.

Sarup, M. (1988) *An Introductory Guide to Post-structuralism and Postmodernism.* Hemel Hempstead: Harvester Wheatsheaf.

Scheff, T. (1990) *Microsociology: Discourse, Emotion and Social Structure.* Chicago: University of Chicago Press.

Schutz, A. (1972) *The Phenomenology of the Social World.* London: Heinemann.

Scott, J. (1991) *Social Network Analysis.* London: Sage.

Scott, J.F. (1963) 'The changing foundations of the Parsonian action scheme', *American Sociological Review,* 28: 716–35.

Scott, P. (1992) 'Measurer of angels and demons', *The Higher,* 10 April.

Seeman, M. (1959) 'On the meaning of alienation', *American Sociological Review,* 24: 783–91.

Sève, L. (1978) *Man in Marxist Theory and the Psychology of Personality.* Brighton: Harvester Press.

Sibeon, R. (2004) *Rethinking Social Theory.* London: Sage.

Silverman, D. (1985) *Qualitative Methodology and Sociology.* Aldershot: Gower.

Smith, D. (1988) *The Everyday World as Problematic.* Milton Keynes: Open University Press.

Strauss, A., Schatzman, L., Ehrlich, D., Butcher, R. and Sabshin, M. (1973) 'The hospital and its negotiated order', in G. Salaman and K. Thompson (eds), *People and Organisations.* London: Longman. pp. 303–20.

Stryker, S. (1981) *Symbolic Interactionism: A Social Structural Version.* Englewood Cliffs: Prentice-Hall.

Swingewood, A. (1975) *Marx and Modern Social Theory.* London: Macmillan.

Tannen, D. (1987) *That's Not What I Meant.* London: Dent.

Tannen, D. (1992) *You Just Don't Understand.* London: Virago.

Thompson, E. (1978) *The Poverty of Theory and Other Essays.* London: Merlin Press.

Turner, J. (1987) 'Analytical theorizing', in A. Giddens and J. Turner (eds), *Social Theory Today.* Cambridge: Polity Press.

Turner, J. (1988) *A Theory of Social Interaction.* Cambridge: Polity Press.

Turner, R. (1962) 'Role-taking: process versus conformity', in A. Rose (ed.), *Human Behaviour and Social Processes.* Boston: Houghton Miffiin.

Turner, R. (1985) 'Unanswered questions in the convergence between structuralist and interactionist role theories', in S. Eisenstadt and H. Helle (eds), *Microsociological Theory: Perspectives on Sociological Theory, Volume 2.* London: Sage.

Vaitkus, S. (1991) *How is Society Possible?* Dordrecht: Kluwer Academic.

Weber, M. (1964) *The Theory of Social and Economic Organisation.* New York: Free Press.

Weber, M. (1967) *The Protestant Ethic and the Spirit of Capitalism.* London: Unwin.

Whitebook, J. (1985) 'Reason and happiness: some psychoanalytic themes in critical theory', in R. Bernstein (ed.), *Habermas and Modernity*. Cambridge: Polity Press.

Wootton, A. (1975) *Dilemmas of Discourse*. London: Allen & Unwin.

Wrong, D. (1967) 'The oversocialised concept of man in modern sociology', in L. Coser and B. Rosenberg (eds), *Sociological Theory: A Book of Readings*. London: Collier-Macmillan.

Zimmerman, D. (1971) 'The practicalities of rule use', in J. Douglas (ed.), *Understanding Everyday Life*. London: Routledge.

Index

abstract theory 32–3, 51, 292
accomplishments 91–110
action 3–4
  context-bound 100–1
  joint activity 82–3
  Munch 206
  Parsons 34–5, 37
  social behaviourism 72–3
  see also structure-action dualism
action theory 215, 220
adaptation needs 21–2
adaptive theory 292–5
affectivity–affective neutrality variable 23
agency 169–70, 274–6, 282
agency–structure dualism 3–5
  Archer 263–7
  Giddens 163, 164–5, 173, 185–6
  macro–micro relationship 193–212
  Marxism 62–4
  structuration theory 181–3
  varieties 239–55
Alexander, Jeffrey 10, 190–1, 204–5
alienation 44, 225
allocative resources 171
Althusser, Louis 46–50, 128
analytical dualism 263–8
anomie 225
anxiety 275
Archer, Margaret 240, 263–8
'artful practices' 108, 109
artistic styles 58
authoritative resources 171
autonomy 291

Barthes, Roland 48
Becker, Howard 70, 76, 77
behaviourism 71–6
Bentham, Jeremy 122

Berger, P. 103–7
bio-power 123
Bittner, Egon 102
blocking 246–7
Blumer, Herbert 71, 74–5, 87
body 18–19
Bourdieu, Pierre 10, 176–7, 190, 194–6,
  259, 287–90
'bracketing' of methodology 176, 186
Bureau of Public Assistance 102
bureaucracy 122, 216, 229

California 184–5
capillary form of power 124
capitalism 16, 41, 44
'careers' 82–3, 85
central conflation 265
Chicago School 73, 76–7, 83
civilising process 140–3, 152
class divisions 43–4, 209
closed individual (homo clausus) 140, 141
collective action 52, 54
collective phenomena 35, 204–5, 222
collectivity-orientation–self-orientation
  variable 24
Collins, Randall 10–11, 191, 208–11, 254, 256
colonisation of the lifeworld 224–6, 233
commonsense knowledge 100–1
communicative action 216–20, 223–4, 225–6,
  228–9, 235
communicative rationality 217, 225
compulsion 178
computer technology 122–3
conflationary theorising 264–5
conflict 27–9, 44, 88–9
conformity 26–7, 35, 47, 145
consciousness 92, 166–7
constraint 108, 177–9, 249, 284–5

consumerism 28, 53, 226
context-bound meaning/action 100–1
contextual resources domain 281–2
control 169–70, 182, 279–80, 294–5
  see also power
conversational (cultural) capital 210
creativity
  Alexander 205
  Bourdieu 195, 288
  Giddens 177–9
  Marxism 54, 55
  Mead 72–3
  phenomenology 251
  structuration theories 285–6
critical experiences 274
critical theory 214, 236
cultural (conversational) capital 210
cultural system 20–1, 48, 281

decentring the subject 116–19, 125, 258
demystification of society 216
determinism 25–6
developmental perspective 140–2
deviance 28–9, 54, 145
dialectic of control 53, 169–70, 182
diffuseness–specificity variable 23–4
disciplinary power 120, 121–3
discourse/practice 117, 124–6
discourses 119–20, 123, 128–9, 132–3
discrimination 24, 28, 246
discursive consciousness 166–7
displays 244
dispositions 177, 289–90
dissent 53–5
distributive dimension of social systems 175
doctor–patient relationship 24–5, 33
domain theory 271–301
domination 126–7, 129–31, 132
  see also power
downwards conflation 264
drives 26–7
drug users 74–5
dualisms 1–7
  false problems 140
  Foucault's challenge 133–6
  links 190–2
  opposition 70–1, 112–13, 129, 133–6, 156–7
  review 295–8
  in social analysis 162–3
  structuration theory 158, 176, 186
  symbolic interactionism 78–9

dualisms *cont.*
  varieties of 239–55
  see also agency–structure; individual–society;
    macro–micro
duality of social relations 282–3
duality of structure 164–5, 173, 183, 260–1
durability
  interaction order 242
  social systems 83, 174–5
Durkheim, Emile 16, 159–60, 225, 251

eclecticism 113, 158
economic institutions 42–3, 47, 48,
  53, 222–3
Elias, Norbert 9, 139–54, 181, 259, 297
emergent properties 17, 19–21, 35–6,
  196, 265
emotion 85–6, 227, 274–6, 279–80, 294–5
emotion/interpersonal control theory 294–5
emotional energy 210, 211
empirical research
  adaptive theory 292
  Parsons 32–4
  social organisation 101–3
  structural Marxism 50–1
  structuration theory 180
  symbolic interactionism 77–8, 89
enablements 284–5
encounters 168
  see also social interaction
the Enlightenment 215, 225
epistemological inclusiveness 293
epistemology 161, 162
ethnomethodology 98–101
  collective phenomena 205
  empirical research 101–3
  Habermas critique 224
  overview 109–10, 297
  Smith 201
  structure concept 102–3, 108
  Turner critique 254–5
European society 140–2
everyday life
  Foucault 127, 136
  Garfinkel 99–100
  Giddens 159
  Marxism 56
  neofunctionalism 207
  Smith 198–9, 203
  symbolic interactionism 87
existentialism 95, 117

expectations 19–20, 23
experience 69–90, 92
expert systems 223, 226
external factors 243–4, 278
external relations 200

face-to-face interaction
    Collins 210–11
    communicative rationality 217
    Elias 149, 150
    emergent definitions 32
    Giddens 169
    Goffman 241
    neofunctionalism 207
    social ties 150–1
    women 199
    see also social interaction
facticity 254
false problems 139–54
families 53, 96
feelings 253–4
    see also emotion
feminist sociology 86, 87, 108, 196–204
feudal society 141–2
fiduciary attitude 94
'fields' of practice 288
figuration concept 140–3, 148–50, 152
Foucault, Michel 115–38
    break with Marxism 126–9
    evaluation 129–31
    Giddens comparison 181
    overcoming dualism 133–6
    overview 9, 137–8, 297
    power 233
fragmentary nature of power 126–7
Frankfurt School 214, 215
Freudian concepts 147
friendship 282–3
functionalism 28–9, 161, 163, 184, 297

Garfinkel, Harold 99–101, 254
general theory 294
Giddens, Anthony
    Bourdieu comparison 194–6
    California influence 184–5
    dualisms 256
    Goffman critique 242–3, 248–9
    Habermas comparison 232, 233–4, 236
    minutiae 87
    Mouzelis critique 259, 260
    overview 9–10, 186–8, 297

Giddens, Anthony cont.
    Parsons critique 26
    structuration theory 155–88
    the unconscious 227
Glaser, B. 83–4
glossary 302–10
goal attainment needs 21–2
Goffman, Erving
    criticisms 247–50
    distinctiveness 249–50
    domain theory 286
    interaction order 241–3
    loose coupling 239–40, 243–7
    macro–micro dualism 256–7
    Mouzelis critique 262
    role distance 80–2
    security 167–8
    self-identity 179
    social theory 250–2
Goldthorpe, John 99
governments 30
grand theory 126–9, 130
gratification 19
grounded theory 293–4
group interests 59–60

Habermas, Jürgen 213–38
    communicative action 216–20
    domain theory 287
    lifeworld 220–6
    overview 11, 191–2, 237–8
    Parsons influence 37
    theory appraisal 227–35
    Turner link 255
habitus 176–7, 195–6, 259–60, 289–90
harmony 27
Hilbert, R. 108
historical materialism 41
historical processes 42, 59–61, 105,
        129, 148
homines aperti 141, 146
homo clausus (closed individual) 140, 141
hospitals 83–4
humanism 117
    dualism rejection 70–1
    Foucault 133–4
    Giddens 163
    individual–society merge 78
    Iowa School 77
    Mead 73
    see also symbolic interactionism

ideal speech situation 228
identity 53, 179–80, 266–7, 274–6, 291
ideology
    Althusser 47–8
    Foucault 119, 127–9
    Marx 44–5
    Parsons 30–1
    resistance/dissent 54
impermanence motif 184–5
impersonal relationships 150–1
impression management 80–1
in-depth research 293
indexical meaning 101, 277
the individual 72–3, 118, 140, 141, 143–6, 274–6
    see also the self; the subject
individual–society dualism 2–3
    Elias 141, 143, 146–7, 152
    false problems 140, 144
    linkage of theories 106–7
    Marx 46
    merging 78–9
    Parsons 36–7
    phenomenology 97
    structuration theory 181
individualism 48–9, 52–3
inequality 26–9, 30, 88–9
informal practices 31
'instantiation' of structure 172
institutional analysis 160, 163
    see also structuralism
institutional order 190, 242–9, 251–2
integration needs 21–2
    see also social integration
interaction order 190, 241–52
    Bourdieu 196
    domain theory 286
    Elias 148, 149–50
    Habermas 235
    importance 247–8
    loose coupling 243–7, 249–52
interaction theories 240, 252–5
interactional skills 165–6
interactive meaning 135–6
interdependence 148, 149–52
    see also figuration
intermediate social classes 43–4, 55–6
internal dynamics 157
internalisation 105
interpretative analysis 163, 164, 181, 182
intersubjective meaning 93–5, 98, 135–6
involvement obligations 286

Iowa School 76–7, 83
irrationality 85–6

joint activity 82–3

kissing 75, 278
knowledge
    Berger and Luckmann 104
    Foucault 124
    Garfinkel 100–1
    Giddens 165–6
    Renaissance philosophy 143
    Schutz 93–4

Laing, Ronald 95–7
language
    Berger and Luckmann 105, 106
    face-to-face interaction 217
    Foucault 119–20
    Schutz 93
    social development 222
    social reproduction 285
    symbolic interactionism 73–5
    the unconscious 227
late modernity 58
'layers' of society 175, 252
legitimacy 29–31
Leonard, Peter 52–5
levels of awareness/consciousness 166–7
levels of organisation 17–18, 35, 46
life situation 280
lifeworld 220–6, 230–2, 234–5, 287
linkage
    dualisms 112
    theories 103–7
local practices 108
locales 168
loose coupling 239–40, 243–7, 249–52
Luckmann, T. 103–7

macro theories 11, 134, 139–54, 201
macro–micro dualism 5–6
    agency–structure relationship 193–212
    false problems 139–54
    Habermas 215, 232–3
    linkage of theories 103–7
    Marx 62–4
    Mouzelis 262–3
    Parsons 22–3
    phenomenology 97–8, 107–9
    symbolic interactionism 78–9, 88–9

macro–micro dualism *cont.*
   Turner 255–7
   varieties 239–55
manipulation 219, 280, 290
manners books 142
Marx, Karl/Marxism 39–65
   alienation 225
   Althusser 46–50
   capitalism 16
   Foucault 126–9, 130
   Goffman link 250–1
   Habermas 214–15, 225, 235
   Leonard 52–5
   overview 7, 64–5, 297
   rationalisation 216–17
   Smith 197–8, 199–200
   structural Marxism 39–52, 55–6
material interests 26–9, 41
Mead, George Herbert 71–6
meanings 69–90
   context-bound 100–1
   intersubjective 135–6
   motivation 76
   nature and sources 87
   situated activity 277–8
   symbolic interactionism 73–5
   Weber 92–3
medium of social activity 166
mental illness 95–7
Merton, R. 28–9
methodological bracketing 176, 186
methods of sociology 159–60
micro theories 11, 86–7, 134, 139–54, 257
   see also macro–micro dualism
micro-dynamics 253–4
Middle Ages 140–2
mind 72
modernity 58, 124–6, 133, 169, 215, 225
monarchical power 120–1
monopolisation processes 141–2
morality 242–3, 248
morphogenetic approach 263–8
motivation 19, 76, 227, 275, 289–90
Mouzelis, Nicos 229, 230, 240, 257–63
multi-dimensional approach 271–301
Munch, Richard 10, 190–1, 205–8
mutual tact 167–8

naturalism 160–1, 163
needs of social systems 21–2
negotiated order 83–5

negotiated outcomes 79–80
neofunctionalism 191, 205–8
networks of interdependence 148, 149–50, 151–2
new politics 225, 226, 230
Nietzsche, Friedrich Wilhelm 124, 127–8
non-verbal communication 219
normalisation 122–3
norms 16–17, 45

objectivation 105, 107
objectivism
   Althusser 49–50
   Giddens 160–1, 163, 174–5, 178, 185
   rejection of 70
   social analysis 196, 202
   subjectivism link 104–7
ontological security 167–8
ontological variety 293
ontology 161, 162
orderliness 16, 56, 99–100
organic system 18–19
outcome of social activity 166
overview 7–12

Panopticon 122, 123
Parsons, Talcott 15–38
   criticisms 25–37, 158
   ethnomethodology links 99
   Habermas critique 221
   ideology 47–8
   macro–micro dualism 22–3
   neofunctionalism 205–6
   overview 7, 38
   pattern variables 23–5
   social order 61–2
   social system 17–22
particularism–universalism variable 24
patriarchy 30–1, 197–9
pattern maintenance needs 21–2
pattern variables 23–5
perceptions 91–110
performance–quality variable 24
personality 19, 52–3
phenomenology 91–8
   Foucault 116
   Goffman 250–1
   Habermas 224, 234
   macro–micro problem 97–8, 107–9
   mental illness 95–7
   overview 8, 109–10, 297
   Smith 198

philosophy 143, 217
physiological system 18–19
plural nature of power 126–7
police work 31, 102
political institutions 223, 245
politics of everyday life 127
Popper, Karl 281
positions 47, 50, 280–1
  see also roles
positivism 77
post-structuralism 57–9, 116, 118, 258
postmodernism 57–9, 73, 115–26,
    127, 258
power
  Bourdieu 287–9
  dialectic of control 169–70, 182
  discourses and practices 132–3
  domain theory 274, 283–4
  European Middle Ages 142
  everyday life 136
  Foucault 118, 119–27, 129–33, 134–6
  Habermas 233–4, 287
  Layder 294–5
  lifeworld 223
  Marx 43, 45, 55, 60, 61–2
  microsociology 257
  modern forms 124–6
  Mouzelis 261–3
  Parsons 29–31
  plural and fragmentary 126–7
  the self 134–5
  situated activity 279–80
  Smith 198, 203
  symbolic interactionism 88–9
practical approaches 161–2
practical attitude 94
practical consciousness 166–7, 227
practices 32, 132–3, 165–6, 280–1, 288
  see also discourse/practice
presence availability 169
presentation of self 80–2
primary socialisation 105
principle of emergence 17, 19
'problematic of everyday life' 198–9
psychobiographical domain 144, 145–6,
    274–6, 289–91
psychological criticisms of SI 85–6

qualifications 246
quality–performance variable 24
queuing study 246–7

racism 120
rational choice theories 257–8
rationalisation 216, 217, 223, 225, 226
rationalism 51–2
Rawls, A. 241–2, 247–8
realism 51–2
recognition 279–80
'recursive nature of social life' 166
reflexive self-monitoring 167
reification 36, 82, 85, 106
relatedness–separateness dialectic 97, 290–2
relations of ruling 197–8
relationships
  Giddens 172
  mental illness 96
  pattern variables 23–4
  phenomenology 97
  structural Marxism 56
  ties of interdependence 150–2
  see also social relations
Renaissance philosophy 143
reproduced practices 32
  see also social reproduction
resistance 53–5, 130
resources 171–2, 243–4
restraint 147
retreatism 29
role distance 80–2
roles
  expectations 20, 22–3, 24–5, 29
  individual–society dualism 152
  subjectivity 50
  symbolic interactionism 79, 80, 84
  see also positions
routines 167–8
rule-distancing 261
rules 99–100, 165–6, 171–2

Sartre, Jean-Paul 49, 95, 117
schizophrenia 95–6
Schutz, A. 92–4
scientific approaches 71–2, 160–1
security 167–8, 275
the self
  Bourdieu 289–91
  Foucault 119
  Goffman 241–2, 247–8
  Habermas 227
  power 134–5
  presentation of 80–2
  social behaviourism 72

the self *cont.*
  Turner 253–4
  unity of 86
  see also the individual; the subject
self-control 147, 279
self-esteem 253
self-interest 16
self-monitoring 167
self-orientation–collectivity-orientation
    variable 24
sensitising 156
separateness–relatedness dialectic 97, 290–2
service transactions 246–7
sexism 120
sexuality 123, 124
shared understandings 217–20, 228
SI *see* symbolic interactionism
situated activity domain 147, 148, 267–8,
    277–80, 291
situations 69–90, 135–6, 243–4, 247
skid row study 102
skills 165–6
Smith, Dorothy 10, 108, 190, 196–204
social analysis 58, 148, 161–3
social behaviourism 71–6
social constructionism 143–6, 274
social development 41–2, 57, 207, 222–3
social exclusivity 144–5
'social facts' 159–60
social institutions 107, 150–1, 172–3,
    174, 183
social integration
  Giddens 172–3, 176
  Habermas 229
  lifeworld 221–2, 224
  Marx 44, 61–2
  Parsons 34
  tribal societies 222
  types 172–3
  see also face-to-face interaction
social interaction
  emergent nature 79–80
  Goffman 241, 286
  lifeworld 234–5
  separateness–relatedness dialectic
    291–2
  situated activity 277, 279–80
  see also symbolic interactionism
social order 61–2, 205
social organisation 83–5, 101–3
social production 26, 82, 164, 285–6

social relations 150–2
  duality 282–3
  Giddens 172
  Marx 63
  mental illness 96
  psychobiography 274
  theory of practice 194
  see also relationships
social reproduction
  Althusser 46
  domain theory 285–6
  Giddens 164–6
  Marx 60–1
  Parsons 26
  practices 32
  role distance 82
  social settings domain 280
social reputation 210
social settings domain 280–1
social system 17–22, 34–5
  see also systems
social ties 150–2
socialisation 22, 23, 105
sovereign power 120–1
space 168–9
specificity–diffuseness variable 23–4
state institutions 53, 222
state power 131
strategic action 217, 228–9
stratification model 180
Strauss, A. 83–4
'stretching' in time and space 168–9
structural Marxism 39–52, 55–6
structuralism 48
  Foucault 116, 117, 129–30, 133
  Giddens 160–1, 163, 167, 181, 182
  social reproduction 164–5
  symbolic interactionist schools 77
structuration theory 155–71
  critical problems 183–6
  critique 249
  empirical research 180
  evaluation 173–86
  influence of 157–8
  Mouzelis critique 260
  overview 186–8
  social production/reproduction 285–6
structure concept
  ethnomethodology 102–3, 108, 254
  Giddens 170–2, 173–4, 176–7
  Goffman 244, 245–6

structure concept *cont.*
  versus habitus 176–7
  phenomenology 108
  reification 85
  rejection 70
  symbolic interactionism 83–5, 88–9
  see also agency-structure dualism
Stryker, Sheldon 84
the subject 116–19, 125, 134–5
  see also the individual; the self
'subject matter' 159–60
subjective understandings 92–3
subjectivism 86, 104–7, 116–18, 163
subordinate groups 203
symbolic interactionism (SI) 71–6
  collective phenomena 205
  criticisms 85–9
  individual–society merge 78–90
  major schools 76–8
  overview 8, 297
  phenomenology distinction 92, 94
  rejecting dualism 70
  structural factors 103
  summary 89–90
'synthetic' approaches 156, 158
system integration 34, 172, 176, 221–2, 224, 229
systematic theory 214–15
systems
  durability problem 174–5
  Giddens 170–1, 172–5
  joint activity 83
  reification 85
  rejecting dualism 70
  uncoupling 222–4
systems theory 206, 207, 214, 215

taken-for-granted knowledge 100–1
Tannen, Deborah 87, 97

technologies of power
    118, 122, 126–7
texts 198
theory of practice 194–6
theory-testing approaches 294
ties of interdependence 150–2
time 168–9, 185–6, 265
total theory 126–9, 130, 136–7
traditional approaches 74, 156–7, 160–1
transcendence 103
transformative capacity 276
tribal societies 222
trust 94, 167–8
'truth' 45, 128
Turner, Jonathan 240, 252–7
Turner, Ralph 79, 80, 84

the unconscious 85–6, 118–19, 166, 227
uncoupling of the system 222–4
understandings 217–20, 228
uniqueness of individuals 274–6
unity of the self 86
universalism–particularism variable 24
unofficial practices 31
upwards conflation 264

Vaitkus, S. 94, 98
validity claims 218–20, 223–4
validity debate 161–2
values 16–17, 45, 61
voluntarism 16, 24

Weber, Max 8, 60, 92–3, 216, 225
women 96, 97, 196–204, 244–5
  see also feminist sociology
Wrong, Dennis 26–7

Zimmerman, D. 102